Praise for *Mastering Leadership*

"This is the definitive book on leadership principles and practices! Expansive and practical at the same time, Mastering Leadership *is for forward-thinking leaders who want the most essential leadership lessons analyzed and presented in one astute place. Anderson and Adams' Universal Model synthesizes everything that leadership theory thus far has to offer. Read it, apply its principles, and you witness the transformation in yourself and everyone in your circle!"*

—Marshall Goldsmith, Author of *The New York Times* #1 bestseller *Triggers*, top-ranked Executive Coach, Author of bestsellers *MOJO* and *What Got You Here Won't Get You There*

"There is no shortage of information on leadership theory—Google will return over 15,000,000 results in .32 seconds. However, in their new book, Mastering Leadership, *Adams and Anderson turn theory into practice by framing great leadership as a purposeful pursuit rather than a genetic anomaly. Their leadership model provides a well proven framework that allows leaders to assess their strengths and needs. Importantly, it also provides the practical knowledge and tools to enable a transition to greater effectiveness. This book should be a well-worn staple in every leader's '10 Essentials.'"*

—John Mendel, Executive Vice President – Automotive, American Honda

"This is not a book written for bedtime reading. Its ideas need to be examined in the bright light of day and then ... for the courageous ... put into practice. The authors have very skillfully woven a tapestry with threads from extensive research, years of experience, philosophy, and metaphysics. The Leadership Circle Profile (LCP) and the Universal Model of Leadership (UML) are tools that empirically guide the reader on a journey of self-discovery and growth. Their application breeches the barriers of traditional thinking and carries the reader into the realm of Unity Leadership. The demands on today's leaders to produce high-performing and highly-productive organizations has never been greater. Therefore, understanding the correlation between business performance and leadership effectiveness has never been more important. This book helps leaders answer the question posed in one of the book's case studies, 'What would you do if you could?'"

—Stephen Ewing, Chairman of the Board of AAA Michigan and ACG, Retired President and Chief Operating Officer of MCN Energy Group Inc., Retired Vice Chair of DTE Energy

"This book is a testimony that love and power and clear purpose can co-exist. It gives form and proof that leadership is a human function. You can define it, measure it, teach it, and yet, in the end, our capacity to be honest with ourselves and fulfill our promises to each other is decisive. The book offers the integration of mind and matter, depth and relatedness; rare combinations in the modern world of speed, convenience, and scale. Read the book. Put it under your pillow. Speak of it to others."

—Peter Block, Partner of Designed Learning and Author of *Flawless Consulting: A Guide to Getting Your Expertise Used; Stewardship: Choosing Service Over Self-Interest*; and *The Empowered Manager: Positive Political Skills at Work*

"Many people talk about the significance of an 'effective leader' but often struggle to describe one ... until now! Anderson and Adams' excellent new book, Mastering Leadership, *offers a simple yet dynamic model that can guide and assist you in understanding what makes great leaders great. This universal model encompasses the skills, capabilities, and principles that stem from real leadership. A transforming and insightful read!"*

—Stephen M. R. Covey, *The New York Times* bestselling Author of *The Speed of Trust* and Co-author of *Smart Trust*

"Anderson and Adams have written a book, in my course of reading, to be without compare. The integrated Universal Model of Leadership, the solid research base, the linkages made between organizational performance, leadership effectiveness, and leaders' consciousness, and the good guidance for readers on how to improve their leadership, make this book a complete package. I believe and hope that it will raise the consciousness of leaders in organizations of all types, because there is a striking claim made in Mastering Leadership *that has far-reaching implications for every leader in every organization. It's a claim backed by the research of 500,000 subjects over decades of study. There is a direct correlation between the level of consciousness of an organization's leaders, the effectiveness of those leaders, and the performance of their organizations. Anderson and Adams have crafted a guidebook for all of us to raise our consciousness, and in doing so, become more effective leaders. Let this book be your companion along that path. Envision the best you can become and do the deep, personal work required to make the system of leadership in your organization a competitive advantage—one that will serve you well for years to come. Commit yourself to this unique approach to leadership and you'll be on that journey for the rest of your life. May the wind be at your back."*

—Robert "Jake" Jacobs, Author of *Real Time Strategic Change* and *You Don't Have To Do It Alone*, Founder and President, Real Time Strategic Change, LLC

"Don't miss this read! This book clarifies two correlations that measure leadership effectiveness. One is the relative performance of the business, compared to others in their industry. There is no better or clearer measure than how they outperform everyone else in pre-tax earnings. Porsche, GE Aerospace, and Morningstar are excellent examples. It comes down to the bottom line, and this book nails that reality by showing the close correlation. The other is the overall performance and tenure of their staff. The authors show that the most effective leadership traits focus on inspiring and empowering people. At our Institute, we've proven that leaders who spend a third or more time visiting and meeting their staff are the most effective people leaders."

—Jim Liautaud, Clinical Professor and Chair, The Liautaud Institute
University of Illinois, at Chicago, www.liautaudinstitute.com

"Anderson and Adams offer us the fruits of their careful investigation, diligent research, and thoughtful application of the core truths of leadership. They fully recognize the importance of the leader's personal journey of growth and of having a set of solid guiding principles. No quick fixes or magic formulas here—this is a serious work that invites a serious commitment from any leader who aspires to reach for the top of their game."

—Karl Albrecht, Ph.D., Co-author of *Service America: Doing Business in the New Economy*

"Imagine a book that takes all leadership theory, combines it with real-world practicality, and then wraps it in a blanket of honest conversation. You'll find it here. Go slow. There's much wisdom for leaders who want to create an organization and culture that makes a difference in today's world, ensures that individuals find meaning in the work they do, and evokes the hope that business can become a place that matters in our lives."

—Eileen McDargh, CEO Chief Energy Officer, *The Resiliency Group*,
Author of *Your Resiliency GPS: A Guide for Growing Through Life & Work*

"Mastering Leadership *is what leaders have yearned for—a comprehensive framework that ends the debate about how to effectively lead people. This book cracks the leadership code wide open and solves the riddle of what effective leadership is all about. If you only have one leadership book on your shelf, make it this one—it may be the only one you'll ever need!"*

—Steve Arneson, Ph.D., Author of *Bootstrap Leadership*
steve@arnesonleadership.com

"Anderson and Adams challenge us to define leadership success *and* leadership effectiveness *in a far more holistic and integrated way. Their book,* Mastering Leadership, *asks leaders to consider their own transformation needs first and provides assessments, exercises and guides to support their journey."*

—Marc Effron, President, The Talent Strategy Group
marc@talentstrategygroup.com

"Bob Anderson and Bill Adams debunk the myth that leaders are naturally-born. Their Universal Model of Leadership is built on the foundation of behavior and consciousness nurtured through stages of development rather than innate qualities. The research is compelling and presented in a highly digestible fashion. This book is much more than about what great leaders do—it answers the elusive question about how great leaders develop. It's a must-read book."

—Al Bolea, CEO Applied Leadership Seminars,
www.albolea.com

"Top-of-the-house leaders have no room for fluff. If they are going to develop their leaders, they want to know that increasing leadership effectiveness will drive organizational performance, and they want their leadership talent to be their strategic business advantage. Bob Anderson and Bill Adams have brilliantly bridged the gap from development to results and created a path for leaders and practitioners to follow with their comprehensive, systemic approach in Mastering Leadership. *A must read!"*

—Bonnie Hagemann, CEO, Executive Development Associates
www.executivedevelopment.com

"Bob and Bill do a masterful job of demystifying the complexities of leadership. Their Universal Model will change the way you think about leadership."

—Tim Tobin, VP Global Leadership, Marriott International
and Author of *Your Leadership Story*

"Mastering Leadership *is a bold book that advances nothing less than a 'Unified Model of Leadership.' The model provides a pragmatic framework for understanding, assessing and measuring the dynamics of leadership effectiveness. The authors draw on research from a variety of fields and bring the model to life with examples from their extensive consulting experience. They dissect both the 'inner' and 'outer' games of leadership, provide a rigorous 360-degree leadership assessment tool, and offer a five-stage development framework which yields rich insight into how extraordinary leadership develops and how the development process can be accelerated."*

—Howard M. Guttman, Principal of Guttman Development Strategies
and Author of *Great Business Teams: Cracking the Code for Standout Performance*

"Bob Anderson's and Bill Adams' book, Mastering Leadership, *defines an integrative, universal, meta-model for leadership and makes a compelling case for the necessity of leaders to develop from the inside out—not just the usual leadership competencies, but their inner knowing and consciousness. Their research shows that the more developmentally evolved and conscious a leader is, the more effective and productive they are as a leader. The author's Leadership Circle Profile 360 (LCP) assessment tool provides a profound, research-based understanding of* what *makes effective leadership and* how *it develops. I highly recommend this book!"*

—Dennis S. Reina, Ph.D., Co-author of *Trust and Betrayal in the Workplace*; and *Rebuilding Trust in the Workplace*; Co-founder,
Reina, A Trust Building Consultancy

"Mastering Leadership *is an integrated, comprehensive approach to developing and delivering effective leadership. Anderson and Adams emphasize direction and meaning, engagement and accountability, and focus and execution. In addition, they highlight the interpersonal skills that build relationships of trust to achieve the desired results. Anyone who is serious about leadership and leadership development will benefit from their research and insights. This book is a must-read for all leaders!"*

—John R. Stoker, Author of *Overcoming Fake Talk* and President of DialogueWORKS

"Mastering Leadership *is a* must-read *for every leader. Having studied leadership development and having worked with organizations worldwide for the past 40 years to help them develop their leaders, this book reinforces my premise that performance, teamwork, and engagement together create a culture that produces results. Their Universal Model of Leadership combined with the Development Framework and Effectiveness Assessment provide great insights and tools for accelerating effective leadership development—and superior leaders produce superior results!"*

—Phil Harkins, Founder and Executive Chairman, Linkage Inc.

"Mastering Leadership *is a compelling book that deals with some of the most challenging issues facing leaders in the business world today. This book goes a long way in defining the challenges and requirements associated with transforming leadership into a relationship building and servant focused leadership style. I have been leading people for 30 years and wish this book would have come out long ago. The concepts in this book have changed me and my leadership team! And the output in regards to what we have accomplished is staggering. The lessons in this book will only be of value to you if you put the knowledge into action!"*

—Michael C. Jett, Vice President of Honda Precision Parts of Georgia

"I first worked with Bill and the FCG group at a key inflection point in our business and my career. We needed to figure out how we could sustain, at scale, the great success we were having in a fast growing and very dynamic part of the world. We knew that raising our leadership game was a prerequisite but what the leadership circle process taught me, is the incredible power of individual learning and self-awareness rooted firmly in the context of a team who fully understand, engage with and appreciate each other. Much of this can be attributed to Bill's powerful and probing questions which led us to find, for ourselves, ways to make each other, individually and collectively, much better. This book serves as a powerful reminder of what we learned and the questions we need to keep asking ourselves to ensure that our development as leaders is a never ending journey."

—Aidan O'Meara, President Asia Pacific, VF Corporation

"Mastering Leadership *is a phenomenal read. I am so pleased to see a book of this kind – integrative and holistic, yet practical. Simple, but not easy, in what it calls us to do. Inspiring and motivational as it describes an inclusive and evolutionary path to higher forms of self, leadership and impact. It's a gift."*

—Michelle L. Maldonado, J.D., Associate Vice President, Corporate & Strategic Relationships, American Public University System

"Last year (2014) we finished the Season with a 9 and 4 record and finished No. 21 *in the nation while playing in the ultra-competitive Pac 12 South Division. I told Bill that we could not have done it without the leadership tools he provided to our entire football staff. Leadership makes a positive difference in performance, as we experienced firsthand the defining advantage between wins and losses during our 2014 Season. The time-proven principles in this book will put you on that track whether you are a head coach, a business leader, or a member of a team. Leadership matters! If you will apply the principles taught by Adams and Anderson, your performance can only go up and on a personal note, I will take every competitive edge I can get."*

—Kyle Whittingham, Head Football Coach, University of Utah Utes

"Mastering Leadership *works! I've experienced the application of its principles and impact firsthand. Adams and Anderson offer a framework for high performance and high commitment like no other. Leadership development is an investment. It is an ongoing commitment to increase an organization's capacity for success. This amazingly comprehensive and thought-provoking masterwork builds on the collective wisdom of the best minds in the field. It is rich with insights, tools and practices to help your organization grow and thrive; a resource you will draw on for years to come. I'm all in. After reading this, you will be too."*

—Richard D. Gumbrecht, Chief Growth Officer, EverBank Commercial Finance, Chairman, Equipment Leasing and Finance Foundation

Mastering LEADERSHIP

Mastering LEADERSHIP

An Integrated Framework for Breakthrough Performance and Extraordinary Business Results

ROBERT J. ANDERSON
WILLIAM A. ADAMS

WILEY

Mastering Leadership
An Integrated Framework for Breakthrough Performance and Extraordinary Business Results

Authorized reprint by Wiley India Pvt. Ltd., 4435-36/7, Ansari Road, Daryaganj, New Delhi - 110002.

Published by John Wiley & Sons, Inc., Hoboken, New Jersey.

Reprint: 2016

Printed at: Print India Press, Sahibabad, U.P.

ISBN: 978-81-265-5851-3

Contents

Acknowledgements

We would like to acknowledge two people who played a huge part in the development of this book. First, Ken Shelton has been the author behind many best-selling books. Ken's exquisite editing helped this book immensely. It is a far more readable book because of Ken. Second, Sydney Isle provided all the project management support for the book. She kept us on track (no small task) and managed all the details that it takes to pull a book like this together. We are grateful to both of you for your professionalism and passion.

We want to thank the worldwide Staff, Partners, and International Licensees of TLC and FCG. You each bring such commitment and integrity to the organization every single day. We are the organization we are because of you. Thank you. Without you being who you are and doing what you do, we could not be having the impact that we are.

Bob: I would like first to acknowledge and thank my wife, Kim. She has watched and supported this book come into being for the entire 32 years of our marriage. I truly doubt that this could have happened without her constant love, listening, and support. I am grateful beyond words.

I would also like to acknowledge all of the thought leaders mentioned in this book and in the bibliography. We all stand on the shoulders of giants and you all have made important contributions to the field that have greatly informed this book. In particular I want to thank Peter Block for his mentorship early in my career. Peter, more than any other person, helped to shape the direction of my career. I want to thank David Whyte whose life's work, wonderful poetry, and friendship have added more to my life than he knows. Bob Kegan's seminal work on *Stages of Adult Development* has deeply informed my life and my work. I could not be more grateful for his contribution, support, and friendship. Ken Wilber's Integral Model is unparalleled. The Universal Model of Leadership presented in this book is deeply informed by and nests into the brilliance of Ken's framework. I thank Ken for his contribution to the world. I would also like to thank all those involved in Innovation Associates, particularly Charlie Keifer, Peter Senge, and Robert Fritz. Your work got me started on this journey and forms foundational elements of the Model. I want to thank the late Clayton Laugherty for the brilliance of his assessments and research. His work has deeply informed The Leadership Circle. Finally, thank you to Susanne Cook-Greuter for her life's work with the Maturity Assessment Profile (MAP) and for her generosity and competence in supporting the Stage research presented in this book.

I want to thank life-long colleagues. Dan Holden was my first client and earliest colleague. Dan's friendship and mastery have supported the development of my work for an entire career. I could not be more grateful for his presence in my life. In addition to Dan, I thank Jim Anderson, David Womeldorff, Barbara Braham, and Leo Burke who have been the core of a circle of support that has contributed greatly to my life for well over a decade. I deeply appreciate your unconditional support for me and for this work.

I want to thank the University of Notre Dame. Our 13-year involvement with the Mendoza Business School's Stayer Center for Executive Education has been a wonderful association. We became involved with Notre Dame when the Leadership Circle Profile was brand new. The ongoing relationship with the Executive Education staff has hugely contributed to the work presented in this book.

I want to thank two employees who have supported me the longest. Marilyn DeMond was my first employee 25 years ago. The elegant joy, passion, and competence you bring every day are remarkable. I could not have done any of this without your tremendous assistance. Jonathan Hulsh, thank you for betting on me and on The Leadership Circle. The marketing, sales, business guidance, and friendship you provided have been immeasurable.

Thanks to my partner and co-author, Bill. Bill is one of the best men I know. He is also as good a consultant as there is. More than any other person, Bill understood what I was up to with my life's work. He has applied my life's work in ways that are well beyond where I could have taken it. His contribution to this book is huge. It is a far better book because of what Bill contributed.

Finally, I want to thank my children, Katherine, Rob, and Scott. You know how much I love you. I have had the great privilege of being your father and of traveling around the world with each of you. Our times together are the best of my life.

Bill: I want to first acknowledge my Savior Jesus Christ. I stand all amazed at the grace that is offered me, and eternally grateful that I can be still and know He is God.

I want to acknowledge my partner and wife, Cynthia Adams. From the bottom of my heart, thank you. Every moment of my life is enriched because of you and has been from the beginning. You are my best friend, faith partner, greatest support, and greatest teacher. You are my one and only. No matter what is required and where it has taken us, we have traveled it as partners. I am a better man, father, husband, and person because of you. My gratitude and love for you is endless.

I have to acknowledge and thank my partners from Maxcomm, Full Circle Group and the Leadership Circle, in particular I want to thank Sydney Isle, David Spach, Dave Schrader, Steve Athey, Nate Delahunty, Betsy Leatherman, Adelle Richards, Roma Gaster and Cindy Adams. Your friendship, love, and partnership are the difference that has made the difference. In particular, I want to acknowledge Jenny Haase; we have worked together for many years. I could not have done any of this without you. Your contribution has been immense and instrumental, as have your love and support.

I want to say thank you for the countless clients and dedicated leaders all over the world who are committed to doing their work to be better human beings and more effective leaders. After 30 years in this business, they number in the thousands. Thank you for jumping in and playing life full out.

In particular, I want to acknowledge those leaders who became my friends and who have been all-in from the beginning. These are a group of men and women who, from the minute I met them, have taught me, supported me, and allowed me to bring my mission to life in the world. I have learned so much from each of you and want you to know of my appreciation and love. Thank you to Steve Ewing, Jim Geiger, Larry

L. Payne, Rod Ross, Gayle Young, Val Christensen, Gregg Baron, Jeff Grimshaw, Tanya Mann, and Scott Slaymaker. Also, I have to acknowledge my friend, client, and partner, the late Jim McGrane. Jim's support and active engagement continue to be crucial in our work and in my life. I miss you every day, Jim.

I want to thank and acknowledge my children who make my life rich and full. Family is everything and we are family. You all know how much I love you. My children: Aubrie, Chase, Tyson, and Kasse; their partners: Greg, Abi, and Mitch M. My grandchildren: Hailey, Gavin, and Whitney and the two newest ones on the way with Abi and Kasse, both pregnant as I write this. Life is rich and filled with love because of you. Cindy and I are blessed to be your parents and grandparents.

Finally thanks to my co-author and partner, Bob. I never expected to find a new partner in Act III who would teach me so much and influence the very way I think about how I am in the world. Bob, you are brilliant, full hearted, and filled with the commitment to steward the planet. Because of you, I have been able to be more impactful and more effective. I am honored and privileged to be your partner and want to thank you for your dedication, commitment, sacrifice, and contribution to making the world a better place and allowing me to be part of that with you. I most admire the father and husband that you are to your family. Thanks for your example.

Introduction

A Universal Model of Leadership and the Leadership Circle Profile Assessment

There is nothing so practical as a good theory.
—Kurt Lewin

If you tend to skip introductions, we plead with you: *read this one!* In it, we introduce a complete leadership development model, system, and process designed to be powerfully transformative and take your leadership to the next level of effectiveness.

> Sarah returns to her office from the meeting and drops her head into her hands. She wonders if she and Matt took on too much when they decided to launch a new product line and globally expand at the same time. Matt walks in looking as shell shocked as Sarah. The two sit and stare into space, questioning themselves, their leadership, and their decisions. Meanwhile, emails roll in, text messages ring out, and the phone silently vibrates, but goes unanswered. Suddenly, their silence is interrupted when someone stops by to let them know they are late for their next meeting.

This book is written for all those who, like Sarah and Matt, feel this way or who suspect they will soon. This book is for leaders swimming in complexity, wanting and needing to thrive, knowing it could be different. There has to be a better way, one that does not just require working more, harder, faster. This book is also for leaders who are thriving in complexity and are hoping to teach others how to do the same. It is for leaders who want to produce great results, impact the world, be better mothers, fathers, partners, friends, sisters, brothers, sons, and daughters—and do all this with a lower energetic cost.

This book elevates our understanding of what makes for effective leadership and how to accelerate its progressive development. Using the first *Universal Model of Leadership* to emerge in the field, this book comes complete with a Development Framework and Leadership Effectiveness Assessment.

In this book, we address the new Leadership Imperative: Senior leaders today face such rapidly escalating complexity, uncertainty, and market volatility that to stay competitive they must accelerate their own development. The pace of leadership development, individually and collectively, must match or exceed the pace of change in business conditions. Individual effectiveness is necessary, but not sufficient. Individual development transforms business when it catalyzes a team of leaders who, together, can effectively navigate the whitewater of changing market conditions and the rapidly evolving needs of customers and stakeholders. Developing leaders who can navigate complexity is now a strategic priority—and, if done well, a competitive advantage. Beyond developing competency and capability, we need to develop leaders with courage and compassion, consciousness and character.

Leaders set the agenda for the future. Their influence is so pervasive that our global future is intertwined with their development. We need better leaders at all levels—leaders who are dedicated to creating a thriving business *and* our sustainable collective welfare, leaders who exhibit the creative capacity to invent the future *and* the capability to hold the delicate balance between short-term profitability and the long-term common good.

HOW THIS BOOK CAME TO BE

To build the context for the promise of this book, we feel a need to introduce ourselves as colleagues and co-authors.

Bob: Early in my career, I arranged to have dinner with a world-renowned Trappist monk who was involved in leading-edge work focused on developing leaders within the Catholic Church. Upon meeting him, I was surprised by his colorful character. He was a sailor before he was a monk, and he still had a sailor's mouth, drank scotch, and smoked cigars. As we talked, I learned his story. While a monk, he developed a rare blood disease that could not be cared for in monastic life and was forced to leave the monastery. For a while, he did not know what to do with himself. Eventually, he decided to return to the university and study psychology. As fortune (or providence) would have it, he studied Developmental Psychology and worked directly with Laurence Kohlberg, an early pioneer in what became a body of research on the progressive stages through which adult development proceeds.

I will never forget this monk sitting across from me with a Scotch in one hand and a cigar in the other, saying: "They are finding out the same damn thing we monks have known for millennia: that human beings can grow, and if they do, they grow through predictable stages of consciousness all the way up to union with God. They are learning how to measure it!"

This conversation would define my career. I have been a student of how human beings develop, how they grow in wisdom and personal effectiveness. This passion and central focus of my life led me to leadership. Not only have I studied what makes for great leadership and how it develops, but I have had to put everything I learned into practice as an entrepreneur. Along the way, I discovered that leading is much harder than all the theory, research, and models portend.

After meeting this monk, I decided to meet, learn from, and work closely with many of the leading thinkers and researchers in the field of leadership. I noticed early on that the field is a random collection of great stuff: a plethora of models, research studies, theories, and bodies of work, each aimed at explaining some aspect of human behavior, capability, or awareness that when applied to leadership promises greater effectiveness. Yet the field wasn't integrated. None of the various models, theories, and research related to any of the others. Each used its own framework and language. There was no universal model that tied everything together into one complete framework that explained what constitutes great leadership and how it develops.

Without fully realizing what I was up to, I set out to integrate it all. I began to weave together the threads of the best theory and research from the fields of Leadership, Organization Development, Psychology, Success Literature, and Human Potential. I also wanted the integrated framework that was developing to be aligned with the wisdom of the world's great spiritual traditions. I kept asking, "How does all of this fit together into a better model of leadership effectiveness and its development?"

I worked on this model for 20 years and field-tested each phase as it evolved. I applied it to myself and used it in my work with leaders and their teams. As the model matured, it gained traction. Its impact became more profound for my development and for that of my clients. Leaders were finding it unique, business relevant, and helpful in guiding their development.

The model underwent various transformations as I struggled to integrate what I was learning, and it went through a final metamorphosis when I remembered my conversation with the monk. After 20 years, I finally realized what he was trying to tell me, and I turned to the research on Adult Development, particularly the work of Bob Kegan, one of the foremost researchers in the field. Upon reading Bob's book, *In Over Our Heads* (Kegan, 1994), the model completely reorganized itself in my head, and I immediately knew it was complete.

My next step was to create the *Leadership Circle Profile* (LCP), a 360° leadership assessment that measures and provides leaders feedback through the lens of the entire model. Three years later, when this was complete, I launched The Leadership Circle, a leadership assessment and development company.

One of my early clients was **Bill Adams**, who owned a consulting company called Maxcomm. He and his partners had a 20-year history at the forefront of the Business Transformation field, redesigning whole systems for breakthrough performance.

After completing the LCP certification training, Bill took me aside and said: "I want to give you some feedback. Having been at the forefront of this field for two decades, I don't believe you're aware of what you have created. This is the first fully integrated and universal model of leadership in the field. I have never seen anything like it."

I was dumbfounded by Bill's comment because I was simply following my passion and curiosity. "Really?" I said, as I fell into a chair. During that conversation, Bill helped me see that the development model associated with the LCP is the first integrated model of what constitutes leadership effectiveness and how it develops, complete with ways to measure and track progress against that model. Bill eventually became my business partner and co-author.

Bill: In June 1973, just before my 18th birthday, I attended a five-day leadership retreat held in the Rocky Mountains. The retreat was designed for student body presidents who were seen as emerging leaders. It was my first experience going to a "development" session.

After the five-day retreat, I had a prompting: *This is what I want to do the rest of my life.* From that point forward, I oriented myself toward a career in leadership development. I knew that I had discovered my passion. What I did not know until years later was that this passion went hand in hand with a passion for business, stemming from being raised in our family business.

I have devoted my adult life to this work, focusing primarily on business performance and leadership effectiveness. The center of my work is personal transformation and leadership development. I have started, run, and sold multiple businesses over the last 30 years. I have practiced applying these principles, and know from experience how hard and rewarding the practice of leadership is. The level of challenge that we face today is unprecedented, and the principles apply more now than ever. Leadership is both a very private and public journey. It is private because it requires personal transformation. It is public because leaders have to *learn out loud.* This book is a very personal journey, for both of us.

I had heard of Bob, but did not meet him until 2005. That year, we were working on a multi-year transformation project for Yale University, and we needed to find or create a model of leadership that enabled us to deepen and scale our work with leaders to sustain transformational change.

I assigned Gayle Young, one of our senior consultants and our best researcher, to find a leadership model with assessments that we could adopt and use with our clients. Honestly, I doubted that she would find such a thing. However, after about three months, Gayle came back and told me with her contagious enthusiasm that she had found a model, *The Leadership Circle*, that would transform the way we thought about and developed leaders.

When I studied the model, I was astounded by its breadth and depth and immediately agreed to have our organization complete Bob's *Leadership Culture Survey* (LCS). After completing the assessment, we phoned Bob to debrief the results. During that 40-minute conversation, I could see that Bob understood both our culture and me as the CEO. Having never met us, his insight was amazing. His assessment revealed to us our strengths, what was most important for us to work on, and where we needed to make changes.

Frankly, this assessment was one of the most impactful things we had ever done. It changed the way we led, improved our performance, impacted our business model, and influenced how we consulted with our clients. From that day forward, we went from tool- and model-agnostic to tool- and model-centric. We adopted The Leadership Circle as our model of leadership. Eventually, we merged our businesses, forming the Full Circle Group.

Bob and I became instant colleagues, best friends, brothers, and business partners. We share a joint vision, common purpose, and business mission. Bob's life work has changed the way I navigate within, as well as lead and influence, the world.

A BETTER MODEL OF LEADERSHIP

Models help explain how things work. Once a good model gets inside you, it can inform and guide you throughout a lifetime. For example, the model of supply and demand explains the movement of price in any market. If supply expands and demand remains constant, price falls. If demand increases and supply does not, price rises. This simple model enables us to make sense of what is happening in markets and more effectively manage our businesses.

A good model is dynamic; it moves. That is, as one aspect of the model varies, another part moves in predictable ways—price goes up when supply contracts. A dynamic model explains how changes in one thing cause changes in something else. Once you understand the dynamics, you can manage and lead more effectively.

A better model of leadership means more effective leadership and better business results. Our efforts at developing effective leaders often fall short because we do not understand what leadership is and how it develops—our maps and models are inadequate to the challenge. *What if* there was a *better* model of leadership—one that:

- Integrates the best theory and research on leadership, human, and spiritual development, and is as complex (and elegant) as the complexities that leaders face today?

- Radically shifts our understanding of what extraordinary leadership is and how we can champion its development?
- Is dynamic, such that, if we change a limiting belief and its associated behavior, certain predictable effective behaviors and results naturally emerge?

What if there was a better way to measure effectiveness in leadership and assess progress as it develops?

The Universal Model of Leadership is a breakthrough. We know that this is a bold claim, but we have experimented with the best our field has produced. While much of it is useful, we can assure you that, until now, there has never been a comprehensive model of leadership that integrates the fragmented field of leadership development; that is business relevant; that is supported by metrics, measurement, and research; and that has been applied with a track record of success.

THE PROMISE OF THIS BOOK

This book is for CEOs and senior leaders who know that leadership effectiveness drives organizational performance and that there must be a better and faster way to develop effective leaders. It is also for the leadership practitioners, Human Resource professionals, and Organizational Development professionals responsible for bringing to those senior leaders new and innovative approaches that can fulfill the promise of developing leaders for the future.

This book promises to:

- Develop the Universal Model of Leadership, the first fully integrated model of leadership development. We develop the model progressively as the book unfolds.
- Show how the Universal Model pulls together the best theory and research in the fields of Leadership, Organizational Development, and Psychology over the last half-century. Table I.1 shows the key thought leadership integrated into the foundation of the Universal Model (see Appendix 2 for a much more extensive list).

TABLE I.1 Foundational thought leaders who form the core of the Universal Model of Leadership

Thought Leader	Theory/Research	TLC Unified Model of Leadership
William and Cindy Adams	Whole Systems Approach	Systems Awareness Dimension, Creative and Integral Level Leadership
Peter Block	Authenticity, Caution, Control, Political Scripts	Authenticity Dimension, Reactive Dimensions
David Burns	Cognitive and Rational Emotive Psychology	All Reactive Dimensions; Underlying, Self-limiting Beliefs and Assumptions and associated behaviors
Robert Fritz	Creative and Reactive Orientations	Two Stages of Development; top half and bottom half of the LCP circle
Karen Horney	Character Structure; Three Core Types	Heart, Head, Will Types; Complying, Protecting, Controlling, Relating, Awareness, Achieving
Robert Kegan and Lisa Lahey	Developmental Psychology; Stages of Adult Development; Immunity to Change	Kegan's Development model is the vertical axis of the LCP; *Immunity to Change* describes Reactive Structure's pattern of Performance
Peter Senge	Systems Thinking and Systems Dynamics; Personal Mastery	Systems Awareness Dimension; Reactive Structure and Creative Structure
Ken Wilber	Integral Model	The Unified Model of Leadership is an Integral Model. Ken's seminal work has greatly influenced its development

- Show how the Universal Model integrates all we have learned about *what extraordinary leaders do*—their competencies—into a comprehensive model that explains *how they have developed* into a person of such mastery.
- Reveal the link between *leadership effectiveness* and *business results*, and between the level or stage of a leader's development and organizational performance.
- Present breakthrough research and metrics, with light psychometric/statistical touches, that relate book content to business performance and leadership effectiveness.
- Explicate a complete Leadership Agenda—self, team, and organization—that can turn leadership in your organization into a distinct competitive advantage.
- Provide a complete Leadership Development System for cultivating leaders in your organization and show you how to deploy it so as to develop leaders for the future.
- Approach the leadership development and the business conversations as one, allowing you to have one simultaneous, rather than two separate, conversations.
- Provide a compelling pathway to a comprehensive, long-term, and systemic approach to developing individual and collective leadership effectiveness.
- Argue that senior leaders need to modify the way they go about changing their organizations; that, unless leaders do their own development work, they are not likely to create business transformation; that businesses do not transform, people do; that leaders must commit to doing their own work; and that they must own the organization's Leadership Development Agenda from the top.
- Share stories of some of the courageous leaders with whom we have worked and how they advanced the Leadership Development Agenda for themselves and their organizations.
- Help both leaders and practitioners enter the field of play, treating leadership as a professional field of practice. On this field, leaders become skillful practitioners, as skillful as those they hire to coach and consult. Practitioners step up to leadership.

- Help you enter into your own leadership transformation, one that improves every aspect of your life—personal, family, and professional.
- Help you fulfill the Promise of Leadership by providing a pathway for you to make the *highest and best use* of yourself, your life, and your leadership.
- Help you more fully and meaningfully deploy all of who you are and leave a leadership legacy consistent with your highest aspirations.

TWO BOOKS IN ONE

This is two books in one. The first half is written for the business leader. In it we emphasize the importance of embracing an expanded, more focused, and rigorous *Leadership Agenda*, one that consciously evolves the organization's leadership system. We provide the business case for developing effective leaders and present the *Universal Model of Leadership*, metrics and research on the model, and case studies describing how organizations benefit through the systemic application of the model.

In the second half of the book, we describe the deep inner work we must all undertake to mature as human beings and as leaders. We develop each stage in the leader's journey toward greater effectiveness and describe the practices that evolve higher-order leadership.

Successful entrepreneurs and senior leaders often resist discovering that they still have much to learn. The higher they go, the less feedback and formal development they get; hence, when leaders try to transform business results, they usually need to do most of the changing. Admittedly, *transformation* is an acquired taste—not for the faint of heart. However, significant culture and performance shifts require it. That's the deal.

Our hope is that this book will stimulate a transformative journey in you. Our goal is that this book will have the same transformative impact on you and your team that it has had for us.

TAKE THE LCP SELF-ASSESSMENT

To receive the full promise of this book, we strongly encourage you to plug yourself into the Universal Model now by completing *The*

Leadership Circle Profile Self-Assessment. The *Leadership Circle Profile* (LCP) measures and provides feedback on your leadership. It enables you to receive feedback on your leadership through the lens of the Universal Model and guides your personal leadership transformation. It provides a reliable pathway for increasing individual and collective leadership effectiveness.

To take the LCP assessment, go to www.theleadershipcircle.com. There you will see a link to this book and your self-assessment. Then simply follow this link. It will log you into the assessment. It will take about 20 minutes to complete.

After you complete the LCP assessment, you will be taken to your own personalized TLC web portal. There, your LCP report will be waiting for you, along with an interpretation manual. You can reference this report at any time online, or download it for future use. We refer to the assessment throughout the book. Having your own self-assessment will enhance the personal and business relevance of this book and deepen reflection on your own leadership as you read. Taken together, the book and the assessment comprise a thorough Leadership Development System.

GOING FULL CIRCLE

The LCP is designed to be a 360° feedback assessment. We do not make the 360° portion of the assessment available with this book because it is so powerful that it requires a coach to work you through the feedback. To learn how key stakeholders (bosses, peers, direct reports, and others) experience your leadership, simply request a consultation by clicking the link provided in your TLC web portal. Using the 360° portion of the LCP as you read this book will greatly accelerate your learning and take it full circle.

We promise that if you take the LCP assessment, dive into this book, and use it as your leadership development system, you will become much more effective and masterful in the art and practice of leadership. This book will serve your leadership development for life.

Chapter 1

The Promise of Leadership

Meeting the High Bar of Expectations

When we step into positions of leadership, we make a whole set of promises we may not know we are making. These promises are profound and come in the form of high, often unspoken expectations. Understanding, managing, and living up to these promises defines our leadership.

We all expect great things from our leaders, and these expectations constitute the *Promise of Leadership*. Leadership expectations come in two forms:

1. **Explicit:** Expressed expectations for certain outcomes that come with the role and that show up in the leader's job description (things like fiscal responsibility, accountability, strategy, and execution).
2. **Implicit:** Unspoken expectations that stakeholders have of their leaders (things like competence, fair treatment, commitment, engagement, listening, acting on suggestions, and providing inspiration, meaning, and direction). Leaders rarely understand the impact these implicit expectations have on their perceived effectiveness.

Stakeholders judge their leaders' effectiveness on both explicit and implicit expectations, even if these expectations are unrealistic or not understood. When you take on a leadership role, followers silently believe and expect that *you will fulfill both my explicit and implicit expectations*. However, since these expectations are sometimes unrealistic and often unexpressed, leaders may feel that they are set up to fail in their efforts to fulfill the perceived Promise of Leadership. Leaders succeed or fail depending on whether or not they clarify role expectations and keep their promises. Organization success or failure likewise depends on leaders fulfilling the Promise of Leadership.

How can leaders discover the explicit and implicit expectations that people have of them? The obvious answer is to ask. We often find that leaders don't ask those who work with and for them about their expectations of them. All leaders can accelerate their progress toward effectiveness by asking, learning, and then managing expectations, thus allowing the clarified expectations to become the bar by which they are measured.

HIGH BAR OF EXPERIENCE AND EXPECTATIONS

When we ask people to identify the extraordinary leaders they have worked for or with, most cannot identify more than one or two, suggesting that we hold leaders, and are held as leaders, to very high standards. The expectations are so high that few leaders meet or exceed them; in fact, only 5–10% of leaders are seen as fulfilling the Promise of Leadership.

Given these violated expectations, we might wonder why anyone would *want* this job. Leaders carry enormous responsibility and operate in a world of increasing change, complexity, and connectivity. They are asked to work with more transparency and disclosure as they endure greater scrutiny. Despite these challenges, many leaders love their jobs and see what they do as a calling. They relish the chance to influence people, create positive results, and change things.

LEADERSHIP MATTERS

Leadership makes a difference in the results we create and the quality of life we live.

Bill: My first corporate job out of graduate school was as a Management Development/Organizational Development Consultant at Blue Cross Blue Shield of Florida. In my role, I was primarily responsible for improving the effectiveness of managers and their teams across the organization. It was a dream job because the company was hiring high potentials out of college to fill the talent pipeline. This aggressive recruiting effort resulted in a group of about 100 young, high-potential leaders. As you can imagine, we bonded as a group of new hires and developed relationships that last to this day.

I worked across this group of high-potentials in every area of the company, and over 18 months, I noticed a pattern. About 12 months into their employment with the company, many of these new hires started to move around the organization, searching for a position where they could grow, have impact, and have a life. In many cases, they moved to areas that they had not previously considered their primary career path; however, the leaders who ran these areas were considered to be the best, and these high-potentials wanted to work for them.

The conversations went something like this: "As soon as you can transfer into Aubrie's organization, you should do it—she is really a great leader." These high-potentials started to refer to these zones of great leadership as "refugee camps" because these groups provided refuge from the culture of compliance that permeated the organization. The best and the brightest were escaping poor leadership. They were voting with their feet and moving to work for great leaders.

Eventually, I found myself in the same position. After three years, I went to work for a leader named Larry L. Payne. I wanted to report to someone who would help me learn and grow and to work in a productive, fulfilling culture. Larry created a life-sustaining, high-performing culture. Our group produced great results and we loved our jobs. It was my refugee camp.

Of course, not all new hires could move into one of these refugee camps, there simply were not enough to go around. The number of great leaders was limited to a handful. Due to this dearth of quality leaders, many high-potential hires chose within three or four years to move on to another company. In their exit interviews, they listed *poor leadership* and a non-productive, *harsh culture* among their reasons for leaving. Thus, much of the investment in building the talent pipeline was wasted because of poor leadership and a dysfunctional culture.

This lesson early in my career has influenced how I assess leadership effectiveness. It was a firsthand experience with why leadership matters. Often as leaders, we have a tendency to pass on the predominant culture, rather than changing it into an effective one. I learned that great leaders create great cultures regardless of the dominant culture in the organization. As leaders, they know that they can sustain what works or change what does not in the culture every day.

The Promise of Leadership highlights the Leadership Imperative and puts a premium on leadership development. We know that leaders are not just born—they are made. They learn and develop over time. Great leaders can be cultivated to meet and exceed our high expectations of them. In order to fulfill the Promise of Leadership, leaders must know what people expect of them, manage those expectations, and develop into the person who can perform against them. When this happens, execution is extraordinary—performance is high, stakeholders are engaged, and work is fun and fulfilling.

FOUR UNIVERSAL PROMISES OF LEADERSHIP

From our research and field experience, we have identified *four universal promises of leadership*: 1) Set the right direction and create meaningful work; 2) Engage all stakeholders and hold them accountable for performance; 3) Ensure that processes and systems facilitate focus and execution; and 4) Lead effectively—maintain relationships of trust to achieve and sustain desired results (see Figure 1.1).

We often explore these promises in our early conversations with senior leaders. While most are familiar with them, few see them as *promises*. We now describe each promise from the perspective of a CEO (L1) and their direct reports (L2).

Promise 1: Set the right direction and create meaningful work

L1 and L2 leaders come together on the Executive Team. They are responsible for setting direction, defining the vision and strategies required for sustainable growth and profit. They also identify markets and products, and establish the mission, vision, values, and culture. These elements constitute the essential components of *meaning* in the organization. Setting direction and creating meaning are vital if the organization is to thrive. Stakeholders hold leaders to this promise.

From direction and meaning flow the organization's *identity* or brand. Executive Leaders need to define how the organization creates value and

FIGURE 1.1 Four promises of leadership

answers the question, "What is it that you uniquely as an organization can contribute to the world?"

When we work, we invest our life's blood (time, talent, and energy) into an organization. Therefore, we want to readily identify the meaning of the work we do, see rewards beyond money, and contribute to the organization's higher purpose. Leaders set the context and create the conditions in which individuals and organizations thrive. When the Executive Team ties the company's direction to the work at hand in meaningful ways, every employee then has a clear line of sight into how *their* contribution makes a difference. This *shared identity* provides the foundation for corporate meaning—a requirement to fulfill the second leadership promise.

Promise 2: Engage all stakeholders and hold them accountable

When direction and meaning are confined to Executive Leadership, value is minimized. With this promise leaders are expected to fully engage employees in owning the company's direction. They are expected to earn trust and the commitment to perform by providing the *why* behind the *what* of work.

The *why* comes from directly connecting the value created by the organization with the personal contribution of each individual. Employees expect that *leaders* will draw forth their *inherent potential*—the hidden talent, discretionary energy, and passion that people put into their work—by creating a culture where people thrive, strive to contribute, and are valued for their contribution. When leaders, for example, set challenging goals, they specifically address the reasons to work toward those goals, each individual's role, and the significance of each person's contribution. They also recognize individual and collective contribution toward the goals because there is a strong link between recognizing individual strengths and talents and capturing their potential as full, committed participation.

This leadership promise can be difficult to keep. While Executive Leadership (L1 and L2) and even Senior Leadership (L3 to L5) often clearly understand the direction of the organization and why work is critical to that direction, they often underestimate the energy and commitment required to create meaning throughout the organization and fully engage everyone. Sadly, clarity and commitment often end at the leadership team level. We see evidence that this promise has been broken whenever employees cannot answer the question, "How does what I do make a difference?" Sadder still, is when employees stop asking the question altogether and resign themselves to work that provides little meaning beyond their paycheck.

Promise 3: Ensure that processes and systems facilitate focus and execution

An employee's well-being is ultimately tied to the organization's performance, which itself is directly related to the organization's ability to execute. Underpinning every stakeholder's commitment is the belief that the leadership "promises" to deliver results in the marketplace by successfully executing on key initiatives. Hence Promise 3—*keep the organization focused on execution.* Effective execution systems efficiently channel action into results and provide feedback on the work the organization is doing; action provides clarity; effort is linked to results, which gives individuals a clear line of sight to long-term, meaningful success.

Leaders break this promise in four ways: 1) by not providing the resources (time, people, and money) necessary to ensure execution; 2) by allowing the organization to be distracted by yet another "silver bullet" or "bright shiny object" (an attractive lower priority); 3) by having too little or an ineffective process in place so everything is done "for the first time" every time; and 4) by being so process-bound that execution becomes secondary to the process. Steve Ewing, the President and COO of Michigan Consolidated Gas Company and DTE Energy Gas, said it this way: "Results without process can't be replicated and process without results is worthless."

When these issues are the case, any line of sight to the results of the work, or to higher purpose, is lost. Breaking this promise exhausts the organization and robs it of discretionary energy, enthusiasm, and performance. When this happens, the organization operates beyond its capacity, activity takes precedence over results, and short-term fixes are substituted for long-term success. Repeatedly breaking this promise creates a culture of frustration, resentment, and hopelessness. Then, *cynicism-by-experience* regarding all strategic change initiatives poisons the well—even for new leaders.

Promise 4: Lead effectively

We expect our leaders to be effective, very effective, and the bar by which we measure them is high. Furthermore, we expect our leaders to be more effective this year than last year. We expect them to be so committed to enhancing their effectiveness that they become the most effective leaders they can be by engaging in ongoing personal and professional development. We expect all this because we know that failure to lead effectively virtually ensures violation of the other three leadership promises.

Leadership development must proceed at a pace consistent with what it takes to stay effective and relevant in today's complex, rapidly changing business environment. Leaders who are committed to improving their performance must commit to growing as individuals, becoming increasingly more competent, self-aware, and conscious.

We recently started working with the extended leadership team (top team and level 3) of an iconic brand. As part of this company's succession, three members of this team have been identified as a potential successor to the President. One of these leaders is viewed by everyone as an exceptional leader who continues to grow year in and year out. When we asked him about his own leadership practice, he explained to us that he had been keeping a journal for over 20 years, noting when he witnessed extraordinary leadership and what was done. By now, he has filled up several journals of effective leadership moments and incorporated some of these elements of "effective leadership" into his own leadership practice. Needless to say, he is one of the most effective leaders with whom we have ever worked. This conscious and deliberate development process has made him an extraordinary leader. His leadership continues to develop and improve year after year.

Leaders must also recognize that leadership effectiveness is more than individual effectiveness. Collective leadership effectiveness drives business performance. Therefore, critical to keeping all four leadership promises is *keeping them with one another*. Leadership teams must work deliberately and unflaggingly on the quality of their own engagement. They must tell the truth, especially when it is hard to do so. They must persevere together through the often excruciating exchanges required to create shared meaning, direction, and viable strategy. They must work together in a way that focuses their individual and collective leadership energy on ensuring that they, and the organization, have what is needed to be successful and fulfilled.

Operating individually and collectively at this level of mastery describes the high bar that is set by the Promise of Leadership effectiveness. Since this promise underpins the other three, this promise requires ongoing development. For the best leaders we know, the desire to be an effective leader serves as strong motivation to developing both as an individual leader and as part of a leadership team.

BROKEN LEADERSHIP PROMISES

Leaders who keep their promises boost their credibility and build trust; those who break promises to their employees lose credibility and trust. We are all too familiar with the consequences of broken leadership promises. We often hear about leaders who fall from grace because of egregious behavior, but trust is usually broken in far simpler ways. Leaders who claim to value the talents and contributions of individuals, yet lead as if intelligence resides only at the top, are breaking a promise. Leaders who seek near-term profits at the expense of sustainability and long-term growth are breaking a promise. Leaders who avoid discussing potential pitfalls during a change initiative are breaking a promise. Leaders who do not make it safe to fail are breaking a promise. Leaders who are unclear in their messaging, avoid difficult situations, or react defensively to feedback are breaking a promise. When a Promise of Leadership is neglected or unfulfilled, trust is broken, engagement erodes, and performance suffers.

When Promise 1 is broken, the organization lacks meaningful direction, fails to be competitive, and declines. When Promise 2 is broken, employees are disengaged. They underperform, turnover increases, competition wins market share, and the organization declines. When Promise 3 is broken, dollars, human capital, and time are wasted as execution suffers. The organization declines as it becomes mired in a culture of resentment and hopelessness. If Promise 4 is broken, there is no chance of meeting Promises 1, 2, and 3.

KEEPING THE PROMISE

Employees, as well as other stakeholders, depend on leaders to keep their promises, to set the right strategic direction, to keep the organization on track, to execute efficiently, and to effectively lead the organization to produce results that sustain the business. All of these expectations exist on the *transactional* side of leadership. On the *transformational* side, leaders are expected to set a vision that captures people's imagination and provides inspiration, to engage employees in meaningful work, and to set the tone for the way people are treated and valued.

To meet explicit and implicit, transactional and transformational expectations, leaders must increase both their competence and evolve in consciousness. This means becoming just as committed to their own personal development as they are to developing the people they serve. As leaders increase in competence, they become more effective. As they increase conscious self-awareness and act upon it, they become more cognizant of the messages their actions, communications, and behaviors convey, as well as how others perceive these messages. Once promises have been acknowledged, and leaders are aware of how they are "showing up," then they can act authentically from their position of responsibility and authority.

Consciously competent and authentic leadership engenders credibility and trust. The relationship between leaders and followers then becomes reciprocal. Leaders have the right to expect that others will compassionately recognize them as fallible human beings. When leaders openly acknowledge their weaknesses and mistakes, constituents reciprocate by seeing these as opportunities to learn and grow. Credibility is earned with time and experience; grace is granted to be human.

The best leaders identify what promises they are being held to, manage expectations, and honor those promises. In so doing, they create a rich and inspiring culture, one in which the organization's values, beliefs, ethics, contribution, and results are aligned. They create an organization and culture that makes a difference in today's world. They ensure that individuals find meaning in the work they do. They realize the hope that business can be a place that matters in the lives of all involved. Great leadership is its own reward and returns a multiple on the effort expended.

THE LEADERSHIP AGENDA

In the next few chapters, we will make the argument for the breadth and depth of development required for leaders to fulfill the Promise of Leadership, individually and collectively, over the long haul. These four promises and the level of effectiveness (if not mastery) that they require—individually and collectively—constitute the Leadership Agenda for the organization. This Agenda, mastering the art and practice of leadership, needs to be held by the Top Team and led as a key strategic priority and business imperative. The performance of the business—as well as the meaning and value creation of everyone associated with the business—depends on it.

TAKING STOCK

- What is possible and who cares?
- Are you creating an organization you would want your children to work in?
- Do you demonstrate love for those you are leading? How?
- How do you model the courage that you want from those around you?
- If this organization no longer existed, what would be lost to the world? Would that matter? Can you articulate why?

Chapter 2

Leadership Effectiveness and Business Performance

The Primary Competitive Advantage

We will only seek a better model of leadership and make the Leadership Development Agenda a strategic priority if we believe that more effective leaders achieve higher performance and that we can develop effective leaders at a faster pace.

The fourth Promise of Leadership is that we lead effectively and *continue* to become more effective. When asked, leaders always agree that the effectiveness of leadership (both individual and collective) is a primary contributor to business performance and success. Yet, developing leadership effectiveness is rarely a leadership priority. In fact, it is often relegated to a staff function that struggles for attention and relevance amid competing priorities. Furthermore, most organizations, if they are focused on leadership development, focus on individual effectiveness and ignore the huge potential of collective leadership effectiveness.

WHAT THE RESEARCH SHOWS

The entire arch of leadership inquiry and research is rooted in the premise that *leadership effectiveness matters*. At The Leadership Circle, we are adding to this research. We developed a business performance metric by asking leaders to evaluate the performance of a business (or business unit) compared to industry standards on a series of performance criteria, including revenue, market share, sales, profitability, quality of

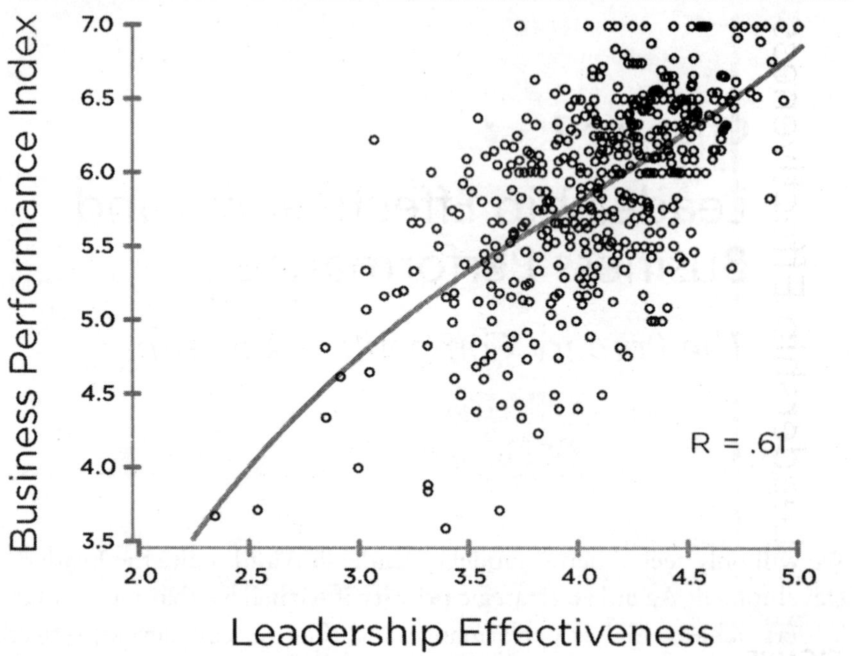

FIGURE 2.1 Leadership Effectiveness and business performance

products and services, new product development, and overall business performance. We then used these criteria to construct a Business Performance Index and correlated that index with a measure of Leadership Effectiveness on our Leadership Circle Profile (LCP) 360 assessment, and we found the pattern shown in Figure 2.1.

This study shows a strong correlation between *Leadership Effectiveness* and the *Business Performance Index*. It was originally conducted with about 500 businesses and has since been expanded to include over 2,000. The results are the same: *Leadership Effectiveness is a primary contributor to business performance*. In fact, this data strongly suggests that if you can improve leadership effectiveness, you have a 38% probability of seeing that improvement translate into higher business performance. In other words, leadership effectiveness is a 38% lever, contributing heavily to the organization's overall performance. Since 38% is well beyond most companies' profit margin, developing effective leaders clearly deserves investment.

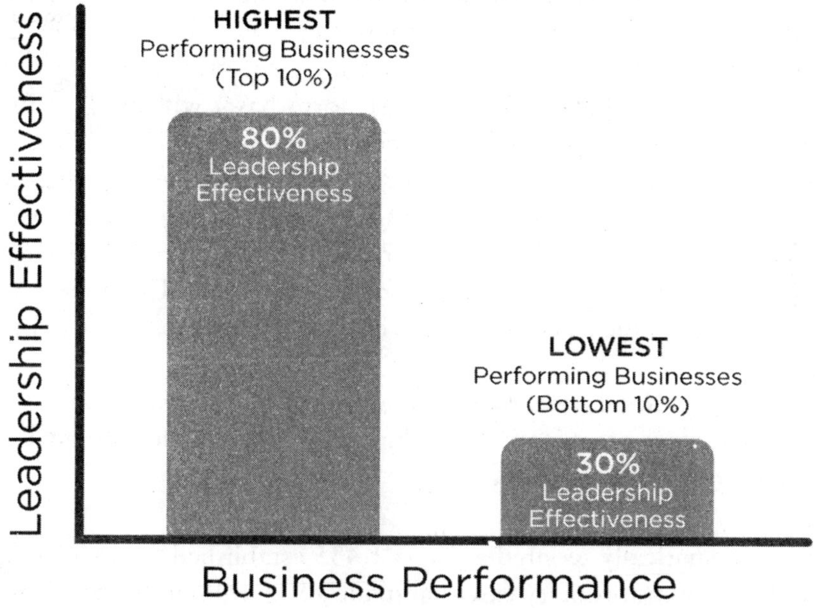

FIGURE 2.2 Leadership Effectiveness in the highest/lowest performing businesses

This study became even more provocative when we computed the average Leadership Effectiveness scores for leaders in the highest performing business—the top 10%. We also compared that to the average Leadership Effectiveness scores of leaders in the lowest performing businesses—the bottom 10%. We found the following (see Figure 2.2):

In businesses evaluated as highest performing—top 10%—the average Leadership Effectiveness score was at the 80th percentile. Thus, those leaders in the highest performing business had Effectiveness scores higher than 80% of our norm base (over a half-million rater surveys). In the lowest performing businesses (bottom 10%), the leaders' Effectiveness scores averaged at the 30th percentile—lower than 70% of our norm base.

This research is consistent with the Zenger-Folkman research that shows leadership becomes extraordinary when effectiveness scores go beyond the 80th percentile. In their book, *Extraordinary Leaders*, Jack Zenger and Joe Folkman report an extensive survey of the leadership competency literature, including their database of over 250,000 surveys (Zenger, 2009). They make an astonishing conclusion: those leaders who are rated on a good 360° competency assessment at or above the 80th percentile (compared to a robust norm base) will produce twice the results of those in the middle 60 percentile range.

When we do the math on Zenger's research, we see that there are only two out of ten leaders beyond the 80th percentile and six out of ten in the middle ranges. So, there are three times more leaders in the middle range who are being outperformed two-fold. This means that each 80th percentile leader is *six-fold* outperforming those in the middle zone!

In *Good to Great*, researcher and author, Jim Collins, set out to discover what great organizations do that allows them to sustain high performance over time. He writes:

> We systematically scoured a list of 1,435 established companies to find every extraordinary case that made a leap from no-better-than-average results to great results. How great? After the leap, a company had to generate cumulative stock returns that exceeded the general stock market by at least three times over 15 years—and it had to be a leap independent of its industry. In fact, the 11 good-to-great companies that we found averaged returns 6.9 times greater than the market's (Collins, September 2001).

Collins actually set out on this line of research with the specific goal of *not* looking at leadership. He did not want to write another book about the primacy of great leadership on business performance. However, as his research progressed, he could not ignore the impact of great leadership on the success of organizations. He called this *Level Five Leadership*—a unique blend of fierce resolve with humility (Collins, 2001).

The conclusion from the research is obvious: leadership effectiveness is a primary contributor to business performance, and it provides a competitive advantage, especially in times of increasing complexity (see Chapter 3). The best organizations are the best led, but this is not something that just happens on its own. Developing effective leaders deserves to be a key strategic priority, owned by top leadership.

WHAT IS YOUR LEADERSHIP QUOTIENT?

Is leadership a competitive advantage in your organization, or is it costly? To measure this question, we created a metric called the Leadership Quotient (LQ). The math is simple.

$$LQ = LE/LI$$

$$\text{Leadership Quotient} = \frac{\text{Leadership Effectiveness}}{\text{Leadership Ineffectiveness}}$$

For example, let's assume that the average Leadership Effectiveness score for an organization is at the 50th percentile (meaning they have an *average* level of effectiveness compared to their industry). Therefore, it is likely that they will have ineffectiveness scores at the 50th percentile as well. This gives them a collective Leadership Quotient of one (1).

$$LQ = LE/LI$$
$$1.0 = 50\%/50\%$$

A LQ score of 1.0 means neutral impact (one times anything results in the same number). Therefore, when we see a LQ score of 1.0, we can assume that leadership is competitive, but it is not yet a competitive *advantage* (or competitive disadvantage). However, an LQ of 1.0 also means that you are vulnerable to being outcompeted by organizations with higher LQ scores.

Let's recall the highest and lowest performing organization research (Figure 2.2) and calculate their associated LQ scores. Leadership Effectiveness (LE) in the highest performing organizations averaged at the 80th percentile. This means that by default, keeping the math simple for now (it will get a little more sophisticated as we develop the Universal Model), Leadership Ineffectiveness (LI) is at the 20th percentile (100 minus 80). Therefore, the LQ for the highest performing businesses, those evaluated in the top 10%, is 4.0.

$$LQ = LE/LI$$
$$4.0 = 80\%/20\%$$

In the lowest performing businesses, or those in the bottom 10%, the average LQ score is 0.4.

$$LQ = LE/LI$$
$$0.4 = 30\%/70\%$$

There is a *10-fold difference* between the LQ of the highest and lowest performing businesses. Ten-fold may seem like a huge difference, but it makes sense because we are measuring the top and bottom 10% of business performance. Consequently, we think the LQ score for an organization measures the degree to which leadership is a competitive advantage or disadvantage. In organizations with LQ scores less than one (1.0), leadership is a costly competitive disadvantage. Organizations with LQ scores above one (1.0) are moving into the range where leadership effectiveness is a distinct competitive advantage. As you can see, scores as high as four (4.0) indicate that leadership is a serious competitive advantage.

PROVOCATIVE QUESTIONS

We invite you to ask yourself these six provocative questions:

- Are you in the group of extraordinary performers with LQ scores well above one?
- Are your key leaders functioning at or beyond the 80th percentile?
- How effective is your personal and collective leadership? How do you know?
- How does your leadership effectiveness compare to that of your competition?
- Are you tracking the effectiveness of leadership over time to gauge improvement?
- Is your leadership a competitive advantage or disadvantage?

If you do not know the answers to these questions, you probably are not serious enough about the effectiveness of leadership—you are not making leadership a business imperative and a key strategic priority.

We have worked with Jim McGrane for over a decade in three different companies. When we got involved with his most recent company in 2006, he took the LCP, and his Leadership Effectiveness score, as evaluated by the key leaders on his team, averaged at the 80th percentile—putting him in the top 20% of effective leaders. We will present Jim's story in an extensive case study in Chapter 7. In that case, using the more sophisticated measure of LQ, Jim had an LQ of 2.0. This is quite high, making his leadership a big competitive advantage. Given his profile results and his high LQ, it is not surprising that he was leading a company that was a rising star in the industry. He made the Leadership Development Agenda a strategic priority. For the entire period of our engagement, he and his team could answer all the questions outlined above and they could correlate how they were performing as leaders, individually and collectively, with the business results they were getting.

COLLECTIVE EFFECTIVENESS

In business, *collective leadership effectiveness* is underutilized and rarely capitalized upon. Most development focuses on *individual* leaders, ignoring collective effectiveness and the leadership system—all leaders and managers in formal leadership positions.

We focus our work primarily on the top four levels of leadership—the CEO (L1), their direct reports (L2: C-Team and EVPs/SVPs), that level's direct reports (L3: primarily VPs), and in some cases the next level down (L4: primarily Senior Directors). This *Extended Leadership Team* (ELT) makes up the organization's Leadership System. While leadership is required at every level, a reference to collective leadership or the Leadership System throughout this book indicates a discussion of the Extended Leadership Team.

The number of leaders on the ELT varies depending on a company's size. In large organizations, there are several hundred people within these ranks. In smaller enterprises, this group might be fewer than 20. Regardless of its size, the Extended Leadership Team is responsible for providing leadership to the entire organization. This group has more impact on how the organization performs than any other group.

The bulleted provocative questions mentioned above apply equally to individual leaders and the ELT. Since the ELT determines the organization's direction and execution, collective leadership effectiveness is impacted by how well the ELT sets direction; aligns around vision and mission; agrees on key strategies and initiatives; develops a clear shared understanding of strategy; translates strategy into execution; understands each other's roles; collaborates together; makes decisions; creates an accountable, engaged, performance-based culture; focuses on achieving results; mobilizes and engages all stakeholders to achieve those results; and develops leadership that can do all the above.

The level and consistency of collective effectiveness of the leadership system makes the difference between organizations that perform optimally and those that do not. It is not merely *individual leadership effectiveness* that results in high organizational performance. Individual effectiveness is necessary, but insufficient, for extraordinary business performance. Individual leadership effectiveness catalyzes collective effectiveness. *Collective effectiveness* carries the day. The organization cannot perform at a level higher than the collective effectiveness of its leadership.

Over the last 30 years, we have worked with hundreds of top and extended leadership teams. We have seen many examples of effective and ineffective collective leadership in businesses ranging from small start-ups to large multi-nationals. Regardless of size or maturity, we have found some common traits that impact the collective effectiveness of leaders, and the results they produce.

Start-ups in particular offer an interesting case study of collective leadership where its effectiveness, or a lack thereof, is immediately on display. Unlike a mature company, where it takes time to see the impact of change, a start-up experiences it very rapidly. The learning that takes place in a start-up is accelerated and amplified both on the upside, when there is rapid growth, and on the downside, when the start-up struggles.

Initially, a start-up is dependent upon its founders for vision, leadership, direction, and management. It requires their guidance on a daily basis. As the start-up begins to realize some order of success, or begins to struggle, its future quickly moves beyond the brilliance of its founding leadership. It now requires the capability and capacity of its collective leadership. When present and functioning effectively, collective leadership removes the single point of failure—dependency on the founder—that many start-ups experience and expands the capacity and capability of the organization to lead its growth.

Often, we can point to a lack of collective leadership effectiveness in start-ups that struggle, or fail outright. We have worked with a few leadership teams at start-ups that faced the need to fundamentally shift strategy and transform their businesses. Using the LCP at these companies, we found that those with a collective LQ of less than 1.0 simply lacked the capability or capacity to execute on strategy, much less transform. This finding has proven to be true with clients that have experienced successful double-digit growth reaching revenues in excess of $1 billion, as well as those who were well funded but simply could not get out of their own way.

We once worked with a mortgage start-up in the southeast U.S. that was intended to be the standalone mortgage banking arm of a small regional bank. The bank had recently been acquired by a manufacturing company that was seeking to diversify its business portfolio. The acquiring company sent one of their financial officers to join the top team of the start-up as its CFO. The other team members consisted of a group who had a long history of working together running the mortgage division of the bank that had been acquired.

We began working with the top team at the end of their first year. Already, a significant number of issues had surfaced both within the team, and about the fundamentals of the business. As we began our work, we conducted interviews with the 8 leadership team members to identify what was working and not working. One question we posed in the interviews was, "How confident are you that the business will succeed with the strategy and team currently in place?" Each of the 8 members of the leadership team, including the CEO, expressed "little" or "no" confidence. All 8 leaders were handicapping their chance of success at 25%. The team was not in alignment on the vision or key strategies, and had energetically, collectively and individually, come to believe that the business would fail.

We immediately worked to get the team on the same page—to establish alignment and effective collective execution. Unfortunately, they had run out of runway and within the next 12 months, the owner sold off the servicing portfolio and exited the business. When we interviewed the owners, they shared that the top team had never provided them with the confidence that the business would succeed. Obviously that was no surprise, given the lack of alignment and the low quality of the leadership conversation that was taking place within the company. In less than 2 years, the leadership team went from being acquired and fully funded for success to being sold and out of work. What was most fascinating about this leadership team was that each individual believed they knew what needed to happen, both strategically and operationally, to be successful. Yet, the team was unable to reach collective agreement and alignment on these issues. Consequently, it was over before it even started.

Simply put, our success as a leadership team is tied directly to our level of alignment on vision and direction, our agreement on key strategies, and how well we execute together. Our ability to do this depends on the quality of our interaction, communication, honesty, and trust. This is what we call the "leadership conversation." This conversation largely determines our collective leadership effectiveness, and the capability and capacity we provide to the business.

The importance of collective leadership effectiveness, driven by the quality of the leadership conversation, cannot be underestimated. The organization simply cannot outperform the collective effectiveness of its leaders. When the leadership conversation is overlooked, collective leadership becomes ineffective and a less than optimal outcome is likely to follow.

COLLECTIVE EFFECTIVENESS AND INTELLIGENCE

Leadership is a conversation. Leaders spend most of their days in conversation—meetings, phone calls, emails, and strategic communications. How *you* show up in these conversations determines your level of effectiveness. How *we* show up together in these conversations drives our collective effectiveness. The quality of our collective conversation largely determines our collective leadership effectiveness and business performance.

We work with an extraordinary female leader of a large professional service firm who consistently leverages the best out of her Extended Leadership Team because of how she deploys herself in leadership conversations. She told us that in every conversation she has three objectives: 1) increase understanding and buy-in, 2) achieve the desired outcome, and 3) improve the relationship. For instance, she told of having a difficult performance review with a key executive. With this framework in mind, she ensured that the content was clearly understood, outcomes were achieved, and the relationship improved. She consistently is seen as being clear, direct, fair, and compassionate. Her people know where they stand with her, and she outperforms her peers in this business at a multiple of *three times* their results. She is highly effective, in no small measure, because of how she models and orchestrates individual and collective leadership conversations.

Collective leadership effectiveness and intelligence represent huge untapped potential in most organizations. Management expert, Peter Senge, notes that the collective intelligence and performance of most groups is well below the average intelligence and performance of the members (Senge, 1990). We usually *dumb down* when we come together. We act at the lowest common denominator. The dynamics played out in most groups—overly aggressive advocacy of positions, poor listening, reactive responsiveness, political caution, ambitious self-interest, mistrust, withholding of opinions—subvert collective effectiveness. Consequently, most leadership teams function collectively well below their members' average intelligence. This results in an LQ of less than one, and most organizations with such a low LQ lose market share and end up on the auction block.

Collective intelligence is required for breakthroughs. Senge talked of finding *leverage points* within the system (Senge, 1990). A leverage point is an action taken or a change made that has a magnified positive and lasting impact on intended results. If you have a long lever, you can move a very heavy object with little effort. In financial language, this is the equivalent of getting a *multiple*. Businesses invest to get a multiple return on investment. Finding leverage means discovering an innovation, initiative, change, or action that, when taken, has a large, lasting, positive impact well beyond the energy of input.

The collective effectiveness of the ELT is often overlooked as leverage. We ask leaders to find leverage here by evaluating the return on their time spent in two ways. First, are you increasing the creative capacity and capability of your organization at a multiple? If you are not getting a 5-to-1 ratio of return on your time spent, your ROI is sub-par. Far too many leaders spend their time on the areas that provide a 1-to-1 return (or worse). These areas are low leverage and need to be upgraded or eliminated. Expanding capacity and capability depends on this ratio of return. Second, are you developing effective leadership at all levels within your organization? As a leader, you cannot scale the organization until you understand and perform your role in developing other leaders. When you enter the executive ranks, your job is to develop other leaders—and, to minimize your losses, know when someone cannot be developed in the timeframe required. When we ask leaders what they would do differently looking back, their most frequent response is, "I would have made changes in my executive team more quickly." They hang on to low-ratio return, high-cost leaders for too long, and it costs them dearly. Having the right people on the leadership team and investing in the Leadership Agenda is high leverage. It is key to developing the collective effectiveness and intelligence required to compete. Otherwise, the business cannot grow at the pace required, the return on leadership will be sub-par, and even the best executives will likely burn out.

Collectively intelligent leadership teams consistently find leverage, those with low collective intelligence are not likely to innovate, create, and find leverage at the rate required to stay competitive. Organizations and their competitive environments are so complex that they defy rational understanding. Actions or changes in the system that would produce lasting improvement are not obvious. If they were, we would have already taken them. It is not easy to find the leverage we need amid complexity. It takes more than one brilliant leader to consistently find non-obvious points of leverage and to expand the business's leadership capacity and capability. It takes an effective leadership team, one that functions well together, to achieve a level of collective intelligence well beyond the average level of brilliance of its members.

It takes honest, often courageous conversation to find leverage. For example, when we worked with Carlson Companies, one of the largest privately held companies in the world, the organization was being led by Marilyn Carlson Nelson, daughter of founder Curt Carlson. Her top team was working through several difficult strategic issues, and the conversation turned to performance and the culture. This team had learned over the years to have honest conversations and to address what really mattered. In one conversation, at a particularly controversial moment, Marilyn made a courageous statement that changed the entire dialogue and outcome. She said, "We are defined by what we tolerate."

At that moment, the entire leadership team, prompted by her clear and honest statement, coalesced around a difficult decision that elevated both culture and performance.

The quality of the leadership conversations determines collective effectiveness, which determines collective intelligence, which determines business performance. As Senior Leaders, the quality of our conversation and our relationships correlates directly with the results we create.

None of this can happen without developing *individually effective leadership*. Individual effectiveness is required to catalyze collective effectiveness. In our leadership consulting practice, we work simultaneously on individual leadership effectiveness and collective effectiveness to improve the quality of the collective conversation.

After a year of work with any given leadership team, the most consistent feedback we receive is: "The difference that made the difference is that we can now tell the truth to one another and have courageous conversations that get results. We can now take on complex and politically charged issues, central to moving the business forward, and we quickly cut through the complexity and personal sensitivities to arrive at high-quality decisions."

Collective effectiveness is vital to fulfilling the Promise of Leadership. Developing such effectiveness, mastering leadership, in the Leadership System is a high-leverage investment. The effectiveness of the Leadership System (the Leadership Agenda) should be a key priority owned by the Top Team.

TAKING STOCK

- How effective is your leadership? How do you know? How does this compare to your industry peers?
- Is your leadership developing at the pace to stay relevant? How do you know?
- What is it about the way you show up that prevents others from providing you with well-intended feedback?
- Are you effective in achieving what matters or just very busy?
- Would you follow you?

[illegible]

Chapter 3

Mastery and Maturity, Consciousness and Complexity

The Leadership Development Agenda

Some say that my teaching is nonsense.
Others call it lofty but impractical.
But to those who have looked inside themselves,
this nonsense makes perfect sense.
And to those who put it into practice,
this loftiness has roots that go deep.
—*Tao Te Ching*, Lao Tzu, translation by S. Mitchell (2008)[1]

We often confer the title of *Master* onto people who are highly effective at what they do. Mastery in anything—from sports, to the arts, to leadership—requires well-practiced capability mediated by a highly mature interiority: a well-honed "Outer Game" arising on a highly-evolved "Inner Game." Both are essential. Masterful leadership is *Conscious Competence.*

The inner game runs the outer game. The maturity of the inner game is mediating and managing the outer game. Since this truth is largely ignored, most efforts to develop mastery in leadership focus on the *outer game of competence* with little focus on the *inner game of consciousness.* Until we take a more balanced approach, one that evolves both the inner

[1]Excerpts from #22 [2 I.]., #67 [6 I] from Tao Te Ching by Lao Tzu, A New English Version, with Foreword and Notes, by Stephen Mitchell. Translation copyright © 1988 by Stephen Mitchell. Reprinted by permission of HarperCollins Publishers.

and outer game (consciousness and competence) simultaneously, we will falter in our efforts to develop leaders for the future at the pace required.

TRIUMPH AND FAILURE OF THE INNER GAME

In the 1988 Winter Olympics, three female figure skaters entered the final night of competition. In first place, and the favorite to win, was Debi Thomas, the 1986 World Champion and two-time USA National Champion. She had a commanding lead, and was the most technically accomplished skater. In second place was Katarina Witt, a prior gold medalist and four-time World Champion from East Germany. She was skating the final event of her amateur career. In third place was a woman from Canada named Elizabeth Manley, a dark-horse contender. No one (except her) expected her to be in contention.

We are always learning about the impact of the inner game on performance, so we paid close attention as each skater was interviewed before taking the ice. Debi Thomas said, "I just want to get through this performance without making a mistake." Katarina Witt spoke eloquently about closing her amateur career with a magical performance. Elizabeth Manley said, "I was not expected to be here. I have nothing to lose. I am going to go out there and have a blast. I am going to skate the performance of my life."

What you hold in your consciousness tends to manifest—the inner game runs the outer game. Debi Thomas, trying hard not to make a mistake, fell and skated beneath her potential. Katarina Witt skated a beautiful swansong performance. But Elizabeth Manley stole the evening, skating an inspired performance. She had the highest score of the evening and rose from third place to capture the silver medal, a fraction of a point from getting the Gold. Katarina won the gold, and Debi Thomas fell to third place.

How mature was Debi's outer game to compete for Olympic Gold? She was more than capable of winning gold. How mature was her inner game for that moment, for that stage? By her own account, not mature enough. *How mature is your inner game for the stage you are on, or to which you aspire?* Is it mature enough to handle the pace and complexity of leading your organization through the volatile whitewaters that most organizations are now navigating?

Debi Thomas was stuck in what Larry Wilson calls a *Play-Not-To-Lose* game (Wilson, 1998). In this game, we strive to win by trying hard not to fail. This is essentially a defensive game—the game we play when our inner game is functioning from, as we will call it, a *Reactive Structure of Mind*. Elizabeth Manley and Katarina Witt were competing in what Larry Wilson calls a *Play-To-Win* game. In this game we play full-out, as if we have nothing to gain or lose. We play this game when our inner game matures to what we call a *Creative Structure of Mind.*

Debi Thomas now coaches aspiring skaters on the inner game. As a successful surgeon, she cannot afford to have a single day when either her outer game or her inner game lets her down.

Which game are you playing?

COMPETENCY IS ONLY HALF THE GAME

Competency alone does not make for effective leadership. Yet, the current focus for developing leadership effectiveness is primarily on improving competency, which is necessary, but insufficient.

Years ago we facilitated a team-building session with the Extended Leadership Team of a large company. We asked the group to brainstorm the salient qualities of a great leader. As we completed the list, the CEO said in amazement: "Our top selection criteria for senior leadership positions is *competence*, and competence did not make the list. There are no competencies on that list!"

Competence is necessary to attain and be effective in senior roles; however, competence alone is insufficient. When we describe *great leadership*, we describe something beyond skill, capability, and competence. We use words like *integrity, honesty, passion, vision, risk-taking, fearlessness, compassion, courage, authenticity, collaboration, self-awareness, selflessness, purposefulness, humility, intuition,* and *wisdom*. These are qualities of the inner game. Great leadership is connected with the deepest parts of ourselves. It has more to do with *character, courage*, and *conviction* than it does with specific skills or competencies. Leadership requires *wisdom, self-knowledge*, and *character development* at psychological and spiritual levels. Mastery of leadership requires that we work at these depths and develop mature, conscious awareness.

TWO GAMES OF LEADERSHIP

We are playing two games at all times: an outer and inner game. The outer game of leadership consists of using all of our knowledge and

OUTER GAME

LEADERSHIP PROCESS
- Science of Leadership
- Business Rhythm and Management Process

LEADERSHIP COMPETENCIES
- Outside Game of Leadership
- Leadership Competency Research

INNER GAME

LEADERSHIP CONSCIOUSNESS
- Inside Game of Leadership
- Evolving Consciousness

FIGURE 3.1 Two games and three domains of leadership effectiveness

experience, as well as our technical, managerial, and leadership competence, to accomplish results. The all-consuming outer game is obviously where most leaders spend most of their time, since the day-to-day requirements of the outer game are fierce and the learning curve is steep. Developing well-honed capability to think and act effectively, skillfully, and competently in different situations is a baseline requirement for effectiveness in managing and leading. We ignore honing this outer game at our peril. If we lack capability in technical competence, management, and execution, we will not be effective.

Today leaders need to be effective in three areas (see Figure 3.1):

Leadership Process. This is the science of leadership and the domain of management. Leaders are responsible for the allocation and effective utilization of resources: people, time, and money. How effectively they allocate and use these resources impacts organizational effectiveness. To effectively utilize resources, leaders deploy *management systems* that include business cadence, strategy, direction, execution, process, metrics, and decision making. Without an effective management process in place, the business is not organized for success.

Leadership Competencies. These are the competencies required for a leader to be successful. We describe this as the *outside game* of leadership. We will review the competencies that are most strongly correlated with effective leadership later in this book.

Leadership Consciousness. This is the *inside game* of leadership. It is the leader's inner operating system—what drives the leader, how they define themselves, what is important to them, what they believe. We will address this in detail throughout the book.

In high-pressure leadership roles, we might assume that the outer game is the only game; however, it is just the tip of the iceberg. What is happening beneath the surface is mediating and organizing the effectiveness of the outer game. The inner game consists of:

- Our meaning-making system—what we use to make sense of the world.
- Our decision-making system—how we analyze, decide, and act.
- Our values and spiritual beliefs.
- Our level of self-awareness and emotional intelligence.
- The mental models that we use to understand reality, think, act, and create.
- The internal beliefs and assumptions making up our personal identity—the system that we use to know who we are, and to define and deploy ourselves into circumstances.

Together, these aspects make up the complex internal system by which we relate to the world. The more well-honed the outer game, the more effective we are. The more mature the inner game, the more effective we are. Both are required for mastery. Mastery is a well-honed outer game arising from a very mature inner game.

INNER GAME RUNS THE OUTER GAME

Again, most efforts at developing leaders target the outer game. The dominant approach to leadership development is competency-based. We measure competencies, provide feedback, and then create action plans. While this approach is helpful, it seldom produces breakthroughs because it ignores the inner game. Furthermore, while leaders may need help with learning a new competency, more often than not they need help with their inner game. They are stuck at the level of their inner game. The inner game is letting them down, and because most of the inner game goes on beneath the surface, they may not know they are stuck.

A breakthrough in the inner game can result in sudden shifts in the effectiveness of the outer game, which, in turn, can result in big performance gains.

A year ago, we sat down with Rob, a senior supply chain manager, to debrief his Profile results. His feedback showed him to be an aggressive, autocratic, arrogant, and critical manager. His scores for Relationships, Teambuilding, and Leadership Effectiveness were low, and his Leadership Quotient score was well below 1.0, indicating that his leadership was costly and toxic.

This was a shock to Rob. As we reviewed his results, Rob gained insight into himself, how he was leading, the energetic cost he was incurring, and the impact of his leadership on others. It was a hard conversation for Rob, but he faced it with unusual openness and courage.

Recently, we called Rob for an update. He reported that he had been through our year-long leadership development process and then said:

> "I will never forget our conversation. I cannot thank you enough for what it gave me. When I returned to the office, I did a lot of soul searching and self-observation. I saw more clearly all that we had talked about. I realized that I am hyper goal-oriented, hard-wired for results. I care about people, but when problems erupt, I take over. I am constantly worried about what others will think if we fall short of expectations. Failure is not an option for me. Through our conversation, I realized how the fear of failure runs me and how I measure myself by always succeeding. So, when problems arise, I become the ogre! I laugh now thinking back on what an ogre I was."

Rob went on to say:

> "About six months ago, I received a promotion. I am now in charge of all supply-side management for the start-up of our new plant in another country. I could not have succeeded here had I not changed. This is a very relational culture. People hug each other when they come into work. They look each other in the eye when they say hello. If I were to lead here the way I used to lead, I would fail. Now,

when problems come up, I can deal with them. Instead of blowing up, blaming people, and taking over, I work with and through the team. I am direct and firm, but in a way that builds accountability, trust, relationships, and teamwork. I still feel the urge to blow up, but now I manage it. It does not manage me. I am not as defined by my results now, and ironically that enables me to be more effective at achieving them."

Rob then told us that before he worked for his current company, he worked for a manufacturer in Detroit. He mentioned how painful it was to live through the downturn in the industry, the closing of plants, and the impact on people and their families. Rob began to cry as he said, "Now I can have a positive impact in another community. I am finally becoming the leader I have always dreamed I could be. I am a much happier person now."

Rob was no longer stuck in his outer game. The maturity in his inner game boosted the effectiveness of his outer game. When Rob did the uncommon work of deeply engaging himself, courageously facing what he saw, and restructuring his inner game, he naturally emerged as a far more effective leader. His company is better off for it, and so is Rob.

We incur huge opportunity costs when we ignore the inner game or treat it as irrelevant. Individual and collective effectiveness cannot emerge unless we explore how our inner game is being played. Yet there is little support for this exploration in our attitudes and approaches to developing leaders, despite all that is being written on the importance of the inner game.

LITANY OF THE LITERATURE

Library shelves are replete with great books that describe the intimate, interdependent relationship of the inner to the outer game and exhort us to go within for the source of our effectiveness, mastery, or greatness. Here is a short sample of this literature:

- In his book, *As a Man Thinketh*, James Allen posits the core tenet of personal mastery:

  "Thought and character are one, and as character can only manifest and discover itself through environment and circumstance, the outer conditions of a person's life will always be found to be harmoniously related to his inner state. This does not mean that a man's circumstances at any given time are an indication of his *entire* character, but that those circumstances are so intimately connected with some vital thought element within himself that, for the time being, they are indispensable to his development.

Man is buffeted by circumstances so long as he believes himself to be the creature of outside conditions. But when he realizes that he may command the hidden soil and seeds of his being out of which circumstances grow, he then becomes the rightful master of himself."

"The soul attracts that which it secretly harbors; that which it loves, and also that which it fears. Circumstances are the means by which the soul receives its own."

"The outer world of circumstance shapes itself to the inner world of thought. As the reaper of his own harvest, man learns both by suffering and bliss."

"Circumstance does not make the man; it reveals him to himself. Men do not attract that which they *want,* but that which they *are.* Men are anxious to improve their circumstances, but are unwilling to improve themselves."

(Allen, 1905)

- In *Think and Grow Rich*, a classic in success literature, Napoleon Hill shows how great leaders in many fields think in ways that make them so successful (Hill, 1937).
- In his book *On Becoming a Leader*, Warren Bennis, the great teacher of leadership, said that the process of becoming a great leader is the same as that of becoming a great person (Bennis, 1989). His book's title parallels that of a book by his friend Carl Rogers, *On Becoming a Person.*
- In *Man's Search for Meaning*, Viktor Frankl wrote: "Everything can be taken from a man but one thing: the last of the human freedoms—to choose one's attitude in any given set of circumstances. When we are no longer able to change a situation, we are challenged to change ourselves." Frankl learned this lesson in a Nazi concentration camp (Frankl, 1959).
- The field of Psychology is premised on the relationship between the inner and outer game. The interior reality of conscious and unconscious beliefs, assumptions, and thoughts runs our lives; it determines

our emotional states, actions, and the results we create. Changing the deep habits of mind changes the results we attain in our lives.

- Tim Gallwey wrote a series of "Inner Game" books on the relationship between the inner game and the outer game (Gallway, 2000).
- In his seminal book, *The Fifth Discipline*, Peter Senge holds that one of the five disciplines of creating great learning organizations is Personal Mastery (Senge, 1990). Peter was a business partner with Robert Fritz who, in his book, *The Path of Least Resistance*, described personal mastery as the shift from a Reactive to a Creative Orientation (Fritz, 1989).
- Larry Wilson, founder of Wilson Learning, describes two internal mindsets that are very similar to Fritz's Creative and Reactive Orientations. He called these mindsets *Playing-to-Win* versus *Playing-Not-to-Lose* (Wilson, 1998). Each orientation gets very different results.
- The Human Potential Movement is founded on the principle that our inner world shapes our outer world. Change the inner world and all things follow suit.
- The *Tao Te Ching* describes the highest states of leadership consciousness and effectiveness (Mitchell, 2008), as does the *Bhagavad Gita*, a spiritual classic of the Hindu tradition (Mitchell, 2000).
- The spiritual, mythic, and poetic literature exhorts us to go inside to discover the roots and keys to freedom, joy, peace, harmony, and our well-being and welfare.

Again, what we hold in our consciousness tends to manifest (individually and collectively). The outer world shapes itself to the inner world. Consciousness creates reality. Everything emerging in human affairs has its source first in thought.

FOUR FOUNDATIONAL PREMISES

We base all of our work with leaders as we help them to develop higher individual and collective effectiveness on four premises that underpin the Unified Model of Leadership.

Premise 1: Structure determines performance

This is a systems and design principle: the design of any system is the primary determinant of the performance of that system.

For example, the Honda Insight averages 60 MPG—more than double the mileage of most cars. The Insight is designed for economy. It will never compete at NASCAR, no matter how hard the driver pushes the pedal to the metal. Design, its operating possibilities and limits, and not the driver, primarily determines its performance. Likewise, you are designed, individually and organizationally, for the performance you are getting. Structure determines performance.

Premise 2: You are a structure

You have a mind for thinking and a body for acting. You are a psychophysical structure. You have an inner game and an outer game, and both have a structure to them. The inner game is a complex system that includes your conscious and unconscious meaning and decision-making system, values, mental models, beliefs, assumptions, self-awareness, emotional intelligence, and identity. This complex system has its own structure. You have been designing the structure of your inner game all your life. We call this our *Internal Operating System* (IOS). It functions like a computer's operating system, operating mostly below the surface, mediating and managing everything going on at the surface in the outer game. The IOS manages the various programs we are running, what tasks those programs are capable of performing, as well as the efficacy and mastery with which they can be performed. The IOS is the inner game that runs the programs called on to accomplish specific results in the outer game.

Like an operating system, the inner game is a structure, and its design determines performance. As the operating system becomes more evolved, increasingly complex tasks can be achieved with greater speed, agility, creativity, artistry, and mastery. Upgrades in the operating system enable us to be more effective. This is why Apple and Microsoft are constantly pushing to upgrade their operating platforms. Each evolution in the operating system enables us to accomplish more with less—higher mastery amid greater complexity.

You are a structure. The inner game is your IOS, and the structure of your IOS is mediating your level of personal and leadership effectiveness.

Premise 3: Consciousness is the operating system of performance

Consciousness (the inner game) is the deep structure of performance. David Bohm, a prominent physicist, once said, "Consciousness creates reality and then says, 'I didn't do it'" (Senge, 1990). Because the operating system operates mostly below the surface, we rarely perceive its influence, but it is running the show. Thought precedes all we do, say, and create. The nature and structure of our thoughts, beliefs, and assumptions, both conscious and unconscious, create our moment-to-moment reality. The structure of our operating system focuses our attention, influences our choices, drives our behavior, and determines the effectiveness of our actions (both short- and long-term). Therefore, consciousness is the operating system of performance. Performance, individually and collectively, is always consistent with our level of consciousness. We cannot perform at a higher level of performance than is built into our operating system. Likewise, an organization cannot perform at a higher level of performance than the collective consciousness of its leadership.

Premise 4: To achieve higher performance, you must be restructured

Since structure determines performance, and since you are a structure, if you want to break through to higher levels of performance, you must allow yourself to be restructured.

In the Debi Thomas story, we saw how important maturing the inner game is to athletic performance. In Rob's story, we saw what can happen when a leader restructures the inner game. Rob's deep insight into the hidden assumptions that made him ineffective enabled him to rethink those assumptions. New assumptions led to different results. Rob's old assumptions did not go away, but he can now manage them more effectively and operate more consistently from his new assumptions. The restructure of his IOS enabled him to be much more effective in a new role with greater responsibility, pressure, and complexity. Rob's shift also enabled him to develop greater collective effectiveness around him and have a multiplied positive business impact.

To perform more masterfully, your *Inner Operating System* (IOS) must evolve to a higher order mental-emotional structure. Thankfully, there is a well-researched pathway to the maturity of our inner game, to higher-order structures of mind. In describing what is required to reach higher personal mastery, we might borrow a term from the spiritual traditions—*Metanoia*, a transformation of heart and mind, a metamorphosis that requires a change in structure and form.

Metamorphosis is what happens when the caterpillar spins its cocoon, crawls inside, and disintegrates. It is a disintegration–reintegration or death–resurrection process. The structure of the old self disintegrates and reintegrates at the next higher order (the caterpillar transforms into the butterfly). Robert Kegan writes, "If a caterpillar knows its future has wings, it hardly experiences itself as land-bound."

So, to attain higher effectiveness, you must be restructured. This is the path of mastery—the only pathway to greater leadership effectiveness. When we see extraordinary leadership, we see well-honed capability arising on a higher-order platform of consciousness.

CONSCIOUSNESS AND COMPLEXITY

The level of maturity of your individual and collective IOS must be more than a match for the complexity of the challenges you face. Consciousness must evolve to a high level of complexity to meet the complexity of today's business challenges.

Several years ago, we were working with the CEO of a midsized insurance company that was going through major changes in two lines of their business. As we were getting acquainted, we asked this CEO how he was doing. He said, "Well, I am like a duck." Surprised, we asked him what he meant. He said, "If you look at me at the surface, you think that I am gliding along smoothly. But, if you look beneath the surface, you see that my feet are paddling as fast as possible, and I am not sure it is fast enough."

He then told us about the arduous task that he and his Senior Team faced in guiding the organization through major change amid volatile financial and economic conditions. He spoke openly of his doubts about his ability to provide the leadership required. He spent many nights in the 4a.m. club, the club where we leaders worry and wonder how to navigate through the complexity we face.

This CEO is not alone. In 2010, IBM interviewed over 1,500 CEOs worldwide to learn what their challenges are and their strategies for addressing them (*Capitalising on Complexity: Insights from the Global Chief Executive Officer Study*). Two challenges emerged at the top of the list: 1) escalating complexity, and 2) building the creative capacity in leadership to deal with it. These two themes have shown up in IBM's 2012 and 2014 CEO studies as well. In this study, many CEOs openly wondered if they were "in over their head," if they had the capability to lead their organizations through so much change.

The 4a.m. Club has many members. Most leaders, including the authors, sometimes lie awake at night wondering how to navigate complexity, if we have what it takes to lead, whether we are "in over our heads," and if we are the right person for the job. We have learned, from many conversations, that this quiet, internal struggle is common among entrepreneurs and senior leaders.

Complexity will continue to escalate. In his book, *Leaders Make the Future,* futurist Bob Johansen makes this disconcerting statement: "In my 40 years of forecasting futures, the direst forecasts yet are in this book." He then describes a VUCA world—a global business environment of escalating *Volatility*, *Uncertainty*, *Complexity*, and *Ambiguity* (Johansen, 2009). We add *market disruption* (see Figure 3.2).

VUCA will continue to accelerate for all of us. We will all be hit by ever-increasing waves (in frequency and amplitude) of *Adaptive Challenge.* Ron Heifetz describes adaptive challenges as a *set* of interdependent challenges that are seemingly unsolvable, but must be solved (Heifetz, 1998).

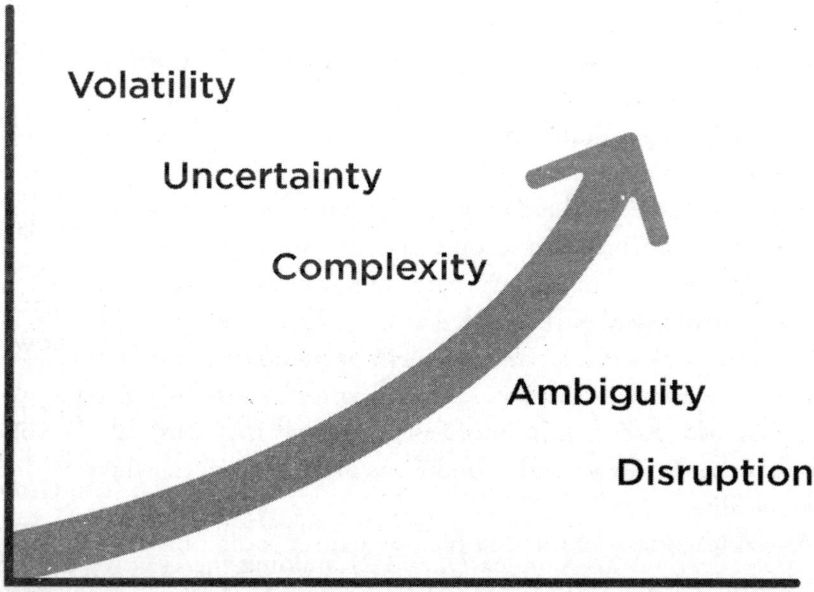

FIGURE 3.2 VUCA business environment

What makes them adaptive is that they cannot be solved from within our current operating system. We must evolve our individual and collective operating system. This gets to the second theme in the IBM CEO study: we must evolve our creative capacity, individually and collectively, to meet complexity.

UNDERSTANDING COMPLEXITY: REDUNDANT POLARITIES AND PROBLEMS

Barry Johnson distinguishes between *Problems* and *Polarities*. Problems are solvable. There are usually a few optimal solutions that, once arrived at, admit to a stable solution. Polarities are dilemmas. They are not solvable because a polarity is comprised of a tension between equally legitimate, but opposite, end points. For example, *should the management of vital business functions be centralized or decentralized?* The answer is, *yes*. Too much centralization is problematic, as is too much decentralization. This polarity, like all polarities, is not solvable, but it is manageable. Furthermore, the optimization point of any polarity is a moving target as companies grow through stages of development, change strategy, and as market conditions change. Polarities are continually being managed and optimized.

Most polarities and problems come in sets. They are interdependent and redundant. *Redundancy* is a term borrowed from engineering. In designing a stable structure, like building an aircraft, engineers are designing for tension resolution, such that the resulting structure is strong and stable. Redundancy results when one tension resolution in the structure depends on a second tension resolution in the structure and vice versa. Part one of the structure cannot be stably resolved until part two is resolved, and part two depends on the resolution of part one.

In mathematics this is the equivalent of *simultaneous equations*—two equations with two unknowns. One equation cannot be solved in isolation. Redundancies are so interdependent that they can only be solved simultaneously. These same conditions are experienced when we think systemically.

Amazingly, many of our complex structures could only be designed by resolving a long string of redundancies. For example, when the Boeing 747 was tested in 1969, the aircraft had some 700 redundancies! Imagine designing something with 700 interdependent elements such that the final stable structure cannot be resolved unless all 700 parts of the structure are simultaneously resolved.

Redundant polarities are polarities that depend on each other for optimal resolution. Two or three polarities are hard enough to optimize separately, but when they each need to be resolved simultaneously, complexity increases dramatically. Now multiply the number of redundant polarities by a factor of 10, throw a few challenging and redundant problems into the mix, add a rapidly escalating VUCA world, and you have the makings of Complexity Stew—adaptive challenges within adaptive challenges. This is the complexity that leaders face. If we do not lead with the whole system in mind, simultaneously designing for and resolving multiple interdependent variables, then the unintended consequences go up in multiples.

NON-OBVIOUS POINTS OF LEVERAGE

Those of us who lead and consult in system transformation often describe organizational systems as "un-figure-out-able." Solutions that could have long-term positive, intended consequences exist, but are seldom easily seen and rationally deduced. When we approach systemic complexity with problem-fix logic, we usually install solutions that make the system more complex or have consequences in other areas that were unseen or unintended. Non-systemic solutions usually result in better before worse performance. Things get better for a while and then either revert to the way they were or get worse. The US war in Iraq is a good example of a reactive and hasty solution appearing to make things better for a while and then making things much worse.

Finding systemic solutions that evolve the system in ways that result in lasting improvement is possible, but not easy. Often these solutions are not obvious, and no one person is smart enough to consistently discover and implement them. Collective effectiveness is required. Finding long-term high leverage solutions takes a whole systems approach. This means bringing a representative body of stakeholders into one room and following a deliberate process so that the solutions to systemic, complex issues can be created. This practice relies on the notion that the wisdom resides within the system for many of the issues that we face. Leaders rarely know how to tap the collective wisdom and intelligence of the system to find leverage amid escalating complexity. Most leadership teams lack the collective effectiveness to pull this off. It takes a highly evolved operating system, individually and collectively, to thrive in a VUCA world.

THE LEADERSHIP IMPERATIVE

The mix of mounting adaptive challenges, multiple redundant polarities and problems, and complex systems with non-obvious points of leverage mandates that leaders evolve more elegant operating systems. Einstein said: "The solutions to our current problems cannot be solved from the level of consciousness that created them." They can only be solved from a higher order of consciousness, one that is more complex than the complexity we face.

To meet the adaptive challenges we face today, we need to evolve more elegant ways of thinking and being. Failure to adapt and evolve is to go extinct. The *Leadership Imperative* is simply this: *The development of leadership effectiveness must, at a minimum, keep pace with the rate of change and the rate of escalating complexity.*

Not to keep pace with the rate of escalating complexity is to become less relevant and effective. The complexity of mind of a leader, and of the collective leadership system, must evolve at a rate that matches or exceeds the rate of escalating complexity. If the challenges we face are more complex than we are, our leadership is inadequate and a competitive disadvantage. But, if we can evolve the complexity of mind of the leader, and the leadership system, to be at least as complex as the challenges we face, we can thrive in a VUCA world.

Rapidly increasing complexity puts the effectiveness of leadership at a premium. When the maturity of the leadership IOS, individually and collectively, evolves to a higher-order platform of consciousness, higher-order complexity of mind, leadership becomes more collectively masterful, effective, and intelligent. This requires a Leadership Quotient greater than 1.0, and when the LQ reaches 2.0, leadership becomes a serious competitive advantage.

Leadership's primary job is to enhance creative capacity by developing collectively effective leadership. As complexity increases, effective leadership becomes a major competitive advantage. Jack Welch believed this and backed it up as CEO of General Electric. He deployed systemic development and then parlayed leadership development, systems thinking, and action into one of GE's primary competitive advantages.

Developing effective leadership, individually and collectively, is a business imperative. This Leadership Agenda must be a strategic priority. Senior teams need to make their own development a strategic priority as they lead development efforts within the leadership system. The organization will not perform at a higher level than the consciousness of its leadership.

THE CORE ARGUMENT

Escalating complexity requires that the creative, adaptive capacity of the leadership of the organization evolve at or beyond the rate at which complexity is increasing. The maturity of the outer game and the inner game of leadership, individually and collectively, must mature at a pace to stay relevant and competitive. The mastery or effectiveness of leadership depends on evolving the complexity of mind or consciousness (IOS) of leadership to be more than a match for the complexity of market and business challenges. Since consciousness is a structure, and structure determines performance, to attain higher effectiveness and better business performance amid complexity, you must be restructured. This is a metamorphosis process—a radical change in the structure of mind. This mind-shift initially happens within individual leaders. More conscious individual leadership catalyzes collective leadership effectiveness, which transforms business performance.

Those leaders who see the extreme upside potential of this Leadership Agenda and act on it create a competitive advantage that sets them and their companies apart. Such proactive development requires an investment in time, money, and people, with time being the most precious resource. In leading companies, this investment continues even when budgets tighten.

Katherine is the CEO of a high-profile media company and one of our clients. In 2008, she faced an economic downturn that turned out to be the worst in its 50 years as a company. In response, Katherine proactively led the organization through a cost reduction process that resulted in the first major layoffs in company history. However, that was only the beginning. During the downturn, she decided to double down on her own development and the development of her leaders. Fortunately, over the years she had purchased her freedom with a record of results, and despite the resistance she received, she continued an aggressive development agenda, believing it would make a difference.

Over the next three years, the Extended Leadership Team worked closely together on the business of the business and on their own effectiveness as leaders. They were quick and decisive, set strong direction, and followed through on that direction while working on their inner and outer game of leadership. During that same time, they retook the Leadership Circle Profile (LCP), and their collective leadership effectiveness improved from the 45th percentile to the 75th collectively, even as they reduced staff and decreased resources.

As they emerged from the difficult times 18 months later, they found themselves in the position of increased leadership capacity and capability that enabled them to win multiple new national clients from their competition, and they posted the best year in company history.

Katherine recently reported: "We could not have made it through these times as well as we have and moved way ahead of the pack if not for our focus on becoming more effective as leaders. We were 12 months ahead of our nearest competition when the market started to improve, and we have not looked back. Even as we reduced costs by 30%, we strategically developed ourselves as leaders, and we have the metrics of the difference this has made. Now we will blow everyone away with what comes next."

This amazing CEO had to make a courageous stand with her organization, her board, and some of her own people. She anticipated the results before they happened, and now the organization is benefiting from the leadership she continues to display.

UNCOMMON SENSE

Several years ago, we were interviewed for a video documentary. The interviewer opened with this curveball question: "Isn't leadership just a matter of common sense?"

We were not sure how to respond. Based on the volumes written on the subject, leadership seems to be both extremely common and extremely rare. Bookstore shelves are full of the latest secrets to leadership success. We are critical of much of this literature for reducing the development of leaders to a set of superficial skills and steps. From this perspective, leadership appears to be easily developed and common. On the other hand, we are facing a worldwide *leadership crisis*. What sense can we make of all this? While some managers and leaders are taking their leadership development seriously, others are seduced by the promise of a shortcut to greatness.

After a moment of hesitation, we responded to the interviewer: "If great leadership were just a matter of common sense, it would be common. The fact that it is not common, despite all the activity to develop it, suggests that, if shortcuts were possible, we would have all bought the package long ago and would now be enjoying the fruits of success."

When the development of leadership effectiveness into mastery is understood to be more than skill and competency development, when it is seen as a profound process of Metanoia, when we acknowledge that it requires metamorphosis, a restructuring of the self into higher-order form, then we will begin to understand why earlier generations called it a *Hero's Journey* or a *Heroine's Journey*. It is not for the faint of heart. It is an acquired taste. Mastering leadership is neither *common* nor *common sense*. It is *uncommon sense*. There are no shortcuts to greatness. As T.S. Eliot said, it will "cost not less than everything." It is worth the cost.

COLLECTIVE WISDOM

Collective effectiveness is the foundation of collective intelligence. As collective intelligence emerges, collective wisdom becomes possible. Since the leadership challenges are formidable, it will take unprecedented collective effectiveness, intelligence, and wisdom to avert global calamity and create a thriving future for Earth's inhabitants. Only when leaders do their heroic inner work will the kind of collective leadership emerge that can positively change the trajectory of events now unfolding. Nothing short of a profound shift of mind is required. Higher-order consciousness and wisdom are related. We must evolve the practice of conscious leadership and the collective wisdom necessary to steward the planet.

Sadly, developing our leadership effectiveness often gets side-lined because we resist the vulnerability of learning and changing. It takes courage to face the truth about ourselves. The truth shall set us free, but first it may make us miserable. As we seek to improve collective effectiveness, we will likely be learning publicly. Senior leaders guard their credibility carefully, not wanting to lose face. Our IOS is who we take ourselves to be and how we have attained our current success. Change is scary. *Who will I be if I am not this? This has made me effective; do I really want to mess with what got me here? Will I remain effective if I make fundamental changes within myself? How will it all work out?* We intuitively know that there are no guarantees. However, we also intuitively know that transformation promises capability beyond what is now possible, that the only way out is through, and that there are no shortcuts to greatness.

A GLOBAL LEADERSHIP IMPERATIVE

The commitment to develop effective leadership as a strategic priority should be made because of its dramatic impact on business performance. The choice for mastering leadership can also be made in service to the larger needs of humanity. The world is hungry for more effective, conscious leadership. As we develop more effectiveness in the leadership system of our organizations, we also develop more effective leadership on the planet. As leaders emerge, conscious of our inherent unity and our collective welfare, we will collectively steward the planet toward a thriving future.

In the next two chapters, we will define various levels of the IOS that, as they progressively evolve, become complex enough for the level of global complexity facing leaders.

TAKING STOCK

- What is your fundamental reason for existing?
- We have two choices. Face reality or ramp up our delusions. Which do you regularly choose?
- What is this problem forcing you to learn? What do you need to learn in order for this problem to completely go away, to completely dissolve?
- What if you knew with certainty that you are the *cause* and never the *effect* of what is happening around you?
- What is your cannot *not*—the one thing that you just cannot keep yourself from doing?

Chapter 4

Stages of Development

The Backbone of the Universal Model of Leadership

Thus far we have been making the core argument that the levels of consciousness and performance—personal, organizational, and systemic—are harmoniously related. We have argued that your business will be structured and perform at the predominant level of consciousness of its leadership, through which all leadership, culture, organizational structure, action, and creation are being organized. This is a greatly overlooked truth. If we want to perform better, individually and organizationally, we must be restructured. With each fundamental evolution in the Structure of Mind (IOS), more, much more, becomes possible.

The good news about this is that the Level or Structure of Mind can evolve. There is a considerable amount of good research in the field of Adult Development that has mapped out the entire trajectory of development—how consciousness structures itself at one level of mind and then restructures itself into the next higher-order structure, and the next, and the next. This chapter is a brief introduction to the Stages and Structures of Mind, how they are integrated into the Universal Model, and their relationship to leadership effectiveness and business performance. In the next chapter, we will describe each Structure of Mind and Stage of Leadership.

Bill: We have spent 30 years working on what is required for systems to transform in order to enhance performance and create a level of leadership that is a competitive advantage. I was first introduced to Stage

Development research in my PhD program. However, until I started working with the Leadership Circle model in 2005, I was missing a major link. The integration of the Stage of Development framework into the LCP and the Universal Model provides a pathway for leader development that can be scaled with tangible results. This framework integrated our Whole Systems transformation work and greatly enhanced our ability to support shifts in culture, engagement, and performance. When used within a Whole Systems approach to develop the leadership system of an organization, it is the most powerful source for cultural change I have found.

Multiple studies and our experience with companies engaged in transformation efforts show that 70–85% of them do not yield tangible results. This is because we have not understood the profound transformation required of everyone, especially leaders, when we try to re-envision and reinvent the organization for higher performance. Many well-intentioned improvement efforts and transformation initiatives fall short of intended results because leaders fail to account for the transformation in consciousness required to create and sustain high performance. Organizations do not transform—people do. Only by operating from a higher order of consciousness can we lead transformations that produce short- and long-term shifts in performance.

The Stage Development framework explains much that has been missing in the field of Leadership Development. Many great researchers on leadership, from Warren Bennis to Jim Collins, readily admit that while they can describe what great leaders do, they do not know how great leadership develops. The Stage Development framework helps explain how extraordinary leadership develops and how to accelerate its development. Yet, Stage Development is still not center stage in our thinking or the practice of developing greater leadership effectiveness. It has been incubating on the sidelines of the leadership conversation in the field of Developmental Psychology, and is just now finding its place in Leadership Development.

STAGES OF DEVELOPMENT FRAMEWORK

If you agree that individual and collective leadership effectiveness correlate closely with business performance and that developing leadership is a strategic imperative that must be owned and led from the top, then you must understand how development happens. Otherwise, you are apt to under-design and under-invest in the Leadership Agenda. You risk developing the effectiveness of your leaders in ways that do not result in sustainable performance improvements. The Stage of Development framework, when integrated into the Universal Model of Leadership, provides what has been missing in our efforts to develop more effective leadership. Progressively higher *Stages of Development* enable progressively higher leadership effectiveness and business performance.

We first encountered the Stages of Development framework through the work of Robert Kegan (Kegan, 1998), and it is a good thing we found him first. Otherwise we might have missed how Adult Development integrates the field. Kegan's particular model is the best we have found for integrating the entire field of leadership and organizational development. There are many other good models (Cook-Greuter, Torbert, Beck, Wilber, Gilligan, Hall, etc.) and all of them describe the same trajectory of consciousness in different ways and focus on different aspects of development. All these models can be tied to, or integrated into, Kegan's framework, but his framework is uniquely structured such that most of the good theory and research in the field of Leadership and Organizational Development, Psychology, Self-Help, Success and Human Potential, and even spiritual literature, can find a place within the structure of Kegan's Developmental Framework.

In Bob Kegan's five-stage model, the first stage includes all stages of childhood development. Kegan called the second stage *Self-Sovereign Mind* (Kegan and Lahey, 2009). We call it *Egocentric* as it describes an adolescent level of development. The other three stages (the heart of his framework) describe progressive stages: *Socialized Self, Self-Authoring Self*, and *Self-Transforming Self*. In the Universal Model, we modify Kegan's labels in order to integrate with other leadership frameworks. We call these three stages *Reactive Mind*, *Creative Mind*, and *Integral Mind*, respectively (see Figure 4.1). Each stage in succession is more mature than the prior stage. We have added another stage (*Unitive*) to include the higher stages described by spiritual traditions. Hence, our Universal Model includes five stages: *Egocentric, Reactive, Creative, Integral*, and *Unitive*.

THE UNIVERSAL MODEL OF LEADERSHIP

As we show how these Stages of Development are integrated into the Universal Model of Leadership, we will introduce some of our research

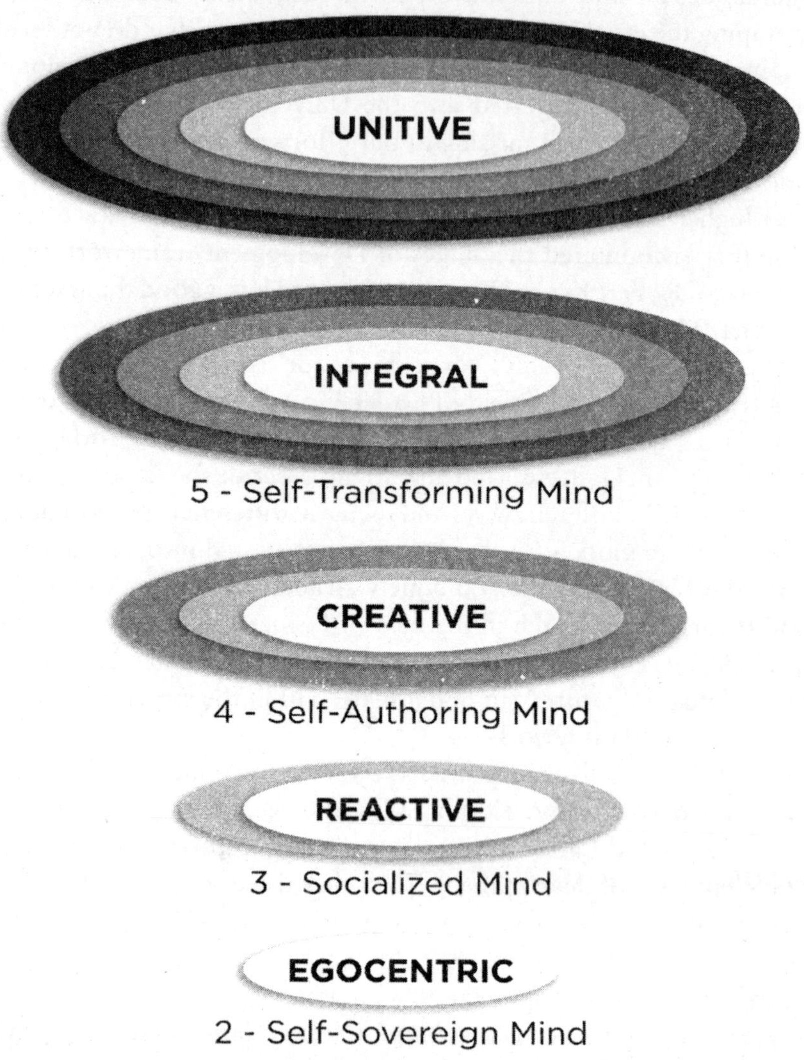

FIGURE 4.1 The Stages of Development Framework

with the Leadership Circle Profile and show how it relates to the real world because the metrics are strong and the research is breakthrough.

The LCP 360° assessment is a unique lens through which to do research. It is the only one that measures both behavior and beliefs at various stages of development, and it is the only one built on an integrative, universal, meta-model of leadership. Hence, our research yields

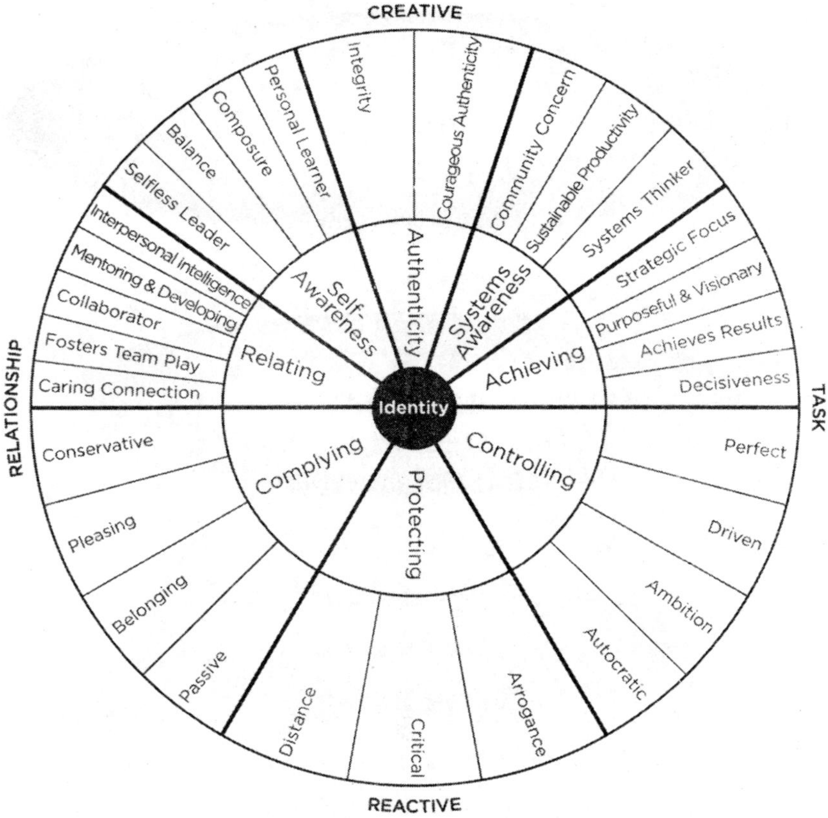

FIGURE 4.2 The Leadership Circle

provocative and profound understandings about *what* makes for effective leadership and *how* it develops.

Figure 4.2 shows how the Universal Model and LCP are drawn in a circle. The LCP displays 360° feedback results in a circle. The circle, as depicted in the LCP, is a complete rendition of the Universal Model (see Appendix 1 for definitions of all dimensions). As we will see, displaying the model (and results) in a circle has unique advantages.

Kegan's Stages of Development framework forms the backbone of the Universal Model of Leadership. Since most adults inhabit the stages of Reactive and Creative, with a small percentage at Integral, the LCP was designed to include the Reactive and Creative stages primarily, and point to Integral. In the Adult Development literature, when we transcend from

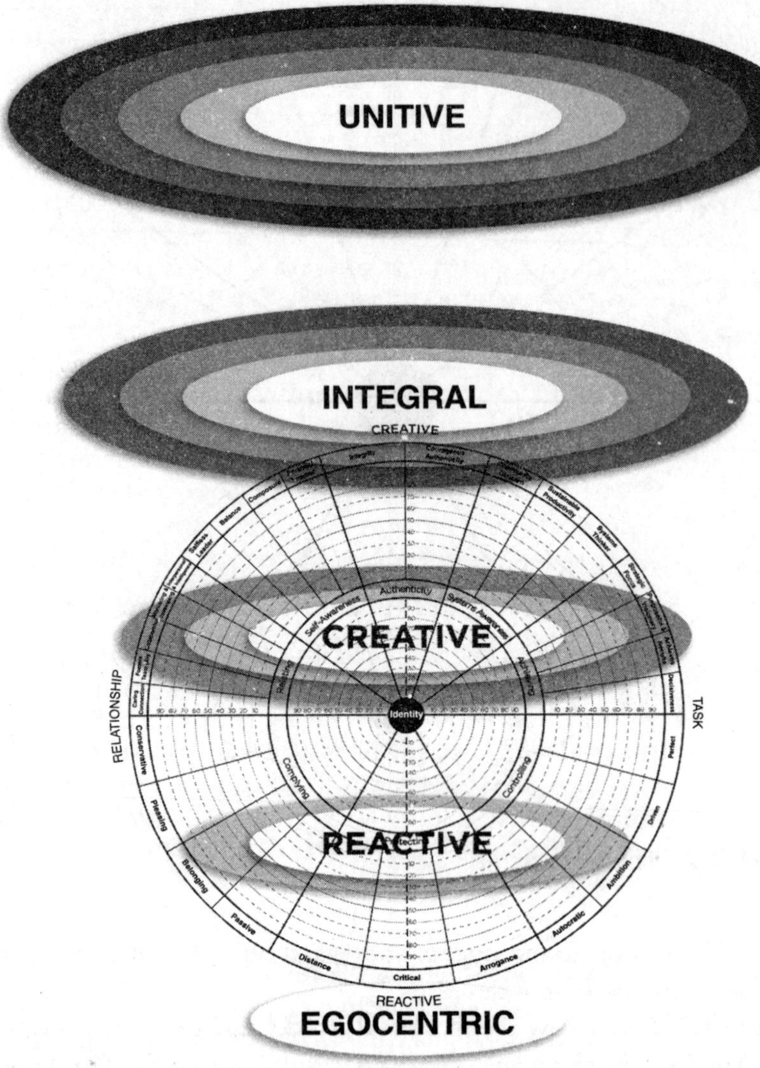

FIGURE 4.3 The Stages of Development Framework and the LCP

one level to the next, it is called *Vertical Development*. Therefore, the vertical axis of the Universal Model, and of the LCP, represents Vertical Development—Stage Development (see Figure 4.3).

Figure 4.3 shows how The Leadership Circle and the Universal Model map the stages of development. It is important to note that the LCP does not measure Stages of Development since that is a more complex undertaking than can be accomplished in a 360° assessment. However, the LCP is built around the stage framework and correlates to measures of stage. It is designed to measure 1) leadership behaviors and the internal assumptions that run those behaviors at the Reactive and Creative stages of mind and 2) aspects of the Integral mind; however, since only 5% of leaders function at this level, the top half of the LCP is labeled Creative, the bottom half, Reactive.

CORRELATION CONCLUSIONS

To see how the Stages of Development relate to leadership effectiveness and business performance, we conducted a study in conjunction with the University of Notre Dame's Mendoza College of Business Stayer Center for Executive Education. The Stayer Center's approach to developing leaders is at the forefront of the field. Their Executive Integral Leadership (EIL) program is based on the Integral Model (Wilber, 2000) that incorporates Stages of Development. EIL is a profoundly impactful program. Because of our long association with Notre Dame, it made sense for us to conduct research together. We constructed a study using the LCP and the Maturity Assessment Profile (MAP), developed by Susanne Cook-Greuter. At the time, the MAP was the most psychometrically sound measure of stage available in a paper and pencil assessment.

We administered both assessments to 90 leaders. The results were groundbreaking. The correlation between the measure of Stage of Development (as measured by the MAP, which is a sentence completion self-assessment) and Leadership Effectiveness (as measured by the LCP 360° feedback scores) was surprisingly strong at .65.

Figure 4.4 shows the line of best fit between the MAP's measure of stage and Leadership Effectiveness scores on the LCP. We see that with each progressive stage of a leader's development, effectiveness increases dramatically, especially in later (higher-order) stages where the curve becomes exponential.

The implications of this study are profound. It strongly suggests that a very large component of a leader's effectiveness is the Stage or Structure of Mind out of which the leader is operating. In short, the entire argument of the first section of this book is strongly substantiated—that a leader's effectiveness is greatly influenced by the Stage of Mind through which the leader is operating: consciousness and competence rise together, the inner game runs the outer game, mastery is related to

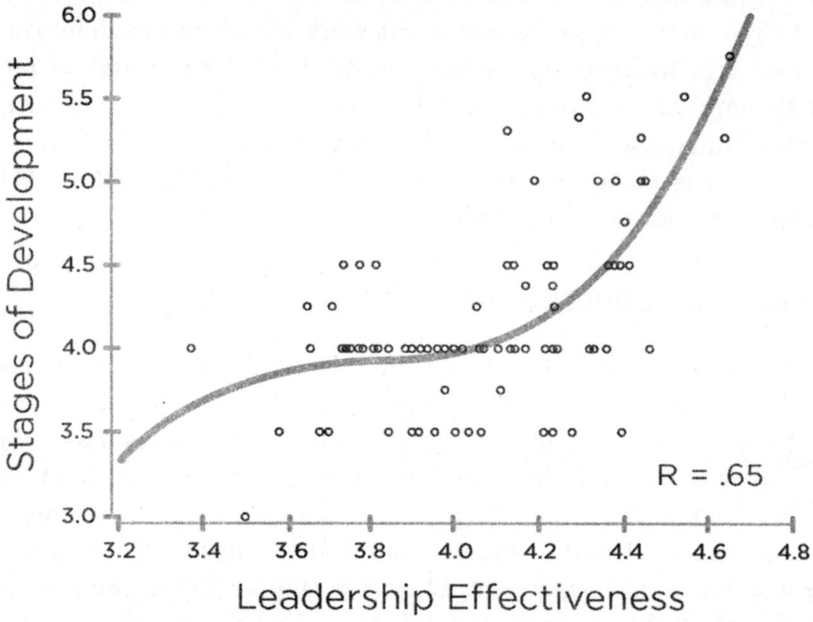

FIGURE 4.4 Correlation between Stages of Development and Leadership Effectiveness

maturity, and extraordinary leadership is well-honed capability arising on a higher-order platform of consciousness.

We then looked at this same data a different way. We asked, "What is the average level of Leadership Effectiveness at each progressive stage?" We found a provocative picture of the relationship between Stage and Effectiveness, as depicted in Figure 4.5.

Those leaders who had measured at the Reactive level on MAP had an average Leadership Effectiveness score on the LCP at the 40th percentile (higher than only 40% of our worldwide norm base of a half million scores). In other words, those who measured at the Reactive Structure of Mind had Leadership Effectiveness scores 10% below the worldwide average and below 60% of the managers in our norm base. The average LQ for this group was .67, suggesting that their ineffectiveness is a competitive disadvantage.

Leaders who measured at the Creative level of development had average effectiveness scores at the 65th percentile—higher than 65% of their

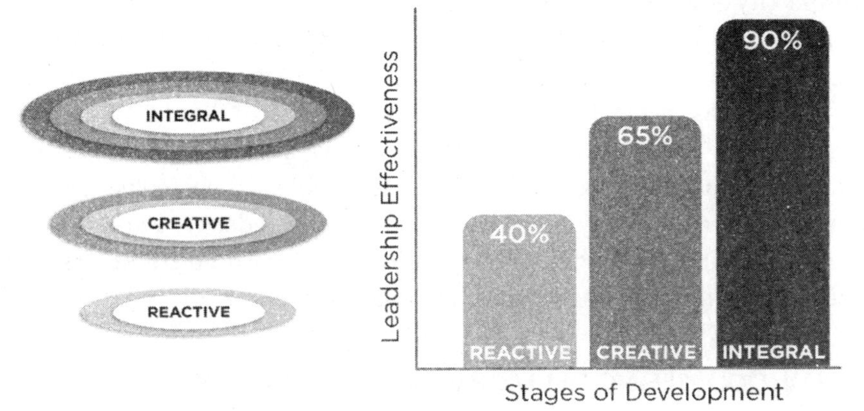

FIGURE 4.5 Average Leadership Effectiveness scores by Stage of Development

peers worldwide. The LQ for this group of leaders is 1.9, suggesting that their level of effectiveness provides a strong competitive advantage.

The highly evolved leaders who measured at the Integral level had average Leadership Effectiveness scores at the 90th percentile and their LQ scores averaged 9.0!

When we added this study to earlier ones, we reached a game-changing conclusion: not only is Leadership Effectiveness highly related to Stages of Development, but business performance is strongly correlated to Leadership Effectiveness. Taken together, these two studies strongly suggest that the performance of an organization depends highly on the level of consciousness of its leadership.

Consciousness is the deep structure, the operating system, of performance. With each evolution in consciousness (IOS) comes greater capacity, capability, and mastery to meet complexity with greater effectiveness. This conclusion is validated by our research and backed up by our work with senior leaders. The level of consciousness begets the level of performance.

TRAJECTORY OF LIFE-LONG DEVELOPMENT

The premise at the heart of the Universal Model of Leadership is that consciousness can evolve into higher-order capacity to meet complexity—development proceeds from lower to higher-order Structures of Mind through a series of well-mapped stages. Many psychological researchers (Piaget, Kohlberg, Gilligan, Lovinger, Maslow, Hall, Fowler, Jaques, Beck, Torbert, Cook-Greuter, Kegan, Wade, Wilber, and others) have described a series of progressive stages as we move from infancy to mature stages of moral, ego, and spiritual consciousness. Remarkably, these many theorists, through independent research, arrived at similar stage descriptions. The world's great wisdom traditions have also described the same sequence of stages for centuries.

CHILDHOOD: SEEING DEVELOPMENT THE EASY WAY

The best way to understand and witness Stages of Development (Vertical Development) is to start with childhood development. A child's development proceeds rapidly. Those of us who are parents or who have spent any time around children know how dramatically and rapidly their minds evolve. In a few years we watch the child morph from one operating system to the next. The changes are obvious, sequential, and substantial. Just as we figure out how to relate to our child (at any age or stage) they move on, and we must learn how to relate to them all over again.

At age five, children live in a magical world, a Disney World reality, replete with Santa Claus, tooth fairies, and imaginary friends. Santa Claus can go around the world and drop off gifts to every child on Earth in one night! Things magically appear, disappear, or turn into something else altogether. In this imaginary world, anything is possible.

While this magical world is a beautiful operating system, it is not well adapted to the demands of adult life, so, as parents, we involve children in a curriculum of development including school, sports, and hobbies. By the age of 10 their favorite book is the *Guinness Book of World Records*. The magical world fades away, and Concrete Operational Thinking boots up. Now they know the truth about Santa Claus and are surprised that this myth ever made sense. The world they live in does not morph and change. Things have stable length and measure, and they are intrigued by the largest, smallest, most, and tallest. They want to figure out this new reality.

We start the discussion of adult and leader development with childhood development for four reasons. First, childhood development is more obvious, and it is easy to see how each new stage brings with it new capability. In leader development it is harder to notice, but each stage brings with it new capability to meet complexity. Second, it is easier to notice that all stages are necessary, good, beautiful, worthy, and dignified. We would never make our five-year-old feel bad for thinking and acting like a five-year-old. This is easy to accept with children, but not so easy to accept with adults. Third, it is easier to see that the stages are sequential. This is obvious in how children develop. Magical thinking precedes operational thinking. We do not expect a five-year-old child to do calculus. There is an order and sequence to stages of development. Each stage develops out of the previous stage and into the next stage. This sequential order is built into the way the human body-mind is designed. Each stage is inevitable: we must grow into it, and eventually beyond it. Fourth, it is easier to see how at each stage transition something is being lost and gained. As parents, we applaud the development of our nine-year-old because the child is now more adapted to the demands of adult life, but we grieve the loss of our five-year-old because those beautiful, magical days are gone. The gain and loss we feel as parents provide a clue about how development proceeds. With each developmental evolution, the old operating system (the way we know ourselves and our reality) is being deconstructed. It comes apart so that a more effective operating system can be reconstructed.

Development is a disintegration–reintegration process. It is Metanoia and metamorphosis. There is loss and gain with each progression. At each developmental inflection point, we are challenged to let go of old ways of knowing before new ways of sense-making have booted up. This is destabilizing. Consequently, these transitions, in childhood and adulthood, are often hard. We tend to resist them whether we know it or not.

Bob: My teenage son, Scott, recently told me about a conversation that he had with his best friend. They concluded that they were happiest when they were five years old. When I asked Scott why they felt that way, he said: "Dad, when we were five, we were not self-conscious. We were freely ourselves in every moment, and we did not care what other people thought about us. Now we are constantly trying to measure up, to *be somebody*. We worry about what we look like, how we are dressed, and how we fit in with the other kids at school. It's hard. At age five, none of this mattered. I miss being five years old."

I, too, miss my five-year-old children; however, I am glad that they are growing into a maturity that will serve them well in their adult lives. At each transition, we are losing ourselves and gaining a new self. This disintegration–reintegration development pattern occurs many times as vertical development proceeds. As children, we have little choice. We are born into an adult world, and we are in that adaptive challenge until we evolve our IOS to a level that adequately meets the everyday challenges of adult life.

Development beyond the norm is less common for two reasons. First, development is hard-earned and often resisted. Second, development into what is normative reduces the adaptive tension that stimulates development. Consequently, most adults do not progress beyond what is normative—the Socialized, Reactive Mind. As a result, development in adults is not so obvious.

IDENTITY IS AT THE CORE

Kegan's research primarily focuses on how the ego's *Identity* restructures itself from one stage to the next. Other researchers focus on other sequential aspects of development (moral reasoning, decision making, values, emotional intelligence, cognitive complexity, spirituality, etc.). As one Stage of Development evolves into the next, many aspects of consciousness are evolving. We focus primarily on one aspect—identity—but other substantive things are evolving in parallel at different rates.

Identity is what we use to construct our self-understanding, our concept of self. We build different constructions of identity at each progressive Stage of Development. At each stage we are identified with that way of being. We say: "This is me. This is who I am. If I am not this, who am I?" When we are identified with something, we *are* that something. It defines us. We measure our self-worth and maintain our security by being that something. That something is so fused with our self-concept that it is indistinguishable from ourselves. We "mis-take" it for ourselves. Of course, the something with which we are identified is not who we actually are, but it sure seems to be that way.

Identity is often referred to as ego because it defines who we are, organizes much of our behavior, moment to moment, and drives the core strategies that we use to establish ourselves in the world (see Figure 4.6). Identity is at the core of our IOS—the part of the IOS that harbors our

FIGURE 4.6 Identity is at the core

sense of self, organizes how we understand ourselves, and how we establish our sense of self-worth, self-esteem, personal value, and security. Identity drives how we take up our role in situations and how we deploy ourselves moment to moment. The structure of identity is responsible for mediating much of our thinking and behavior. Therefore, we generate patterns of results consistent with how our identity is structured. When identity evolves, so do we, as do the results we get in the world.

In the Universal Model of Leadership, identity is at the core. If it evolves, identity restructures itself into more mature operating systems. Each progressive evolution enables increased capability to handle increased complexity.

In the core of the LCP is a black dot with the word "identity." The profile is designed to measure leadership behavior that derives from progressive stages of identity. The Universal Model of Leadership tracks the evolution in identity as we transform from one stage to the next.

Leadership is the deployment of self into circumstances. Since identity is the core of how we understand ourselves and the world, it manages how we deploy our leadership in every situation. Structure determines performance. The structure of our identity determines how we show up as a leader, how we deploy ourselves into circumstances. Hence, as our identity transforms, so does our leadership. All things change when we do.

In the next chapter, we will describe how identity evolves as each progressive Structure of Mind is constructed, deconstructed, and then reconstructed. We will show how each progressive stage relates to leadership effectiveness, organizational structure, culture, and performance.

TAKING STOCK

- How long has it been since your world was rocked to its core by something you learned?
- What refusal have you been postponing (Block, 1993)?
- What's the toll of not living your truth each day? Each moment?
- When it is all over, what do you want people to say about you and what you contributed?
- Where do your passions and talents intersect with the world's greatest need?

Chapter 5

Five Levels of Leadership

Structures of Mind and Performance

Leaders develop, if they develop, through a series of sequential stages, and these same stages exist in all cultures. They are, therefore, universal and invariant, built into human nature. To ignore this reality is to jeopardize our efforts to transform organizations and develop effective leaders. Transformative change requires all stakeholders to shift to a higher stage of development. Unless this personal transformation occurs, any improvement will be temporary. The organization will likely revert back to *normal*, its prior equilibrium, since the inner game runs the outer game.

Personal transformation is the movement from one stage to the next. At each progressive developmental stage, a new, higher-order structural design principle is established to relate the self to the world. Reality does not change. What changes is the way we organize the self–world relationship. As the self adopts a higher-order IOS, the interface between the self and the world is at once more complex, simple, and elegant. Now it can handle more complexity with more grace, greater ease, and less energetic cost—in short, mastery. Unsolvable dilemmas (adaptive challenges) at previous stages evaporate in the new reality. What was not possible in the prior stage becomes doable. The person experiences a new burst of creativity, efficacy, freedom, power, and joy. The organization experiences a person standing more fully in their leadership capacity. The world gains someone capable of greater contribution and service.

As leaders move to higher levels (higher versions of themselves), so too evolve the system and culture. The evolution of the individual and organization is interdependent. The organization cannot organize at a higher level of performance than the consciousness of its leadership. Until the system organizes at the new level, it hinders the development of most people in the system. Moreover, advanced business structures place an evolutionary demand on all stakeholders. As conscious leaders invent higher-order systems, the design mandates development in everyone. As critical mass develops to a new stage, a new tipping point is reached, enabling the system to sustain its evolutionary leap.

There is no organizational transformation without first transforming the consciousness of the leadership. The process of cultural evolution first happens in the awareness of individuals. These individuals exert influence on the system and change it. The new system encourages a critical mass of people to develop. As that critical mass develops, the full potential of the new order is realized, the likelihood of regression to an earlier level of development is reduced, and the platform is built for the next evolutionary leap.

Yes, 70–85% of change efforts fail, but we can do better if we manage change in Creative and Integral ways, addressing the inner and outer demands of transformation. We must be willing to go through the same Metanoia (shift of mind and heart) that we want for the enterprise and engage in the difficult, ongoing dialogue that surfaces what is hidden in our culture, thus allowing personal transformation to translate into cultural and systemic change.

For organizational change to be real, we need to personally transform ourselves. Much "resistance to change" is actually the struggle people have with reorganizing their identity. People need help and support to make this inner journey. They seldom get it in change efforts. We know that personal transformation precedes organizational transformation; however, until recently we lacked the development pathway for creating sustainable personal and, therefore, business transformation.

The inner dynamics of identity are powerful forces. They operate at both individual levels (who I am) and at collective/cultural levels (who we are). For most of us, these powerful forces were organized years ago. They have decades of momentum behind them. If these internal dynamics are ignored, they can easily scuttle the most well-intentioned change process.

Deep systemic change occurs only if we can be the change we want to see. This shift is what we mean by evolving from one level to a higher-order level. In this chapter, we describe *five levels of leadership*: 1) Egocentric, 2) Reactive, 3) Creative, 4) Integral, and 5) Unitive.

EGOCENTRIC LEADERSHIP

This Stage begins at about 8 years of age and ends as the adolescent matures into early adulthood. Adolescence is a transition phase (between Stages 2 and 3) as the teenager adapts to the demands of adult life. We will jump into the stream of adult development by focusing on this time of transition.

As most parents know, adolescence is egocentric. Identity at the Egocentric level is "I am my needs." We are identified with our ability to meet *our* needs. This identity does not notice others' (often competing) needs. Kegan calls this stage *Self-Sovereign* because at this stage *our needs are primary* (Kegan and Lahey, 2009). We are islands unto ourselves, and we relate to others primarily to get our needs met. We do not yet know how to make others' needs equally important to ours.

The strength of egocentricity is the capacity to get our needs met and gain independence. We can defer impulse gratification long enough to plan and organize to meet our needs.

The theme song for this stage is "I Am the World." The ego is the center of the world, and the focus on meeting personal/physical needs is primary. Meeting our own needs is *subject*, meaning, *we are not aware that we are defined by meeting our needs*. Thus, the primacy of meeting our own needs is on autopilot. We are subject to this identity and its dictates. Needs are not yet an object of our reflection, and so our needs run us. We are overly independent and cannot yet see that we are that way. We are not yet separate enough from our needs to manage them—they manage us. Looking out for Number One is the first and last focus. Decisions are made primarily on the basis of physical and personal need satisfaction. This self-preoccupied stage is marked by the absence of a shared reality.

We are so identified with our needs that others' needs do not show up on our radar screens. Our needs and others' needs are not integrated. We do not make decisions based on the impact of our behavior on others with whom we are in relationship (no *Mutual Perspective Taking*). We make decisions based primarily on what will happen to us if we please or displease others. For example, if we tell a lie, our concern is not about the loss of trust or the feelings of others, but about the consequences to us if they catch us in the lie and whether or not we can risk those consequences. There is no shared reality to which we are responsible, only effects that come back at us as we pursue our needs.

For most of us at this stage, *it is only wrong if we get caught*. How you feel, and the impact of our behavior on your reality, is not in focus. This stage is marked by the over-independence that comes from not considering the needs, values, rules, and morals of the rest of the world.

The absence of a shared reality is the structural limit of this phase. Since we are our ability to meet our needs, it feels like death to the self to subordinate its self-interest to that of others. Yet this is the evolution that takes place in adolescence. Growth at this phase is taking others' needs and expectations into account. This growth requires giving up an absolute relationship to our point of view and subordinating that view to a larger way of knowing. It requires defining ourselves co-relationally, such that our principal loyalty is no longer to ourselves, but to the relationship (friend, parent, family, organization, church, and community). This is the process of socialization, of turning the overly independent adolescent into the citizen.

As this happens, our needs move from subject to object. Kegan explains consciousness evolution in terms of major subject–object shifts in our Identity—our understanding of the self–world relationship. Like fish in water, when we are subject to something we do not see it. We see through it. We are, thereby, "subject," at any stage of development, to a way of meaning-making, a way of seeing ourselves and the world around us. Like children living in the world of fantasy, we assume that this is the way things are, the way we are, and the way the world is. We assume this is the "Real World." In fact, when we are subject to any level of identity, the assumptions and mental models by which we define ourselves and the world are so automatic that we do not even notice them. They run us in unseen ways; we do not run them. They have us; we do not have them. Since we do not see them, we cannot manage them. We are subject to them. They manage us without our realizing that we have options. A subject–object shift moves that to which we were formerly subject to an object of our reflection. We are then no longer subject to that limited understanding of ourselves and the world. We can now think and act differently. More behavioral options are available. We are more free and more autonomous.

This subject–object shift happens at every stage transition. It happens in adolescence when we notice that we are not just our ability to meet our needs. We are not our needs; we have needs, but needs do not have us. Because of this subject to object shift, we can have a relationship with our needs in the context of a larger community of competing needs, to which we are responsible.

The end of adolescence is a time of transition in which we learn how to pursue our wants and needs within a larger system of competing needs. It is a difficult time because something is being lost: our egocentric relationship to the world. The world does not revolve around us. In order to succeed in the world, we realize that we need to give up our egocentric agenda and our hard-won independence in order to take up membership in society.

About 5% of leaders who do not fully make this transition and continue to operate with an Egocentric Mind tend to be autocratic and controlling—"my way or the highway." They are not self-organized in a way that permits more participative forms of relationships. Individuation allows for higher levels of relatedness. They are still too fused with their own needs to consider and value the needs and opinions of others. Unquestioned loyalty to *the leader*, not the organization, is the first priority. The organization and its employees exist to serve them. Their relationships are distant, marked by interpersonal insensibility. They are demanding of others, making unrealistic expectations on subordinates who feel oppressed. They manage through strict hierarchies that require unquestioned authority. Egocentric employees tend to play out victim or rebel roles. Teams and organizations that operate out of an egocentric culture are dictatorial and oppressive.

The Egocentric Mind in adolescence is normal. In adulthood, it is pathology. In leadership, it is oppressive and destructive. Development goes awry when it does not proceed beyond the adolescent mind, which in adulthood is very egocentric and ethnocentric. On the world stage, egocentric leadership is responsible for oppressive dictatorships, fascism, Nazism, terrorist extremism, ethnic cleansing, gang violence, and immoral governance.

The ability to hold both our needs and the needs and feelings of others simultaneously is the hallmark of the next stage, the Socialized, Reactive

Mind. Most of us enter adulthood with this socially defined self, the self that the adolescent is both moving toward and resisting.

REACTIVE LEADERSHIP

Each new level is a triumph of development. As parents, we breathe a sigh of relief when our adolescents mature into good citizens and learn that the world operates a certain way and, if they want to get on in the world, they need to take on its rules, values, expectations, and ways of operating. As this developmental shift happens, the teenager takes on adult roles.

The developmental challenge of the Reactive Mind is to merge with society. As adolescents, we reluctantly give up our over-independence and learn that to get along we must go along. As we transition into the Reactive Mind, we learn societal rules and play by them in order to meet expectations. We construct a life that best fits and works within these expectations.

We dive into our chosen professions and work hard on honing our outer game. We gain the *Domain Knowledge* required to succeed in a chosen field. We create businesses and careers, climb ladders, get married, have families, and establish the homestead. We gain professional and managerial competence, learn industry knowledge, and take on roles at work, in the family, in our churches, and in the community. We learn what it takes to succeed in these roles and in the domains of our life. There is a steep learning curve to all of this, and so we take on this development agenda to gain effectiveness and become happy, contributing members of society.

This evolution is essential if we are to build a successful life. This ability to take up membership, to work and live co-relationally with others and within organizations, is the triumph of this stage of development. It enables us to build a life of meaning, self-worth, and security. This is the strength of this stage, and it is also the liability.

As we embrace the Reactive Mind, we build our new identity by living up to and into the expectations of others and the culture. Messages and expectations from key influences, institutions, and individuals shape who and what we become. These messages shape how we think about ourselves and what we conclude will make us worthwhile, safe, successful, valuable, good, and contributing members of society. We craft our identity in harmony with these expectations. We internalize them and define our personal worth and security by living up to them.

We are not aware of what is happening, we are simply breathing in the surrounding self-defining messages and constructing ourselves accordingly. We define ourselves, not from the inside out, but from the outside in. Our externally validated sense of self-worth and security are in others' hands; thus, we must live up to their expectations in order to feel successful, safe, and worthwhile. As such, the self is actually located outside the self, fused with its surroundings. We are defined from the outside in. This is why Kegan calls the Reactive Mind the *Socialized Self* (Kegan and Lahey, 2009).

At this level, external expectations make us up. The identity is this: "I am my unique, well-honed role and capability. I do not merely have a capability; I define myself (my worth and security) through that capability. It is not just a strength that I have; it has me. It defines me. It makes me up. I am not aware that I am identified with a way of being. I am subject to it. I am subject to this new identity. I do not see it. I see through it. I understand myself and deploy myself through this new construction of the self. It is the way I am. I would not know who I am if I were not seen by others as being this way."

One of our talented leadership coaches was debriefing a senior manager (let's call him Carl) on his LCP 360° results. Carl had a long track record of turning around steel manufacturing plants. As they talked, the coach asked him about a very low *Work–Life Balance* score. Carl smiled and said, "Yes, I do not have much of a life." Through a series of questions, the coach learned that Carl worked all the time and that Carl was engaged to be married for the third time. Even when Carl was at home with his new fiancée, he was on the computer corresponding with the plant at all hours of the day and night. Carl admitted, "I work all the time. I do not know what I would do with myself if I was not working. I do not know who I would be if I did not have my work."

Carl is a leader who is externally defined by his capability to get results. His construction of identity sounds like, "I am my ability to get results—to get the job done and done right. This makes me who I am. This is how I know myself to be a worthwhile person. My ability to be successful not only defines me, it protects me and provides for my security. If I am not this, who am I?" This identity has significant strengths and liabilities associated with it.

Since the Reactive Mind constructs the self from the outside in, we tend to define ourselves in one of three ways: through our relationship, intellectual, or results capability. Therefore, there are three primary forms of Reactivity—Complying, Protecting, and Controlling.

Complying Types. If we form our identity around relationship capability, we are likely leveraging our big-hearted nature. We see ourselves as good, worthwhile, and safe because we are a kind, caring, and supportive person. We identify with our capacity for relationships: we know we are safe and worthy if we are liked, accepted, or admired by others. A relationship-based identity says: "I am OK, worthwhile, and secure if you like and accept me, and see me as supportive." In this case, "I am my relationships. I do not merely have relationships. They have me. They define me." We manage our behavior so we are always seen as caring and supportive of others. In order to be effective at getting results, Complying types tend to give up too much power in exchange for being accepted.

Controlling Types. Carl is an example of a leader who was identified by his capability to get results. His ego identity says: "I am my achievements. I not only create them, they create and define me." Carl has leveraged his strength of getting results to a high level and is identified with that capability, which has liabilities. Controlling types tend to use power to create what they want at the expense of people. This undermines collective effectiveness and intelligence.

Protecting Types. Some leaders construct their identity out of their native brilliance. They learn that being smart has its advantages. The Reactive Mind leverages this strength and builds an identity out of it. Intellectually-based identity says, "I am my smartness. I am not merely smart. My smartness defines me. It is what I use to be seen as a valuable, contributing, and worthwhile person." Protecting types tend to position themselves as intellectually superior while maintaining emotional distance. This limits their ability to influence.

Each of the Reactive types is externally defined. We make ourselves into whatever we have been socialized to think is good and right. We identify with these expectations and become them. Stephen R. Covey called this stage of ego development *Dependent* because, at this stage, we are defined from the outside in and are dependent on external validation for our sense of self-worth, esteem, and security (Covey, 1989). Kegan calls it *Socialized Self* (Kegan and Lahey, 2009). Psychologists call this *External Locus of Control*. We call it *Reactive*, because when we are subject to an externalized identity, outside influences run our behavior more than we realize. We are constantly reacting to circumstances without realizing it, and thus short-circuit more creative and effective responses.

The over-extension of a strength becomes a weakness, and the Reactive Mind over-extends its strengths. When we are identified with a given strength, we use it a lot. We over-develop it and under-develop other strengths. Consequently, we tend to overuse that strength. Since that strength defines us, it feels natural to use that strength all the time, and it feels awkward, if not risky, to use other less developed strengths.

About a year ago we worked with the General Manager of a manufacturing facility in Canada. He had about 3,000 people working for him and was considered to be one of the best performing plant managers in the industry. We were talking about highly Controlling types, and this leader said, "I get this. My controlling behavior is such a go-to strategy for me that I call it my 'blade down' mode. When faced with problems, I say to myself, 'Blade down.'"

This leader was referring to the blades on a snowplow. On a snowy highway, all the rest of us can line up behind the snowplow with the blade down and have a clear, safe path of travel. We can all relate to the image of a snow plow clearing a path in front of us by going "blade down." He said that with his "blade down," he could move any obstacle. Yes, he would often leave a body count along the way, but "blade down" mode worked for him, and he was rewarded for it. He was afraid of how he would be defined without it, worried he would lose his power.

When he was promoted to GM, he saw that what had worked for him for so many years now worked against him. When he needed people on his side, partners to work with, or others to think things through, his "blade down" strength became a weakness.

"Blade down" had its strengths—he knew how to get things done and create great results. Now when he went "blade down," however, it had unintended consequences. His dictated orders were not followed when he was not there. His span of control and need for additional capacity and capability outmatched his primary mode of operating. "Blade down" only covered a small part of what he needed to do. Now his leadership was being rejected, and he had to make the move from "blade down" to "blade up." He needed to work collaboratively through others, not only rely on his own strength.

We all tend to react to situations by deploying the strength with which we are identified. We do this automatically and habitually. Hence, we over-extend our strength, and this becomes a main limitation and liability of the Reactive Mind.

Hershey and Blanchard developed the popular *Situational Leadership* model (Hershey, 1969). This model suggests that leaders are more effective when they can change their leadership style to match the unique needs of the situation: sometimes leaders need to ask, and sometimes they need to tell. While this model is useful, Reactive Mind is incapable of such flexibility. The fact that we are identified with a certain way of being limits our behavioral options. So, we react to a situation with our auto-pilot response. Anything else would seem ineffective and risky.

Cognitive and Rational Emotive psychologists have defined the core assumptions through which we form our externalized identity at the Reactive Stage. These internal assumptions form the core of our IOS. They are *beliefs* we hold about ourselves that equate our self-worth and security with being perceived a certain way. These equations take the following form:

Worth and Security = X (where **X** is a strength)

When we form our Reactive Mind, we simply form these equations around the strength with which we are identified (relationship, intellect, and/or results). Different people simply substitute different Xs into this equation. The structure of the self is the same in each case; only the self-defining beliefs are different. As we build these equations, we become externally defined. The Reactive Identity can be stated: "I am worthwhile and safe if I am X, and if others see me as X," or, "*To be is to be X*." If we run this belief backwards, "*Not to be X is not to be*," we see why these beliefs are so powerful and why they cause us to react to most situations by using X (the strengths with which we are identified) instead of some other strength that might be more effective in a given situation.

Reactively structured beliefs are inherently self-limiting because they restrict our behavioral options in situations. The problem is not the strength, but identifying with the strength. These beliefs cause us to run behaviors that limit our leadership effectiveness. The more we are defined by other people's approval, the more likely we will fear

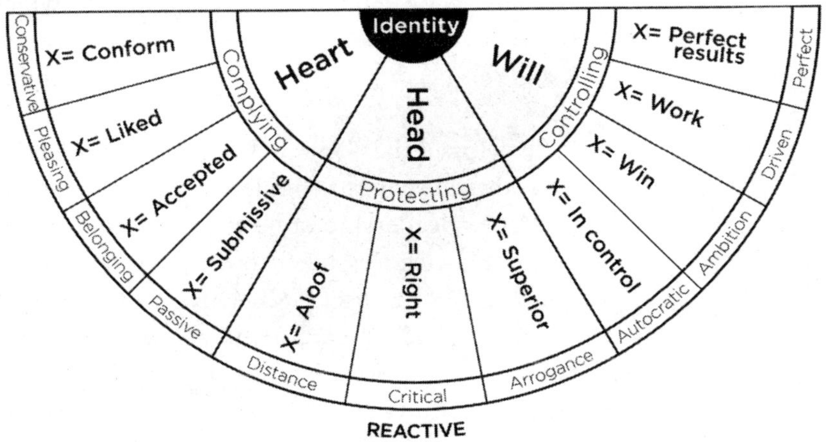

FIGURE 5.1 Reactive half of the circle and associated beliefs

rejection and be risk-averse, indecisive, cowardly, and compliant. The more we define ourselves by our results, the more likely we fear failure and fail to delegate, collaborate, build teamwork, and allow others to engage meaningfully and creatively. We will tend to relate to others in autocratic and controlling ways. If we define ourselves on our intellectual capacity, we will fear vulnerability, fail to connect with others, acknowledge their brilliance, and relate to others in self-protecting, arrogant, analytically critical, and condescending ways. Reactive beliefs are self-limiting and have serious liabilities. The more we are run by them, the less we lead effectively, and since leadership effectiveness drives business performance, Reactive leadership puts us at a competitive disadvantage.

The bottom half of the Universal Model and LCP is labeled *Reactive* and is made up of 11 dimensions that constitute a map of the Reactive Mind. Each dimension measures a set of leadership behaviors that naturally result when we are subject to a given Reactive belief.

Figure 5.1 shows how the Reactive half of the Universal Model and LCP is organized. The diagram shows the dimensional structure of the complete Reactive Model. The outer circle displays the 11 Reactive dimensions and how they fit within each of the three types (displayed in the inner circle). Each Reactive dimension lists the Xs that are plugged into the core identity-forming equations that run Reactive behavior.

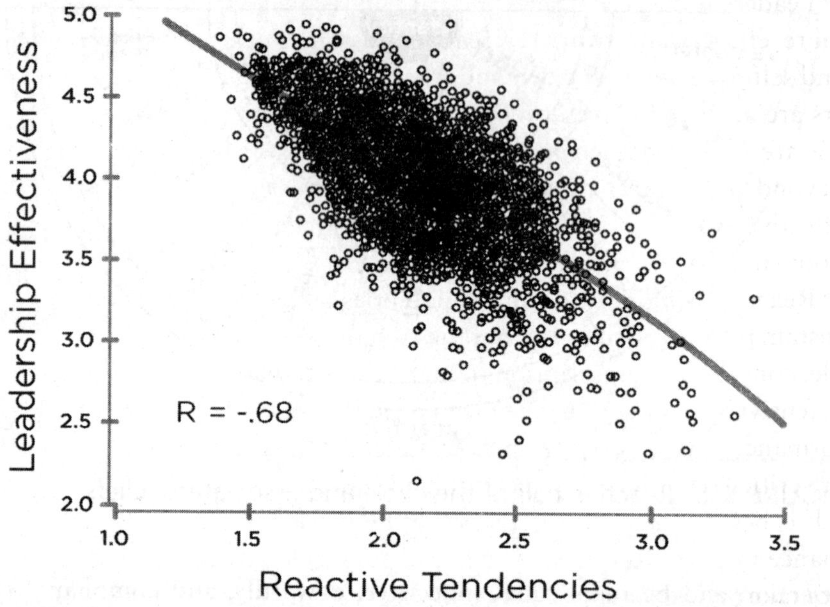

FIGURE 5.2 Correlation between Reactive Leadership and Leadership Effectiveness

Appendix 1 defines each of these dimensions and provides brief descriptions of the associated Reactive leadership styles.

In our research, Reactive leadership is measured by the average score on the Reactive dimensions that make up the bottom half of the circle (provided by a leader's 360° raters). Average Reactive leadership scores are correlated to the measure of Leadership Effectiveness embedded into the LCP. Figure 5.2 summarizes our research results.

Note that as Reactive behavior increases, Leadership Effectiveness goes down. We see a solid (-.68) inverse relationship between Reactive Tendencies and Leadership Effectiveness. This strong correlation is derived from 500,000 rater surveys worldwide. We see some scatter to the correlation because there are strengths at the core of the Reactive Structure. In some situations, these strengths are just what are needed, but if we overuse and misuse a strength, it becomes a liability. The stronger your Reactive tendencies, the less likely you will be experienced as an effective leader.

Leaders today are trying to create high-engagement cultures that are more efficient, innovative, creative, customer-centric, agile, involving, and self-managing. The demands that these change efforts make on leaders are at the Creative Level of Mind and leadership, meaning the ways we are expected to behave in the new, transformed organization are beyond the natural capability of the Reactive Mind. These new, more effective ways of leading become readily available as Creative Mind boots up.

Reactive Mind has too many liabilities associated with it to lead and sustain the transformation that these change efforts represent. For example, consider the prescription to high control managers to "stop reacting defensively" and use "active listening skills." If we identify with our performance and believe that our aggressive strength protects us, when we are criticized or have our performance questioned, we feel that our very self is being attacked. If my worth is my performance, when my performance is called into question, I am being called into question. I cannot *not* take this personally. This capability to "not be defensive" comes more naturally at the next stage of development.

If I "am my relationships," I will likely never use assertiveness skills because asserting my opinions may get me disapproval. This feels like death to the person identified with pleasing others. Yet leadership and teamwork require that leaders learn to listen non-defensively and assert their wants. These Creative level behaviors cannot happen consistently until the Reactive Self is shed.

Most adults operate from the Reactive Mind. Since 5% still operate at the Egocentric level and only about 20% are at the Creative level or higher, about 75% of adults are living from a Reactive Mind (or in transition from Reactive to Creative). Since structure determines performance, and consciousness is the operating system of performance, Reactive Mind naturally gravitates toward organizational forms that are consistent with the way Reactive Mind organizes its world.

Leaders at the Reactive Stage typically no longer function as Egocentric, oppressive dictators. Loyalty is not so much to the leader, but to the organization and its objectives. Institutional authority replaces the personal loyalty required by Egocentric leaders. Leaders at the Reactive level often care deeply about their employees and manage and function as benevolent parents or patriarchs/matriarchs. The organization is ordered and efficient. It is competency driven and mechanistic. It uses all of the scientific management tools. Employee input is solicited, but decision-making and creative expression is still vested with top leadership. Leadership is often humane, but lacks the capability of broadly sharing power. People are informed, but not significantly involved in decision-making. People feel supported financially and treated fairly, but most are not expected to be involved in important decisions. High levels of engagement are unlikely.

The institutional style that emerges with leadership at this level is a large, efficient hierarchy—an ordered and layered bureaucracy. Its political climate requires loyalty and obedience. While such organizations are still common, most change efforts seek to create structures and cultures that are flatter, leaner, more agile, more engaged, and require more ownership and creative involvement at lower levels than the Reactive Structure of Mind can tolerate.

Nearly 75% of managers operate out of a Reactive Mind, with *Leadership Effectiveness* scores averaging at the 40th percentile and with a LQ of .67 (see the study reported earlier). Reactive Mind is outmatched by the complexities of organizational life today. The level of complexity leaders face daily is more suited to Creative Mind or higher. Most of us are being challenged daily to evolve to a higher order of mind. This developmental shift, from Reactive to Creative, should be seen as a strategic imperative in any organization that wants to thrive long-term.

Most change efforts are attempts to create a Creative level culture. Most of these change efforts fall short because they can only be created and sustained if the leadership is functioning at or beyond the Creative Level of Mind. Since most leadership teams are not, what usually happens is the implementation of a lot of activity that should put a high-performance organization in place but fails to do so. When this happens, Reactive leadership does not see itself as the reason for the failure. Instead leadership moves on to the next and latest fad in the management literature. This "flavor of the month" approach to change continues without leaders noticing that in order for any of these new approaches to work, leadership must evolve. Consciousness is the operating system of performance, and if these change efforts are to succeed, senior leadership must transition from a Reactive to a Creative level consciousness. This is no small undertaking.

In our Business Transformation work, we design and structure every meeting and change event very carefully to engage the entire organization in a Creative level structure. We have done this for years without realizing that we were creating a practice field at the Creative Level of Mind. People in those meetings would consistently rise to the occasion and play at a Creative level in that practice field. For years we wondered why the organization could not sustain the Creative way of operating. We have learned that unless leaders are on a Creative development path, they cannot lead in Creative ways when they leave the practice field and return to the current culture. Most transformation and major change initiatives cannot be sustained because leaders, operating from Reactive Mind, cannot replicate Creative practices and structures (like the practice fields we design for them) on their own. They cannot transform their organization from within because their Reactive IOS cannot replicate Creative Structures and operate creatively within them. This is the root cause of why transformative change fails to sustain.

CREATIVE LEADERSHIP

The transition to the Creative Structure of Mind is marked by two changes in the IOS: first, we shed some old assumptions that have been running us all our lives; and second, we initiate a more authentic version of ourselves as we shift from *Reactive* to *Creative*.

By shedding well-patterned assumptions, we start to see the habitual ways of thinking that we adopted while growing up that were socialized into us. These embedded habits of thought form the core of the Reactive IOS. They have served us well and are now reaching operational limits. They are not complex enough for the complexity of life and leadership into which we have grown. These assumptions must be shed and replaced with new assumptions.

As we are liberated from the limitations of the Reactive assumptions, we ask new questions: "If I am no longer defined by the outside expectations that I grew up with, what do I really want?" The central questions of the Independent, Self-Authoring, Creative Mind are: "Who am I? What do I care most about? What do I stand for? How can I make my life and my leadership a creative expression of what matters most?" We start to march to the beat of Thoreau's "different drummer." We become visionary leaders.

Years ago, we worked off-site with the senior leadership team of a large hospital. Each team member had completed the LCP, and all had high scores on the Reactive dimension called *Perfect*, a measure of perfectionism. When asked what this meant, we explained: "Perfectionism results when we hold a belief or assumption that our personal worth, esteem, and security are established by being seen as perfect, flawless, and capable. So, we set extremely high standards for ourselves and for others—so high as to be unreachable. Mistakes, limitations, failures, and imperfections are so intolerable that even good performance is not good enough. Everything must be performed to an extremely high standard. Leadership is driving results in a way that is not sustainable, pushing people and systems beyond capacity."

At this point another manager spoke up: "This feels risky to say, but it needs to be said. If you remember, the Strategic Plan that we submitted to the Board had 26 key strategic directions. They sent it back to us saying that there was no way we could fulfill on all of them. They told us that the plan lacked focus. Strategy has as much to do with what you are not going to do as what you choose to take on. What did we do in response? We reorganized the list under five headings, sent it back, and they said, 'Good, now you are focused.' I knew we could never fulfill on all those strategies, but there is no way I was going to 'cry uncle' and be the first to admit in this group that I had limits. My need to always appear perfect, heroic, capable, and inexhaustible in your eyes had me colluding to agree to a strategic plan that I knew we could not accomplish."

After this courageous statement, the entire group admitted to similar thinking. Together they had colluded to pretend that they could do it all. Moreover, they knew they were not strategically focused, because they had not identified their strategic priorities. They also confessed to how exhausted they were. Some were even thinking of leaving the company. They committed to redoing their strategic plan and making it both strategic and achievable.

At its core, the perfectionistic assumption is false. Personal worth and security are not made up by how others see us, let alone by having them always see us as being so perfect and flawlessly overachieving. Each member of this senior team was operating on the false assumption, "I am better off if I am perfect." It likely felt true when it was created, but it is false. As leaders trade their old assumption for a new, more mature assumption, they become more capable of leading effectively amid complexity.

As we shed the self-limits of Reactive assumptions, new possibilities open up. We begin to orient our life and leadership less on what we assumed was expected of us as we grew up and more out of our own deeper sense of personal purpose and vision. *Transitioning to the Creative Self is the major transition in adult life and leadership.* To make this transition, we no longer ignore or distort the unique call of the soul. We face the fact that following our own path often means disappointing others, risking failure, or contradicting the norms that we assume make us (as a Reactive self) worthwhile, successful, and valuable.

This transition is arduous because, to make this journey, we have to let go of how we have come to define ourselves. We let go of the deeply held beliefs that our worth and value are tied up with how we are seen by others, by what we do, how smart we are, or how acceptable we are. We are less defined by cultural expectations. We configure a self from the inside out for the first time. Vision springs from within. Action becomes an authentic expression of an emerging sense of inner purpose. We begin to experience the power, creativity, freedom, and satisfaction of living from our own deep center. We value and encourage the same in others. We begin to treat others as equal participating members whose rights, insights, and purposes need to be engaged and creatively aligned. Self-expression and cooperation become our new principles.

Such self-authoring, visionary, authentic, and courageous leadership only becomes consistently possible when we begin living and leading out of a Creative Mind. The top half of the circular Universal Model of Leadership and the LCP maps out the Creative Mind. This mind is run by the Creative IOS and is formed around the inside-out, Self-Authoring, Creative identity.

In the outer circle of the top half of the LCP (see Figure 5.3) is an array of Leadership Competencies that have been well researched by the field to predict high levels of Leadership Effectiveness. These 18 Creative Competencies are strongly and positively correlated to leadership effectiveness and business performance.

The Leadership Field has been describing the kind of leadership that naturally emerges as Creative Level Mind evolves without realizing the developmental, sequential relationship between Reactive Mind and Creative Mind. In his book, *In Over our Heads*, Bob Kegan says that these behavioral capabilities arise naturally on the Creative, Self-Authoring Mind, but they do not boot up as well on Reactive Mind (Kegan, 1998). Therefore, the key leadership competencies that, through extensive research, have risen to the top of the list are those that describe how

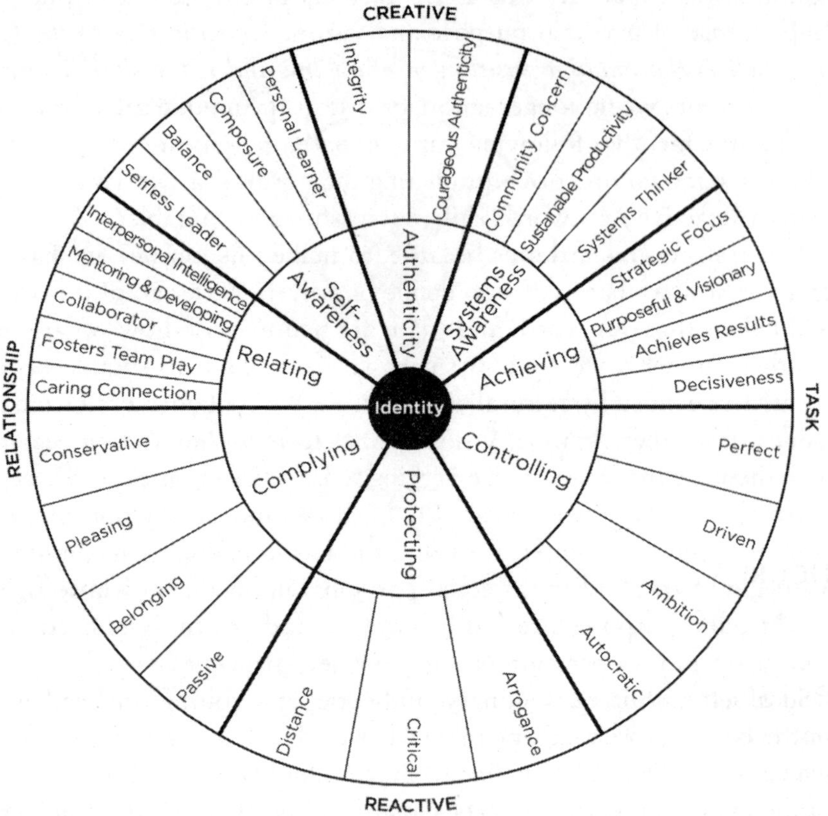

FIGURE 5.3 The Leadership Circle Profile

Creative level leaders lead. In other words, the competency research is highly adequate for filling in the top half of the model.

The Inner Circle (see Figure 5.4) in the top half of the model groups the 18 competencies into *five categories:* 1) *Achieving*, the ability to envision and get results; 2) *Systems Awareness*, the advanced leadership capability to think systemically and design organizational systems for higher performance; 3) *Authenticity*, the willingness to act with integrity to courageously tell the truth even when it is risky; 4) *Self-Awareness*, balance and composure that result from highly developed self-awareness, emotional intelligence, and ongoing learning and development; 5) *Relating*, the critical leadership capability to relate well to others, build teams, collaborate, and develop people. These five categories summarize the entire

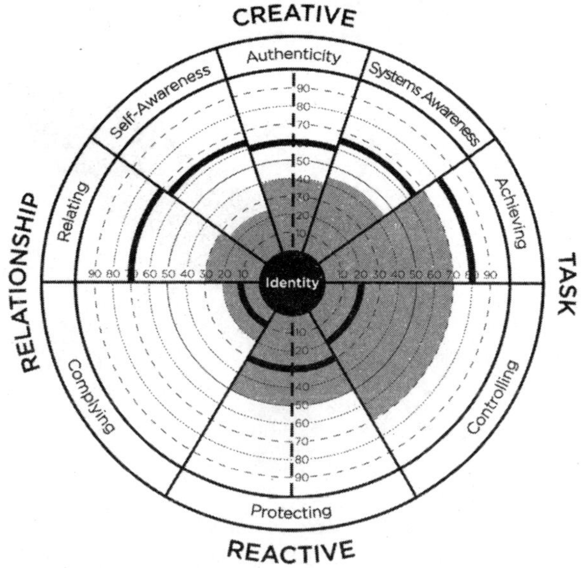

FIGURE 5.4 The Inner Circle

field of Leadership Development and serve as the Summary Dimensions of the Inner Circle of the LCP into which the 18 Creative Level Competencies fit. The top of The Leadership Circle maps out the Creative half of the Universal Model.

In our research we create a metric that averages these 18 Competencies to measure the degree of Creative Leadership—the average score of all 18 Creative Competencies on the LCP (provided by a leader's 360° raters). Creative Competency is .93 correlated to the measure of Leadership Effectiveness that is embedded into the LCP. The correlation, based on over a half-million surveys worldwide, is displayed in Figure 5.5.

Perfect correlation is 1.0, thus a .93 correlation is extremely strong, suggesting that if you can improve your Creative Leadership Competency, you will improve your Leadership Effectiveness. The relationship is nearly one-to-one: for every improvement in the key Creative Competencies, you get an equal increase in Leadership Effectiveness.

The Correlation between Reactive Leadership and Effectiveness is strongly inverse at -.68. Creative Leadership is just the opposite with a positive correlation to Effectiveness at .93. We conclude that Creative Leadership is much more effective than Reactive Leadership.

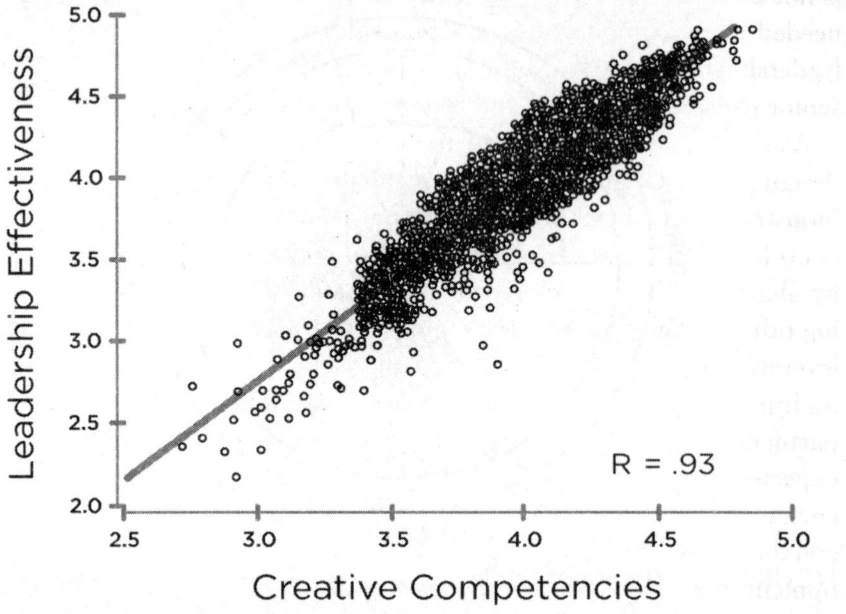

FIGURE 5.5 Correlation between Creative Competencies and Leadership Effectiveness

In the study reported earlier, we find a strong relationship between the leader's measured Stage of Development and their Leadership Effectiveness—a significant positive correlation at .65. This suggests that Leadership Effectiveness improves as consciousness evolves. In this study, leaders who are assessed as operating from Reactive Mind have average Leadership Effectiveness scores at the 40th percentile compared to our norm group. Leadership Effectiveness scores for the leaders who are assessed to be operating from Creative Mind average at the 65th percentile. Their LQ is nearly 2.0, which means their leadership is a big competitive advantage.

Creative Leadership is the minimum level required to create lean, engaged, innovative, visionary, creative, agile, high-involvement, high-fulfillment organizations and to evolve adaptive organizational designs and cultures that can thrive today. However, only 20% of leaders are operating out of the Creative Mind. This is the Leadership Imperative. The collective consciousness of most extended senior leadership teams is not complex enough to lead the kind of cultural and systemic change needed to remain competitive. Creative or higher is required. Evolving leadership to Creative Mind or higher is the Leadership Agenda that senior teams need to hold and forward for the organization.

As the consciousness of leaders moves to Creative levels, they tend to design and create organizational structures and cultures that facilitate industry-leading business performance. Leaders begin to *share power*. It is no longer perceived as "letting go" of control, but of gaining power by sharing it. The development of self and others is prized. Developing other leaders becomes the main job of leadership. This focus is high leverage as leaders are developing the capacity to scale and getting a multiple on their time invested. Leadership is shared, but not yet a full partnership. Creativity and critical decision-making are developed and expected at all levels. The leadership styles that emerge are empowering, engaging, and collaborative, involving ever larger constituencies. With collaboration, the emphasis is both on individual expression and development as well as group performance. The leader is no longer the sole decision-maker, but facilitates groups in developing, becoming more self-managing, and becoming more creatively involved in the success of the organization. The leader can support, challenge, and confront the group and its members. The focus is on high performance through teamwork and self-development. Leadership is collaborative. The leader now takes responsibility for authoring the vision, enrolling others in the vision, and helping them discover how the vision enables them to fulfill their personal purposes collectively.

The institutional style here is *High Engagement*. People at every level (and there are fewer levels and broader spans of control) are deeply involved in decisions that affect them. There is a successful, quality culture that sometimes evolves into a self-managing organization.

The business environment, and the complex challenges we collectively face on the world stage, are applying enormous adaptive pressure on leaders to evolve into Creative Mind and then beyond that into the Integral Mind. We are convinced that the current level of complexity in the global business environment and on the global economic, environmental, and geopolitical scene requires leadership from the Creative Mind at a minimum. We are more and more convinced that the level of consciousness required of leadership, if we are to successfully usher in a thriving planetary future, is Integral Level Leadership.

INTEGRAL LEADERSHIP

Integral Mind ushers in a level of leadership that is capable of leading amid complexity. At this stage, the vision of the Creative visionary leader expands to include systemic welfare. The visionary-strategic capability that emerges in the Creative leader evolves into Systems Thinking and Design. The Integral leader holds a larger vision of the welfare of the whole system and becomes the architect of its future. Integral leaders focus on a vision not only for their organization, but also for the welfare of the larger system in which their organization is embedded and interdependent. At this stage, Servant Leadership fully emerges. The leader becomes the servant of the whole.

Integral Mind is built for complexity. It is a level of mind and leadership that can lead through the redundant polarities and problems that make up complex challenges. Integral Mind can hold opposites in tension without reacting to resolve them quickly (superficially). It can hold conflicting visions of the future within a diverse set of stakeholders without championing one over the other. It looks for the merits of all perspectives and works toward synergistic synthesis.

This ability to hold opposites, conflict, tension, and polarity, without avoiding them, over-simplifying them or resorting to quick fixes is the hallmark of this leadership. By facilitating constructive dialogue with diverse stakeholders, it creates a platform for synergistic and systemic solutions to emerge. Collective intelligence goes beyond the average intelligence of group members and, thus, high-leverage systemic breakthrough thinking and action emerge.

The ability to see and hold the whole system (its functional aspects, its dysfunctional elements, its integrity and brokenness, its unresolvable tensions seeking resolution, its degree of alignment and conflictedness) with both a fierce commitment to transformation and with compassion for what is, results from yet another metamorphosis that has happened in the structure of the self.

The hard-earned authentic, self-authoring, visionary, creative self, with which we are identified at the Creative Stage, begins to fray. We begin to realize that we are not only this authentic visionary person; we are also its opposite. Here, the inner self-definition shifts from "I am a whole and complete self that coordinates with other whole and complete selves," to an internal realization that, in fact, "I am not whole and complete."

Rather, "I am many selves: I am an ecology of selves that are often in discord." As Zen teacher, Norman Fisher, states: "We are all many persons. Some of these people we know, and others we don't—only someone else knows them. Some of them we long for, and others we want to run away from. All this is music; it's the music of our lives if we could only stop to listen" (Wenger, 2002).

The realization that we are made up of many disparate and conflicting parts is not a kind of schizophrenia, but a deeper engagement of the *shadow side* of the self—the parts of us that we have ignored and not developed. *Shadow* does not mean dark or bad, but *ignored* or *left behind*.

In our discussion of Reactive Mind, we showed how it tends to identify with certain strengths, over-develop them, and under-develop others. These under-developed aspects of ourselves go into shadow. As Carl Jung said, "Most of the shadow is solid gold" (Jung, 1976). In the shadow, there are many undeveloped strengths, which often present as weaknesses and darker elements of the psyche. As we move into this stage we realize, to paraphrase Pogo: "We have met the enemy, and they are us" (Kelly, 1972). The enemy is not *out there* only, it is within us. The conflicted function and dysfunction in the larger system is also in us. We are, individually and collectively, a microcosm of the very system we are trying to lead and change.

As we embrace our partialness, we no longer need to pretend completeness and can move toward the unacknowledged aspects of ourselves with compassion and curiosity. We can now hold the whole complexity of our personality, good and bad, light and dark, hard and soft. We can see this inner complexity without flinching or needing to engage in some strenuous self-improvement regime. We see others this way—as complex multi-dimensional beings. We also see the world this way—as a dynamic interplay of conflicting forces. Seeing the self as a rich ecology of discord and harmony opens us to the richness and complexity of the workplace and world. The self-compassion for our incompleteness allows us to engage others and the larger system with the same acceptance. This interior evolution is what enables Integral Leaders to see the whole system in a way that honors huge diversity, with many opposites in tension, and to engage it in a way that moves toward creative resolution.

Only about 5% of adults develop to the Integral Mind. This low percentage points out the developmental challenge. Integral Mind results in highly effective leadership. Again, in our research, leaders who were assessed as functioning from Integral Mind had average *Leadership Effectiveness* scores at the 90th percentile, and their average LQ was 9.0. Their leadership is clearly a competitive advantage. This is truly an extraordinary level of leadership.

Not only is Integral Leadership highly effective, it also is best suited to lead the transformation of complex systems. Bill Torbert, a foremost researcher on Adult Stages of Development, conducted a long-term study on the relationship between the Stage of Development of the CEO and the ability of the organization to transform itself (Rooke & Torbert, 1998). In this study, Bill consulted with 10 organizations over 10 years. He had measures of Stage on each of the 10 CEOs. He collected metrics to assess whether transformations actually happened. He concluded that only the CEOs who lead from Integral Mind are able to create and sustain business transformations. The five CEOs in his study who led from Integral Mind created and sustained 15 measurable organizational transformations. Those functioning from earlier levels of mind achieved no measurable sustained change.

Integral level leaders have harvested all the visionary, strategic, authentic, team, and interpersonal competence as they matured through Creative Mind. They, therefore, build upon the Creative cultures and structures, and take them further. Frederic Laloux, in his book, *Reinventing Organizations* (Laloux, 2014) describes well the kinds of organizational cultures and structures that emerge at this level of leadership. Leaders at this level become systemically and community oriented. The workplace becomes a self-renewing organization where members are true engaged and participating partners. The legacy of the leader is connected to developing the organization into a vehicle for service to a larger constituency and world. The organization is seen as a network of stakeholders nested within a larger system of networks. Vision often becomes global and oriented toward service to human welfare. Sustainability and long-term common good become salient values. This is servant leadership.

All CEOs grapple with escalating complexity. CEOs consistently report feeling in over their heads, wondering if they have what it takes to lead their organizations. Integral level leadership is best suited to lead amid the complexity. Clearly, it is a competitive advantage and we believe the level of leadership capable of resolving the planet's perilous situation.

UNITIVE LEADERSHIP

Any overview of the Stages of Development would not be complete without including the highest stages of awareness. In the spiritual literature, there is a progression of awareness that moves through sequential stages, up to the highest level of sacred union with *All that Is*. We concur that this level of human development is possible. It may, in fact, be the purpose of human existence: to evolve into the highest knowing of who we are.

Research and experience strongly suggest that spiritual practices, such as mindfulness, meditation, and contemplative prayer, accelerate our development through stages. In fact, the Unitive Self seldom, if ever, develops without a long-term spiritual practice.

At the Unitive stage, another major shift takes place. Up to this point, the self has seen itself as a separate self, as located within the body-mind. Now the self realizes that "I am not the body, nor the mind." In the early phases of the Unitive stage we identify with the "soul"—an essential self in communion with the Divine Reality. The Integral self is not discarded. That richly nuanced self is used to act in the world. It is highly functional and effective. It becomes a useful tool of the spirit.

Further into the Unitive Stage, the astonishing oneness underlying and just behind diversity becomes obvious. This is the stage where the person ecstatically experiences the world as one. This oneness is not just an idea, not something gleaned from a book. It is a literal experience of oneness with life itself—the oneness of all things with Itself. This is the birthplace of universal compassion, for one knows "I am my brother, and my sister. We are all each other! The earth and all beings are one life."

This level of leadership is rare, although it becomes more available through long-term spiritual practices. Unitive development does not mean disengagement from the world. On the contrary, leaders at this level function as global visionaries and enact world service for the universal good. From the perspective of Unity, we are all each other. The children dying in wars on distant shores are our children. There is only one family. The Ecosystem is our body.

Mastering leadership is required, and it requires conscious development. We live in a time of great opportunity and great peril. The next 50 years are going to be "interesting" and pivotal. We could well bring into being a new and vital global order of planetary welfare. We could destroy ourselves. Certainly business, with its growing global reach, plays a major role in the world's future and has a huge stake in the outcome. It is only from the presumption of our inherent unity and the indivisibility of all things, resting on the enormous Integral Leadership capability, that we will find the solutions, on a planetary scale, to our current predicaments.

TAKING STOCK

- When was that last time you risked it all to become way more than you are now?
- How do you get in your own way?
- Are you waiting for others to give you permission to be great?
- If you were living life more authentically, what would you be doing differently? How would you be different?
- Are you are prepared to live in the world with its harsh need to change you? (Whyte, 1992)

Chapter 6

The Universal Model and Metrics

Global Leadership, Cross-Cultural, and Gender Application

In the last chapter, we introduced the Stages of Development framework and some of the architecture of the Universal Model of Leadership. Here we develop the entire Universal Model of Leadership by delving more deeply into the research conducted with the Leadership Circle Profile.

TASK AND RELATIONSHIP—HORIZONTAL AXIS

The Stages of Development framework is the vertical axis of the Universal Model and the LCP. The horizontal axis of the Leadership Circle Universal Model shows the leader's Relationship and Task balance: the left half is labeled *Relationship*; the right half is labeled *Task*. If leaders effectively organize and execute to accomplish tasks, and establish great relationships, they will be effective. If leaders are ineffective on either task execution or relationship capability, their leadership effectiveness diminishes. Research backs the 1950 Ohio State leadership studies which show that no other combination of variables better accounts for a leader's effectiveness than task and relationship. This finding has never been refuted.

This forms a four-quadrant grid which underlies the Universal Model of Leadership and the LCP (see Figure 6.1).

A leader can manage people Creatively—in a way that engages, empowers, and brings out the best in them. Or that leader can engage people Reactively—in a way that is people oriented and heart centered,

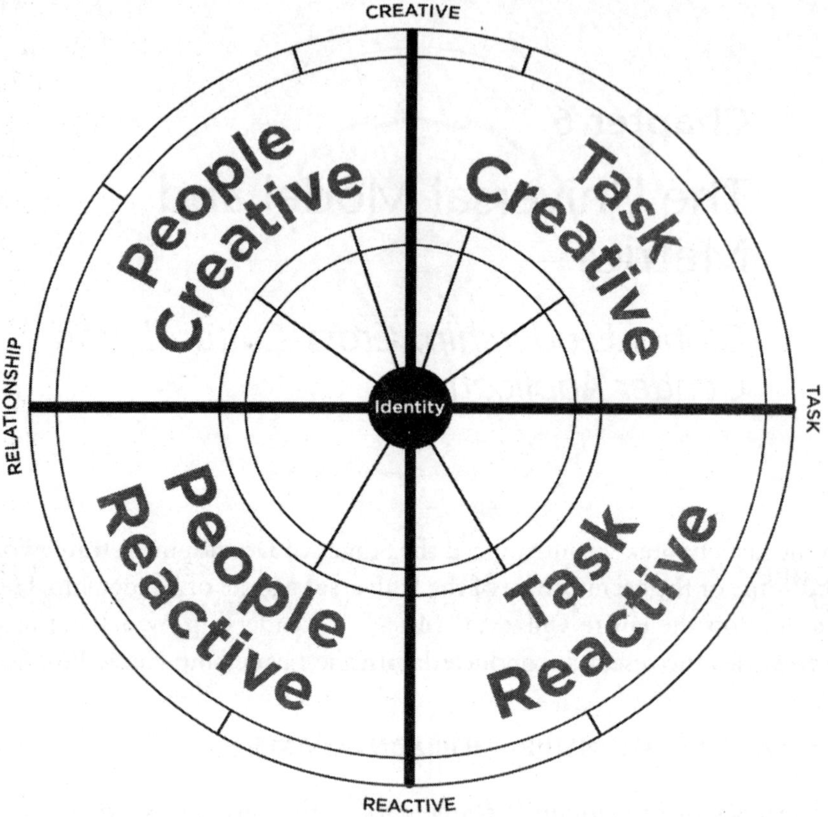

FIGURE 6.1 Four quadrants of the Universal Model of Leadership

but gives up too much power in service of being liked and accepted. A leader can manage tasks Creatively—purpose driven and vision focused that translates into effective execution on results and systemic improvement. Or, a leader can manage tasks Reactively—over-controlling and driving the organization and people beyond sustainable limits.

In the outer circle of the top half of the LCP is an array of Creative Leadership Competencies that predict leadership effectiveness and business performance.

The Inner Circle (see Figure 6.2) in the top half of the model groups the 18 competencies into five categories. These are arranged along the Relationship-Task axis with Relating and Self-Awareness on the left

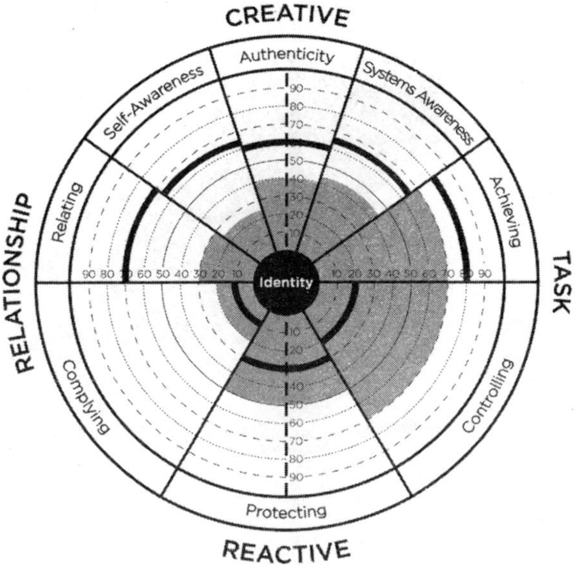

FIGURE 6.2 The Inner Circle

or *Relationship* side of the circle, and Achieving and Systems Awareness on the right or *Task* side. Authenticity is located in the center since it is so central to establishing individual and collective leadership effectiveness.

The bottom half of the circle mirrors this arrangement with three forms of reactivity. Complying is reactively people oriented and is located on the left below Relating. Controlling is on the right below Achieving because Controlling is reactively task driven. Protecting is in the middle.

This way of mapping the inner circle dimensions forms the core of the Universal Model. It visually renders most of leadership theory and research and the dynamic interdependence of the findings.

A DYNAMIC MODEL

Kurt Lewin, Einstein and others have said that "there is nothing so practical as a good theory." The Universal Model is dynamic in that every dimension is interrelated and interdependent with every other dimension (both theoretically and statistically). Therefore, the Universal Model maps out the key relationships among the various aspects of leadership that heretofore have not been combined in one model. The dynamic

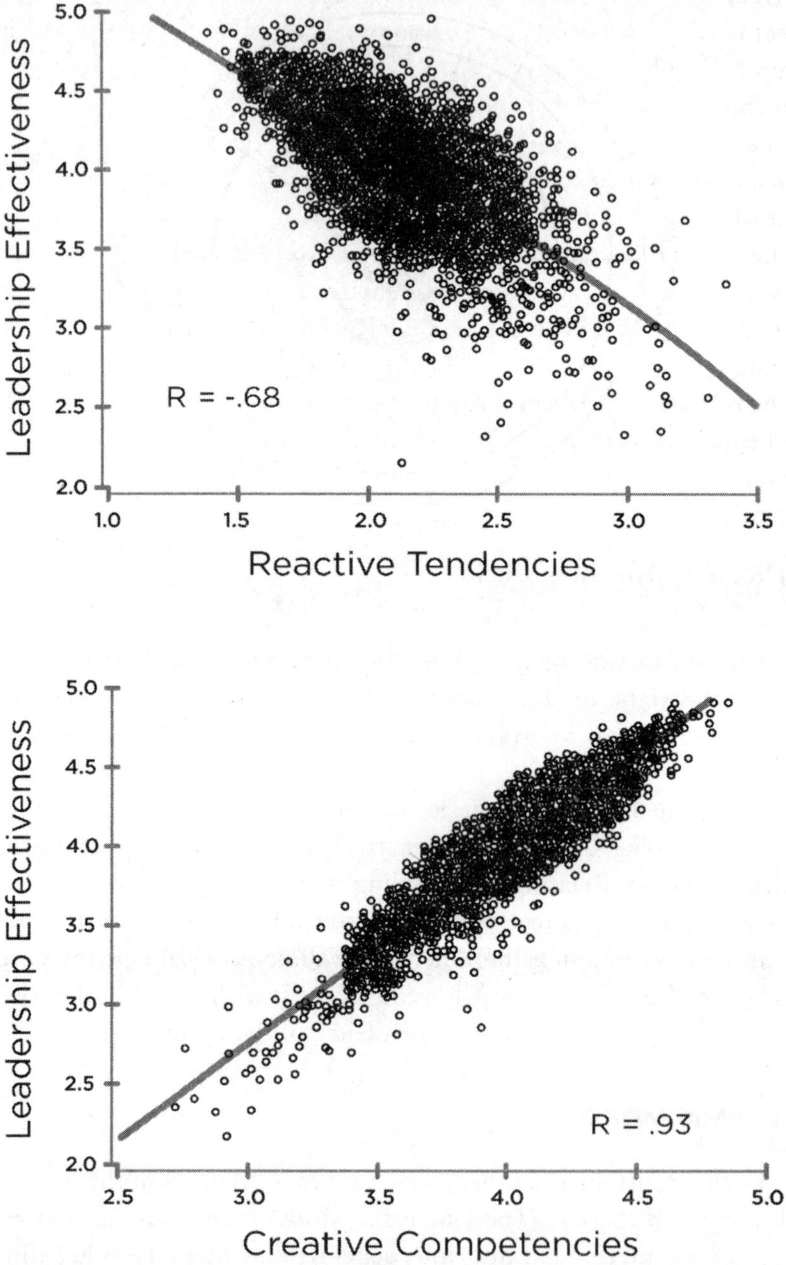

FIGURE 6.3 Reactive and Creative correlations to Leadership Effectiveness

interrelationship between all aspects of the model means that when one aspect of our leadership changes, it affects all other aspects of our leadership in predictable ways.

In the last chapter, we showed how scores on our measures of Reactive Leadership are inversely correlated to Leadership Effectiveness. We also showed how strongly Creative Leadership Competencies correlate to Leadership Effectiveness (see Figure 6.3).

The model becomes dynamic when we look at the relationship between Creative Leadership and Reactive Leadership. Figure 6.4 shows the relationship between the average Reactive (rater) score and the average Creative (rater) score.

The relationship is very strongly (−.76) inverse, meaning that as Reactive Leadership increases, Creative Leadership very likely decreases. This inverse relationship is what makes the Universal Model so dynamic and so instructive. When a leader receives feedback that suggests they are low in a particular Creative Competency in the top half of the circle, they can look to the bottom half of the circle to see what Reactive strategy may

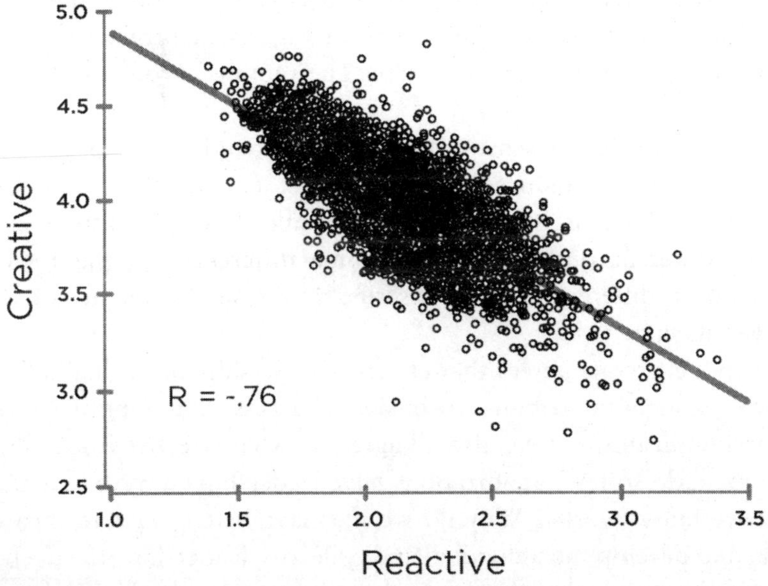

FIGURE 6.4 Correlation between Reactive Tendencies and Creative Competencies

be diminishing their effectiveness. And since all dimensions of the Model come from the best research in leadership and organizational development, the feedback plugs right into all this research. The data gives them access to the model, and the model powerfully instructs. *There is nothing so practical as a good model.*

OPTIMAL LEADERSHIP

What might the LCP of an optimal, highly effective leader look like? Optimal leadership creates a profile that has strong scores in the top half and low scores in the bottom half. The Optimal Profile also has good balance between the left and right halves. The strength of a score in the LCP is displayed by its distance from the center. Strong scores, calculated as a percentile (compared to our worldwide norm group), extend far out from the center, while low scores are closer to the center. Optimal Leadership is highly Creative with strong and balanced Task and Relationship capability.

To test this, we asked over 50,000 managers worldwide to evaluate *Optimal Leadership*, the kind of leadership that would enable their organization to thrive. We then created an aggregate profile to illustrate what Optimal Leadership looks like. The Optimal Profile is shown in Figure 6.5.

The worldwide consensus describes optimal leadership as highly Creative with very reduced Reactive styles. This image is deceptively informative. First, it is cross-cultural. While different cultures create slightly different optimal profiles (some differences in the Reactive dimensions), different cultures describe a very similar picture of Optimal Leadership.

Second, everyone agrees that effective leadership, individual and collective, strongly contributes to business success. Our Optimal Leader research indicates that we also all agree on what effective leadership is. Why then, do so few organizations have leadership cultures that reflect what we know works? Why do we not have better ways to measure, track, and develop the individual and collective leadership effectiveness? Why is the Leadership Agenda so often not a Leadership Imperative held by senior leaders as a strategic priority for creating competitive advantage?

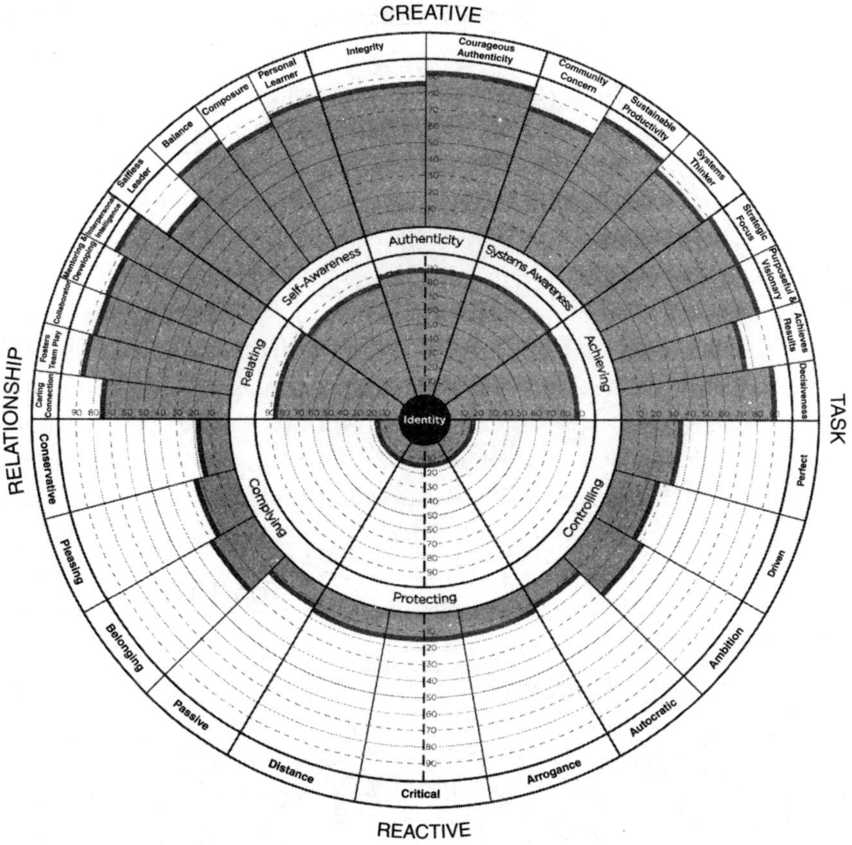

FIGURE 6.5 Optimal Leadership Profile

LINK TO PERFORMANCE AND EFFECTIVENESS

We have shown that our research shows a strong (.61) correlation between Leadership Effectiveness and Business Performance. Now let's look at the relationship of Leadership Effectiveness and Business Performance to the Creative and Reactive dimensions of the Model. We presented some of this research earlier by showing what the average Leadership Effectiveness score is for the leaders in the highest performing businesses—the top 10%. We then compared that to the average Leadership Effectiveness scores of leaders in the lowest performing businesses.

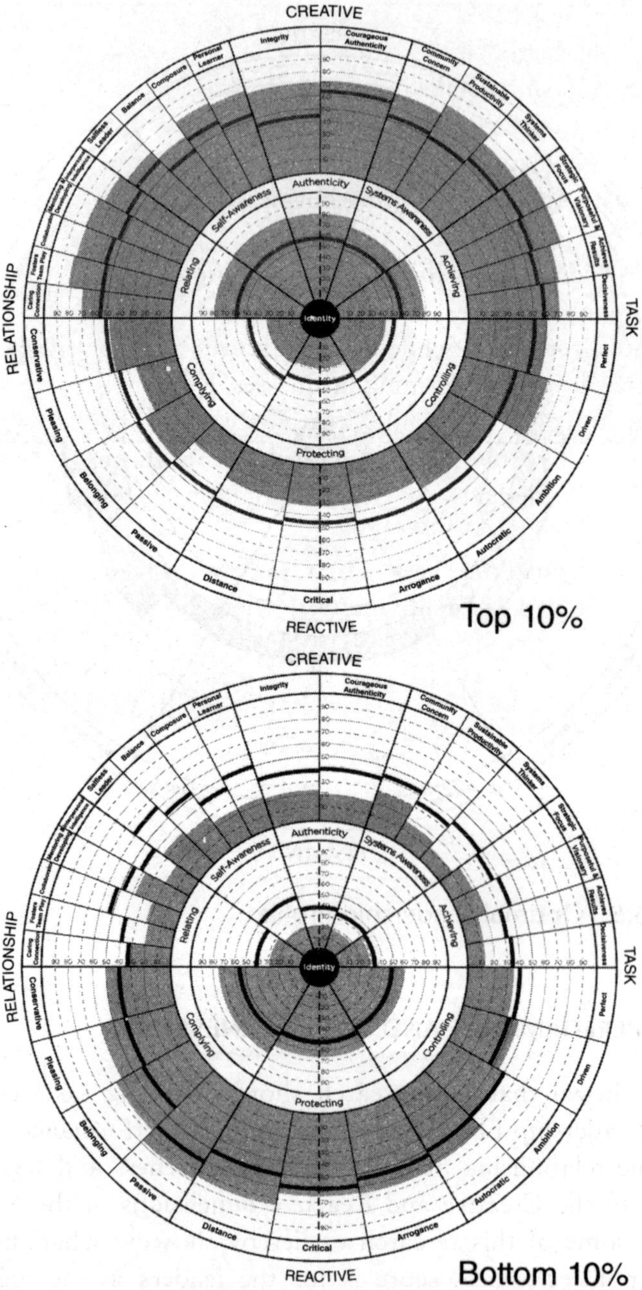

FIGURE 6.6 Leadership culture in the highest and lowest performing businesses

We now ask: "What is the aggregate Leadership Circle Profile in businesses rated as highest performing, or the top 10%? And what is the aggregate Leadership Profile in businesses rated as lowest performing, or the bottom 10%?" Figure 6.6 shows what we found.

Businesses evaluated as highest performing have very Creative leadership cultures; in underperforming businesses, Reactive leadership styles abound.

Figure 6.7 summarizes this same information differently. In the highest performing businesses, the average Creative score was measured to be at the 80th percentile, while Reactive scores were low at the 30th percentile. In the lowest performing businesses, Reactive scores were found to be at the 70th percentile while Creative scores averaged at the 30th percentile. Clearly, Creative leadership greatly outperforms Reactive leadership. Creative leadership is a decided competitive advantage. Reactive leadership is a competitive disadvantage.

Earlier, we defined the Leadership Quotient (LQ) as Leadership Effectiveness divided by Leadership Ineffectiveness. Now that you understand

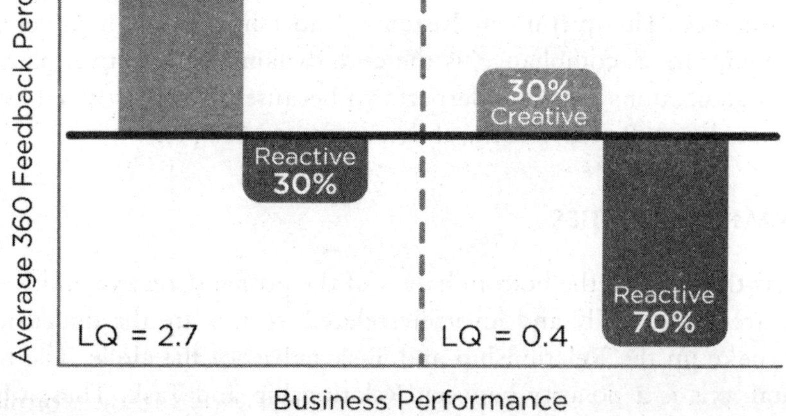

FIGURE 6.7 Reactive and Creative scores in highest and lowest performing businesses

the full Universal Model, we can use Creative Competency scores as a measure of Leadership Effectiveness, and Reactive Scores as a measure of Leadership Ineffectiveness. The LQ score in the highest performing businesses is 2.7, while the LQ score for the underperforming businesses is .4. Remember that a score higher than 1.0 makes leadership a competitive advantage. Clearly, this suggests that leadership, individual and collective, in the highest performing businesses is a distinct competitive advantage. The LQ score in the highest performing business is more than *six-fold higher* than the LQ score of the lowest performing business. The difference in effectiveness drives very different performance.

This finding is consistent with Zenger and Folkman's findings that leadership becomes extraordinary when the leadership competency score reaches the 80th percentile and that managers rated at or above the 80th percentile six-fold outperform managers scoring in the middle percentiles (between 20 and 80).

Also, in the highest performing businesses, the self-evaluations (solid line in Figure 6.6) were slightly under the average rater scores (outer edge of the shaded portion). The reverse was true in the under-performing business with Reactive leadership. This suggests that Creative leaders have a greater, more mature capacity to be constructively self-critical, while Reactive leaders tend not to see the liabilities associated with their Reactive style of leadership.

In the lowest performing businesses, the dominant leadership style is Reactive-Complying. Complying, to a greater extent than other forms of reactivity, greatly reduces both Leadership Effectiveness and Business Performance. This picture of Reactive leadership, where high-control leadership drives compliance, is the core dynamic of Reactive, patriarchal organizations which underperform because of the costly liabilities associated with Reactive cultural dynamics (see Chapter 9).

DYNAMIC POLARITIES

Just as the top and the bottom halves of the profile (Creative and Reactive) are dynamically and inversely related, so too are the dimensions that make up the Relationship and Task halves of the circle. The horizontal axis is a polarity between Relationship and Task. These often show up in the leadership literature and research as opposite leadership tendencies—leaders strong on task accomplishment may not be as good

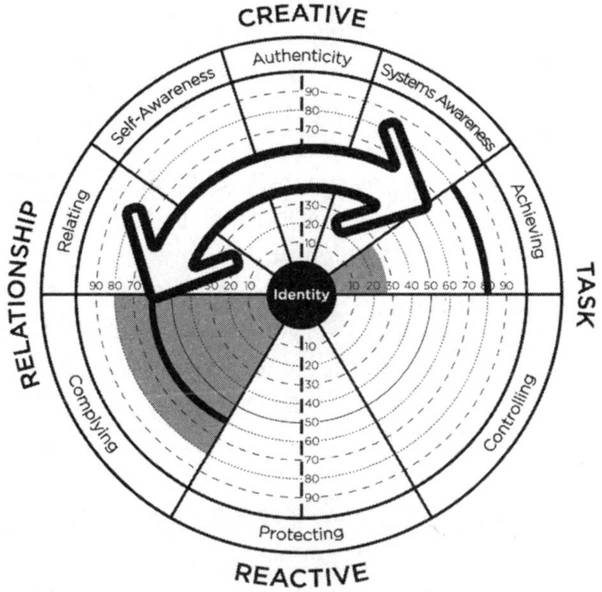

FIGURE 6.8 Polarity between Complying and Achieving

at relationships and vice versa. Therefore, the entire circle is designed as a set of behavioral polarities or opposite tendencies.

Notice in Figure 6.8 that Complying (lower-left) and Achieving (upper-right) are on opposite sides of the circle. This is because they are opposite in every way. 1) They are opposite leadership styles and behaviors. 2) The belief structures that run those behaviors are opposite. 3) Achieving and Complying are most inversely correlated. Table 6.1 shows the correlations between all dimensions in the inner circle and Leadership Effectiveness and Business Performance.

Complying strongly interrupts Achieving (−.75), and since Achieving is highly correlated to Effectiveness (.91), Complying reduces Effectiveness (−.63). Complying, therefore, is very problematic. As Complying increases, Leadership Effectiveness and Business Performance suffer because the most highly correlated dimension to Business Performance is Achieving (.61).

The opposite polarity (Figure 6.9) is the polarity between Relating (upper-left) and Controlling (lower-right). These two dimensions are opposite each other in the circle because they are opposite behaviorally, the beliefs that run these behaviors are opposite, and they are inversely

TABLE 6.1 LCP Inner Circle correlations

	Business Performance Index	Leadership Effectiveness	Relating	Self-Awareness	Authenticity	Systems Awareness	Achieving	Controlling	Protecting	Complying
Business Performance Index	1	.61	.50	.48	.50	.57	.61	−.21	−.31	−.40
Leadership Effectiveness	.61	1	.85	.76	.78	.84	.91	−.41	−.56	−.63
Relating	.50	.85	1	.87	.72	.80	.76	−.64	−.75	−.44
Self-Awareness	.48	.76	.87	1	.66	.73	.66	−.74	−.74	−.36
Authenticity	.50	.78	.72	.66	1	.78	.86	−.23	−.38	−.72
Systems Awareness	.57	.84	.80	.73	.78	1	.88	−.40	−.51	−.61
Achieving	.61	.91	.76	.66	.86	.88	1	−.24	−.41	−.75
Controlling	−.21	−.41	−.64	−.74	−.23	−.40	−.24	1	.83	.09
Protecting	−.31	−.56	−.75	−.74	−.38	−.51	−.41	.83	1	.23
Complying	−.40	−.63	−.44	−.36	−.72	−.61	−.75	.09	.23	1

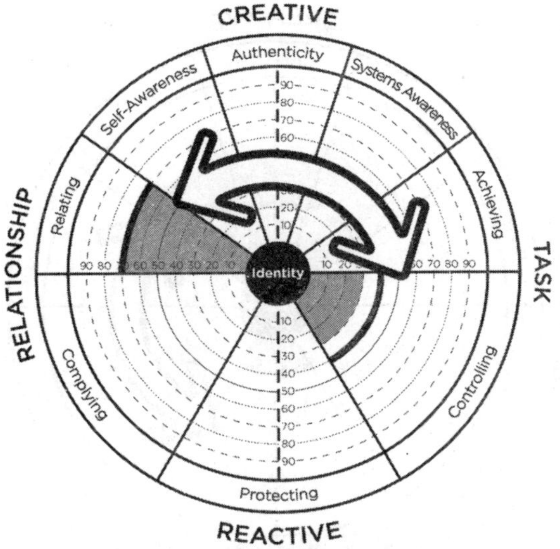

FIGURE 6.9 Polarity between Controlling and Relating

correlated (−.64). Thus, when Controlling goes up, Relating is reduced. Since Relating is highly correlated to Leadership Effectiveness (.85) and Business Performance (.50), when Relating is reduced, Leadership Effectiveness is reduced and, thereby, Business Performance suffers.

As you can see from the Inner Circle correlation table, Protecting is solidly inverse to all Creative dimensions in the top half of the circle. It is most inverse to Relating (−.75) and Self-Awareness (−.74) because it is highly correlated to Controlling (.82). When Protecting is high, Achieving is reduced (−.41), as is Systems Awareness (−.51). Consequently, Leadership Effectiveness suffers (−.56) and this, in turn, hurts Business Performance (see Figure 6.10).

As the Inner Circle Correlations table shows, all correlations are solidly in the expected direction. Since the Inner Circle is the core of the Universal Model, this provides strong evidence for the validity of the Model. It also shows that the dynamics of the Universal Model are supported by the metrics. The correlations validate the model's theoretical framework and business relevance.

UNIVERSALITY OF THE MODEL

We have 15 years of experience using our Universal Model for developing leadership effectiveness worldwide. For example, a recent Full Circle

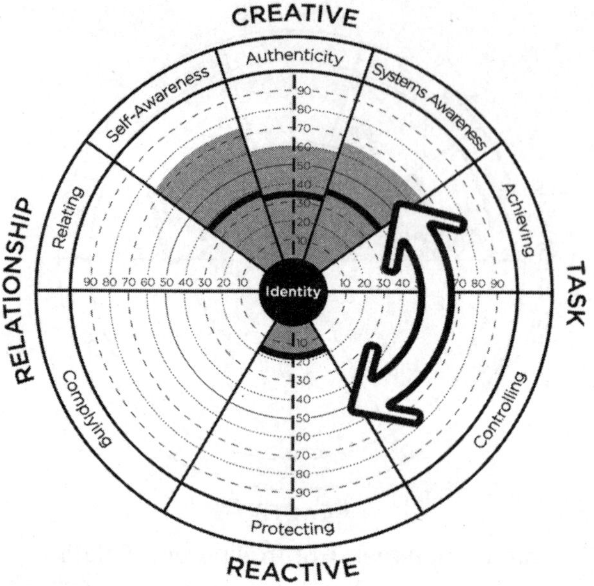

FIGURE 6.10 Polarity between Protecting and Awareness

Group session conducted in Hong Kong included senior leaders in one global organization speaking 17 different native languages!

Applies Across Cultures. The model is embraced cross-culturally and provides a common framework and language for the challenge of advancing the Leadership Agenda in global and culturally diverse organizations.

Table 6.2 shows the correlations between Leadership Effectiveness and the Inner Circle Dimensions—the core of the Universal Model—for various cultures around the world. There is very little variation around the world in the correlations of the key Creative Competencies to Leadership Effectiveness. All are strongly and positively correlated. This strongly suggests that the Creative half of the model provides a globally cross-cultural model of effective leadership. While there is some variation in the Reactive dimensions, all Reactive dimensions are in the expected direction. We consistently see, in developing countries, lower correlations between Leadership Effectiveness and some Reactive Dimensions, principally, Complying and Controlling. This may be because patriarchal leadership is more prevalent, more valued, more accepted, and more necessary in these developing countries.

TABLE 6.2 Inner Circle correlations to Leadership Effectiveness around the world

	Relating	Self-Awareness	Authenticity	Systems Awareness	Achieving	Controlling	Protecting	Complying	All Creative	All Reactive
United States	.88	.83	.76	.82	.90	–.47	–.63	–.60	.90	–.66
Canada	.87	.82	.75	.79	.89	–.45	–.62	–.56	.89	–.63
Latin America	.87	.84	.79	.84	.90	–.30	–.50	–.48	.91	–.51
Europe	.85	.78	.69	.76	.86	–.37	–.58	–.53	.87	–.57
Middle East	.89	.85	.75	.84	.89	–.33	–.57	–.46	.91	–.53
Africa	.87	.83	.74	.81	.89	–.26	–.50	–.49	.90	–.47
India	.88	.84	.74	.83	.90	–.24	–.51	–.45	.90	–.44
Asia	.86	.83	.71	.80	.88	–.32	–.57	–.53	.89	–.53
Australia & NZ	.85	.81	.76	.76	.87	–.40	–.57	–.59	.88	–.61

All correlations are significant at .001

Given the results in Table 6.2, we would expect, and our research shows, that Outer Circle correlations are also very similar worldwide (with variation consistent with what is found in Table 6.1). We conclude that Effective Leadership, as measured through the lens of the Universal Model, is described similarly worldwide. Therefore, it provides a strong framework of support to senior leaders challenged with advancing the Leadership Agenda in globally diverse organizations.

CASE IN POINT: CROSS-CULTURAL APPLICATION IN RURAL UGANDA

Since we claim that the Universal Model is cross-cultural and gender inclusive, let's explore one application of the Model in a most unlikely place, Uganda.

In the early 1980s, a bold experiment in the application of the Whole Systems Approach to Creative Leadership development began in the village of Kahunge, Uganda. The Uganda Rural Training and Development (URDT) organization was founded. Mwalimu Musheshe, Ephrem Rutaboa, and Silvana Veltkamp, a small group of dedicated young leaders, decided to do something about the economic and social development needs of Africa. They concluded that most approaches to rural development were failing because they were not advancing the community's Leadership Agenda that would support the development of a grass roots capacity to create opportunity. Most approaches were foreign-aid based and failing because they created dependency, not self-sufficiency. Musheshe and Ephrem are Agricultural and Civil Engineers, and they had much experience in applying systemic solutions in the hard sciences. With Veltkamp's help, they traveled to the United States where they learned from the top thought leaders in Whole Systems Change. We worked with them at this time, helping them deepen their understanding of the principles of Creative Leadership. Musheshe and his team returned to Uganda to undertake a bold new approach of integrating a soft and hard systemic approach to rural development.

What makes their approach to development, and human and rural transformation, so unique is that it is a grass-roots, Whole Systems, and empowerment approach to developing Creative Leadership capacity at the village level. Little aid is required and is used sparingly and judiciously. In the 1980s, when Musheshe and his team entered Kuyunge, villagers came out to meet them, expecting aid. They asked, "What are you going to do for us?"

Musheshe responded, "Nothing."

As people started to walk away, Musheshe invited them to a meeting. Soon roads, fishponds, and schools were being built. Springs were being protected. Micro enterprises were starting, and local lending structures evolved to provide revolving credit for business development. Health outcomes were improving and sustainable agriculture and land use were being practiced.

We visited the project first in 1986. While we were there, the project was visited by Charlie Deull and his wife Laurel Dutcher. They were on assignment from the United Nations to research new approaches to economic development worldwide. After observing the project for a few days, Charlie said to us privately: "This is a relatively small project compared with other projects around the world, but it is the most innovative and promising project we have seen. The difference here is that people are enthusiastically embracing the challenge of being responsible for their own development and for creating the future to which they aspire. It is being done without the need for a large infusion of resources. Furthermore, it is a complete, Whole Systems approach to economic development, education, community health, and ecological sustainability." All this happened while Uganda was engulfed in the violent revolution, led by the now President of Uganda, Yoweri Museveni, to overthrow the brutal dictator, Milton Obote.

In 2013, we visited URDT again to train URDT leadership on the Universal Model and support URDT's Leadership Agenda: ongoing development of their leadership effectiveness, individually and collectively. We administered the LCP with 25 of their key leaders and conducted a three-day development process with them. The session was very powerful with lots of learning that continues to this day.

The results we observed in this project over the intervening 27 years were amazing. The project had moved from Kuyunge to Kagadi, the poorest part of Uganda. URDT's village development efforts were multiplying in the area. In order to expand its impact, URDT realized that their capacity constraint was rural development leaders who could start and support projects until they were self-sustaining. To solve this challenge, Musheshe founded Africa Rural University (ARU) in Kagadi, an entire school system for girls from grade school through University. The vision of ARU is to develop Rural Development Leaders for all of Africa that are deeply schooled in the principles of the Whole Systems and Creative Leadership Approach. There are 260 girls in the school system. Only young girls from the poorest families who have few future prospects but who show leadership potential are eligible to enter the school system. ARU has been recognized as one of the top 10 Change Maker Schools in East Africa and one of Africa's most innovative universities. When these girls graduate from ARU years later, they are some of the most educated and capable women leaders of rural transformation in all of Africa. URDT immediately hires some of them and deploys them as Rural Transformation Specialists in village development projects and to work with local government leaders, enabling them to enhance authentic service delivery for the development of human and social capital for sustainable and lasting change.

Joel Yanowitz is on the Board and a long-time Partner of URDT. Joel was the President of Innovation Associates when Peter Senge, Charlie Kiefer, and Robert Fritz were pioneering the Systems approach. Joel recently told us: "URDT and ARU are perhaps the longest running and most successful experiments of the application of these principles." Musheshe is now an honored leader in Uganda and across Africa, having received many awards. In addition to his pioneering work with URDT/ARU, he has served in many top-level Government posts for Uganda. He is an example of the vision, courage, and impact of an extraordinary Creative Leader—one of those top 20% leaders who get a six-fold multiple on their leadership.

GENDER AND THE UNIVERSAL MODEL

Not only does the Universal Model integrate the fragmented field of Organizational and Leadership Development and honor cross-cultural and ethnic diversity, but it is also gender balanced. Since the horizontal axis of the Universal Model spans the polarity between *Relationship* and *Task*, the Model illustrates the different leadership orientations of men and women. This yin-yang or Feminine-Masculine framework allows us to explore the question: Do men and women lead differently?

We recently studied gender leadership differences seen in the LCP database. Table 6.3 shows the results for the Inner Circle Dimensions of Relating and Achieving—the Creative dimensions that define the

TABLE 6.3 Gender differences

Dimensions	Women		Men		
	Average	Percentile	Average	Percentile	Effect Size
Relating	4.06	56%	3.89	39%	−0.27
Caring Connection	4.08	60%	3.8	37%	−0.39
Achieving	4.15	53%	4.06	41%	−0.17
Creative Dimensions	4.09	57%	3.97	40%	−0.21
Reactive Dimensions	2.06	42%	2.21	61%	0.25
Creative-Reactive Score	2.01	59%	1.75	40%	−0.27
Leadership Effectiveness	4.09	53%	3.97	41%	−0.15

N = 250,000 raters. All differences between the Average scores of Men and Women are statistically significant at P < .001

Relationship–Task polarity. We included Caring Connection (a subdimension of Relating) as it shows the biggest difference between men and women. Table 6.3 also contains scores for the average of all Creative and Reactive dimensions. The Reactive-Creative score combines both scores into one summary score to measure the degree to which a leader is showing up more Creatively or Reactively. Leadership Effectiveness is also included.

Across the board, women have higher Creative scores, and lower Reactive scores, than men. Combined, the Reactive-Creative Score shows a difference of .26. This difference, when normed against the entire raterbase, produces percentile scores where men average at the 40th percentile, while women average at the 59th percentile. Women are also rated slightly higher on Leadership Effectiveness. This difference suggests that there is a pent-up demand for what women bring to leadership. With this data, we can make a strong argument for gender diversity and inclusion and an even stronger case for more women in leadership.

This data suggests that women are more effective leaders than men, or that at least they are rated higher on average. How significant are these differences? Effect Size measures whether the difference between scores is likely to be experienced, at work, as a practical difference in the way that men and women lead. Effect sizes greater than .20 or less than −.20 begin to show practical differences in the way the genders show up as leaders, but researchers do not get excited until the Effect Size is greater than +/−.35. Our researcher, Lani Van Dusen made this conclusion:

> Several findings meet minimal requirements for practical significance, but only one is noteworthy. On the "Caring" dimension, the difference in the performance of males and females is practically significant (Effect Size = −0.39). This finding suggests that females score at the 60th percentile of the norm base and at the 66th percentile of male scores on this dimension. Women are exhibiting more Creative behaviors associated with this dimension than male counterparts.
>
> The findings from the gender analyses, showing almost no practically significant differences in the averaged ratings of males and females, suggest that *what makes a leader effective tends to remain consistent across genders (and cultures)*. However, female leaders tend to perform slightly better in the Relating dimension and much higher on the Caring Connection competency. This suggests that female leaders have a natural proclivity to express skills in this area and higher social and emotional intelligence. And, their "soft" relationship skills assist them in showing up strong also on the results side.

Our experience of working with thousands of leaders suggests percentile score differences of 15 to 20 points (as measured in the 360° results for men and women) will impact performance. Women are bringing a much needed Creative contribution to business cultures. Since a highly engaged workforce is a competitive advantage, organizations are shifting from *Patriarchal Cultures* to *Partnership Cultures*. In this shift, the relational, emotional, and social intelligence of women leaders is much needed. In fact, the higher Relational and Creative evaluation of women leaders reflects their contribution to the shift in the leadership culture needed for high performance.

STAGE OF DEVELOPMENT RESEARCH

In our study conducted with the Stayer Center for Executive Education at the University of Notre Dame's Mendoza College of Business, we explored the relationship between the stage of a leader's development (as measured by the Maturity Assessment Profile) and the effectiveness of their leadership (as measured by The Leadership Circle Profile). Earlier, we reported the relationship between the leader's Stage of Development (Reactive, Creative, Integral) and their Leadership Effectiveness (Figure 6.11). The correlation between the Stage of Development of the leader and their measured level of Leadership Effectiveness was high (r = .65). Now let's look at the rest of the study.

The impetus for this study came from the convergence of two lines of research. In their book, *Extraordinary Leaders*, Zenger and Folkman report their research finding that those leaders who scored beyond the 80th percentile (in the top 20%) on a good 360° competency assessment would two-times (2X) outperform managers scoring in the middle 60 percentile ranges (from 20% to 80%) (Zenger and Folkman, 2009). Again, each manager in the top 20th percentile was performing at a six-fold multiple on the performance of a manager in the middle group. This six-fold multiple matches the difference we find in the LQ scores between the highest and lowest performing business. Clearly something is extraordinary about leaders assessed beyond the 80th percentile.

The second body of research that formed the hypothesis for this study was from the field of Adult Stages of Development, which finds that only about 20% of adults are living and leading from an operating system configured at Creative level or higher.

Both lines of research point towards something extraordinary happening beyond the 80th percentile. Is it possible that they are identifying the same group of leaders? Is extraordinary leadership a matter of consciousness or competence? The answer, from our research, is yes.

This study was conducted in two phases. The first phase was conducted with an Executive MBA class at Notre Dame's Stayer Center for Executive Education. This EMBA program is unique because it starts with the week-long residential Executive Integral Leadership (EIL) program which focuses on developing the inner and outer game of leadership. Students in this program (and in our study) are typically mid- to senior-level executives in their mid-thirties looking to develop their leadership capability. The 65 leaders in this class were administered both our Leadership Circle Profile (LCP) and the Maturity Assessment Profile (MAP) administered by Susanne Cook-Greuter.

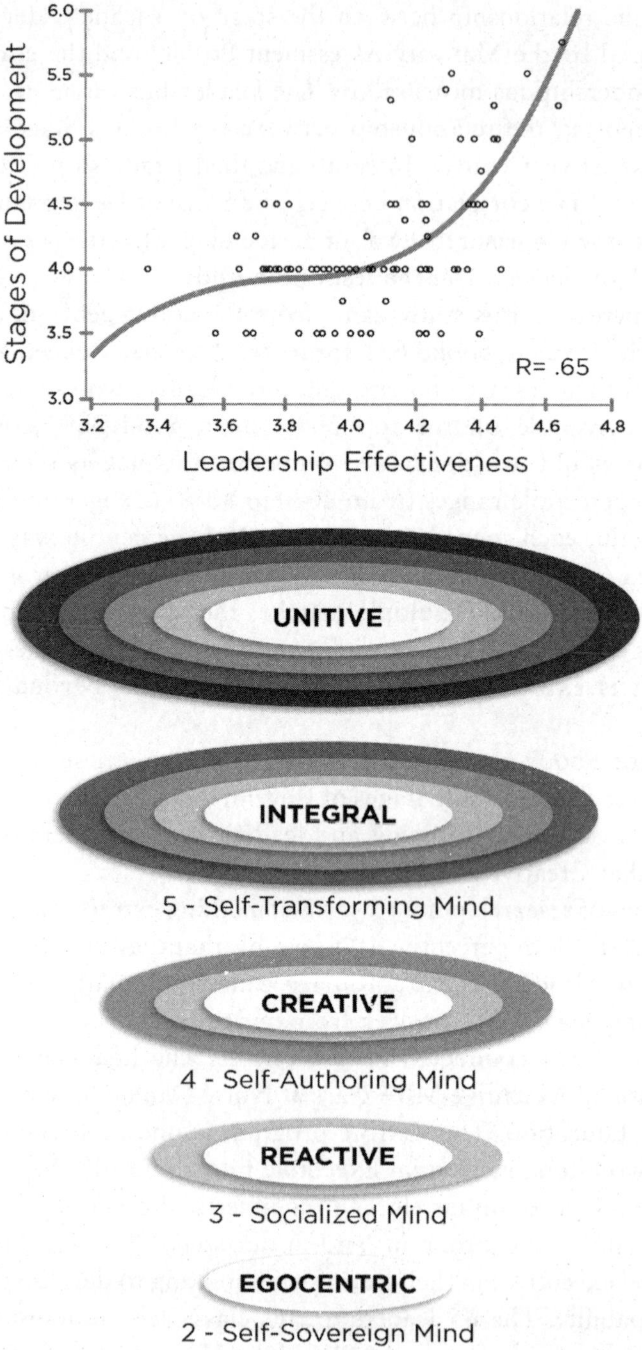

FIGURE 6.11 Stage of Development related to Leadership Effectiveness

When Susanne completed her scoring of the MAP Assessment, she called us and said: "I do not think you will like the results because we do not have a single post-conventional leader in the group. Everyone tested out at Expert and Achiever (with one Diplomat)." In other words, everyone measured at various levels of Reactive Mind—no one scored at the Creative level or higher.

Our response was that this was not at all surprising. This is why: First, about 75–80% of adults score within the same range as the EMBA group. Second, the most highly-correlated variable to Stage of Development is age. Development from one stage to another takes time, it takes years. Given that the average age of this group of students was about 35, their measuring at various Reactive Stages would be the normal, expected result.

We said: "Well, that is very interesting, because the average overall Creative-Reactive score on the LCP is at the 40th percentile, which is very similar to the aggregate result of the MAP Assessment." The group's aggregate LCP is shown in Figure 6.12.

This aggregate Profile, at the 40th percentile, is slightly more Reactive than Creative. It is more Reactive than most of the Notre Dame EMBA Group Profiles (which range from the 40th to 60th percentile over the 13 year period of our association). This group's LQ score of .71 is also lower than most Notre Dame EMBA groups, which typically range from .75 to 1.5. This Profile shows why an EMBA program like the one at Notre Dame can be so valuable in shaping a leader's effectiveness for the rest of his/her career.

Susanne had scored this Notre Dame EMBA class at an average MAP score of 3.89. There are three sequential levels of Reactive Development measured by the MAP—Diplomat, Expert, and Achiever. This EMBA group had one Diplomat; the rest were measured at the Expert and Achiever levels (an Expert is scored as 3.5; an Achiever is scored as a 4.0). This group had more Achievers than Experts, suggesting that this group was functioning, on average, at a mid-to-late Reactive level. The LCP's average overall score, at the 40th percentile, is suggesting the same thing.

We thought this was an interesting finding (that the average LCP and MAP average scores are so similar), however, we did not have a study because our hypothesis was that Post-Conventional leaders (Creative or higher as measured by the MAP) will consistently be rated as more

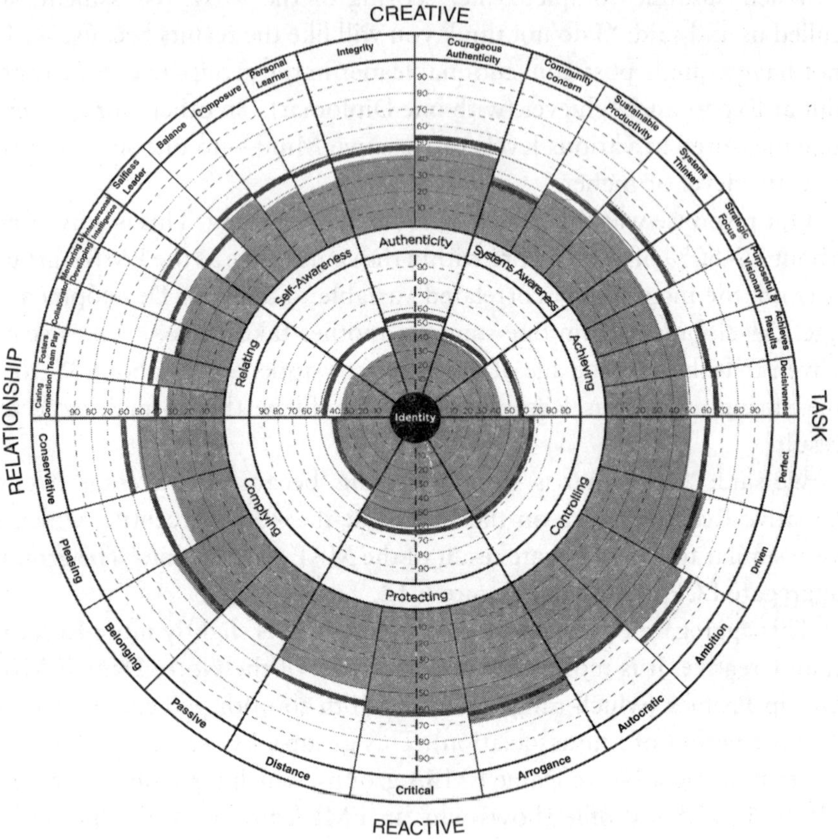

FIGURE 6.12 LCP for the Notre Dame EMBA group

effective (by the LCP). Since we had no Post-Conventional leaders, we had no study.

As we thought about this dilemma, we decided to ask our network of LCP-certified consultants to nominate extraordinary senior leaders for the study. We gave them this simple criterion: No one could have completed either the MAP or LCP previously. They should be champions of a bold vision, be emotionally intelligent, and systemically aware. If the consultants felt that the person they were nominating was an extraordinary leader, we would include them in the study and provide all the assessment and feedback for free. We accepted 25 additional leaders into phase two of the study. This group consisted of mostly senior leaders, in

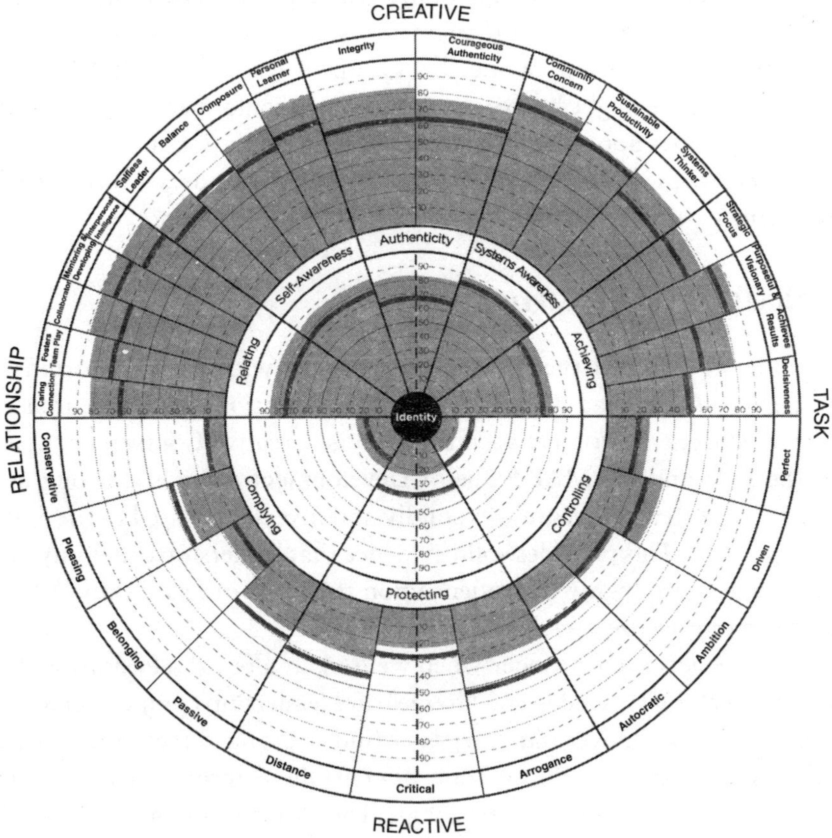

FIGURE 6.13 LCP for the Extraordinary Leader group

significant positions. They also had a much higher average age than the Notre Dame group. Their LCP is shown in Figure 6.13.

As you can see from the aggregate profile, this is an extraordinary group of leaders. The aggregate LCP reflects scores in the 80th to 90th percentiles compared to our norm base. The LQ for this group is 4.24, well beyond 1.0 where leadership becomes a competitive advantage and well beyond the LQ score of .71 for the Notre Dame group. Comparing the LQ scores of the Notre Dame group and the Extraordinary Leader group, we again find a six-fold difference. The Extraordinary Leader group's average MAP Stage score measures midway between the Creative Mind and Integral Mind. The MAP Stage score for this group is

4.75, compared to 3.89 for the Notre Dame group. The Extraordinary Leader group has a Stage score that is 2.7 standard deviation units above the Notre Dame group. While this group of leaders is older than the EMBA group, it might be expected that they would measure somewhat higher (age does not cause stage development, but it does take time), but by all measures this is an extraordinary group of leaders—way beyond the norm.

CONCLUSIONS AND IMPLICATIONS

When we combined the Notre Dame group with the Extraordinary Leader group, we had a study. The high correlations are a researcher's dream. The correlation between the average Creative Competency score on the LCP and the MAP Stage of Development score is a strong .65. The average Reactive score was solidly and inversely related to the Stage score at −.42. This provides solid evidence that leadership capability and effectiveness are highly dependent upon the stage of leadership. All the metrics point to this conclusion.

The case gets even stronger when we look at a few dimensions within the LCP. The LCP was designed to measure leadership competencies that emerge from Creative and Integral Mind. Certain dimensions on the LCP and questions within certain dimensions describe capability that naturally arises at the Integral Stage. The dimensions most positively correlated to this Stage are Purposeful Visionary, Community Concern, Personal Learner, and Mentoring (see definitions in Appendix 1). The Reactive dimensions that are equally but inversely correlated to Stage are Conservative and Ambition. When these dimensions are aggregated into one Stage-Predicting Dimension, the correlation to Stage reached .75. The correlation is displayed in Figure 6.14.

This research validates the primacy of the inner game on leadership effectiveness. It is important to note that this is only one study. It is the largest of its kind to date and other smaller studies have found significant correlations between 360° rater scores and measures of Stage. Nonetheless, this is the cutting edge of leadership research and deserves further exploration.

Extraordinary leadership capability emerges with the Creative Mind. As leadership effectiveness evolves, higher levels of consciousness naturally enable higher levels of capability. In the Leadership Development

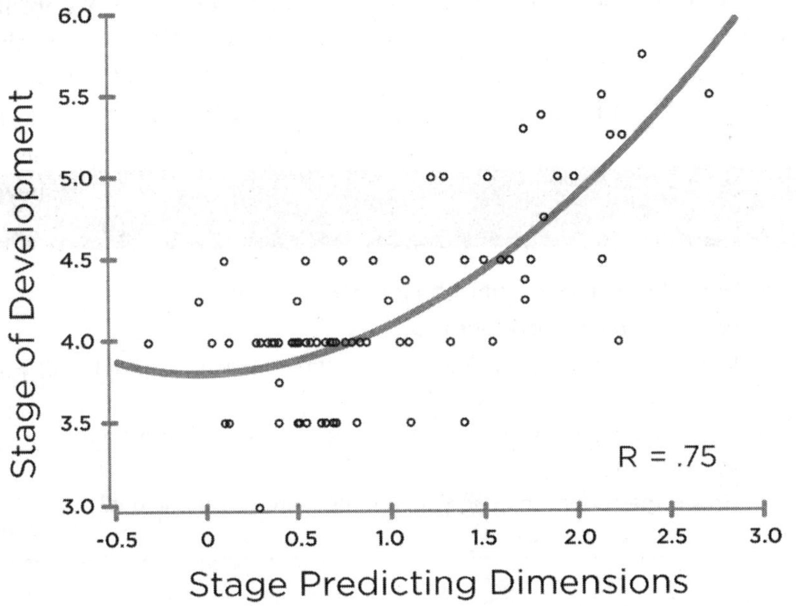

FIGURE 6.14 Correlation between the leader's Stage of Development and the LCP Stage Predicting Dimension

field's zeal to discover what makes for extraordinary leadership, we have missed the main question. When we see extraordinary leadership, we immediately ask: "What are they doing that makes them extraordinary?" The field has done a good job of extracting the key competencies that relate to leadership effectiveness, but has largely ignored the question: "What operating system is that leader running to achieve such mastery?"

In this book we have revealed, metaphorically, the DNA code of development. Development is the dual helix combination of Competency and Consciousness, the inner game and the outer game, mastery and maturity. We now have a model of development that integrates the best theory and practice of leadership development, and we have the metrics to substantiate the model, metrics that are consistent with the best research on effective leadership and business performance.

All of these findings suggest that mastering leadership is long-term life work. As Warren Bennis said, the process of developing extraordinary leadership is the same process as becoming an extraordinary person. To fulfill the Leadership Imperative, we need to rethink how we develop leaders. Our efforts need to be long-term and systemic (not piecemeal and episodic), individual and collective, and integrative of the inner and outer game of leadership. Anything less is not likely to succeed.

TAKING STOCK

- What do you care enough about to stand for now?
- What is non-negotiable for you?
- In any given moment, is the context defining how you show up, or is it informing how you show up?
- If your soul could speak, what would it say about what is important to you and why?
- How is the system shaping you, and how are you shaping it?

Chapter 7
The Leadership System
The Central Organizing System

Businesses are facing a Leadership Imperative that requires them to focus on and accelerate the development of effective leadership. This requires a transformative approach to the development of leaders, individually and collectively. Collective leadership effectiveness is one element of the Leadership System which is the central organizing system of business. When the Leadership System functions effectively, performance is high and sustained over time.

This chapter will illustrate a Whole Systems approach to the development of the Leadership System. In doing so, we will highlight four case studies that show what can happen when the Universal Model of Leadership is applied with a Whole Systems approach to developing the Leadership System of these organizations. We will begin by describing what we mean by using a Whole Systems approach to the development of the Leadership System.

The Leadership System is the central organizing system. It is one of six core systems within organizations. We will explain each of these six systems with a special emphasis on the Leadership System.

To illustrate the importance of the Leadership System when we talk with leaders, we often ask them about their Leadership System and the collective effectiveness of the leaders within that system. We ask, "How many people are on the top leadership team?"

One leader responded, "Nine."

"Now, how many direct reports do those nine people have?"

He started doing the math in his head. "Maybe 84."

"So, there are 93 leaders in the top three levels of Leadership (CEO, his direct reports, and their direct reports, L1–L3). How many employees do you have in your company?"

"32,500."

"Your leadership system and *collective leadership effectiveness* is made up of 93 people who are responsible for 32,500 people and for the effective functioning of the entire organization. It is pretty obvious that the effectiveness of this group is key for your business to succeed and thrive. They must be effective both individually and collectively in order for this to happen."

We are no longer surprised to find that the overwhelming majority (80%) of leaders we talk to either have not entertained this notion or have not focused on taking advantage of leadership as an asset. The majority of the businesses we come in contact with have not recognized that their Leadership System is the central organizing system and that the collective effectiveness of the leaders within that system is critical to their businesses' health and success. These businesses, by not capitalizing on this asset, are leaving good money and contribution on the table. Simply put, the Leadership System is one of the most underutilized assets in business today—underutilized at best, a competitive disadvantage at worst. Given that this group (L1–L3) comprises the leaders within the leadership system, it is not only important to understand how effective they are as individuals, it is also wise to look at how their collective effectiveness, or lack thereof, impacts the overall health of the Leadership System.

We will now describe the Leadership System in more detail within the context of the Six Systems of Organizational Effectiveness.

SIX SYSTEMS OF ORGANIZATIONAL EFFECTIVENESS

Six Systems within organizations must be carefully developed and maintained for businesses to thrive and organizations to be changeable. The systems are broader in scope than functional departments or activities and must be understood independently, as part of an integrated whole (see Figure 7.1). These Six Systems set up the conditions and components necessary to create a healthy, high-performing organization. They also maintain the discipline and metrics that add the predictability, consistency, measurement, and accountability required for maximum

FIGURE 7.1 The Six Systems

productivity and long-term success. These six systems reside within an organization that we define as a *living system* with mechanical parts.

System 1: Leadership. The Leadership System is the central organizing system for ensuring that the organization thrives. To achieve high performance and sustain those results, leaders must focus their attention on each of the six systems. Each of these systems cuts across all organizational boundaries, processes, and departments. The Leadership System ensures the effective functioning of the other systems.

First and foremost, the Leadership System ensures that organization identity is defined; this happens by providing direction and strategy, and ensuring alignment. Leaders address three main questions:

1. *Vision and Value.* What unique value do we bring to our customers to gain competitive advantage? What do we do and for whom? Why?
2. *Strategy and Approach.* In what distinctive manner do we fulfill the unique needs of our customers and stakeholders? What strategy supports the vision for achieving sustainable results and competitive advantage?

3. *Structure and Alignment.* What is the designed alignment of structure and strategy, technology and people, practices and processes, leadership and culture, measurement and control? Are these elements designed and aligned to create optimal conditions for achieving the vision?

Senior leaders, as part of their role in designing and maintaining the Leadership System, define and refine *Key Leadership Processes* and execute them with daily discipline. They translate vision and values into strategy and objectives, processes and practices, actions and accountabilities, execution and performance. They ensure alignment, communicate clarity, engage stakeholders, develop talent, manage performance, build accountability, ensure succession, allocate resources, craft the culture, and ensure that the organization is delivering results.

The Leadership System creates the leadership culture, which acts as the organization's cultural DNA. We have found that evolving the consciousness of leadership is essential to transforming culture and the way a business operates.

Because the Leadership System has such potential to create (or erode) high performance, senior leaders are responsible for the health and effectiveness of this system. Therefore, it makes sense to monitor its health, its capacity and capability. Like any system, the Leadership System requires management, maintenance, and measurement. This requires metrics, a common set of measures, to track operations, opportunities, and improvements, as well as to measure individual and collective leadership effectiveness. How effective are you? How do you know? What is your leadership ROI? How well do leaders *communicate*, providing constituents with an effective exchange of information? Do leaders create effective means and methods for the *delivery* of quality products and services? Do they excel at selecting, retaining, and developing the right people? Are leaders *accountable* to their constituents for creating a culture where individuals and teams deliver on their commitments?

Overall, *the leadership system is responsible for creating meaning, setting context, and maintaining the conditions by which the organization can thrive.* The Leadership System is placed in the center of the Six Systems graphic because it is responsible for the effectiveness of all the other systems. Unless and until it operates effectively, all other systems are degraded, people struggle, and performance suffers. When it functions effectively, anything is possible.

System 2: Communication. Everything happens in or because of a conversation, and every exchange is a potential moment of truth—a point of failure or critical link in the chain of success. Strategic communication ensures that the impact of your message is consistent with your intention and results in understanding. Effective communication creates organizational meaning. Organizational meaning produces the context in which the entire organization operates. If the meaning field is not deliberately created, then it will be created by default. What you say, the way you say it, and where, when and under what circumstances it is said, shape the performance culture. Leaders maximize their contribution by attending to the quality of daily conversations. They engage authentically and, through example, encourage people to lean into moments of truth that create an on-the-table culture. They align people around common cause, deliberately create meaning, provide focus, reduce uncertainty, challenge excuses, learn from experience, treat mistakes as intellectual capital, and leverage the power of leadership decisions to shape beliefs and behaviors.

System 3: Accountability. Leaders translate vision and strategic direction into goals and objectives, actions and accountabilities. Performance accountability systems clarify what is important and what is expected of people. They align consequences for efforts with actual performance. Leaders need to build discipline into their leadership process and management cycle to achieve accountability, predictability, learning, renewal, and sustainability.

System 4: Delivery. The best organizations develop simple processes that are internally efficient, locally responsive, and globally adaptable. Complexity is removed from the customer experience to enable them to engage you in ways that are both elegant and satisfying. Establishing and optimizing operational performance is an ongoing journey. Operations need to be focused on the priority work, using the most effective techniques: aligning initiatives and operations with strategy, continuously improving operations, pursuing performance breakthroughs in key areas, using advanced change techniques in support of major initiatives, establishing a pattern of executive sponsorship for all initiatives, and building future capability and capacity.

System 5. Performance. The Human Performance System is designed to attract, develop, and retain the most talented people. The idea is to hire the best people and help them develop their skills, talents, and knowledge over time. Of course, it becomes critical, as they add abilities and know-how, that they are properly rewarded such that they feel good about their work and remain loyal, dedicated employees.

System 6. Measurement. A system of metrics, reviews, and course corrections keeps the business on track. Organizations need concrete measures that facilitate quality control, consistent behaviors, and predictable productivity and results. Within these parameters, *control* is instrumental to viability and profitability. Every activity has a set of daily rituals and measures. Leaders establish and maintain the measurement system to ensure disciplined processes. They track progress against strategy and planning, review status on operational results through clear key metrics, update the strategy regularly, and ensure action is driven by insight based on relevant, current information focused on achieving the vision.

This Six Systems model helps us understand how everything within an organization is a system that, when fully integrated, optimizes overall performance. These systems operate at the *macro level* (organization) and *micro level* (department/project). Like a human body, these systems are interrelated and none stands alone. They depend on each other to function at full efficiency. For example, we can have an excellent Accountability System, but if the Leadership System does not model or reinforce accountability, the Accountability System cannot be sustained. The Leadership System cannot operate effectively if there is no way to measure results or ensure people are accountable for performance. In order for the Performance System to reward people properly, we must know what they are accountable for and how they are performing. So the Measurement and Accountability Systems must function properly. The Communication System affects the Accountability System. Unless people understand what is required of them and how their actions impact the end product, the Accountability System will be ineffective. All six systems are interdependent and the Leadership System is the nucleus.

WHOLE SYSTEMS APPROACH TO DEVELOPING LEADERSHIP

We need a Whole Systems approach to any development or transformation agenda, starting with a focus on the Leadership System because it drives every other system. This approach constitutes a replicable approach to transforming any business into a profitable and purposeful organization by developing its leadership, fully aligning the internal systems, and engaging the hearts, hands, and minds of people. Every essential system is created, modified, or redesigned and then integrated and aligned. Every stakeholder is involved. Transformation is sustainable because this approach creates the capacity to cope with and capitalize on complexity, and because those who created the new system are developed to run the business after changes are made.

In 1999, we published the book *The Whole Systems Approach: Involving Everyone in the Company to Transform and Run Your Business*. This book captured our learning at that time from 15 years of partnering with Top Teams to design and implement business transformation that fundamentally reshaped their businesses. The book defined our methodology and approach to ensuring that successful transformation took place and was sustained over time. We chose the term, Whole Systems, carefully because it reflected what would be required of organizations in the future. With the shift from the Information Age into the Integration Age, business success would depend on how effectively organizations use, leverage, and combine all the resources available to them—particularly the passion, motivation, experience, and wisdom of their greatest asset—people. Given this perspective, it was not by accident that we adopted the Universal Model of Leadership and the LCP as the framework to integrate with our Whole Systems Approach to Transformation. We now have a fully integrated business and cultural transformation model and methodology, with leadership at the core.

Our Whole Systems approach to developing leadership balances the development of competence and capability with the evolution of consciousness and character. We engage leaders in development through application of the Universal Model, thereby evolving the collective leadership mind to higher stages of consciousness and effectiveness. Kegan identified the need for this as he observed: "We usually ask for more of our leaders than what they have been developed to do" (Kegan and Lahey, 2009).

In order to effectively apply and capitalize on the Universal Model of Leadership, we have found that success is dependent on three key variables: 1) Utilizing a Whole Systems approach to leadership development; 2) Fully defining, understanding, and capitalizing on the Leadership System as a competitive business advantage within your business; and

3) Focusing on individual and collective leadership effectiveness and development versus just individual development.

When this approach is taken, and effective collective leadership is well established, the Extended Leadership Team becomes an Enterprise Leadership Team. They lead together taking a whole systems perspective and capitalizing on it. Our partner, Steve Athey, describes Enterprise Leadership: "The Extended Leadership team has taken on the following characteristics—organizational boundaries, structures, processes, cultures, and resources are all subservient to advancing the vision and serving the mission. The team has an unwavering commitment to being 'in this together' and sharing a common 'whole system' accountability with a strong focus on the emerging future of the organization."

Enterprise leadership teams are "all-in together," aligned and focused on creating outcomes that matter. They are responsible jointly for one another's successes and failures and they take a systems perspective in all they do. Obviously this takes a very mature leadership team. It takes a constant focus on the Development Agenda to achieve this level leadership maturity, but the reward for operating this way is an exponential increase in the organization's effectiveness and the results that it creates.

Throughout our careers, we have partnered with CEOs and their teams across dozens of organizations and can say with confidence that successful transformation efforts were those in which the Extended Leadership Team "did its work" of mastering leadership and improving their individual and collective effectiveness while tending to the health of the Leadership System. These transformation efforts were not only successful, but more importantly, the success was sustained over time. Sadly, we also witnessed transformation efforts that were less than successful and in some cases failed. These failures could be linked directly to a failure of leadership to consciously transform individually and collectively. Without a mature, highly evolved, and fully functioning Leadership System, transformation efforts will not succeed—PERIOD!

Let's explore some examples of successful leadership and business transformation efforts and the kind of performance shifts that are possible.

FOUR COMPELLING CASE STUDIES

We will now demonstrate a Whole Systems approach to developing the individual and collective effectiveness of the Leadership System. We will show what a big difference this can make by exploring four case studies: 1) EverBank Commercial Finance, where CEO Jim McGrane and his team used the Whole Systems/Universal Model approach to developing the Leadership System to achieve remarkable results; 2) Global Shared Services, McDonald's Corporation, where managers Kelvin McLaurin and Debbie Ballard created a culture for developing leaders; 3) Honda Precision Parts of Georgia where General Manager Mike Jett expanded his personal leadership development to his ELT and achieved amazing results; and 4) a global technology corporation in Asia Pacific whose most important customer relationship was turned from a disaster into a major success story.

Case 1: EverBank Commercial Finance

We worked with one remarkable leader, the late Jim McGrane, for two decades in three different companies. We first met Jim 20 years ago when he was leading a prominent division of Heller Financial. In our first meeting, we realized that Jim was a serious student of leadership. He had already worked with several thought leaders in our field to design his organization for high performance. In making the Leadership Development Agenda a strategic priority, Jim proved the close connection between leadership effectiveness and business performance.

Jim called us in late 2005 when he was CEO of US Express Leasing (USXL), a start-up commercial finance company. He was surrounded by a team of highly capable industry all-stars. He had worked with them over many years. Together they grew the business from startup to one of the fastest growing companies in the industry. They raised an impressive amount of money: $125 million in equity and $700 million in debt (over time); gained industry prominence, ranking as one of the top 25 companies in the monthly leasing index; created a culture that provided a predictable, consistent, and reliable customer experience with 95% customer and employee satisfaction; and grew assets under management from $45 million in 2004 to $700 million by the end of 2006. USXL became one of the top 100 largest and the fastest-growing U.S. commercial finance/equipment leasing companies. They attained that success by operating under the values of integrity, passion, fun, accountability, and respect.

In 2006, USXL was preparing for an IPO targeted for 2008; however, their fast growth had triggered heightened investor expectations and a shift in the focus of the leadership team from internal to external stakeholders. When Jim contacted us, he had decided that he needed to take the team's effectiveness to the next level to prepare them to take on future challenges. He expressed confidence in his Top Team going from good to great. We told Jim that improving on a good leadership team is even more difficult than moving a poor team to average because of the team members' lack of a perceived need to work on team effectiveness and their resistance to focusing on team development and leadership effectiveness while growing the business.

For 18 months, from late 2006 to mid-2008, we worked with Jim and his team to increase their performance and effectiveness. We used a qualitative methodology to assess where the team was effective and ineffective. Beyond establishing a baseline of their effectiveness, we also observed and participated in their team meetings and we conducted individual interviews.

Jim's 2007 LCP. In 2007, we ran Jim's first Leadership Circle Profile (LCP).

In Figure 7.2 we see that Jim's Creative scores across the top half of the circle averaged at the 93rd percentile. Leadership ineffectiveness or Reactive scores averaged at the 46th percentile in the bottom half, resulting in a LQ of 2.0. His Leadership Effectiveness scores averaged 80%, putting Jim in the top 20% of effective leaders. Jim's profile is as strong as or stronger than the leaders whose business ranked in the top 10% of highest performing businesses. Given his profile results, it is not surprising that he was leading a company that was becoming a rising star; his leadership was clearly a competitive advantage. Over 18 months, Jim improved team performance and individual and collective leadership effectiveness, aligned and focused the Top Team, and improved relationships.

Tiger by the Tail: 2008 to 2011. After our initial work with Jim and his leadership team in 2006 and 2007, the economy weakened just before the meltdown in markets from 2008 to 2011. There was a huge dislocation in the financial services industry. To capitalize on recession opportunities, Jim and his team turned to the capital markets and in May 2008 they were purchased by Tygris, a new private equity backed venture. Tygris is Latin for tiger, symbolizing strength, swiftness and vitality. Like a tiger, Tygris raised $2.1 billion from 90 investors. This was the largest capital raise in the industry up to that point in time. Jim and his team became part of the Tygris leadership team.

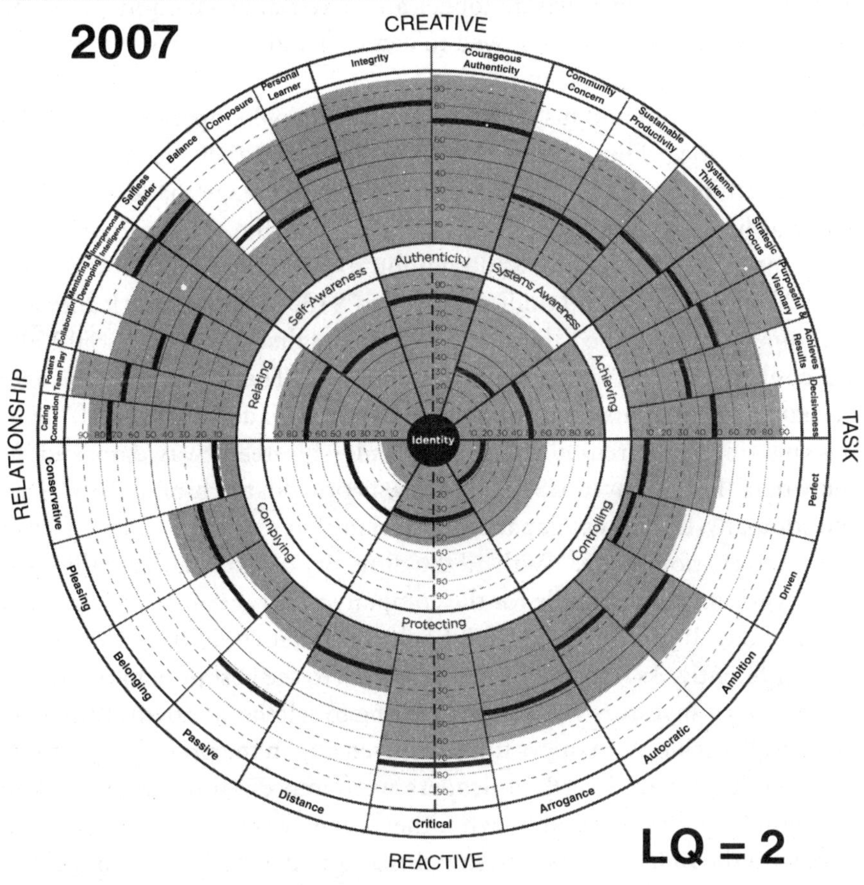

FIGURE 7.2 Jim's first LCP

In July 2008, we worked with the new CEO and the senior leadership team. During that time, the team agreed on the new vision and values, structure, strategy, and the initial action plan.

Tygris was off to the races, filled with hope and a story of a bold move, counter market, right into the teeth of the recession. By early 2009, the newly formed business was moving toward obtaining a bank charter that would have given Tygris funding critical to its success in the midst of the capital market's turmoil. Unexpectedly, the bank charter was not granted, sealing the company's fate. With all of the hope and promise that had marked the start of 2009, Tygris was on life support as a business at the end of that year. There was no longer any material production (sales and business development had slowed to a crawl) and obviously the employees knew that Tygris was in trouble.

At the time, Jim and his original USXL team were operating as Tygris Vendor Finance. They operated with a cloud over their heads as Tygris considered its options. "We thought it was a marriage made in heaven, but that has not turned out to be the case," said Jim. Assets under management fell from a high of $800 million to $500 million, and new business dropped from $400 million a year to $135 million. One leadership team member described the scene: "After the first few months in 2009, we could see that Tygris would not continue. There was lots of anger at management, many emotions came out, and leadership eroded." During this time, the credibility of Jim's leadership team was damaged, as reported: "People loved USXL. There was pride in the brand, the slogan, the company. USXL was flat and egalitarian. That was lost as Tygris went into preservation mode." With all the difficulty described, the reality was that Tygris made it possible for the company to survive and stand to fight another day. If not for the denied bank charter, it could have turned out very differently. As it stood, the net result led to the best possible scenario.

The Tygris investors were actively trying to sell the company. EverBank came to the table as an opportunistic buyer, and in the process something amazing happened. EverBank leaders were impressed by what Jim and his team had achieved and by what they knew was possible for the business with the right owners. Jim saw this as an opportunity to rebuild and achieve his team's original vision. When EverBank officers met with his team, they chose to buy and invest heavily in Jim's legacy business, including its leadership team. As Jim told us: "Initially, they were only looking at purchasing a portfolio, but then our leadership impressed them. EverBank bet on us as leaders and we had to perform against their faith in us."

As Blake Wilson, the President and Chief Operating Officer of EverBank, stated: "I spent the day with Jim and his management team and did a 180. They had built a real company that had a different asset class from us with some similarities. This was an intact leadership team with a company poised to grow. I knew it was a fit. Even after everything they had been through, they brought a strong leadership team with many strengths." This was a big endorsement of Jim and his team and the company they had started out to build.

Back on the Scene. At the start of 2010, we reengaged with Jim and his team and worked with them to pick up the pieces and reengage their Leadership Imperative. We ran another round of Leadership Circle Profiles and Jim had a wake-up call regarding his leadership and the team's collective leadership. Figure 7.3 shows Jim's profiles in 2007 and in 2011.

By comparing the LCP results, we can see that Jim's LQ went from 2 to 1: his Leadership Effectiveness during that time was cut in half, meaning his leadership was no longer a competitive advantage. He was neutral in his influence.

Jim realized that at a time when he needed to be most creative, his leadership effectiveness had slipped from where it was in 2007. This wake-up call got his full attention. In fact, during the week, between when he received his results and the time we met with him to talk about his results, he conducted over 25 one-on-one interviews with his key leaders. He put both profiles on the table, and asked them, "What happened to me?" and, "What do I need to do about it?"

Few leaders are so committed to their effectiveness! Everybody agrees: effectiveness outperforms ineffectiveness. We often ask questions like, "How effective are you; how do you know?" or, "How much of your time and attention, personally and collectively, goes into the strategy of developing leadership?" These questions are interruptions for most leaders. In contrast, Jim concluded: "I am the problem. At a time when my leadership was most needed, I slipped into Reactive mode."

Jim had a second wake-up call. When he saw the Group Profile of his senior team, he realized he had not done what he needed to do to develop the leadership effectiveness of his team. He resolutely went about addressing this over the next two years.

Figure 7.4 shows Jim's senior leadership team in 2007 and 2011. Note that they slipped further into Reactive, and more toward Complying, meaning they were complacent. Their LQ went from .86 to .76, meaning their leadership was less of an advantage. Now the whole team, with Jim at 1.0 and the team at .76, was playing below average—not-to-lose.

Levels 3 and 4 were made up by about 30 managers. Their Group Profile averaged at the 25th percentile with a low LQ of .5.

We then charted, for Jim and his team, the relationship between their collective leadership effectiveness and changes in their business performance. Figure 7.5 shows the relationship between Business Performance and LQ scores from 2007 to 2010.

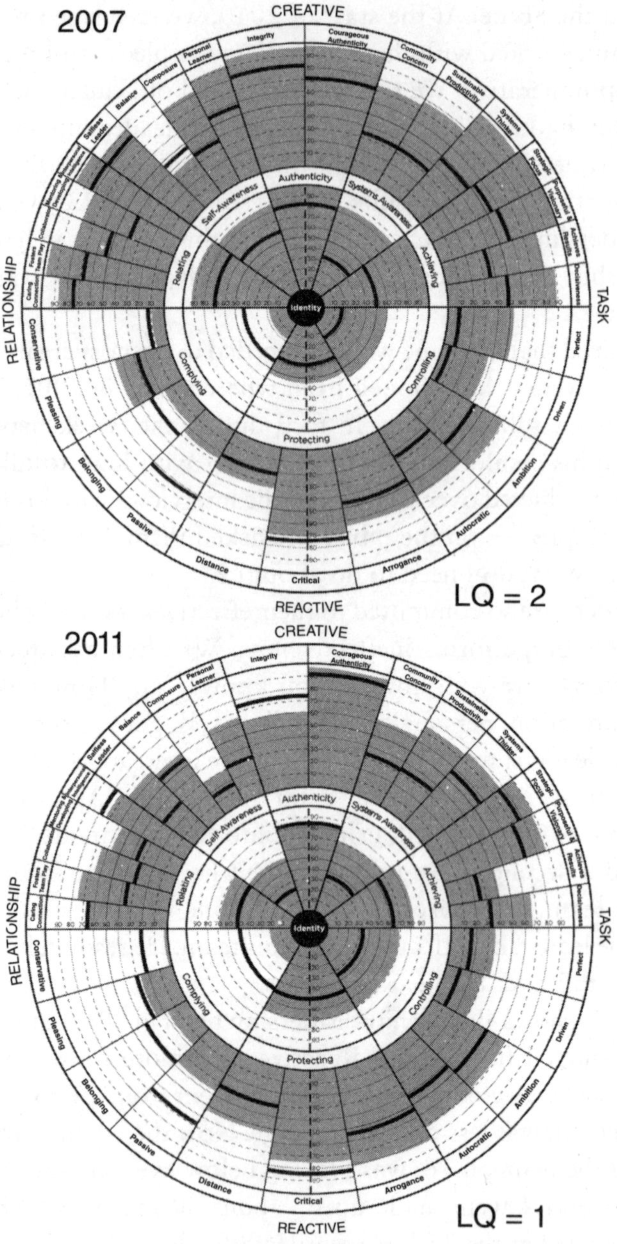

FIGURE 7.3 Jim's 2007 and 2011 LCPs compared

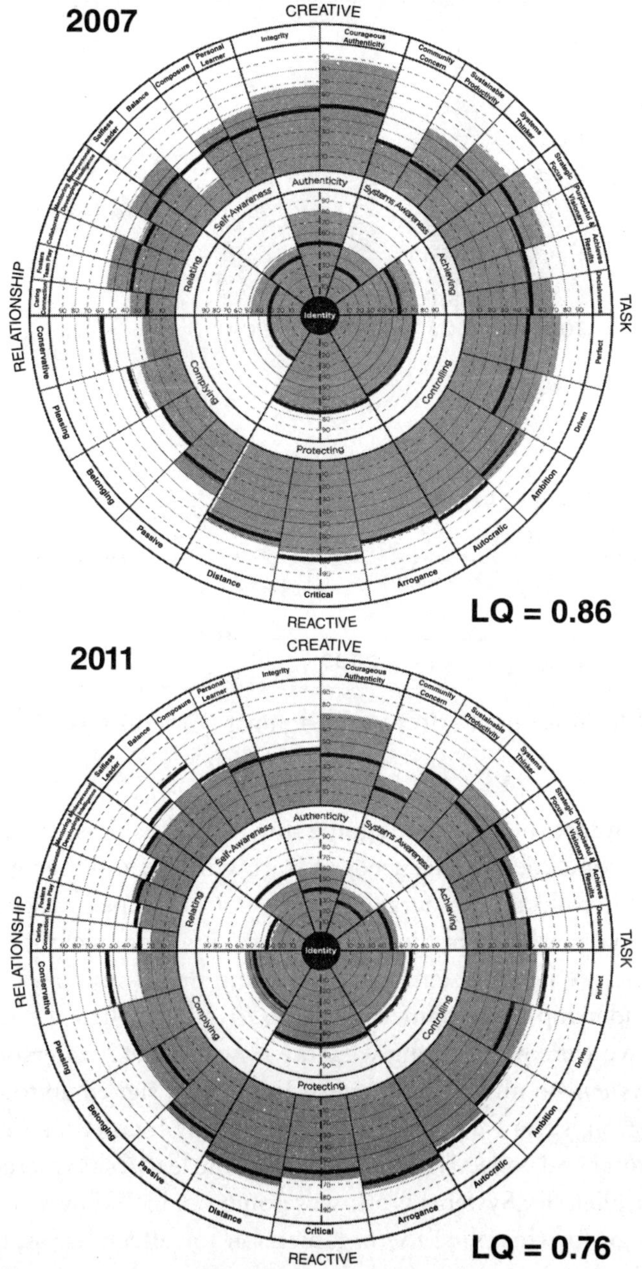

FIGURE 7.4 Senior Leadership Team's 2007 and 2011 LCPs compared

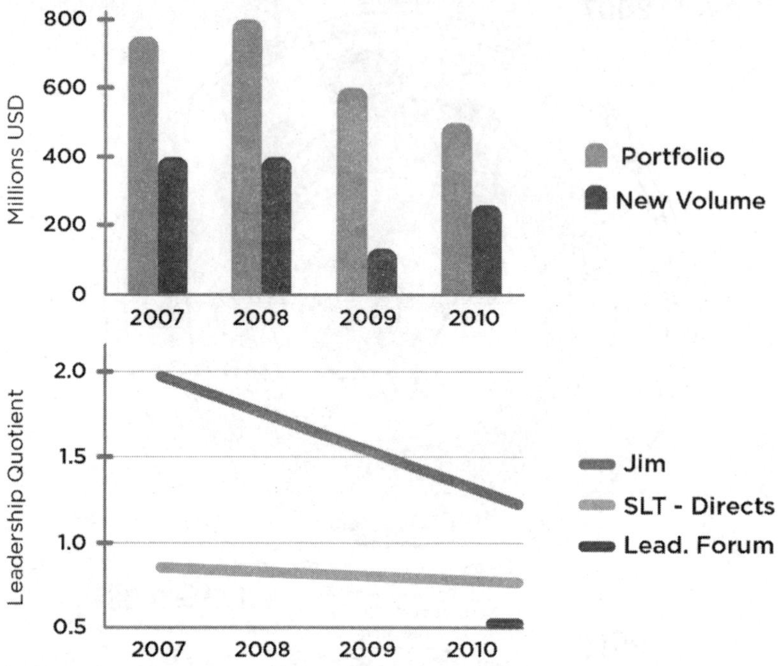

FIGURE 7.5 Business Performance against LQ scores 2007–2010

When Jim saw the LQ scores going down and business results following suit, he concluded: "This needs to start with me, and then we need to work on our collective leadership. I have not developed collective leadership. I have not brought along my people. I will change that. To scale the business, we need to scale leadership, and that is my job."

The Leadership Development System. In 2010, when we reengaged with Jim, we were prototyping what we now call the *Leadership Development System*—a multi-year process. Jim readily signed up to be one of our pilot groups. As we proceeded, we primarily focused on developing the individual and collective effectiveness of the leadership system. However, in parallel, Six Systems work was going on, including a major process redesign to streamline the organization for effectiveness, customer focus, and to position it for growth.

The Leadership Development System implementation (see Figure 7.6) began with readiness building—understanding why we were doing it and what we were trying to achieve, strategic communication, assessments

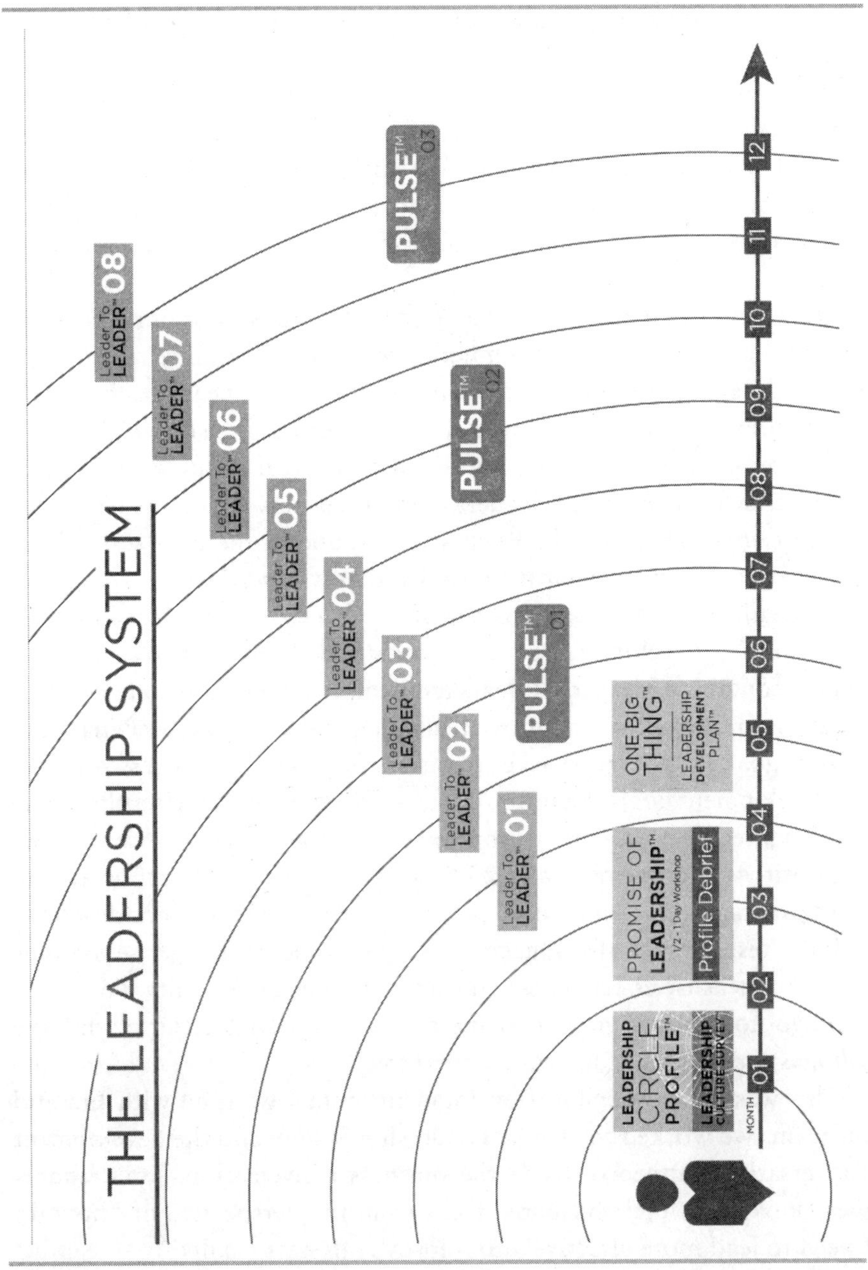

FIGURE 7.6 The Leadership System

(LCP and Leadership Culture Survey), and with an official launch once that work was complete.

We then conducted a half-day *Promise of Leadership*, an interactive development session, with the ELT. This was a half-day introduction to the LCP, wherein we covered the relationship between effectiveness and performance and provided an overview of the Universal Model, feedback on profile results, and held a LCP debrief with each leader by a seasoned coach.

Over a two-year period of time, *Leader-to-Leader* sessions were conducted. Each session was facilitated face-to-face, contained a key leadership development content element, and involved peer coaching and accountability. Each session was short, powerful, focused on the inner and outer game of leadership and focused on real business challenges. At the end of each session, leaders committed to work on something to improve their leadership between sessions, and at the next session, we start with a review of what they tried and how it worked.

As Leader-to-Leader sessions began we also created, with each leader, an actionable development plan and constructed a *Pulse Survey*. A Pulse Survey contains a measurable leadership improvement goal, one Creative Leadership Competency improvement goal, and one Reactive Behavioral change goal. Pulse surveys went out every few months to assess progress on development goals. Figure 7.7 shows an example of the results of the ELT's aggregate pulse survey. Approximately 88% of leaders were showing positive improvement and 25% were showing much improvement. These are big shifts in measured performance over a short period of time.

Pulse results were also plugged in to the Leader-to-Leader sessions as a way to measure effectiveness and create peer accountability. The entire team got to see their individual and collective progress ensuring that the *whole system* was engaged and committed.

This was the Leadership Development System we used with Jim and his team. We worked the whole Leadership System and the development conversation happened inside the business conversation. Jim's leaders were looking at their business issues from the perspective of "how do I need to lead more effectively to improve business results?"

The Results. Figure 7.8 shows the change in Jim's Profile from 2011 to 2013. We see a big reduction in Controlling scores (and everything on the Reactive half) with corresponding increases in the Creative half of the circle. Jim's LQ increased from 1.0 to 2.0.

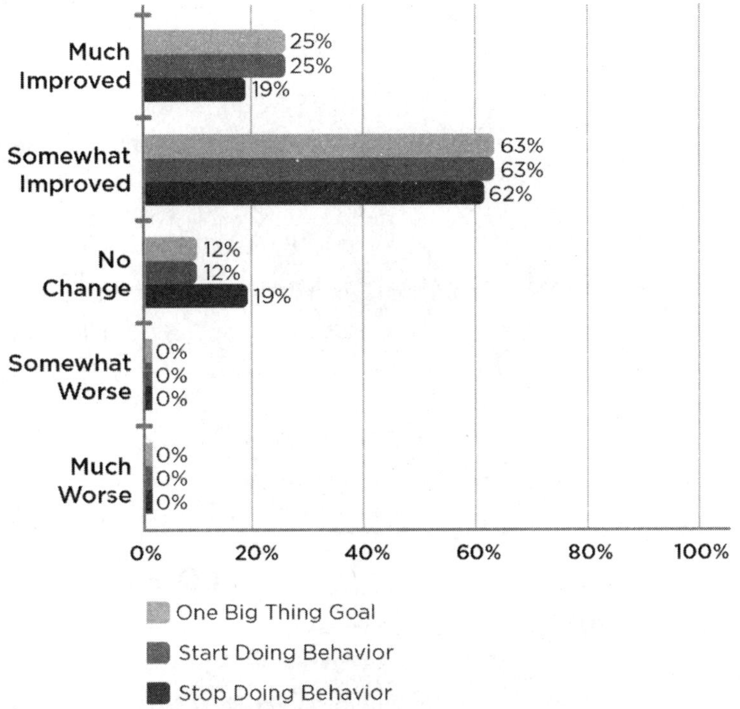

FIGURE 7.7 Percentage of leaders showing change in performance

Figure 7.9 shows the change in Jim's senior team. Creative scores increased across the board. Reactive scores, particularly Complying, were significantly reduced. This group was now really showing up as a group of effective leaders. LQ scores doubled from .76 to 1.6, and their LQ went from a competitive disadvantage to a serious competitive advantage.

The ELT (L-3 and L-4) also doubled their effectiveness, improving from .5 to 1.0. While there was still more work to be done here, they went from being a competitive disadvantage to being competitive.

Figure 7.10 shows the relationship between changes in LQ scores and business performance during this period of time. From 2011 to 2013, assets under management went from a low of $500 million to $2 billion, quadrupling the business! New business origination went from a low of $135 million in 2009 to $1.4 billion in new business—a huge turnaround. Their LQ scores paralleled their performance.

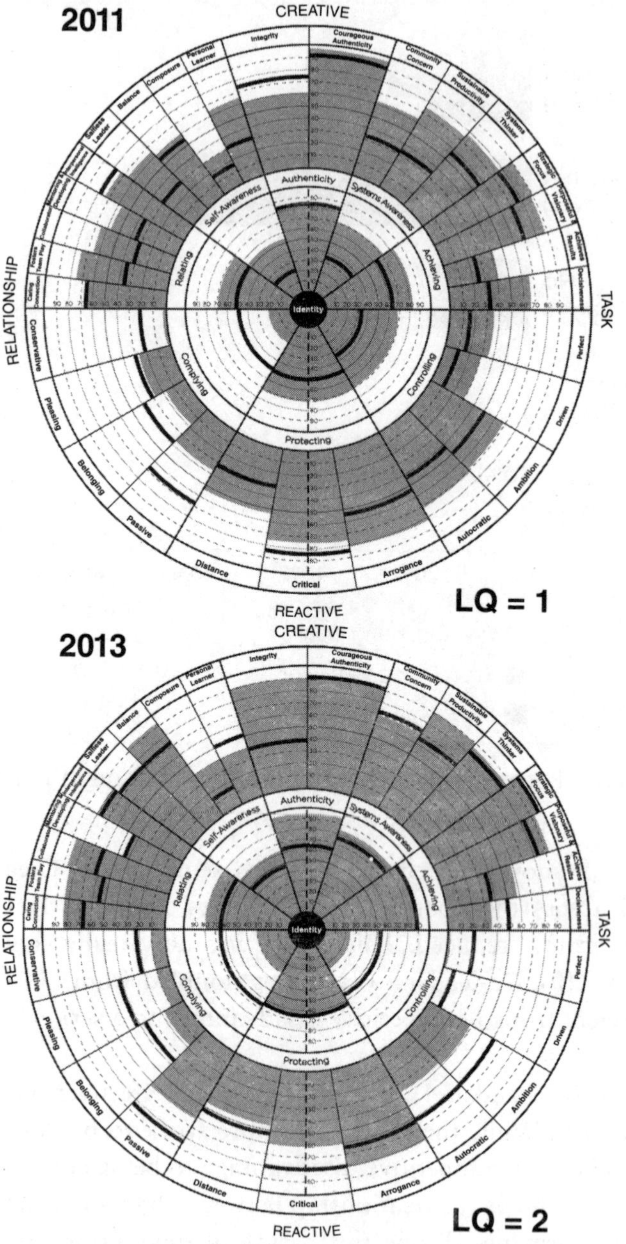

FIGURE 7.8 Jim's 2011 and 2013 LCPs compared

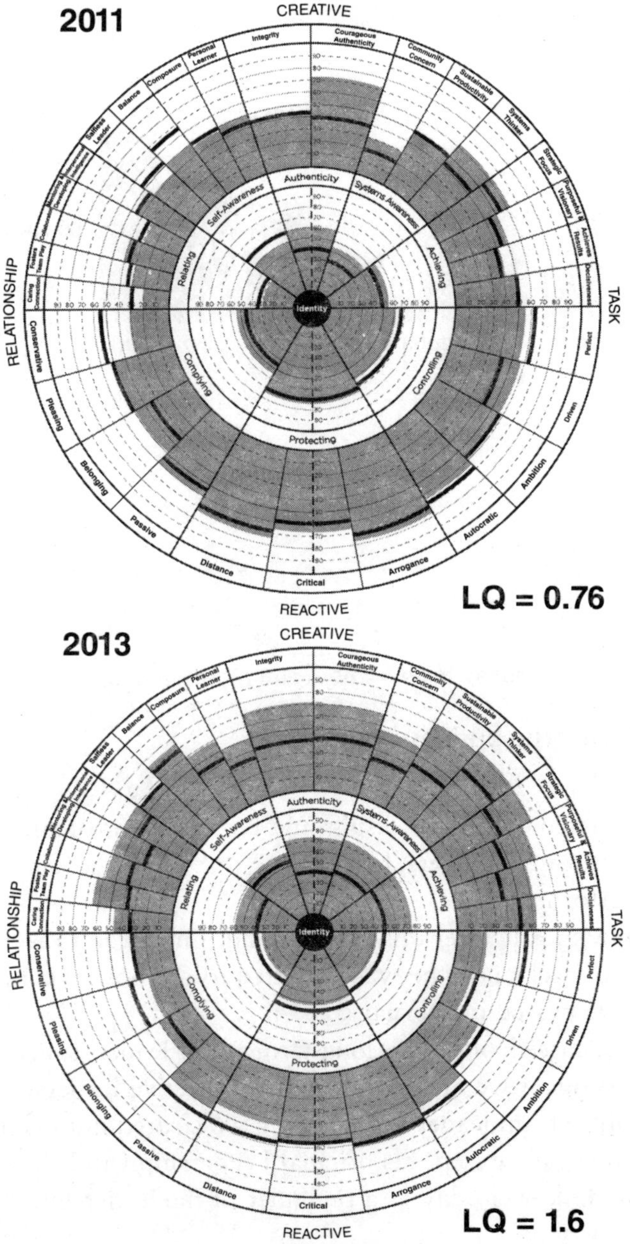

FIGURE 7.9 Senior Leadership Team's 2011 and 2013 LCPs compared

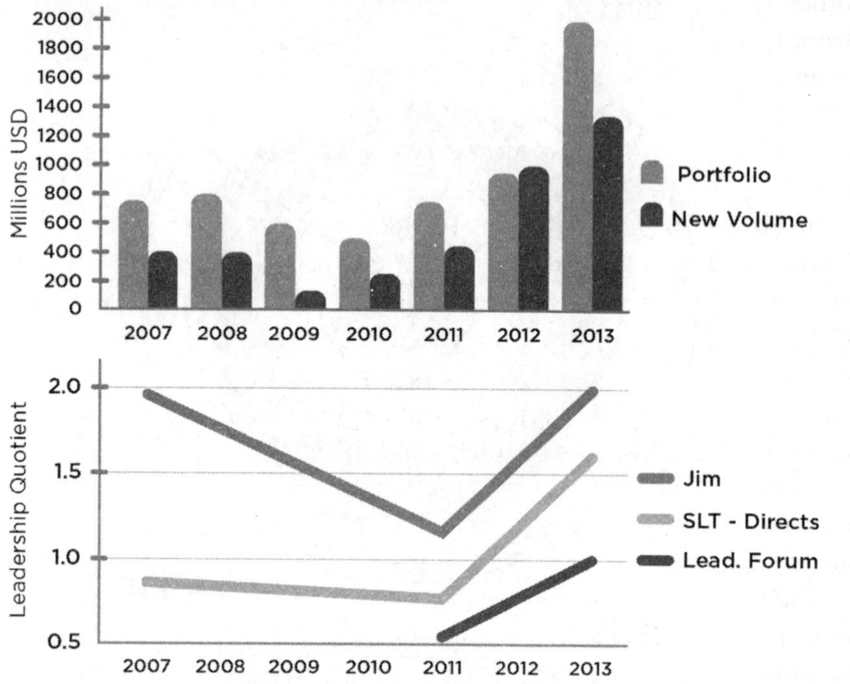

FIGURE 7.10 The business turnaround

Jim was elated with these results and became an advocate, along with several of his team members, for focusing on effective leadership to drive business performance.

Tragically, shortly after this turn-around, Jim began to feel physically unwell. Two weeks later he was admitted to the hospital, and he never came out. He passed in February, 2014.

When Jim passed, one of his long-term senior leaders said to us: "Now we will find out if we are serious about collective leadership effectiveness." Another team leader said: "When we cleared out his office, I did not want anything, except his original Leadership Circle Profile. I want that on my desk every day as a reminder of the leadership that I aspire to."

Jim leaves a huge vacuum, but he also leaves a huge legacy with all the people that his leadership touched. Jim was one of our practice partners. We learned more from Jim and his organization than they ever did from us. This is how we do our work. We practice together on each other. We learn together. So we intend to carry on what we have learned from Jim and his legacy. After several years of working with us to implement a systemic approach to developing effective leadership, Jim said: "You have cracked the code. The work we have done with you has positioned us for sustainable success. We could not have done it without you."

In Honor of Jim McGrane: Equipment Leasing Foundation Study. Rarely does an entire industry assess its leadership effectiveness; however, in honor of Jim McGrane, that happened in the Equipment Leasing & Finance (ELF) industry. As reported by Richard D. Gumbrecht, Chairman of the ELF Foundation, the ELF study, *Leadership: The Next Productivity Frontier*, determined the current level of effectiveness of leaders in the industry and identified how leadership effectiveness impacts performance. It also identified the best practices for creating and enhancing leadership effectiveness and specific management challenges that future leaders must address to ensure success.

The research team interviewed 32 executives from 26 ELF organizations to assess perceived impact of leadership, importance of leadership development, current professional development efforts, and expectations for the future. It also administered The Leadership Circle's *Leadership Culture Survey* to 162 leaders in 17 lessor organizations. This instrument reliably measures how respondents describe both the effectiveness of their current leadership culture and their desired, optimal leadership culture. *In memory of Jim*, here is a brief summary of the results.

1. *Effective Leadership has a positive impact on performance.* Leaders were asked to rate the impact that leadership has on their organization's performance. This metric was found to correlate highly ($r = .73$, $p < .002$) with Leadership Effectiveness scores from the Leadership Culture Survey. This correlation is quite high and further substantiates the research reported earlier—a more effective leadership culture creates a more successful organization.
2. *Growth rates were substantially higher in effective leadership cultures.* The study compared the business performance of the most and least effective leadership cultures. Organizations rated as having the most Creative leadership, better than 50% of the organizations included in this study, averaged 11% year-over-year growth. Those that rated lowest, in the bottom 50% of the organization in this study, had a 2%

growth rate. This study found a 9% growth rate difference between the most and least effective leadership cultures.

3. *Development of tomorrow's effective leaders needs to begin today.* When executives were asked about the challenges leadership will need to address to ensure the future success of their organization and the industry, three common themes emerged:
   - Leading in a changing environment—maintaining a long-term perspective while creatively adapting to new technologies, regulations, acquisitions, and global demand.
   - Attracting and retaining qualified talent—ensuring the right people are in the right jobs and that they have the appropriate grounding in the industry.
   - The generational leadership gap—the need to develop the leadership skills of Millennials to fill the void left by the exodus of a "graying cadre of leaders."

The study concluded that its findings and each of the above challenges, "underscores the importance of launching an intensive leadership development program that provides opportunities for the younger generation to learn from more experienced leaders and to develop the skills that will impact performance. ELF organizations that have quality leadership development efforts are more likely to grow competent leaders, and leaders who possess strong creative competencies are more likely to foster a thriving culture in which productivity soars. Thus, the sooner development work begins, the greater the likelihood that sustainable productivity will be achieved."

Case 2: Global Shared Services, McDonald's Corporation

As the world's leading foodservice retailer serving nearly 70 million customers daily in more than 100 countries, McDonald's recognizes the importance of having good people in place in order to deliver an exceptional customer experience. McDonald's has a rich history of developing leaders. Founder Ray Kroc, once said, "As long as you're green, you're growing." McDonald's supports this philosophy and commitment to their people by providing opportunity, nurturing talent, developing leaders, and rewarding achievement. This is evident in McDonald's tradition of promoting from within: nearly half of corporate managers and 60% of owner-operators started as crew members.

For many people, McDonald's represents a first job—a place to develop basic skills that can help them achieve success in future life pursuits. For others, McDonald's represents a pathway to a long-term career that provides rewarding opportunities to grow, contribute, and advance over many years. McDonald's values state their belief that a team of well-trained individuals with diverse backgrounds and experiences, working together in an environment that fosters respect and drives high engagement, is essential to their continued success.

Shared Services Business Challenge. McDonald's Shared Services team began their partnership with us in 2008. At that time, Shared Services was part of McDonald's IT group, which was decentralized in structure, but needed to function as a cohesive team to drive common global solutions. The CIO recognized the importance of developing teamwork and alignment across IT leaders and engaged us to lead this effort. After the IT Leadership Team had gone through The Leadership Circle process, the CIO asked each of the officers, including Kelvin McLaurin, then VP of Shared Services, to engage their teams in the program.

Soon after The Leadership Circle was introduced, the Shared Services organization evolved into Global Shared Services (GSS) and became the first global function at McDonald's. McLaurin recalls: "We needed to build a diverse, global team with leaders who could expand beyond their current capabilities." He wanted to establish leadership effectiveness as a priority early with the team he was building and leverage the Leadership System to make this a reality.

In 2012, McLaurin transitioned to a role leading McDonald's Finance Transformation. Debbie Ballard, who had been a member of the GSS Leadership Team since 2005, took over leadership of the GSS organization. Having experienced the value of The Leadership Circle, she was already a supporter of the Profile and its benefits. Ballard explains: "The Leadership Circle process helps me professionally and personally. It enables me to step back and see why I am behaving the way I am behaving, and it helps me grow as a leader and to model the things that I am asking my leadership team to do." GSS continued their focus on leadership development and further engrained The Leadership Circle program into its culture.

Strategic Solution: The Leadership Circle. When The Leadership Circle was introduced in 2008, the GSS leadership team was skeptical. Introducing an exercise that required not only getting feedback about individual strengths and opportunities, but then sharing publicly with their fellow team members would not be easy. However, the team committed to the process, knowing the first session would be hard, but trusting that outcomes would make it worthwhile.

Despite the initial hesitation, the GSS has become the group that applies The Leadership Circle most holistically and consistently. While other groups at McDonald's leverage the Profile, GSS is unique in that they continue to use public feedback with each team member talking about their strengths and weaknesses in front of the group. McLaurin explains: "The Leadership Circle has become the common language across the GSS Leadership Team to onboard and develop our leaders." As new members join the leadership team, either from GSS or a support partner, they are expected to participate in The Leadership Circle. GSS also engages their high-potential managers in the process. In 2014, GSS added The Leadership Circle Pulse Survey to hone in on opportunity areas and ensure more frequent feedback to drive development in those areas.

McLaurin, who now leads Finance Transformation, brought The Leadership Circle practice to his new leadership team as well in September 2014. In addition, the Finance Transformation team also incorporated individual LCP assessment with team development opportunities.

Outcomes. The Leadership Circle helped GSS to become a true, shared leadership team and build a culture of openness, support, trust, and high performance. Ballard explains: "It is part of our DNA, part of who we are. We have now done multiple offsite meetings with our leadership team focusing on individual and collective effectiveness. As a result, we have forged a cohesive, high-performing leadership culture and system."

Team members are empowered to mentor each other, talk openly about their opportunities, and gain support using a common language. Each leader's candor, paired with their support for one another, enables GSS to drive business results at an accelerated pace. Instead of ignoring issues that could hinder progress, the team talks through them.

Since the team respects The Leadership Circle process and one another, gaining awareness of strengths creates a culture of trust and support. Ballard notes: "Leaders were afraid at first of publicly showing people their development opportunities, but then they see that this supportive environment is designed to help you become a better leader, not discourage or embarrass you."

The culture that The Leadership Circle has helped to create in GSS contributes to their success: "*We achieved our five-year strategic plan in only three years*, and then set in place the GSS 2020 Strategy to continue our momentum toward our vision to be a world-class shared services organization." Both McLaurin and Ballard continue to be strong advocates for The Leadership Circle process, driving application in their organizations and sharing their experiences with others in the McDonald's System.

Case 3: Honda Precision Parts of Georgia (HPPG)

In response to the Leadership Imperative, one strong plant manager, Mike Jett, made leadership development a strategic priority and achieved impressive results. Mike has been the Plant Manager for HPPG since 2009. He epitomizes what makes Honda such a great company. In 2012, Mike was invited to join a group of high potential leaders in a year-long leadership development effort called the Honda Leadership Summit (HLS). Two groups of senior leaders come together twice every year to start this process of developing their leadership. This program is designed and led by the Honda OD Team, along with several of their executive leaders. In 2011, Honda asked us to work with them on part of the design of the core residential development program, a five-day program followed by a year of work.

HLS includes the Leadership Circle Profile and the Promise of Leadership workshop—an orientation to the model and the developmental framework, and a debrief of the LCP results. In addition, we work with the leaders throughout the entire year of their program. We use our Leader-to-Leader process—face-to-face and virtual development sessions focused on specific topics, peer coaching, and accountability. In addition, the Honda OD team facilitated "home room" coaching groups every other month to work on live leadership and business-relevant issues. The year culminates with a presentation to the Board of Directors on what was learned and what impact the year had on the operations. This is a systemic, whole systems program that follows all of the criteria of what makes for effective leadership development.

Upon his return from the Honda Leadership Summit, and over the course of the following year, Mike engaged his entire leadership team in development at HPPG. His enthusiasm and support for the work could not be contained. He leaned in and played full-out. Initially Mike helped his leadership team at HPPG realize that they faced a huge leadership challenge: *If we do not evolve our ways of leading, individually and collectively, we cannot compete.* They started to treat the development of effective leadership as a strategic imperative.

When Mike received the results of his first profile, he was shocked. "Before receiving the results of my first profile, I was very confident, even cocky, in my management capabilities. I thought that I was a good leader. When I received my LCP results, I think I cried for a week." See Figure 7.11.

In our debrief with Mike, we discussed with him the key patterns evident in his Profile. He said: "The LCP feedback helped me see my strengths and weaknesses. I did not realize how bad I was as a manager until I got the results, but I learned from it. In fact, I kept my first LCP on my desk for well over a year. I would come in early every morning and look at it. That motivation helped drive the things I wanted to change because I did not want to be the person that the LCP said I was. Once I realized where I was, I set goals to get where I wanted to go and identify what characteristics I needed to develop."

Mike continues: "When I shared the material with my team and showed them my LCP results, they were able to give me examples of my behavior. Even though this hit home hard, those discussions were extremely positive. It led to many courageous discussions. I took that feedback and put together a plan for how I would change. For example, I am a very controlling person. It is hard for me to let go. I have really had to force myself to let go. And what I have seen is that the more I let go, the more responsibility and accountability the division managers below me take. So when there is a crisis situation, instead of jumping in and taking control, I am letting my leadership team do that. That was hard for me to do in the beginning. But I see them take more responsibility and accountability on themselves to lead in those situations."

Mike never looked back. He engaged his entire plant as well as his leadership team in this work. "Since then we have had several follow-up sessions and aggressively applied what we learned to our operations here."

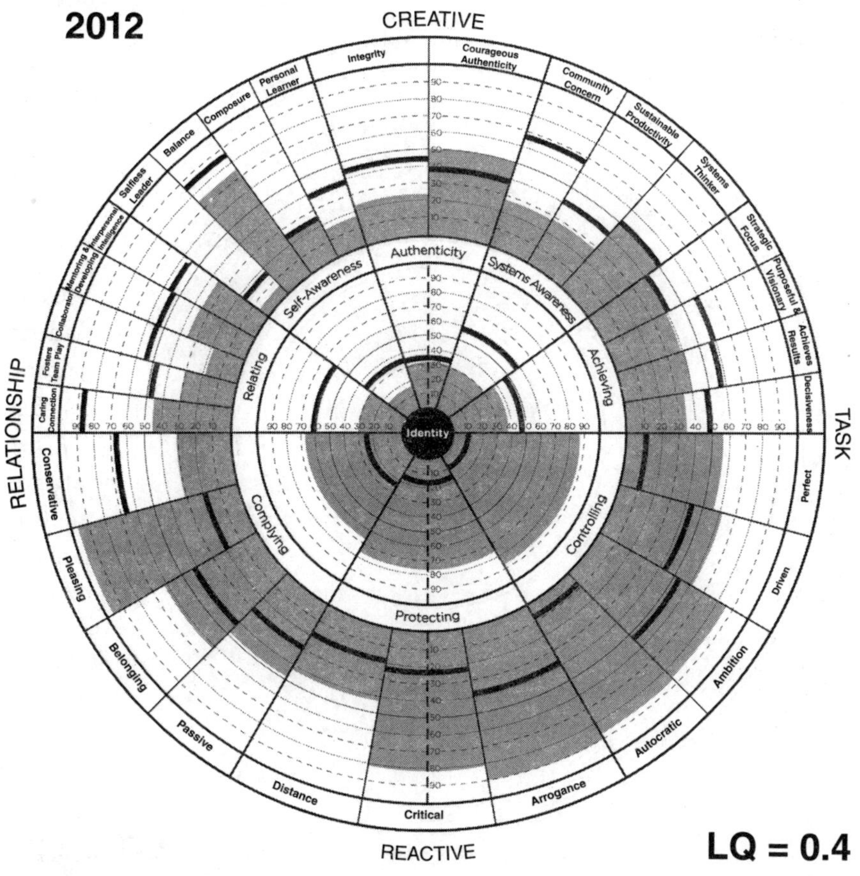

FIGURE 7.11 Mike's first profile

Mike says that he can laugh about that first LCP now because his second LCP was 100 percent better: "The second one was what I wanted the first one to be." (See Figure 7.12).

What is it about the LCP that drives such meaningful change? Mike answers: "The LCP is very *descriptive* of the leadership characteristics you now have and very *prescriptive* of what you should aspire to be. It first gives you a comprehensive understanding of where you are and then, based on the feedback from your leaders and subordinates, shows you pathways for change. It has made a big difference in me personally and in my leadership team. You can see the difference in our business,

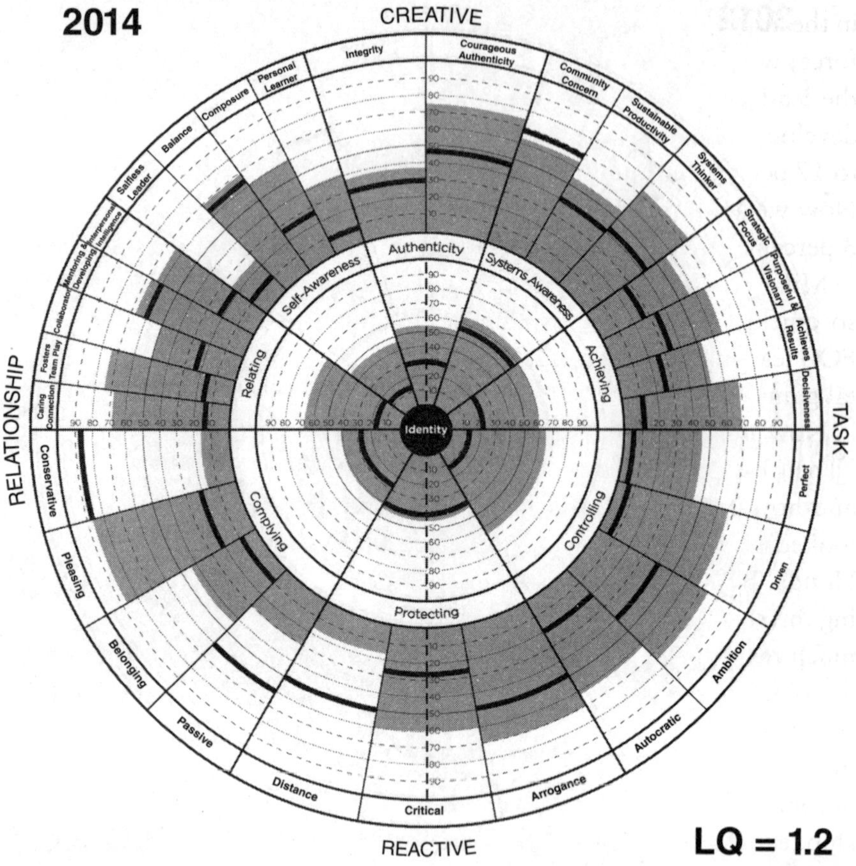

FIGURE 7.12 Mike's second profile

in the quality of our products and the productivity of the plant. All our business characteristics have improved greatly."

Mike reports major gains in every area of HPPG's business over the past two years. Here are just *four indicators*: "First, our *productivity* has increased about 8 percent. Our ability to exceed production expectation is measured on operating efficiency (assembly run rate). We were averaging about 88 percent; now we average 96 percent. Second, in the area of *safety*, the incidence of injury rate has dropped 9 to 6 to 0.5, the lowest in the company. Third, in the area of *quality*, specifically the customer complaint measure, in terms of what we deliver to the other Honda plants, we are setting company and industry records, going from 90 to 19. Fourth, in the area of *employee retention*, the retention of our engineering workforce, we have seen the biggest improvement. Two or three years ago, the leadership team was not doing a good job of communicating and developing relationships with our younger engineers. Attrition was close to 17 percent, meaning we were losing 17 percent of our talent annually. Now we are hovering around 6 percent and moving toward our goal of 3 percent. The incredible gains made in retention impact every area."

Mike confirms: "We could not have achieved such positive results so quickly without the experience. I can tell you that the Honda and FCG leadership approach leads to exponential gains, not just incremental gains."

Now most of Mike's senior managers have gone through the HLS. "Their experience was very positive, both in terms of what we learned and how we applied what we learned, and the results achieved. If you looked at my leadership team before HLS, working with the internal Honda OD and with the Full Circle Group, getting feedback, and working through modules, you would see that our management approach was much regimented."

"Now if you asked my team what is most important, you would find that it is serving the people we work with—developing and maintaining relationships of trust with them. Our relationships now are so much deeper. I can sense a positive culture change, especially in the leadership team relationships. They are much deeper. These changes would not have happened without this work. Our division managers now understand that it is not about you being the boss—it is about them, our people, about their growth and development. You can lead more effectively by understanding and serving others. Now our associates see that the leadership team is not about top-down control but about a servant-leadership approach, about caring for them, their learning, growth and development."

Mike and his leadership team are now accelerating the culture change—from a Reactive to Creative style, from a focus on problems and threats, fear and reactions, to a focus on vision, purpose, passion, and action. He and his team have identified three Reactive characteristics that they want to reduce (Controlling, Protecting, and Complying) and five creative competencies they want to develop (Relating, Self-Awareness, Authenticity, Systems Awareness, and Achieving).

"We are making these changes because we now know that the way we used to respond to problems was less effective. When we were trapped in the vicious cycle of Problem-Reacting (problem/threat to fear to reactions) our typical responses to threats and fears were emotional and occasionally hostile. Emotions ran high, and the end result was much frustration. To create the culture we want to establish, we had to transcend the Reactive styles and practice Outcome Creating: vision/purpose to passion to action. Our focus now is on building relationships, and helping others to realize that we are all one team and we can rely on each other when times are challenging. We have identified three next steps: 1) expand what we learn as individuals and strengthen how we interact with others and do so with increased empathy; 2) increase fulfillment by following the Honda values or the three joys—from product creation through lifetime-owner-loyalty through end of life; and 3) integrate the Honda philosophy more and to strengthen leadership across North America to achieve our ideal image."

In the beginning, Mike reports:

"The HLS development experience was really about learning more about myself as a leader, receiving the LCP feedback and understanding that if I wanted to see change in our team and company, I needed to change first. I was then motivated to get more of my leadership team through that process so they would see how I was trying to change and why we needed to change as a team. We now have a critical mass of people who have experienced the process so that the positive changes can be sustained. We have deeper discussions on core issues, and we act differently on those issues, not just react to them. We have developed modules for discussion. In our monthly leadership meetings, I take one module topic and turn it into a 30-minute discussion—on *being vulnerable* or on *being extraordinary*, for example—because I do not want to lose the momentum we have gained."

In addition to the business results achieved, Mike was able to retake his LCP 15 months later (see Figure 7.13) and e-mailed us to say, "This stuff really works! I am so happy that I improved from the first time I

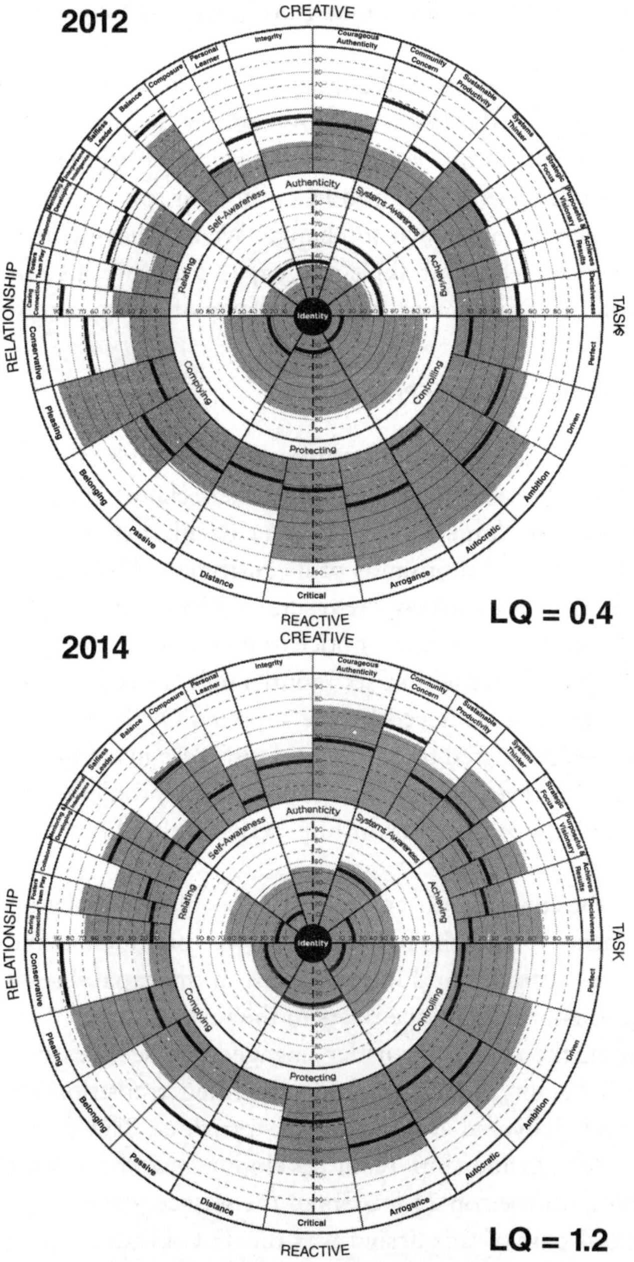

FIGURE 7.13 Mike's 2012 and 2014 LCPs compared

took the profile. I have made much progress and look forward to the work ahead."

In this case, we can see Mike doing his personal development work, and then taking on the Leadership Agenda at his plant: "The positive changes in me and in our culture and business performance come as a result of everything that HLS and FCG brought to the table, their holistic (whole systems) approach to change. We see that by applying what we learned to increase our skills and capabilities, we also increase our contributions and fulfillment, with less waste of energy and resources."

Case 4: Technology Service Provider

A multi-national service provider (we agreed to maintain anonymity at the request of the service provider and their client) encountered a big challenge when its largest client in Asia Pacific experienced a serious problem that affected thousands of its customers. From the client's perspective, the issue was largely the responsibility of the service provider.

The client organization gave notice of its intention to cease the multi-million dollar contract within six months unless five key criteria of service excellence were achieved by the supplier. Of the service provider's 850 employees dedicated to the client, most were in client support roles. An investigation revealed that a large part of the problem was a systemic issue—the quality of the relationships between the client and the service provider.

Meeting the key criteria could only be achieved if there was a culture transformation on the part of the service provider, including a shift in employees' attitudes and improvement in the capability of collective leadership to engage team members in the turnaround.

Soon after, the service provider engaged the services of Full Circle Group Asia Pacific. A custom and integrated transition strategy was designed and delivered for the service provider. The first 12 months included Senior Leadership Team development and one-on-one executive coaching for the top 25 leaders of the service provider.

An integral part of this design was the TLC Leadership Culture Survey (LCS), the Promise of Leadership workshop and the Leadership Circle Profile 360 (LCP). These were used in tandem along with other key culture transformation initiatives, including Vision Journey Mapping, ongoing TLC Pulse Surveys, Leader-to-Leader cohort sessions for senior

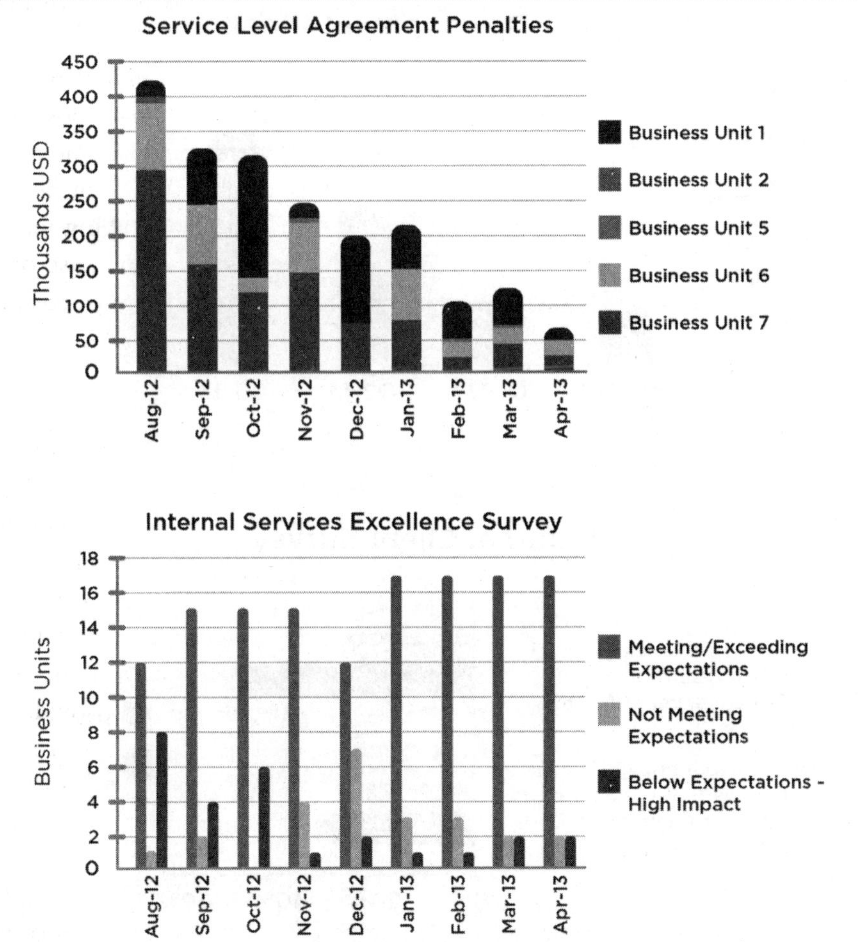

FIGURE 7.14 Changes in service supplier metrics

leadership development, and culture change workshops attended by about 800 employees. The work was designed systemically with the entire system in mind.

The outcome was astonishing, especially to the client. As Figure 7.14 shows, business metrics changed dramatically and very quickly. Service penalties dropped 700-fold in 9 months. The sales pipeline increased five-fold over the same period. Internal Excellence and Customer Satisfaction scores increased as well. The service provider's culture changed so positively that the client postponed the cessation of the contract after only

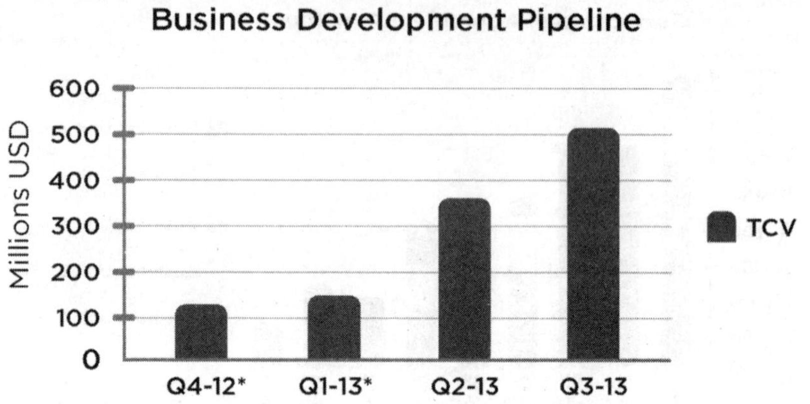

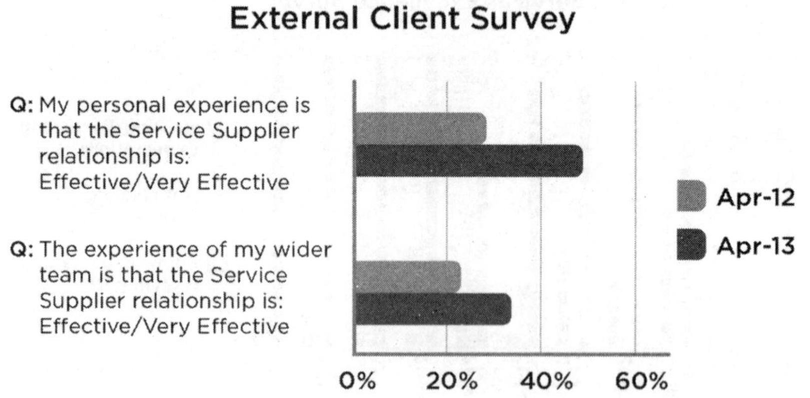

FIGURE 7.14 (Continued)

three months from the start of the culture change program. Within six months, the client began to reaffirm old contracts and entered into two new contracts, both worth over $100 million. As evidence of the shift in the client-service provider relationship, the CEOs and board members of both organizations agreed to meet semi-annually to discuss how the two organizations could work more closely together for the medium and longer terms.

What Changed? Here is a summary of what changed in the service provider's organization dynamics:

- The LCS enabled the leadership team to realize that the negative relational and cultural dynamics that the client was experiencing were evident within their own collective leadership team. The leadership team was a fractal of the whole culture.
- The leadership team collaborated to consciously change from within and then to lead the business to a new level of capability.
- With the support of one-on-one executive and senior leadership coaching using the LCP 360, leader-to-leader sessions, and Pulse Surveys, the leadership team aligned to a powerful vision and client-focused strategy. With this shared purpose and clear future direction, the Executive and Leadership Team, along with the top 50 leaders and appointed "change champions," engaged all individuals and teams in dialogue to agree what it would take to achieve the vision.
- The top 50 leaders (Extended Leadership Team) and change champions were invited to culture change work sessions to become aware of their operating behaviors and values. Soon, most chosen behaviors had aligned with the vision and resulted in quality engagement with peers, direct reports, and clients.
- Leaders who struggled to adjust or resisted engaging with the culture change initiative were shifted to another part of the service provider's business. Some chose to leave the organization.
- Internal culture change champions held forums about how to accelerate the change.
- The leadership and culture transformation started to show results within three months. Within six months, the CEO and board members of the client organization publically recognized the turnaround in both results and relationships. Since then, relations have gone from strength to strength, and the client continues to ask for a closer relationship with the service provider at the highest levels. This was unimaginable before and shortly after the major problem that became the catalyst for the leadership and culture change initiative.

OWNING DEVELOPMENT FROM THE TOP

Effective collective leadership insures that the organization is fit for purpose, will make a lasting and meaningful contribution, and remain competitive. One of our clients, another strong female CEO leader at a large professional service agency, made the case for owning the Leadership Agenda from the top. In speaking to her Extended Leadership Team as they embarked on their leadership transformational journey, she said: "The ever increasing complexity of our business and the demands required of us as leaders can be daunting. As we pull together, we will navigate challenges, enjoy great opportunities, and build collective leadership capacity. The decisions we make as leaders, the culture we create, and the growth that we source, will have more impact on sustaining our business success than any other factor." She goes on to say that their ability to be resilient, develop and inspire people and to creatively solve business challenges will impact their success. "I am committed to equipping our leaders with the development and tools necessary to be the high performing *corporate athletes* who can build collective capacity for getting better, smarter and stronger. We need to work on our own personal leadership, build collective leadership capacity, and create a culture we need to thrive. We are serious about leadership development and will measure our ROI with the same rigor we would for any other decision. This investment in our leaders is designed to create a competitive advantage for our business." She could not have said it better. She could not have done a better job of owning the Leadership Agenda.

The above cases demonstrate the power of using a Whole Systems approach to advancing the Leadership Agenda—a Whole Systems approach to the vertical development of the Leadership System for driving and sustaining a transformation in business results.

Hopefully, we have made the case for a deeper, long-term, systemic, and vertically transformative approach to the development of leaders both individually and collectively. To accomplish this, it is imperative that we understand how the journey of transformation proceeds.

Mastering leadership takes informed, conscious practice. It requires that we transform our selves. This is not territory with which most of us are familiar. If we are serious about mastering leadership, individually and collectively, we need a detailed map of the territory. The second half of this book is a deep dive into the progressively developing Structures of Mind (Reactive, Creative, Integral, and Unitive), how they develop, and practices for supporting the evolution of leadership.

TAKING STOCK

- What is the organization that, if it existed, would put you out of business?
- What would the soul of your organization say about its enduring reason for being—beyond money or stakeholder value?
- What are your individual, team, and organizational non-negotiables?
- If the system had a voice, what would she say to us right now?
- What voice of the system brings both compassion and understanding to the harsh realities in which we find ourselves?

Chapter 8
Reactive Leadership
An Insufficient Triumph of Development

The evolution of *Egocentric Mind* into *Reactive Mind* is a triumph of development. As we enter adulthood, we leave behind the over-independence of adolescence and adopt the messages from our surrounding environment about how we have to be in order to get along in the adult world. This allows us to successfully launch our careers, get married, create families, and take on roles in the community. Adopting the messages, mental models, values, morals, and roles prescribed by the surround is the very triumph of development that as parents we are championing. It also forms the structural limits of this IOS.

Reactive Mind is well suited for growing into adult life, but as life gets more complex—with the competing demands of expanding leadership roles, growing families, and mounting financial commitments—Reactive Structure likely meets its limits. All structures have limits and when we meet them we face adaptive challenges. Furthermore, as organizations today change to be more agile, innovative, empowering, engaging, flexible, creative, lean, and fast to market, the Reactive Mind faces additional adaptive challenges. Reactive Mind is not structured for leading transformative change. It was formed to merge with the prevailing culture. It is not yet mature enough to individuate from the prevailing culture and change it. Reactive Leadership is ill-equipped to lead the transformation into these new high-performing cultures and structures. Creative Mind or higher is required, especially by those leading the change.

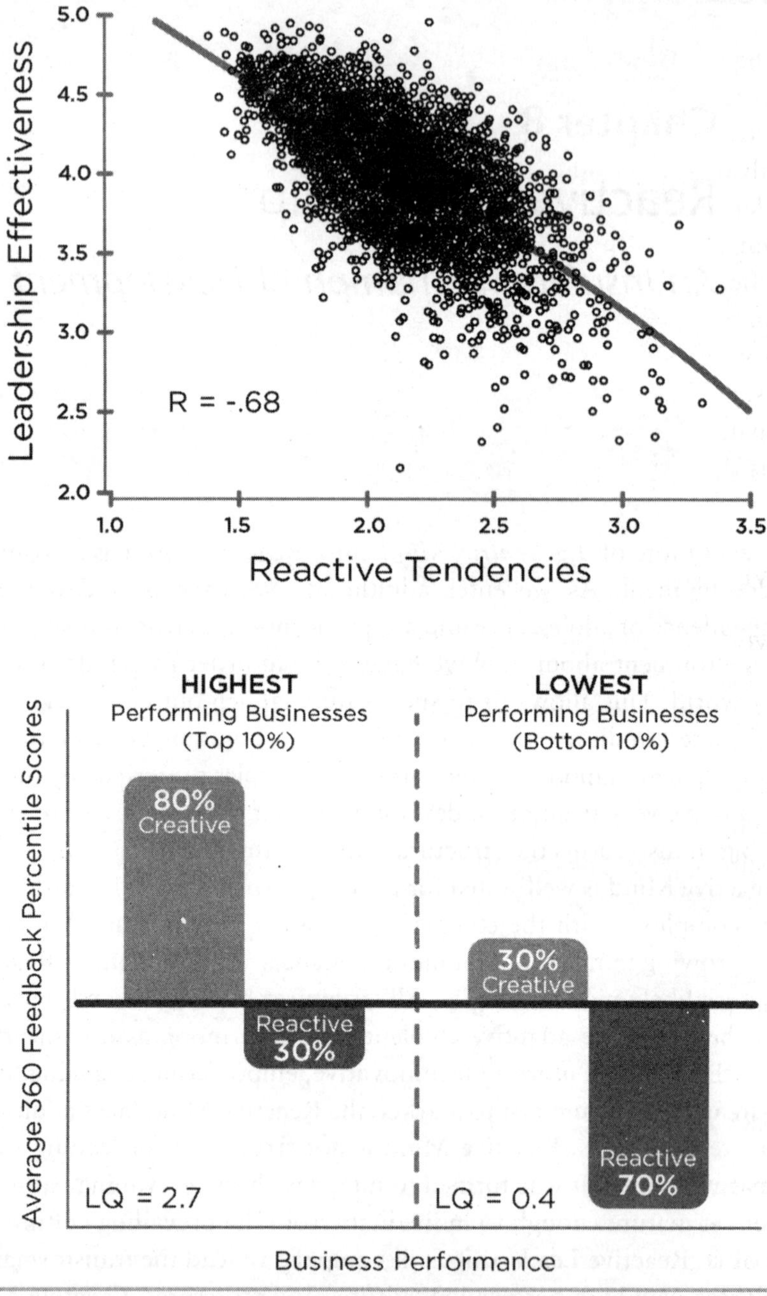

FIGURE 8.1 Reactive Leadership, Leadership Effectiveness, and Business Performance

PERFORMANCE REVIEW

We have already shown that Reactive Mind is inversely correlated to Leadership Effectiveness (−.68) and Business Performance (−.31). Reactive Leadership typically has a LQ of less than one, a competitive disadvantage. In underperforming businesses (bottom 10%), Reactive Leadership scores average at the 70th percentile (see Figure 8.1).

Our research provides solid evidence that Reactive Leadership lacks the effectiveness and complexity to orchestrate the kind of business transformations seen in the last chapter. To evolve beyond Reactive Leadership, we must first see it and know it deeply. We must see how it lives in us. Thus, in this chapter, we will explore Reactive Leadership, its strengths, the patterns of performance that it is designed to produce, and how it limits the high-performance required of leaders today.

LEAVE YOUR EGO AT THE DOOR

At work we often hear, "Leave your ego at the door." What we mean is this: *Leave the unconstructive parts of yourself out of the meeting—only bring the best parts*. Of course, this is impossible. We wear our ego and live through it as our IOS. Vertical development makes more of our subconscious ego conscious. We can then see it, manage it, and even transform it into higher level leadership. If development does not proceed, we are subject to the dictates of the ego. It has us—we do not have it—and it can take over on autopilot. In Reactive mode, we are subject to a host of invisible internal assumptions put in place a long time ago. If we do not see them, we cannot manage them or control them in the pressures of the moment, perhaps to the detriment of our best intentions.

I DARE YOU TO TELL ME THE TRUTH

Years ago, we were asked by the CEO, let's call him Duke, of a health care system to conduct a team building session with his senior team. Duke is one of the best, most visionary, and purpose-driven CEOs we had ever worked with. He was leading a progressive transformation effort, but it was bogged down with what he perceived as a lack of support by his top team.

We interviewed every member of the senior team and, after assessing the team dynamics, we called Duke to arrange a debrief. What he did next was a clue to how his ego/character/identity was organized: he chartered a plane and arrived at Bob's house the next morning. In that meeting, we laid out all that we had learned, including how he was contributing to the group's impasse. He took it well and eagerly agreed to go forward with the teambuilding.

A few weeks later, we arrived the evening before our three-day off-site. Duke picked us up at the airport. His van was packed full of everything we would need for our session. We were driving to his 13-bedroom *cottage* on the lake. "Wow," we thought. "This guy plays big. First, he charters a plane to meet us, and now we are headed to his 13-bedroom *cottage*."

Duke talked excitedly for the entire two-hour drive. Clearly he was genuinely committed to making this off-site successful. He knew that there would be some difficult conversations and that he had a part in what needed to change. He volunteered to go first to get feedback on his leadership style. Given his attitude, we were optimistic.

When we arrived at Duke's cottage, Duke asked us to help him unpack the van. As we were doing so, Duke asked Bob to load the refrigerator with all the food he had brought for the event. Bob picked up a big tub of tuna salad and, as he put it into the refrigerator, Duke said while standing over his shoulder, "Upper right shelf." Then Bob grabbed a jar of pickles and Duke said, "Lower left." Duke directed where everything went in the refrigerator. We wondered if this might have anything to do with what Duke's senior team might want to say to Duke.

The meeting started well, and then it came time for the group to get into the issues. True to his word, Duke volunteered to go first in receiving feedback. The group was slow to respond, reluctant to say anything. Then one brave manager cautiously spoke up. "Well, perhaps there is one thing. Sometimes you tend to control things a bit too tightly."

Duke's body posture changed visibly. He crossed his arms, frowned, and said sternly, "Just give me one example." His tone seemed to say, "I dare you." No one said a word.

We let the silence linger. The fear in the room was palpable. After a long minute of silence, Bob said, "I have an example." He told the story of Duke directing how the refrigerator was packed.

Duke continued to frown with his arms crossed. As the story finished, Duke relaxed and said, "I did do that, didn't I? Wow! Does anyone else have an example like that?"

The ice broken, Duke now seemed genuinely open to more feedback. The group had a lot to say about how he controlled everything, how he made major decisions within their jurisdiction, and how he would come into their meetings, uninvited, and take over. The group felt that Duke did not trust them to lead their areas of responsibility, even as they were leading a change effort designed to empower decision-making at lower levels.

Duke's initial Reactive behavior almost derailed the meeting. In that moment, his Reactive ego had him. He did not have it. Nor was he aware that this behavior prevented him from getting the feedback he needed. He was largely unaware of how much he needed to be *The Guy*—bigger than life, in charge, in control, and the one upon whom all success depended. This ego/identity need was controlling everything and jeopardizing the change effort.

To his great credit, after the ice was broken, Duke had enough maturity to make a shift and open up the meeting for a candid discussion. When it came time for Duke to provide feedback to the team, he had a lot to say about their caution and how they kept playing small. He talked about how they punted important decisions to him, about how they did not discuss the difficult issues in meetings, and how they played a Reactive "play-not-to-lose" game. He said that because they did not step up to the tough issues, he felt the need to take over.

Each member of the group was playing reactively while sponsoring a transformation that required that they play a different game—one that they creatively lead. Their unconscious reactivity was colluding to keep all of them stuck in a Reactive mode. Each was blaming the other, assuming that others were not committed to the vision that they collectively espoused. No one had the insight or courage to voice what was really happening. Had this dynamic gone unchecked, the change effort they cared deeply about would have derailed.

This is an example of how the inner game (ego, identity, IOS, and character), functioning at the Reactive level, runs the show. In this example, each member of the Senior Team was caught in the Reactive ego dance that is the norm. This dance scuttles our best intentions to operate more effectively, innovatively, and agilely. Collective effectiveness and intelligence, required to pull off a transformation, are diffused in this dance. The Reactive operating system reaches a limit in the culture it can create and support. Unless it is seen and transformed, the Creative-level change in the system will fail. Each operating system is based and designed on different structural principles, and, since design determines performance, each Stage of Leadership gets predictable patterns of performance.

TWO PRIMARY MOVEMENTS

Two primary movements happen in the structure of the self as it transforms from a Reactive to a Creative Mind (see Figure 8.2). Understanding these two movements explains how Reactive leadership is organized and how it can be reorganized and transformed into Creative leadership.

The first movement has to do with a shift in how we optimize the tension between purpose and safety (see Figure 8.3). In the second parallel movement, identity shifts and reorganizes from being configured from the outside-in to the inside-out. Let's explore these two shifts one at a time.

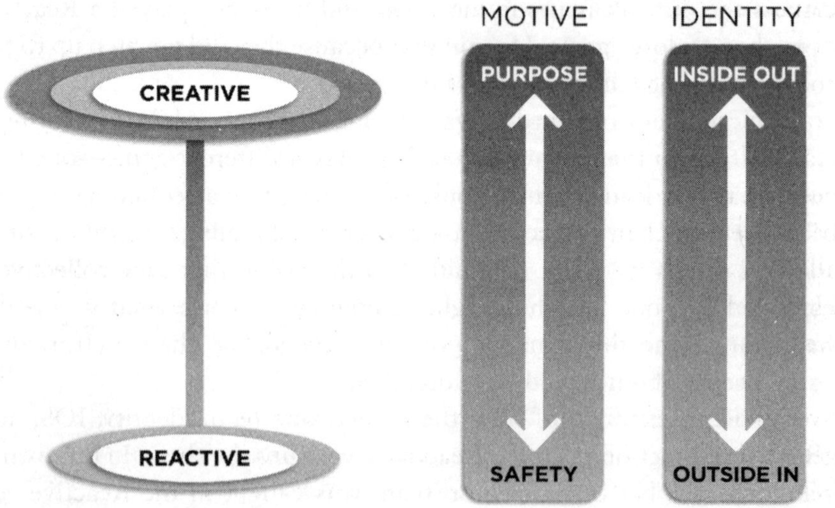

FIGURE 8.2 Two primary movements

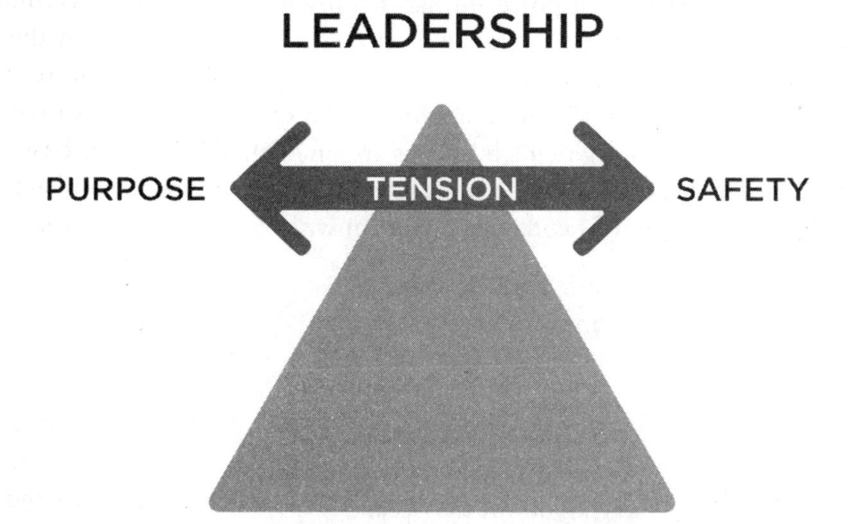

FIGURE 8.3 The tension between purpose and safety

First Movement: Purpose and Safety, Love and Fear

The primary tension in life and leadership is the tension between purpose and safety, between the part of us that wants to be about something great, make a difference, and merits our deepest commitment and another part of us that simply is not up for that much risk.

The tension between purpose and safety is not bad. It is not a problem, not something to fix. As a dilemma, a polarity, it cannot be solved, only resolved. It cannot be solved because we need to achieve both ends of the polarity. Both essential ends of this tension–resolution structure seek to be fulfilled, and they compete for our attention. This tension is inherent in all of us, all the time, in every meeting. It was evident in Duke's meeting. How we habitually resolve this tension defines which operating system we run—Creative or Reactive.

In the face of this tension, we need to make a choice that defines our lives and our leadership. In his poem, *Out on the Ocean*, David Whyte gets to the heart of this choice poignantly (Whyte, 1989). There is a story behind the poem. David was kayaking five miles out on the ocean one day. He got caught in a violent storm, and he spent a few hours fighting for his life. Exhausted, he finally reached the shore. As he recovered, he realized that something powerful had happened within him. He wrote this poem to discover what was awakened.

The first part of the poem is about the huge struggle amid immense turbulence. This image alone is a wonderful metaphor for the volatility and complexity through which leaders are often challenged to navigate. It is also descriptive of the seeming life-and-death struggle that comes with transformation. David ends the poem with this stanza:

with five miles to go
of open ocean
the eyes pierce the horizon

the kayak pulls round
like a pony held by unseen reins
shying out of the ocean

and the spark behind fear
recognized as life
leaps into flame

*

always this energy smolders inside
when it remains unlit
the body fills with dense smoke.[1]

In leadership, there are such moments when everything is at stake, where the kayak of the soul "pulls round" and the eyes of resolve pierce the horizon. The choice to live is made, always in the face of fear. With poetic precision, David nails the core tension between purpose and safety—the spark and the fear reside together. As we orient on what we most want, we face what we most fear. Always this energy smolders inside. Always the spark of our purpose and passion awaits our commitment. Always fear lurks inside cautioning us not to move toward the spark. It is too risky. However, if the spark remains unlit, if we do not move toward the spark, fan it, feed it kindling, and cultivate it, the body fills with dense smoke. When we do not live at the edge of our

[1]Printed with permission from Many Rivers Press, www.davidwhyte.com. David Whyte, "Out on the Ocean", *Songs for Coming Home*, 1989. © Many Rivers Press, Langley, WA USA.

creativity and passion, we become toxic to ourselves and those around us. We either move through the fear toward our passion, or we slowly and inexorably die.

Our experience of life often mirrors David's—the tension between spark and fear, purpose and safety, is always inside. Each time we step up in our life or leadership to a new aspiration or vision, we meet fear at the door. Our biggest wants are met with our biggest fears. This is the deal.

Each of us is unique. With that uniqueness comes a passion, curiosity, or contribution that only we can make. Each of us wants to be a part of something great. We each want to make a contribution, and we have a vision, if we discern and distill it, of what that would look like if realized. *Leadership is the act of creating outcomes that matter most.* If we had our druthers we would orient our lives and our leadership on that which seems to want to come through us. We would birth that which most matters into the world. We work, in part, to fulfill these aspirations.

We all long for noble purpose, and we also need to pay the mortgage. We work to provide a safe and stable life for ourselves and our families. We want to establish a financial safety net for the future of those we care about. This is an important part of why we work. If we do not carefully tend to this part of life, we put ourselves, our loved ones, and our higher aspirations at risk.

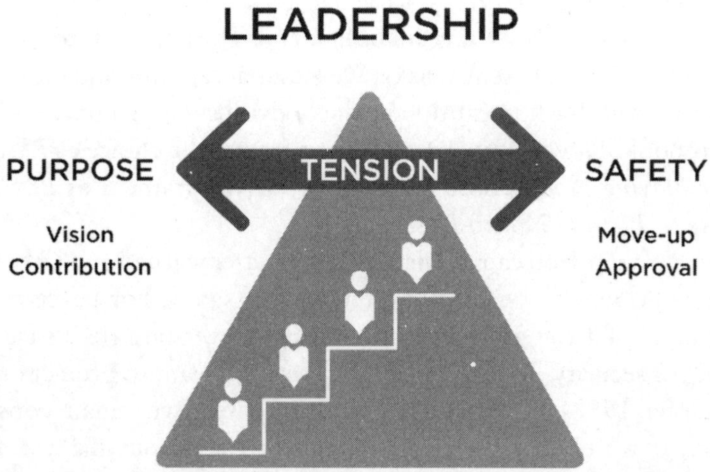

FIGURE 8.4 The tension between purpose and safety at work

Those of us who work in organizations usually want to move up. Perhaps we buy the myth that we are better off at a higher level, that self-esteem increases with altitude in the pyramid. Perhaps we believe we are more secure the higher we rise. We hold this notion despite the experience that caution increases the higher we go. Often we hear, "I no longer do the things, take the risks, that got me here." The higher we rise in organizations, the higher the stakes, the bigger the stakeholders, and the greater the fall. Still, moving up expands our impact, pays more, and makes it easier to finance and secure the future we want.

If we want to move up and we want to do that safely, we need to win and maintain the approval of those around us, especially those above us. When we look up, we are looking at those who control our future advancement. We tend to vest them with the keys to our future. To fall from grace, to lose favor with bosses, higher-ups, and with key stakeholders, is bad for the career. So we are in a dilemma: do we advocate for what we want and what we think is in the best interest of the business, or do we keep our heads low and live to fight another day?

This tension occurs in every meeting: How much do I say? How controversial am I willing to be? What will they think if I challenge the prevailing direction of my peers or those above me? How much do I care about this issue? Does it matter enough for me to take the risk of pursuing it? These questions come up often, and they beg for resolution (see Figure 8.4).

Most of us are looking for a safe path through, a safe place to be great. There isn't one. *There is no safe way to be great, and, there is no great way to be safe.* The safe paths have all been taken. The paths left to us require risk. Leadership is inherently risky. We either accept this and move to the edge, or we pull back in caution as the body fills with smoke.

In his book, *Play to Win*, Larry Wilson frames the choice as *Playing to Win or Playing Not to Lose* (Wilson, 1998). We frame it as *Playing on Purpose or Playing Not to Lose.*

From a Nazi prison camp, Dietrich Bonhoeffer learned and later wrote, "There is no way to peace along the way of safety. For peace must be dared, it is itself the great venture and can never be safe. Peace is the opposite of security. To demand guarantees is to want to protect oneself" (Bonhoeffer, 1998). If we orient our lives on safety, we remain constantly insecure. If we choose the opposite and orient on our highest aspirations, we live the futures we were born to create, and that brings its own security. It is counterintuitive. Caution is not the safe path. In leadership

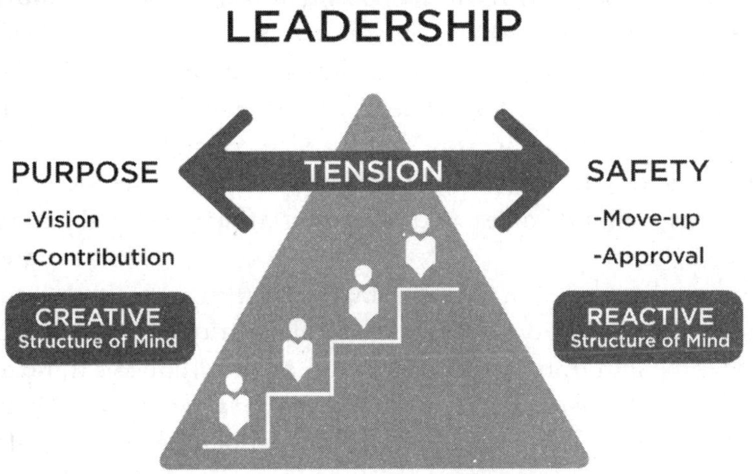

FIGURE 8.5 Purpose or safety, Creative or Reactive

positions, more people get fired for their caution than for their courage. If we play for purpose, we accept the inherent risk of leading, of living full-out, and that brings with it an inherent sense of security. This security is not rooted in powers outside ourselves, upon which our future seems to depend. It is rooted in our capacity to create the future to which we aspire. To lead is to live at the edge. There is no safe path. That's the deal.

How we resolve this choice determines from which operating system we live. If we orient primarily on safety, we live and lead reactively. If we orient on the pull of purpose and vision and accept the inherent risks, we evolve Creative Mind and leadership (see Figure 8.5).

The core of the Reactive operating system is a play-not-to-lose game. We react, reflexively, toward safety without even realizing it. Thus, the Reactive operating system is based on fear—designed to react to fear and reduce it. That is why it is called Reactive.

The core of the Creative operating system is a play-on-purpose game based on love. In this game, we orient on *what we love enough to risk for*. It is designed to create the future to which we aspire. That is why it is called Creative.

Second Movement: From Outside-In to Inside-Out

The second movement is a shift from an ego/identity structure configured from the outside-in to one that is lived from the inside-out. Kegan calls this shift the shift from the *Socialized Self* to the *Self-Authoring Self* (Kegan and Lahey, 2009). The Reactive Self is oriented on living up to, or living out of, all the messages it has adopted from its environment. The Socialized Self is defined by what others have told it, that it must be in order to be worthy, good, and successful. Kegan says that, at this stage of development, the self does not have a self. Key people, institutions, cultural values, and important affiliations hold and define the self.

The Self-Authoring or Creative stage is the first wherein the self discerns its own internalized definition and identity. Stephen R. Covey describes the shift from Reactive Mind to Creative Mind as a transformation from the *Dependent Ego* to the *Independent Ego* (Covey, 1989). By Dependent, he means that the self depends on outside validation for its sense of worth, esteem, security, and well-being. The Independent Ego is self-validating and can act independently or autonomously. It can march to the beat of a different drummer, whether or not others approve. Larry Wilson describes this same shift as changing from a play-not-to-lose to a play-to-win game—a shift from a life lived out of the fear of not meeting expectations to a life lived on purpose. Psychologists identify this shift as moving from an external to an internal locus of control.

Bob: Early in my career, I was living and working within a Reactive operating system, before I knew there was such a thing, and with no awareness of higher-order systems. Slowly, I began to see the outside-in, Reactive Mind through which I was living and leading. I was then employed as the Director of Organization and Leadership Development in a large healthcare system. I reported directly to the Senior Team, and I was frustrated with their leadership. One of our external consultants wrote me and said, "I wish they would get excited about anything; even painting the flag pole would give us something to focus on." I was so frustrated that I had a bottle of Maalox (antacid) on my desk. This was my level of self-awareness at the time.

What does a young, Reactive consultant do when he is frustrated with his leaders? He conducts a culture survey. So I did, to get the ammunition (data) necessary to prove to them how screwed up they were and then fix them. This is how I thought. Is it any wonder that I was ineffective in working with senior leaders?

When I received the results from the culture survey (on big green and white computer print-out paper) from the university, I walked eagerly into my office to see what the numbers indicated. I looked at the top sheet, which contained the organizational results, and sure enough, it showed *they were screwed up*. I was thrilled. I had the ammo I needed!

Then, when I glanced at data for my organization, the Leadership Development Department, I got the shock of my young career. *We were just like them!* The area that I managed had results at the 50th percentile of the organizational norm base. We, the group that was supposed to stand for an optimal culture, were a microcosm of the organization with which I was so frustrated.

This hit me hard. It was a serious blow to my leadership, and I took it seriously. I tried working on it with my staff without success. So I called in a consultant to work with me. She interviewed my team, sat me down at breakfast the morning before the start of a three-day team-building session, and immediately said, "I have interviewed your entire team and, well, frankly, you are the problem."

I said, "What do you mean, *I am the problem*?"

She said, "You do not offer any leadership."

I said, "Oh, I know about that. What else did you find out?"

She responded, "What do you mean you know about that?"

My response was vintage Reactive Mind. I said: "How do you expect me to lead when I have no leadership? It is not my job to have a vision. I am a consultant to them. It is their job to have a vision, and since they do not have one, there is nothing for me to do. My hands are tied."

Initially she did not know how to respond, but then she asked me a stunning question, the central organizing question of the Creative Mind: "What would you do if you could?"

Then, all the stuff I wanted to do in the organization, in my career, and in my life poured out of me.

She absorbed all that, smiled, and simply responded, "Let's have a meeting."

That three-day off-site began a learning process that culminated a few months later in a revelation. I was sitting at home alone, reading a book, *A Guide to Rational Living*, by Albert Ellis, father of Rational Emotive Cognitive Therapy, a branch of psychology that has mapped out the core organizing assumptions of Reactive Mind (Ellis, 1975). As I read, I suddenly realized, "*They* are not the problem. *I* am the problem. I want to lead, I want to be an agent of change, and I want everyone to like me.

That will not happen. That's a catch-22. How can I lead if I need everyone to be pleased with me all the time, especially the leaders above me in whom I vest the keys to my future?"

I realized that I believed that my worth and security were in their hands. I maintained my sense of personal worth, esteem, and security by always being liked and admired. I so needed their approval that I was afraid to lead. My Reactive strategy was to play it safe by always being agreeable, deferential, and non-controversial. One cannot lead from this risk-averse stance.

I had just discovered an assumption at the core of my Reactive operating system: *The approval of others funds my sense of self-worth and security*. I needed others to like and admire me, so much so that I was not leading.

This need for outside validation is why Covey calls this Stage of Development *Dependent* (Covey, 1989). At this stage, we are defined externally and dependent on external validation for our sense of self-worth and security. This puts us in the play-not-to-lose game in which we try to advance our objectives by trying not to lose.

My play-not-to-lose game was my unwillingness to risk the disapproval of those around me and above me. I was reflexively reacting to stay safe by remaining uncontroversial. I had an unconscious habit of staying off the radar screen, thinking I was leading. I was playing not to lose in search of a risk-free path, governed by the assumption that worth and security equal approval.

Seeing a belief like this can be transformative. If we continue to track the workings of that belief in our life and leadership and continue to challenge its validity by experimenting with new assumptions while focusing on creating what we want, this belief eventually gives way to Creative thinking. As the Creative Mind boots up, new possibilities emerge.

This is what happened for me. When I saw how much of my behavior was governed by this belief, I could free myself from it. As I began to notice, in real time, when this belief was cautioning me to play it safe, I became free to make other choices. I kept working at the same organization with the same key stakeholders, and together we achieved transformational results.

Having observed this core operating belief over time, I now know it is false. My essential worth is not measurable, it is immeasurable. It is not defined by how you see me and whether or not you like, approve, love, or admire me. My future is not in your hands. Over the years, many leaders and clients had not supported my way of thinking or the direction in which I was leading, yet my life and career had progressed, quite successfully.

At this time, the core of my Reactive operating system went from subject to object. I was no longer blind to it. I no longer lived through it unseen. It no longer had me or defined me. I was not subject to it. I now had it as an object of my reflection. Now, when the voice of fear emerged in me, cautioning me to lie low and keep my head down, I recognized it as the voice of this old, false belief. It was not the truth, just the voice of a belief I had adopted. I could now put that voice in perspective and make my own choices.

As this happened, a different voice emerged, the voice that always knows the answer to the question, "What would you do if you could?" This voice leads the show in the Creative Mind. This is why Kegan calls this stage *Self-Authoring* (Kegan and Lahey, 2009) and Covey calls it *Independent* (Covey, 1989). I was no longer being authored by the dictates of this old belief. I was becoming independent of past conditioning to author my own life and lead from the emerging vision. Creative Mind is led by vision, by what matters most. I started managing my fear of disapproval and began to lead. My fear and preoccupation with safety receded. I still needed to create a safe and secure future, but that was now in my hands and was not foremost. The spark of my deep longings to live out the purpose and vision I cared about became foremost. The externally conditioned play-not-to-lose game receded, and the internalized vision began to lead. My operating system shifted from outside-in to inside-out, from Reactive to Creative Mind.

STRUCTURE OF REACTIVE MIND

This story illustrates another aspect of Reactive self-leadership—I did not see myself as part of the problem. *They* were the problem. The problem was outside me, and it was my job to fix it. Reactive Mind is outside-in because the forces that defined me and shaped me were outside me (external to me). I am not part of the problem (external). They are the problem (external). They hold the keys to my future (external). They have defined, over a lifetime, how I must be seen in order to be okay (external). All of this is external to me.

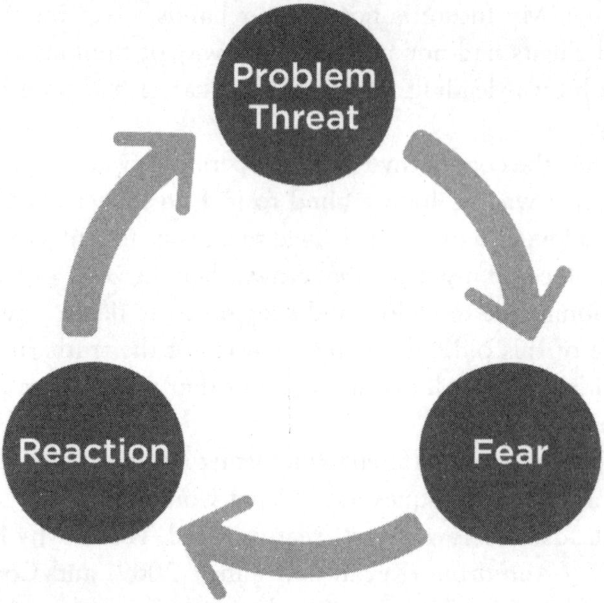

FIGURE 8.6 Reactive Structure

The Reactive Structure is problem-focused, driven by a fear that has its roots in unseen, un-reflected, and externally organized beliefs and assumptions. This way of relating the self to the world forms the core design of the Reactive operating system, displayed in Figure 8.6.

Reactive Mind is focused on problems, not vision. It is focused on removing, fixing, or reducing problems and threats. It is run by fear, motivated to reduce the internal conflict generated by the problem. Behavior is a reaction to this internal conflict, and the focus of behavior is to get rid of the problem. As you examine my story, you see all of these elements.

Another story further elucidates this structure:

Bob: Years ago, I presented the Reactive Mind diagram at an Insurance Sales College started by my early mentor, John Savage, one of the most successful life insurance salesmen in the world. He made the Million Dollar Roundtable on the first business day of every year. He was an extraordinary human being. After my presentation, a man came up to me and said in an animated voice, "You were talking about my life! We need to talk."

Over lunch he launched into a conversation by saying, "I have a problem."

"What is your problem?" I asked.

He said, "I am not learning anything here."

I was surprised by this, and so I asked, "What do you mean?"

He said, "I know how to sell life insurance and I am good at it, so I am not learning anything here."

I asked, "So, other than spending a week and some money, what is the problem?"

He said, "My sales results do not show it."

I said, "Tell me about your results."

He said, "When I look at my results, I get disgusted with myself. I also fear that I may not be able to make ends meet. So I swing into gear. I do all the things that John is telling us, and I am good at it. About nine months later, my results are much better—cash flow is up, and I am making a good income."

"So what is the problem?" I asked.

He responded, "I look at my results nine months after that, and they are way off. I get disgusted with myself and swing into gear all over again. And this has been my career. It has not gone anywhere. My results are up and down. They are nothing like John's."

This conversation depicts a problem-focused and fear-driven Reactive operating system. His behavior was intended to get rid of the problem, but mostly it is designed to get rid of the inner conflict that the problem is creating—the feeling of being disgusted with himself. There is also a complete lack of a Creative orientation. Nowhere does he talk about what he is trying to achieve, his vision, or why he cares about his profession.

Structure determines performance. Reactive Mind gets a predictable pattern of performance, a pattern described well in the salesman's story. Reactive Structure is designed to oscillate. As the problem grows (results fall off), so does fear and inner conflict. As the inner conflict gets bigger, the tendency to react to it grows. As our salesman reacted (by selling), he reduced the problem (increases cash flow). Things are looking good, right? Well, not for long. He is winning at a play-not-to-lose game.

He has cycled through his Reactive loop once, and things are improving. He is feeling better about himself. He is feeling less fear and less self-disgust, and he is more secure. Since Reactive Mind is a play-not-to-lose structure run by fear, the fact that he is feeling better sets up the next downturn in his results. The problem now is smaller (more income), his

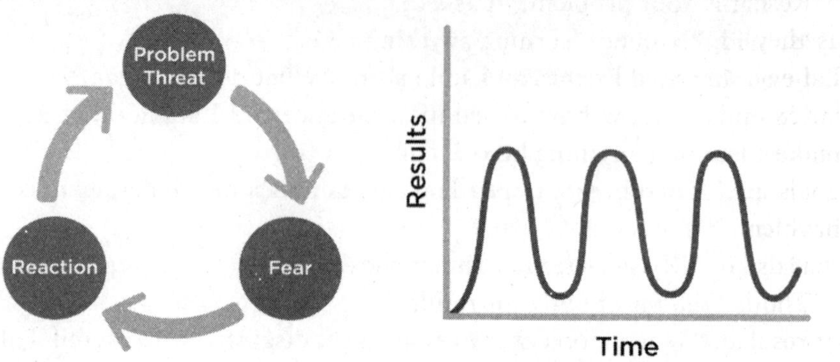

FIGURE 8.7 Pattern of results over time for Reactive Structure

fear and self-disgust is less, and so the tendency to continue his Reactive strategy (swinging into gear) is reduced. He reduces his reaction, the problem returns, and he starts all over.

The design of any structure determines its pattern of performance over time. When we operate from a Reactive Mind, here is the predictable pattern of results (see Figure 8.7).

Reactive Mind seeks equilibrium. It is designed to go back to normal. Reactive Structure is a balancing loop. Peter Senge describes balancing loop structures as being designed to maintain homeostasis (Senge, 1990)—like a thermostat, designed to keep the room at a constant temperature. However, the temperature is never constant; it oscillates up and down within acceptable parameters. As the temperature gets too hot, the air-conditioner turns on, and the temperature goes down. As the temperature gets too low, the air-conditioner turns off, and the temperature goes up. Since the thermostat is designed the way it is, it gets the pattern of results that it was designed for: a relatively steady-state temperature.

Reactive Structure is designed the same way. It is a balancing loop structure that creates an oscillating pattern of results around a set point. It is a good structure for maintaining equilibrium. The human body has thousands, if not millions, of balancing loop structures that help maintain homeostasis. Without them, we would quickly die. So, Reactive Structure is not bad. It is simply inadequate for achieving higher performance and maintaining it, or improving it further. Reactive Structure is designed to maintain current reality.

Reactive Structure functions like an immune system to keep things as they are. In their book, *Immunity to Change*, Bob Kegan and Lisa Lahey describe this same oscillating pattern of results by using the familiar example of New Year's resolutions (Kegan and Lahey, 2009). We all make them, and often make the same ones a year later. Why do we set goals and then act in ways contrary to our commitments? Because we have competing commitments, which are often run by internal beliefs that drive behavior designed to maintain the current equilibrium.

The same structure was running the salesman. Beneath his pattern of results are some powerful unseen beliefs, operating on autopilot and structured from the outside-in (how others see me defines me, and I must live up to their expectations in order to be okay).

Suspecting this, I drew, on a napkin, the pattern of oscillation, pointed to the troughs in the pattern, and told the salesman, "We know what happens to you here. You get disgusted with yourself and your fear of not making ends meet swings you into high gear."

He nodded in agreement.

Then, I pointed to the peaks and asked, "What happens to you here, when you start to succeed?"

He got wide-eyed, as if a scene was passing through his mind, but he said nothing.

I asked him, "What just happened? What did you just notice?"

He said, "Oh, that would not have anything to do with it." Three times I asked him to tell me what he saw, and three times he dismissed what popped into his awareness as having nothing to do with his problem of on-again, off-again performance.

Finally, I said, "Humor me. What did you notice?"

He then said, "I thought of my dad and the church."

I asked, "What does your dad have to do with this?"

He responded with the deliberateness of someone coming into a new awareness. He said, "My dad tried all his life to be successful and never was. You do not think that I would be worried about what my dad would think of me if I were more successful than he ever was, do you?" As he said this, his eyes widened like a deer caught in the headlights.

He had answered his own question. I then asked him, "Tell me about the church."

He said, "I have been taught all my life that it is bad to have money."

I did not talk theology with him about the misinterpretation of this way of thinking. Instead, I said: "So, let me see if I understand. Here (pointing to the troughs in the oscillating pattern), you are disgusted with yourself and here (pointing to the peaks), your dad is going to hate you and you are going to hell. Is that about it?"

He looked at me stunned, sobered, and simply nodded in recognition. He was seeing, perhaps for the first time, the underlying assumptions running the pattern of his performance. This was a breakthrough moment for him. It held the possibility of a transformation in his IOS.

This salesman, like me in my story, was at the mercy of the assumptions he had adopted earlier in his life because they made sense at that time. They were not his assumptions. They were given to him. Reactive Mind forms an identity externally—from the predominant environmental message and from the conclusions we make from those messages about how we should be: we are okay if we live up to the self-defining assumptions supplied by our environment.

Since these assumptions may not be mature enough for the complexities of our adult life, they become the structural limit to what is possible for us. They seek to maintain a state of equilibrium and often drive behaviors that compete with our vision and commitments.

If you are clear on your vision, and you are repeatedly falling short of achieving that vision, the highest leverage place you can look is into your belief system. The inner game runs the outer game. Underneath the fear, doubt, and inner conflict that govern Reactive Leadership, we find unconscious beliefs. The full picture of the Reactive Structure of Mind is displayed in Figure 8.8.

Reactive Structure is designed to maintain equilibrium between current beliefs (unseen and externally defined) and current reality. It is not designed for change or transformation. Insidiously, Reactive Leadership is initially self-reinforcing. It works at first. Things get better, and we feel better. However, the reaction, while aimed at fixing the problem, is designed to reduce the inner conflict. Since the inner conflict is motivating the reaction, predictably the action we are taking will attenuate as soon as the inner conflict is reduced to an acceptable level.

Since the inner conflict has its source in beliefs and assumptions designed to have us live up to environmental expectations, the direction of our reaction is to establish equilibrium with these expectations—to

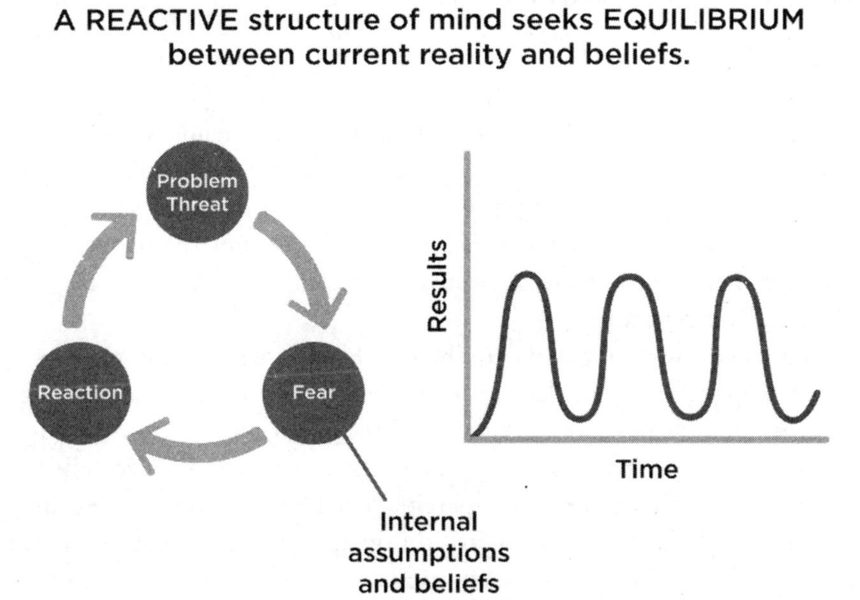

FIGURE 8.8 The full picture of Reactive Structure

re-establish current reality in a way that keeps us meeting the expectations of that current reality. Thus, Reactive leaders habitually seek safety over purpose.

Some people might describe this as *staying within a comfort zone*; however, as Robert Fritz points out, this is not a *comfort zone* but a "Zone of Tolerable Conflict," one designed to manage discomfort, not produce comfort (Fritz, 1989).

Reactive Mind has a high energetic cost. This salesman was working hard and not creating what he wanted. Of course, he was not clear about what he wanted. He just did not want to feel bad about himself, a self that was formed from a set of erroneous, externally defined, and irrational assumptions. Until these assumptions are seen and challenged, the pattern will repeat. Eventually, fatigue sets in as energy is expended without result.

The Creative Mind and its IOS are designed to create what matters most, to create the future to which we aspire, to get better results more consistently and at a much lower energetic cost.

CORE OPERATING BELIEFS

One of the most transformative practices is to see into and rewrite our IOS code. Our IOS is made up of a host of well-patterned beliefs, assumptions, and mental models. Most of these are accurate and serve us well. Some are not. Maturing our IOS requires us to observe, reflect on, and modify the invisible assumptions embedded in our IOS. This is hard because they operate beneath the surface. We do not see them, we see *through* them, and we are subject to them until we can make them an object of our reflection.

The most powerful beliefs are the beliefs and internal assumptions by which we establish our identity. These powerful self-defining beliefs get incorporated into the core of our IOS throughout our life from emotionally powerful, positive, or painful experience. They also are installed by important people in our lives—parents, teachers, coaches, bosses, mentors, political leaders—and by institutional, national, and cultural affiliations. As we adopt these assumptions, we live by them and reinforce them. The brain puts them on autopilot so that we do not have to think about them anymore. They are just seen as *true*.

Bob: One of my deeply embedded assumptions is that I must be perfectly successful in order to be okay. I come by this belief honestly, and most of the experience that created this belief was positive. For example, when I was 13, I tried out for the football team. I had never played football, and most of the guys on the team had been playing for a few years. I did not know that you needed to work hard to get noticed by the coaches, so I stood patiently on the sidelines waiting to be put on the practice field. As such, I was not seen as a player. Since the coaches did not have the heart to cut me, I ended up on the "Taxi Squad." The few of us on this squad practiced together on another field. The real team had eight male coaches. We had Mrs. Dixon, a nice lady who knew nothing about football.

At this time, I was not moving in the circles in which I wanted to move. The cool kids were on the football team, and as long as I was on this Taxi Squad, I had little chance of getting accepted into their group. To make matters worse, all the cheerleaders practiced near where the team practiced, and I did not have their attention either. I was a nobody.

One day, Mrs. Dixon did not show up and the coaches were forced to allow the Taxi Squad to practice with the team. What happened that day changed my life. I was playing left defensive tackle and after a play in which I must have done something right, one of the coaches picked me up, lifted me up above his head and screamed into my face, "That was great! Do that again."

I was so unaware of what I just did that I asked him what I had done.

He took a personal interest in me for the rest of the practice. He taught me how to play that position. Soon, I was wreaking havoc on the offense. That week I went from Taxi Squad to captain of the team. I started on offense and defense for the rest of the season. I also moved into the center of the boys with whom I wanted to be friends. I even piqued the interest of the cheerleaders. I went from *nobody* to *somebody* in one practice.

I learned that day that I am *somebody* if I am first string, captain of the team. I learned that I had to be the best, first string or else I would be a nobody.

This story illustrates how the driven nature of my personality began to form. I could tell other stories about how this drive was refined into the need to be flawless at everything I did. So, I entered adult life believing that my worth and self-esteem, the success and security of my future, depended utterly on being flawlessly successful all the time.

That belief served me well. I worked very hard at everything and created early success in my career. The belief worked well until it met its limits when, in order to scale the business growing up around me, I had to teach others how do to what I had learned to do.

Of course, I assumed I would be a good mentor, however, that was not the case. My perfectionist standards and fear of failure combined to make me inept at letting go to others so that they might learn. What made this so difficult for me was that I had to let go when we were working with key clients. I did not do this gracefully. Every time one of my colleagues was not performing well enough, I became terrified that I would lose the client. Consequently, I took over the session and later pointed out all the ways my colleague could have done better. This approach so undermined their confidence that no one could learn from me, and I was failing to scale the business.

My perfectionism and need to be successful had me. I did not have them. I did not start to face this belief until after two years of failing to scale the business. Once I saw how I was the problem, as I dropped into this belief structure to see its illusion, and as I began to see my

TABLE 8.1 Identity beliefs: X = Relationship, Intellect, and Results

Relationship	Intellect	Results
Liked	Smart	Number one
Loved	Self-Reliant	Best
Approved of	Brilliant	Perfect
Accepted	Superior	A winner
Belong	Above it all	Higher than others
Supportive	Distant	In charge
Submissive	Aloof	In control

fear-driven perfectionism as resulting from another irrational belief, I began to mentor more effectively and the business began to scale nicely.

The structure of these core identity beliefs is simple:

- Worth = X
- Security = X
- I am OK if I = X
- To be is to be X

We fill in these equations with specific Xs, depending on our formative life experience. Different people choose different Xs to complete these equations. There are the three main categories of Xs with which we identify at the Reactive level—relationships, intellect, and results. The most common Xs are shown in Table 8.1.

X is always a good thing. There is nothing wrong with wanting to be successful, liked, admired, or smart. What forms the self-limitation is that these beliefs are structured from the outside-in. We are identified with always being X or seen as X. Not to be X or not to be seen as X, is not to *be*. For me, not to be flawlessly successful, is not to be. This makes not being X (or seen as X) threatening. Not to *be* is not okay. The structure of these beliefs is all-or-none.

These beliefs form the core of the Reactive operating system—the mechanisms by which we form our externally validated identity. Because we need to be seen by others as X, our self-esteem, security, and future are in their hands. They make us up. How they see us defines us. We depend on external validation, living within the confines of a Socialized Self, as the Self-Authoring, Creative Self lives beyond the bounds of these Reactive beliefs. We tend to oscillate and return to normal as we react to meet the expectations of these beliefs. This is how Reactive Mind is structured and, since structure determines performance, how it performs.

PUTTING IT ALL TOGETHER

Reactive Structure is inadequate to lead effectively today because volatility and complexity put a premium on the ability to adapt and recreate the organization in new and innovative ways. Reactive Structure is designed to return to normal for six reasons.

First, Reactive Mind forms in the transition out of adolescence when the challenge is to join with, to merge with, the prevailing cultural reality. Development succeeds to the extent that we take on the mental models, values, rules, and ways of operating that are structured into the world of which we are members. We build our lives, roles, careers, and identities such that we succeed within the current culture. Reactive Mind is designed to fit into and to replicate what is, not change it.

Second, Reactive Mind is problem focused—organized to remove the problem. At best, when we try to fix our way forward, we eliminate the problem, which returns us to homeostasis, not to a new future.

Third, Reactive Structure of Mind is designed to reduce the inner conflict (fear, anxiety, and self-doubt) created by the problem. As such, it orients on safety in a play-not-to-lose game. Since we get what we avoid, Reactive Structure tends to reestablish what we do not want.

Fourth, if our Reactive strategy is successful, it attenuates the inner conflict that is motivating the very behavior we are using to make change. This sets up the likelihood that we will stop reacting as the inner conflict recedes, and thus, the problem returns.

Fifth, the inner conflict we feel is generated by beliefs and assumptions that run on autopilot. These beliefs are externally structured and were formed by taking on the dominant assumptions of the current cultural reality. Worth and safety are maintained through external validation. We live, therefore, reactively. We are motivated to live up to the expectations of others, which we mistake as our own. This dependency on external validation creates fear, keeps us habitually in a play-not-to-lose game, has us seeking safety over purpose, and thus sets up the oscillating/balancing loop structure that maintains current reality in a way that is consistent with our belief structures and consistent with current reality as it is.

Sixth, Reactive Structure orients toward safety. The choice to pursue a larger purpose and vision gets compromised. There is no risk-free path to creating the future we want. The safe paths all lead back from whence we came. To lead transformation is a risky business. It requires the biggest risk of all: that we change fundamentally. Reactive Structure, in its unconscious, play-not-to-lose, fear-attenuating, externally dependent structure, is simply not designed to lead into a more purposeful vision of the future.

The work of transforming into the Creative Mind is to individuate from the current normative cultural assumptions and expectations—to be our own Self-Authoring person. We then become less dependent on meeting the expectations of those in the culture. Purpose and vision become the primary drivers of our leadership. This developmental move paves the way for a far greater capacity to stand for change in the current situation. This is the stance of transformative leadership.

THE LEADERSHIP AGENDA

Most organizational transformation efforts today are aimed at establishing a high engagement, high fulfillment culture of innovation. So many of these efforts fall short of intended results because we try to create change from within a mindset designed to maintain the status quo. The Reactive Mind sets up a return to normal as shown in Figure 8.9.

When we set the vision of a new, transformed culture and business performance, that vision usually requires leadership behavior and capability beyond the boundary of our current belief structure. If it did not, we would likely have created it already. When the new vision is a stretch beyond the confines of our current operating system, we are in an adaptive challenge, like Duke's senior team and when I wanted to scale my business.

Choosing to create outcomes that lie outside the bounds of our belief system produces conscious or unconscious anxiety, fear, doubt, and other forms of internal conflict. Reactive Structure is designed to reduce this anxiety and so we typically default to old behavior, behavior consistent

FIGURE 8.9 Belief boundaries

with our unseen current belief structure, behavior that was patterned to meet the expectations of the very current reality we are intending to change. As this happens, even though we are championing a new vision, we end up behaving in ways that keep the old culture in place. Reactive Structure is designed to go back to normal. Unless, as we champion bold change, we do the work of seeing how we habitually return to old habits of behavior, and then explore the deeper self-defining assumptions that drive these behaviors, we will likely undermine the change to which we aspire. In our decades of consulting experience, we only see transformations succeed when senior leaders choose to "do their work" of mastering leadership, and then go on to sponsor and support the entire leadership system in doing this same deep work. This is the Leadership Agenda inherent in any transformation effort.

The vision of higher performance puts everyone in the dilemma that Einstein described: "The solutions to our current problems cannot be found from within the consciousness that created them." They can only be found from a higher-order structure of consciousness. Reactive Leadership is insufficient to orchestrate these dramatic shifts in performance. The ways we want to lead today require Creative Leadership to support and sustain the new structure, culture, and performance. Unless this happens, the natural tendency, the path of least resistance within

Reactive Structure, is to establish and reestablish Patriarchy. We will explore this more fully in the next chapter.

TAKING STOCK

- Do you love more than you fear?
- What is the energetic cost of how you show up? To yourself? To others?
- How much of what you are afraid of has ever actually happened?
- How do the voice of fear and the voice of love speak to you? Which one gets most of your attention?
- What if I stopped waiting for those around me to do most of the changing?

Chapter 9
Reactive Leadership at Work
From Patriarchy to Partnership

In the last chapter, we showed how Reactive Mind is structured and how it generates the predictable pattern of returning to normal. We showed how this structure is not mature enough to lead transformational change. In this chapter, we will build on that by showing how leadership, functioning collectively from a Reactive Mindset, has a natural tendency to establish patriarchal organizational structures and cultures. We will also show, as we try to transform these cultures, how they tenaciously reestablish themselves, unless we lead them from a Creative Mindset. To understand this we need to delve more deeply into the nature of the dynamics that play out when leadership teams come together and lead reactively.

MOVING FROM PATRIARCHY TO PARTNERSHIP

Since most organizations are still led predominantly by men, and since most cultures are heavy on top-down control, we tend to create cultures of Patriarchy. Patriarchy evolved in times when most of the population was illiterate. The over-controlling tendency of patriarchy has its place when the workforce lacks the basic knowledge and capability required. It also works well in times of crisis and business turnarounds. It may well be the optimal structure for these situations. However, the global consensus in developed economies is that to compete in today's complex business environment and fulfill on the Promise of Leadership, we

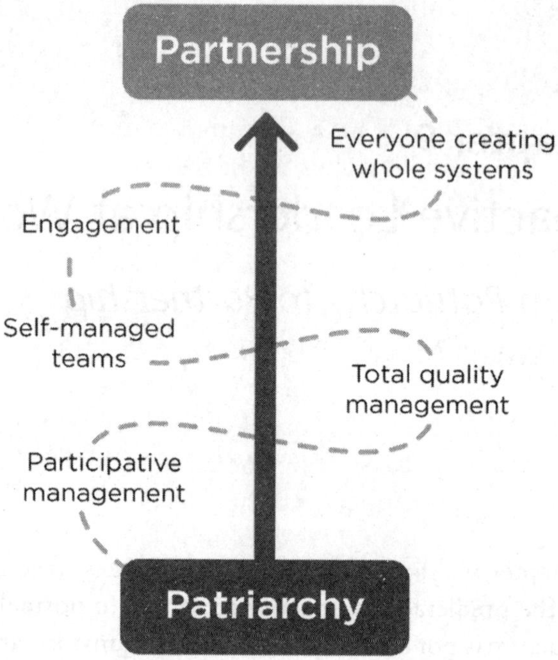

FIGURE 9.1 Moving from Patriarchy to Partnership

need to move toward cultures of Partnership, toward organizations that are more diversely led, and engage more people in cooperatively creating, innovating, and taking responsibility for the success of the business. The emerging form of organization asks everyone (customers, suppliers, employees, managers, and leaders) to partner in the organization's success. We call this transition the movement from Patriarchy to Partnership.

On the journey from Patriarchy to Partnership (see Figure 9.1), leaders, despite the best of intentions, block their own progress (Block, 1993). Early in our careers, before we fully understood how the Reactive IOS operates, we were surprised to watch leaders, deeply committed to transformation, fall into old patterns of behavior (over-control at the top, caution in the middle, blaming from below) that undermined the very change effort they championed. The inconsistency between their behavior and vision was rarely obvious to them. These inconsistent behaviors led to many mixed messages, which created a climate of caution. People avoided taking the change effort seriously. They sat on the sidelines, waiting to see which way the wind would eventually blow.

We are so familiar with patriarchal, top-down systems that we are blind to the ways that we continually "act out" that system, even while trying to change it. Our externally based mental models, identity, beliefs, and assumptions are formed in, and by, that system. We are subject to them. They are on autopilot. Thus we neither see them, nor do we see the inconsistency between the new vision and the way we are showing up as leaders, individually and collectively. This is the primary reason why transformation efforts fail.

When we try to change the system, we run smack into ourselves. *We are the primary obstacle to the very future we are committed to creating*. Moreover, we seldom notice when we are in the way. If we want to transform the performance of organizations we lead, we must do most of the changing. We cannot just sponsor change or merely redesign systems and processes; we must redesign ourselves! *The organization will never perform at a higher level than the consciousness of its leadership*. As we change the system, we must change ourselves; otherwise, the change we champion will become the *flavor of the month*.

NAVIGATING TWO JOURNEYS

Moving from Patriarchy to Partnership requires navigating two journeys simultaneously, the *system journey* and the *personal journey* (see Figure 9.2).

We tend to spend most of our time on changing the system (without a Whole Systems approach) and relatively little on the profound personal changes required of us. We try to change culture as if it is separate from ourselves. We try to change *it*, not *us*. Our observation is that the deep work of change is internal. Since 80% of adults are living and leading from a Reactive Mind, most organizations are structured and function reactively. The shift from Patriarchy to Partnership is a move from a Reactive to a Creative organizational structure and culture. Reactive Mind is incapable of ushering in the needed change. Creative level leadership is the minimum system (IOS) requirement.

System change requires a transformation in consciousness within the leadership. The work required of change leaders is to discover how we personally contribute to the culture we are trying to change. When we lead change, *we are the culture we are trying to change*. To be

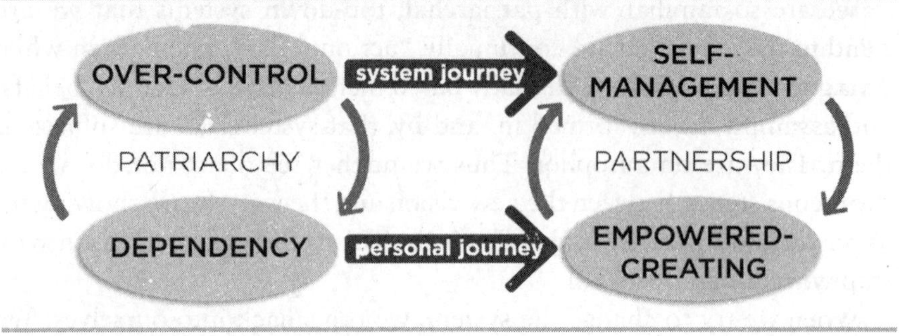

FIGURE 9.2 Two journeys

transformed by the effort, we must see how our ego/identity/character structure is organized to produce the current culture. This requires us to see into how our Reactive IOS is organized and the ensuing cultural dynamics. We need to see how we are the culture we are trying to change.

THREE CORE REACTIVE TYPES

One reason why Reactive Mind naturally gravitates toward establishing and reestablishing patriarchal structures and cultures has to do with how the three Reactive types—relationship (heart), intellect (head), and results (will)—interact. These are the three main ways that we form our Reactive Mind. Therefore, there are three basic types of people, and these three types, as they develop into the Reactive Mind, form their ego structures in different ways. These type differences, when they are reactively on autopilot, create patterns of behavior that result in patriarchal cultures, limiting leadership effectiveness and business performance.

In her book, *Our Inner Conflicts*, Psychologist Karen Horney identified three basic "trends" in the way we form our character or ego structure (Horney, 1945). She labeled them: *Move Toward*, *Move Against*, and *Move Away*. We call these three types the *Heart type* (relationship), *Will type* (results), and *Head type* (intellect). These titles reflect the essence, gift, and strength around which each type organizes its character/ego/identity. Each will leverage their core strength.

These three character structures show up in many different forms and diverse bodies of work. The Enneagram describes nine different types: three of them are *Move Toward* types, three are *Move Against*, and three are *Move Away*. In our efforts to integrate the field, we came across Pathwork, a spiritual system of development wherein we wear three ego masks: *Love*, *Power*, and *Serenity*.

As this three-way typology kept showing up, we became even more curious and turned to science. The atom is composed of electrons, protons, and neutrons. Electrical circuits have a negative lead, positive lead, and neutral or ground lead. The waveform of energy is a down wave, up wave, and the stasis or neutral position at the top and bottom of the wave.

We began to think that there are three basic energies that explain the three core types. *Heart types* are the electrons—the negative, feminine charge. They are the down stroke in the wave. They are yin, the receptive energy. They move toward others to form bonds of relationship. *Will types* are the protons—the positive charge, the up stroke in the wave of energy, the yang or masculine energy. They move outward and proactively act on the world to create results. *Head types* are the neutron—the still, stasis position in the wave of energy. They are the ground and balance between yin and yang. They remain neutral, still, and composed and bring knowledge and truth to any endeavor.

Each of us is a unique blend of all three energies. Metaphorically, each of us is our own unique shade or color, made up of the three primary colors. While each of us has all of these energies, strengths, and gifts, we tend to have one that is primary. Each type—Heart, Will, and Head—organizes its personality around one of these basic energies. This is core to who they are, their essential nature. As we mature, we tend to develop our primary energy orientation first. We leverage our best. Other strengths tend to develop later or remain under-developed. At the Reactive Stage, while we are always a blend of all three, one of these core behavioral tendencies is usually central to our identity and to how we deploy ourselves. Understanding these three types and how they interact at the Reactive level helps us understand the natural tendency of Reactive Structure to create patriarchal cultures.

As we explore each of these types, keep in mind that each of the three character types (Heart, Will, Head) has its origin in our unique essential nature. We organize our ego structure, our core identity, in a way that expresses the best in our individual, essential nature. We put our best foot forward and pack our best into our Reactive Structure and strategies.

Heart Type. Heart types *move toward* others. Like electrons, the receptive, feminine charge, they move toward others to form relationship bonds. They establish their core ego identity in relationship to people. They form their character around their gift of Heart. They are relationship oriented. This is their essential nature and gift. At the Reactive level, they are identified with that gift. They establish their self-worth and security by ingratiating themselves with others. Their self-worth and security depend on others liking, loving, or accepting them. The core beliefs that make up this type are, "I am okay if you like, love and/or accept me," and "I am not okay if you do not." The strength of this type is that it moves toward others to establish relationship as its first priority. The limitation, at the Reactive Stage, is that Heart types give up too much power in order to be liked. The core fear is rejection. Since not being accepted, loved, and liked feels like death, this type of person tends not to push controversial issues, to be conflict-averse, and thereby fails to lead. At the Reactive Stage of Development, we call the Heart type the *Complying type*.

Will Type. This type is the opposite of the Heart type. These people *move against* others. Rather than ingratiating themselves to others, they compete in order to triumph over others. They are protons, the positive masculine charge. Rather than giving up power, they take up power and use it to get ahead. They organize their character structure around their strength of will. Their core strength and gift is their inner drive to make things happen and get results. They are naturally gifted at using their personal power to accomplish and create what they want. This is their essential nature. They are born to lead and to drive things forward. As they develop into the Reactive level, they identify with this capacity. They organize their identity around their gift of will and use of power. Their core beliefs are, "I am okay if I am the one who gets results, if I am perfect, if I move up the organization, and if I am the one in charge and in control." Their core fear is failure. Failing at anything, or even coming up short, feels like death. Their strength and gift is driving results forward. The limitation, at the Reactive level, is taking up power at the expense of others and seeing others as resources to be used to accomplish what they want. Hence, they can leave a host of maimed bodies in their wake. They do not delegate, develop teamwork, build trust, or mentor others gracefully because trusting others with results risks failure. We will call this Will type, at the Reactive level, the *Controlling type*.

Head Type. This type *moves away* from others in rational, analytical distance. They form their character structure around their gift of

Head—Intellect. They are usually intellectually brilliant and quite rational. They seek knowledge and truth. This is their essential nature and gift. At the Reactive level, they are identified with that gift. They establish their sense of worth and personal security by demonstrating their analytical and critical capabilities. Like neutrons, they remain detached. They remain in their head, staying above the fray, and provide rational explanations for what is going on around them. Their self-worth and security depend on others seeing them as smart, knowledgeable, and superior. Their core beliefs are, "I am okay if I am smart, self-sufficient, superior, and above it all and can find the flaw in others' thinking." Their strength is remaining composed and rational amid chaos and conflict, analyzing what is going on from a safe, rational distance and providing brilliant analysis to complex and conflictual situations. Their limitation is that they play from the neck up. They are often experienced as cold, distant, disengaged, overly analytical, critical, or arrogant. Their core fear is vulnerability while life and leadership are inherently vulnerable. They protect themselves from vulnerability with the safety of the rational analytical world. Consequently, they tend to stay in their head and provide analysis, but often come across as being harshly critical, finding fault, and feigning superiority. We call this Head type, at the Reactive level, the *Protecting type*.

GIFTS OF EACH TYPE

We defined each type by describing their core strength or gift. Each of us, at the core, is a uniquely gifted person. We form our character around our native strengths. This leads us to develop some very valuable and admirable qualities. The *Will/Controlling* type serves others and the organization by mastering the ability to achieve results, push for aggressive growth, accomplish important priorities, and organize vast resources toward the accomplishment of a worthy objective. Organizations need such people of drive to succeed in a competitive marketplace. The *Heart/Complying* type becomes loyal, hard-working, gifted at creating harmony, sensing others' needs, and helping and supporting others. Organizations need these qualities as well, so that people can work together. The *Head/Protecting* type brings the strength of the analytical mind to bear on complex problems. They stand apart to gain perspective and engage with unemotional calm, clarity, and often-needed insight.

TABLE 9.1 True gifts of the Reactive

COMPLYING	Claiming Your True Gift
Conservative	Loyalty and fidelity to the organization's purpose. Champion of values and preserver of heritage.
Pleasing	Love for self and others. Willingness to give of oneself in service to others' needs.
Belonging	Builder of community and organization, committed purpose.
Passive	Service. Non-attachment, acquiescing to the needs of others, flowing with, egoless.
PROTECTING	**Claiming Your True Gift**
Distance	Wisdom through detachment, care and reflection.
Critical	Discernment through being inquisitive and challenging limited thinking.
Arrogance	Strength of character without the need for credit. Mentoring others into their own "bigness."
CONTROLLING	**Claiming Your True Gift**
Perfect	Constant pursuit of continuous improvement balanced with acceptance for things/people as they are. Desire to create outstanding results.
Driven	Willingness to work and risk for what you love. Doing whatever it takes to realize your deepest longings.
Ambition	Desire to create outstanding results. Personal energy to pursue worthy results.
Autocratic	Service through personal strength, persistence, and influence. The integrity to do what is needed even if it is controversial.

Each type has its own strengths and gifts, summarized in Table 9.1. Each Reactive dimension in the table is a dimension of the Universal Model and measured on the LCP. The gifts listed describe the full maturity of that gift when it is free of Reactive limitation.

While leaders who function out of Reactive Mind will likely be less effective, this does not mean that there is something wrong with the leader. On the contrary, at the Reactive level, each type of leader organizes around a core gift or strength. The limitations of Reactive leaders come not from their giftedness, or lack thereof, but because they run their strengths through a Reactive Structure of Mind. This creates liabilities.

GIFTS HUNG ON A REACTIVE STRUCTURE

At the Reactive level, we are identified with our gifts, and this becomes the limiting factor of the very gift or strength we try to offer. The inner game runs the outer game, and the Reactive, play-not-to-lose game is a limiting game. When we hang our core strengths on a Reactive Structure, we effectively remove the gift from the field of play and introduce liabilities.

For example, if we are a Heart type, our core belief might be, "I am okay if I am accepted." With this belief, we move toward relationships, but our need to be accepted limits our power. We fear not being accepted because not to be accepted is not to be. This emotional risk is huge. Therefore, we will avoid conflict and we do not deal with important issues in order to have cordial relationships. As a result, our relationships suffer. In this case, the need for acceptance subverts the very thing it wants—relationship. The gift is removed/diminished. Furthermore, since not to be accepted is not to be, rejection feels like death. Consequently, we are in a compulsive relationship with our core strength. We have to be acceptable all the time. We overplay this strength by always trying to stay within the good graces of those around us. We cannot *not* play it safe in our relationships. In a leadership role, this means we will not advocate clearly and strongly for what we think is important; we will hold back in crucial, conflictual conversations; and we will limit our vision to what is safe and acceptable.

Complying seriously interrupts leadership effectiveness, as clearly seen in the Inner Circle Correlation Matrix (Table 9.2). Reactive Complying is inversely correlated to Achieving (–.75), Systems Awareness (–.61), and Authenticity (–.72), and since these Creative Dimensions are highly and positively correlated to Leadership Effectiveness (.91, .84, and .78, respectively), Reactive Complying turns the core gift into a liability. Furthermore, Complying is inverse to Relating (–.44) and, thus, it undermines its own gift—reducing the quality of relationship and teamwork

TABLE 9.2 Inner Circle Correlation Matrix

	Business Performance Index	Leadership Effectiveness	Relating	Self-Awareness	Authenticity	Systems Awareness	Achieving	Controlling	Protecting	Complying
Business Performance Index	1	.61	.50	.48	.50	.57	.61	−.21	−.31	−.40
Leadership Effectiveness	.61	1	.85	.76	.78	.84	.91	−.41	−.56	−.63
Relating	.50	.85	1	.87	.72	.80	.76	−.64	−.75	−.44
Self-Awareness	.48	.76	.87	1	.66	.73	.66	−.74	−.74	−.36
Authenticity	.50	.78	.72	.66	1	.78	.86	−.23	−.38	−.72
Systems Awareness	.57	.84	.80	.73	.78	1	.88	−.40	−.51	−.61
Achieving	.61	.91	.76	.66	.86	.88	1	−.24	−.41	−.75
Controlling	−.21	−.41	−.64	−.74	−.23	−.40	−.24	1	.83	.09
Protecting	−.31	−.56	−.75	−.74	−.38	−.51	−.41	.83	1	.23
Complying	−.40	−.63	−.44	−.36	−.72	−.61	−.75	.09	.23	1

(Based on 500,000 rater surveys)

that the Heart type most cares about. When Heart types hang their gift on a Reactive Structure, the gifts become Complying liabilities.

The same can be said for the other two types. Each organizes their identity around their essential, unique, and gifted nature—whether that's being smart and knowledgeable in the case of the Head/Protecting type, or the power, drive, and ability to get results in the case of the Will/Controlling type. Since these types form Reactive beliefs from the outside-in—"I am OK if you see me as X"—not to be X (e.g., seen as smart or seen as in control) is not to be. This sets up a compulsive relationship to the core gift. We have to be seen as X (smart or in control) or else, and the "or else" is not to be, or we will lose identity and safety.

Since this is unacceptable (failure is not an option, and being seen as stupid is a fate worse than death), these types are always overusing these gifts. They are always super-rational, analytical, and critical or they are always pushing and controlling. Thus, overextension of a strength becomes a weakness. Over-controlling fails to build the trust, teamwork, and bench strength required for high performance—the very thing that the Controlling type is trying to achieve. Remaining overly analytical and critical is experienced by others as cold, aloof, and harsh. It, therefore, fails to get the message across because others are put off by the delivery.

All of this can also be seen in the Inner Circle Correlation Matrix. Controlling is inverse to everything, most notably Relating (–.64), Self-Awareness (–.74), Leadership Effectiveness (–.41), and Business Performance (–.21). Furthermore, Controlling is inverse to Achieving (–.24), thus working against its own gift, the very thing Will types care most about—creating results. The same pattern can be seen for Protecting. It is inverse to all the Creative Dimensions and inverse to its own strengths (Self-Awareness at –.74, Authenticity at –.38, and Systems Awareness at –.51). Protecting, too, undermines its own gift, what they care most about—the honest exchange of learning, knowledge, and wisdom.

Notice how each of these types takes their gift off the table as they hang it on a Reactive Structure. This is why (and how) a Reactive relationship to our core strength over-extends it, creates liabilities, and reduces effectiveness.

If managed well, the differences between the types can cause each to play to their strength; the best qualities of each person are available for the team and organization. This ideal, however, seldom happens. The collective intelligence is usually well below the average intelligence of group members because when these differing types come together, they often trigger each other's liabilities. The conflictual and dysfunctional dynamics we often see in leadership teams can be explained by what happens when opposite types react to each other.

REACTIVE DYNAMICS—TRUE TO TYPE

Several years ago, we consulted with the Senior Team of an oil refinery. Two senior managers could not get along. They could not be in the same room with each other, and this was causing major problems. We were hired by the president and asked to "fix them."

Let's call these two managers Ken and Jack. Ken was the VP of Technical Services, and Jack was VP of Operations. Most of the 500 people who worked at the plant reported to one of these two men. When we first met with Jack, he described Ken, saying: "He is a wimp! He cannot make a decision. I cannot get anything I need out of his organization. I have no use for him."

Ken described Jack as an "animal." He thumped his chest with both hands saying: "He is a big hairy ape. He sits in meetings all day beating his chest. He is an egomaniac. I cannot stand him and I cannot work with him." Needless to say, we had our hands full.

First, we administered the LCP to each manager. We also interviewed several people who worked for and with each of these men.

When the profile results came back, **Jack** scored very high on the *Controlling* and *Protecting* dimensions. He was described as excessively *Ambitious*, *Autocratic*, *Arrogant*, and *Critical*. He was also scored low on Relationship dimensions—on *Caring*, *Teamwork*, *Mentoring*, *Collaboration*, etc. What bothered Jack the most, though, was that he was scored low on *Integrity*. He thought of himself as a high integrity person and had read many books on high-involvement, high-fulfillment workplaces. He cared passionately for people and sought to empower them through his leadership. His interview data validated his high *Controlling* and *Protecting* scores. People described him as Jekyll and Hyde—good Jack, bad Jack. They never knew which they were going to get. One day he would show up in an inspiring way, talking about high involvement, empowerment, and engagement. On other days he would take people apart. He dominated every meeting and left little room for discussion. Jack did not walk his talk, thus his low Integrity scores. Jack was a high Controlling type with a Protecting backup style.

Ken was a Complying type with a Protecting backup style. He scored high on *Pleasing*, *Belonging*, *Passive*, and *Distant*. He had low scores on *Achieving Results*, *Strategy*, *Decisiveness*, and *Courage*. This would suggest that he was not leading, but playing cautiously and letting key issues fester. When we talked to Ken's team, they told us Ken was very smart and technically competent, but he was indecisive and did not confront the difficult issues to improve Tech Services. This was hard news for Ken to swallow.

To both men's credit, they leaned into their feedback. We met with both men separately for some time. Jack got a lot of insight about his demanding, caustic, over-controlling behavior. He defined himself as a turnaround guy who did not want to be one any more. He discovered the belief that he is only as good as his latest turnaround. One failure, he feared, would ruin his career. Failure was not an option. He looked squarely at his core organizing belief: "I am my results, and not to get results is not to be." Since these belief structures are all-or-none, one failure meant the ball game is over. He acknowledged that these assumptions were very emotionally powerful and that they had driven his behavior all his life. Second, he realized that they were false. They are simply too extreme (success every time or else) to allow for him to lead with greater flexibility, agility, and inclusiveness. As soon as results began to slip, he reacted from the fear of failure. He then took people apart or took over. He did not mentor, he dictated. He realized that if he were to become the kind of leader he aspired to be, he needed to change this assumption. He began to challenge his automatic angry, aggressive reaction as it came up in his body. He started to ask good questions instead. He started to listen.

Ken, too, began to see into his Reactive operating system and found a core organizing assumption that he needed to be a nice guy. He wanted people to like him. His leadership was constrained by the belief: "I am my relationships. I am a good person if people like me. Not to be liked means I will be rejected, and that is unacceptable." He, like Jack, came to two conclusions. His need for approval had him playing too safe and did not enable him to say what he knew needed to be said. Since he is a people person, he could say things in a way that would likely be heard. Second, he realized that he could live with people not liking him.

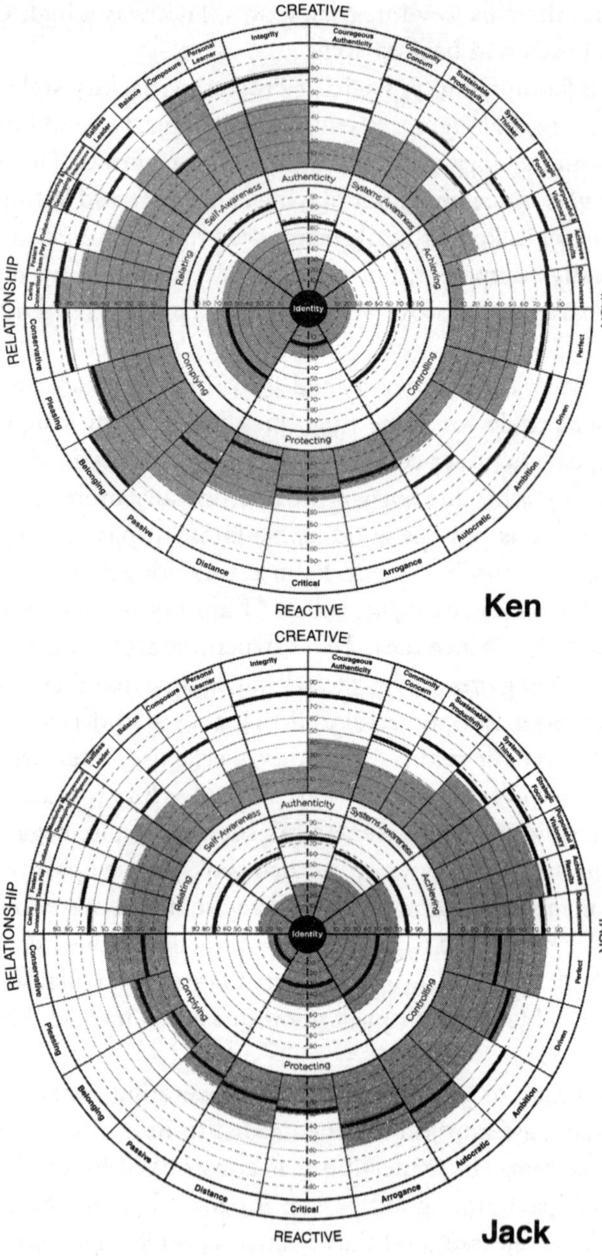

FIGURE 9.3 Ken and Jack's Leadership Circle Profiles

His belief, too, was all-or-none. One person's disapproval meant the end of the world. Ken realized the irrationality in this false belief, and he began to challenge his fear and step into conversations that required courage.

Once Ken and Jack had enough insight into the way they were reacting, we brought them together for a meeting. They each put their LCP's down, side-by-side, and looked in silence at the results (Figure 9.3). Then they looked up at each other and said, "No wonder."

They could see that they were opposite types who triggered each other. Ken was looking for approval from Jack, and as soon as Ken showed any caution or indecisiveness, Jack clobbered him. Ken's indecisiveness threatened Jack to the core. He needed the output of Ken's team to get results and so when Ken hesitated, Jack erupted, which sent Ken further into caution. Each triggered the worst in the other. Both were brilliant men, but the dynamics between them had them playing at a low level of collective effectiveness.

As they saw the dynamics, they saw how each contributed to it. They saw the opposite ways they had each configured their ego/identity structure. They realized that each represented their shadow opposite (more on this later). Each saw his part in the name-calling, and both acknowledged that they were playing from the fear of rejection and failure. As each man took in the other man's fear, compassion and understanding grew. They saw how they were playing in a not-to-lose game that kept them in an oscillating pattern of bouncing off of each other and getting nowhere productive. They agreed to change the game, and they did. It was not always smooth between them, but they made it work. The plant was much better off because of it.

There were other players in this story. Jack and Ken had peers and a boss on the leadership team. Each contributed to the dysfunctional dynamics between Ken and Jack. Some of Ken and Jack's peers were Protecting types. Their play-not-to-lose strategy was to move away. They kept a safe distance from the explosive relationship. They could analyze what was going on, but would not jump in and help resolve it. In this way, they colluded in the dance. The boss, the President who brought me in to "fix them," was a strong Complying type who lacked the power to challenge Jack and Ken to clean up their act. So, every member of the Senior Leadership Team contributed to the ineffectiveness of the team. It was not all on Ken and Jack.

To break through to higher business performance, we must take on the Leadership Agenda inherent in that goal. Ken and Jack took on this challenge. Theirs is a story of vertical development happening inside a business conversation. Ken and Jack had begun the shift of mind from Reactive to Creative.

REACTIVE TYPE DYNAMICS IN THE UNIVERSAL MODEL

The Leadership Circle Profile and the Universal Model integrate the best of Cognitive and Rational Emotive Psychology, within the Type framework at various Stages of Development, and relate all of this to what we have learned from the field of Leadership and Organizational Development about what works and what does not.

There is a solid (−.76), inverse relationship between *Reactive Leadership* and *Creative Leadership Competency* (see Figure 9.4). This relationship shows dramatically how running our gifts and strengths through a Reactive IOS takes those gifts and strengths off the table.

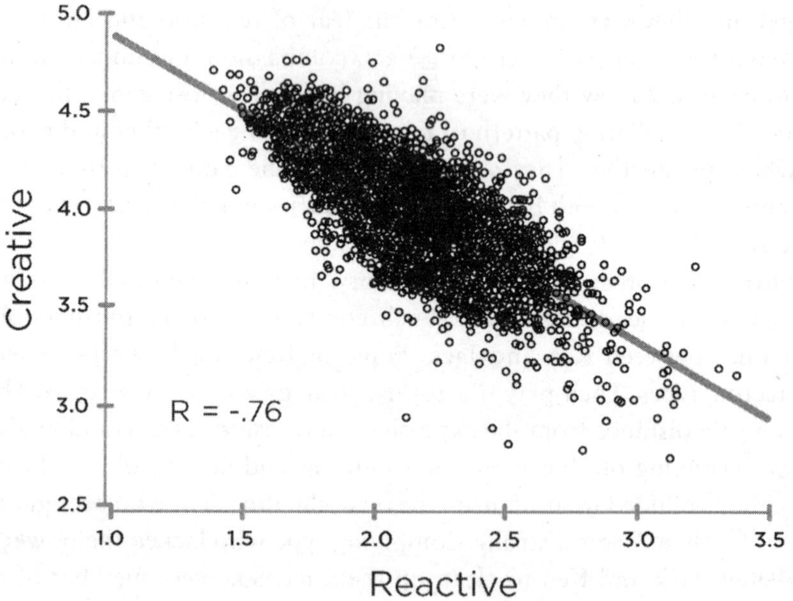

FIGURE 9.4 Correlations between Creative and Reactive

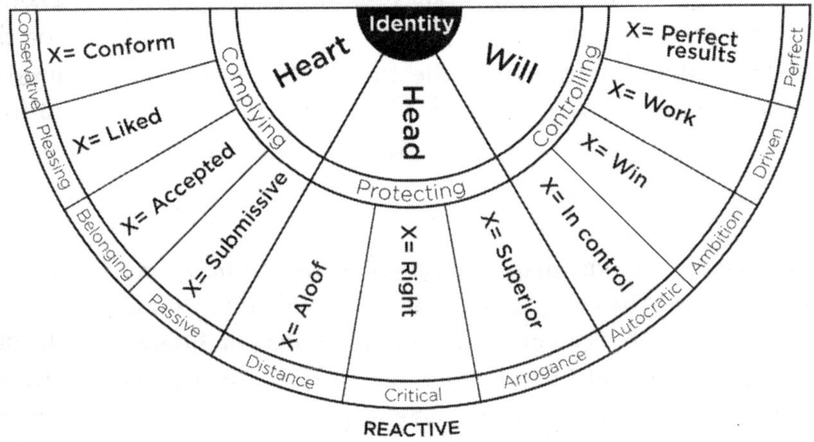

FIGURE 9.5 Reactive domain and associated beliefs and behaviors

The bottom half of the circle is a complete map of how Reactive Mind structures itself (see Figure 9.5). The 11 measures of Reactive behavior, run from well-researched self-limiting beliefs, fit neatly into one of the three types and form the core organizing beliefs and behaviors of each type. Since the opposite types of Complying and Controlling are displayed on opposite sides of the circle, with Protecting in the middle, the Model and the Profile are very useful in explaining the dynamics between types (e.g., Ken, Jack, and the Senior Team).

Providing leaders, like Ken and Jack, with feedback through the lens of this model elucidates the Reactive Mind and enables a leader to make the subject–object shift that Kegan describes (Kegan, 1998). The LCP invites leaders to:

- Learn how they are establishing their identity;
- Explore the Reactive beliefs to which they are subject—beliefs that run on autopilot;
- See clearly the behaviors that these beliefs are running;
- See how they might be playing-not-to-lose;
- See their predominant Reactive type;
- Learn how they may be sub-optimizing the tension between purpose and safety;

- See how their leadership is set up to return to normal—maintain the status quo;
- See how they contribute to the functional or dysfunctional team dynamics;
- See how they may contribute to creating results that are contrary to best intensions.

This dynamic model maps out how Reactive Mind is organized, how leaders behave when they are run by a Reactive IOS, and the organizational dynamics that can play out between leaders of different types. The Universal Model and LCP describe the structure, beliefs, and behavior patterns of leaders, individually and collectively.

NATURAL SELECTION PROCESS—CREATING COLLECTIVE PATTERNS OF PATRIARCHY

The Ken and Jack story (and Duke's refrigerator story in Chapter 8) represent the kind of type dynamics that, when taken to a larger scale, naturally sort themselves out into patriarchal structures and cultures. How do the interactions of types establish patterns of patriarchal behavior and structure?

In his book, *Beyond Ambition* (1991), Robert Kaplan observes that Controlling types tend to move up. Their strengths are ready-made for senior levels, and they are ego-driven to move up. Since their self-esteem is often related to their altitude in the pyramid, they work unceasingly to advance, succeed, and expand their power base. This serves the organization's need for people who will expand, push aggressive agendas, grow the organization, and step up to the rigors and demands of leadership. Consequently, the top levels are populated predominantly by Controlling types.

Complying types tend not to move up as readily. Since they do not measure self-worth in the same way that Controlling types do, they are not as driven to move up. Also, because using power and taking risks may not get them liked (which is how they measure their self-esteem and security), they have not developed the repertoire of behaviors that seem natural to Controlling types. So they are less likely to end up in the most senior positions. Instead, they populate middle and lower levels

FIGURE 9.6 Patriarchal structure

and serve the organization by their loyalty, hard work, and dedication to doing what is right and meeting the expectations of others.

This natural selection process that pushes Controlling types up and Complying types to lower levels directly leads to patriarchal relationships and systems (as displayed in Figure 9.6) that Protecting types fill in across the board. We realize there are exceptions to this pattern and we are oversimplifying it to show the general dynamic tendency.

It is the habitual/compulsive nature of the three types which makes them interact in such a way that an overly hierarchical, patriarchal pattern of relationship often results. People at the top take most of the responsibility and control, while people at the bottom say: "It is not my job to take responsibility. My job is to do what is expected." In this exchange, both types get their identity/ego needs met. Controlling types feel safe and worthwhile because they are in control and on top, and the Complying types feel safe because they do not have to risk being controversial and taking responsibility. The Controlling types feel justified in taking control because they do not see those below them taking risks and making the tough decisions. Complying types feel valued because they are doing what is expected of them and doing it well. The relationship is reciprocal and self-reinforcing. Each type does its part in maintaining the patriarchal dynamic, and both types are not aware of how they "must" continue to maintain that system in order to continue using their Reactive strategies. Both would feel at risk and devalued if the game were to change. This is what makes change so difficult, especially if that change is in the direction of Partnership.

This natural selection process, where Controlling/Protecting types tend to inhabit the high ground, and Complying/Protecting types fill in below, creates the dynamics of Patriarchy. When leaders fail to re-optimize the tension between purpose and safety, when they do not challenge their play-not-to-lose game, and when they lead change from a Reactive IOS, the resulting culture can be costly.

Culture, when it is ineffective, eats strategy for lunch. The number one reason for failure of strategy is not that it was poorly conceived. It is because the collective leadership effectiveness to execute that strategy is inadequate. The kind of Reactive organizational culture and team dynamics described in this chapter are costly. Strategy gets consumed.

Reactive Mind is designed to return to normal—to create an equilibrium between its belief structure and current reality. As a result, the kinds of cultural dynamics described in this chapter tend to reassert themselves as we attempt to change them, in spite of our best intentions to operate in a new and transformed way. We are all carriers of the culture we are trying to change. Transformation efforts give us the opportunity to see how we are, individually and collectively, the culture we are trying to change. As one leader said to us, "How did we think we could transform the culture without being transformed ourselves?"

When the collective leadership mind has its center of gravity at the Reactive Stage, the kinds of type dynamics illustrated by Ken and Jack play out. Collective effectiveness suffers and the collective intelligence drops below the average intelligence. The hidden points of leverage needed for breakthrough are, therefore, not surfaced and acted upon. This is why we see Leadership Effectiveness scores from those assessed at the Reactive Stage of Development averaging at the 40th percentile with a Leadership Quotient of .67—not mature enough for leadership to be a competitive advantage. Great results simply cannot be achieved from within a play-not-to-lose structure run by fear (from unconscious beliefs) and designed to go back to a patriarchal normal. We simply cannot build the kinds of Creative partnership cultures we envision with Reactive Leadership. Personal leadership transformation to Creative Mind is required.

TAKING STOCK

- Without vision the people perish. What, in your organization, is perishing?
- Fear is information. It can also be F.E.A.R. (False Evidence Appearing Real). If you wade through both, what is left for you to do?
- There is no safe way to be great. No great way to be safe. Where do you stand?
- Is our culture one that turns achievement into failure or failure into achievement?
- Why you? Why this team at this point in your company's history?

Chapter 10
Creative Leadership
Fulfilling the Promise of Leadership

The transition from the Reactive to the Creative Mind is arduous. Only about 20% of adults fully make it. It is the major transition in most adults' lives. In the Mythic literature, it is called the Hero's Journey or the Heroine's Journey. It is not for the faint of heart.

PERFORMANCE REVIEW

Before we launch into the nature of the Creative Mind and how it develops, let's summarize briefly what we have said about its effectiveness (Figure 10.1).

While Reactive Leadership styles are strongly inverse to Effectiveness (−.68), Creative Competencies are very strongly and positively correlated to Leadership Effectiveness (.93). In the highest performing businesses, those evaluated in the top 10% compared to industry peers, Creative Competency scores average at the 80th percentile compared to the worldwide norm base of 500,000 rater surveys. Reactive Leadership styles are well below the norm at the 30th percentile. The reverse is true in underperforming businesses (bottom 10%).

In our Stage of Development study (Figure 10.2), those people assessed as living and leading from a Creative Structure of Mind had average Leadership Effectiveness and Creative Competency scores at the 65th percentile compared to norms. This constitutes a Leadership Quotient of

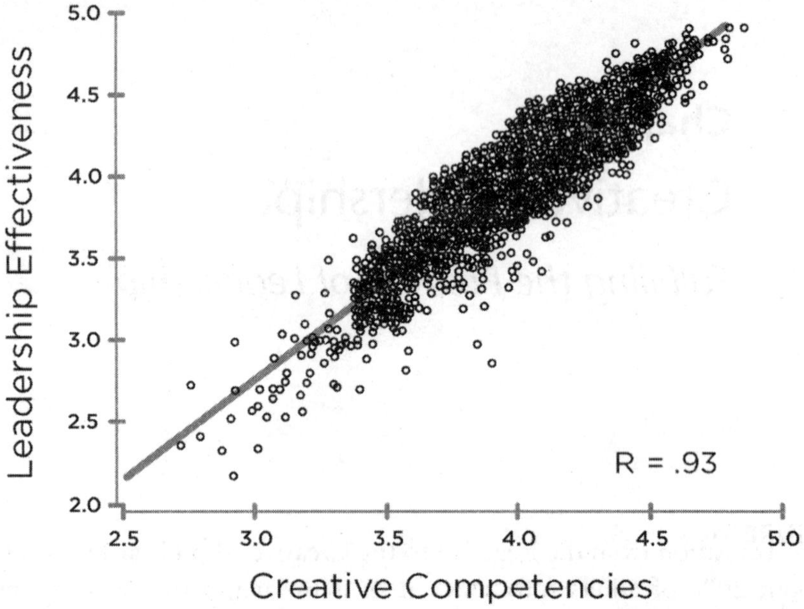

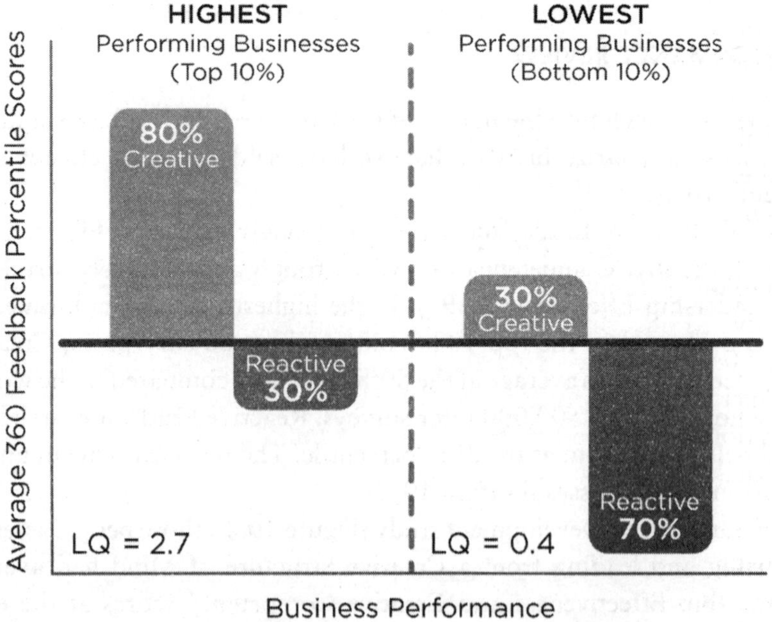

FIGURE 10.1 Creative Leadership and Effectiveness

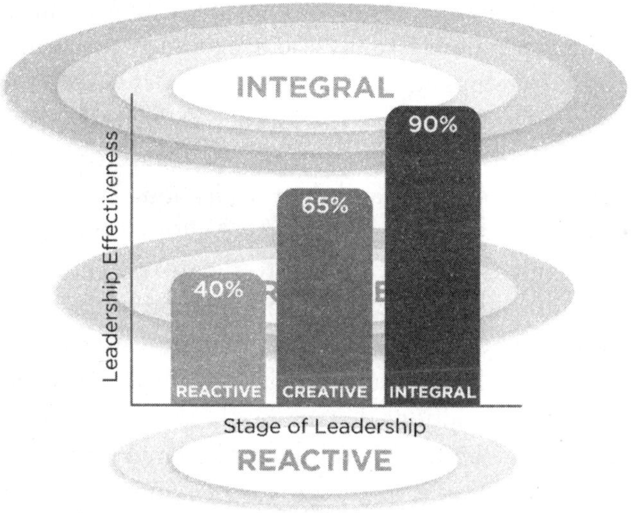

FIGURE 10.2 Stage of leadership and effectiveness

nearly 2.0, suggesting the leaders who function out of a Creative mindset create a big competitive advantage.

The Creative Mind is much more capable of leading in today's complex organizations. Since only 20% of leaders operate out of a Creative mindset, the Development Agenda in most organizations should be to accelerate the development of Creative Leadership, individually and collectively. This is a leadership imperative.

To execute this Development Agenda, senior leaders and HR executives need to lead the way by developing Creative Mind themselves and then by developing it within the organization. For that to happen, we need to understand the nature of Creative Mind, how it is different than Reactive Mind, why it gets a different pattern of results, and how Creative Mind develops—what needs to happen to support its development. The metamorphosis of Reactive Mind into Creative Mind is the major transition in most adults' lives. It is a profound development, and those who make the passage into Creative Mind seldom, if ever, go back.

THE HERO'S JOURNEY

In his book, *Hero With a Thousand Faces*, Joseph Campbell describes this transition as the Hero's Journey (Campbell, 1949). In the Mythic stories of many traditions, the hero goes on a journey in pursuit of a deeper call or aspiration. Usually the kingdom is in peril; the land is in famine, war is rampant, the kingdom is under a spell, and there is much suffering. The hero takes the journey to heal what is broken. At the start of the journey, heroes may not be aware of the relationship between the kingdom's need and their aspiration. They respond to the call of the soul from a deep place of longing without fully understanding why. The movement from the known to the unknown makes no sense. The journey only makes sense at the end, looking back.

Shortly after the heroes cross the "Threshold of Adventure" (code for leaving behind the conventional mind, with all its socialized assumptions and well-worn solutions that are reaching adaptive limits), they get thoroughly trashed—abducted, lost, swallowed by a whale, attacked, dismembered. Mythologically, this is the way of expressing the arduousness of the passage and the reality that the one who starts the journey is not the one who finishes it. The person who starts the journey is too small, too reactive, too full of themselves, too scared, too controlling, too cautious, too protected, too subject to conventional wisdom, and too caught in an unseen play-not-to-lose game to be ready to lead with the necessary uncommon wisdom. The old self, the Socialized, Reactive Self, is too much on autopilot and can only replicate what is, not lead with courage and clarity into a new and thriving future. That self must die. It must come apart and be reconstituted into a new self, one that marches to the beat of a different drummer. What makes this passage so disorienting is that the hero is shedding all the known and familiar ways of knowing that have worked well. The old self is being shed for a new self that has not yet been discovered. It feels like death, and when the hero/heroine goes through this transition, they are not gifted with the certainty that it will all work out. There are no guarantees. There is only the pull of the unknown longing to contribute.

This transition is "Spiritual Boot Camp." It is hard but required if we are to move from the old conventional reality to a new creative reality. The spiritual traditions refer to this process as *Metanoia*—a profound shift of mind, a transformation in the Structure of Mind. The butterfly is the symbol for this transformation. The caterpillar, following some unknown impulse, spins a cocoon, crawls inside, and disintegrates. Halfway through the cocooning process, there is no form, only gelatinous goo. Disintegration precedes integration. Death precedes resurrection. As the butterfly gives itself over to the metamorphosis process, a new, higher-order structure begins to take form. When the transition goes "full circle," the butterfly emerges. No longer limited to crawling, it arises to a winged life. This life is more free, more agile, more fluid, and capable of going farther and faster and doing so from a higher perspective.

In this transition, the tension between purpose and safety is re-optimized. The self that was previously playing-not-to-lose (in a Complying, Protecting, and/or Controlling game) reorients on higher purpose. It orients on the question, "What would you do if you could?" The outside-in identity is traded for an inside-out identity. The Socialized, Reactive self moves from subject (operating unseen) to object (seen and capable of being reflected upon). The emerging Creative Self can now take a perspective on the old Reactive Self, which no longer runs the show on autopilot. It is incorporated and utilized from the higher perspective of the Creative Self. This is the shift from an External Locus of Control to an Internal Locus of Control, from a Dependence to Independence (Covey, 1989), from the Socialized Self to the Self-Authoring Self (Kegan and Lahey, 2009). If it happens, it is often seen, and experienced, as a crisis.

WHAT THE TRANSITION LOOKS LIKE

When we first met Joe, he was the Chief Technology Officer for one of the largest U.S.-based telecommunications companies. It was the morning before the first day of a public workshop. We were in the meeting room preparing for the day. We had arranged the tables and chairs and were writing on the flipchart when we heard the door open. We did not turn around, but continued writing. We heard Joe say in a loud gruff voice, "This room arrangement sucks! I do not think I can find a seat in this room."

We were surprised by his outburst, but continued to work.

You can imagine what Joe's 360° feedback might look like, given the way he entered the room. It showed, among other things, low scores on Creative *Relating* competencies and high scores on Reactive *Controlling* and *Protecting*. His feedback, handed out on the afternoon of the first day, sobered him. He became quiet and reflective.

The next day, we asked the group to write down the results they would commit to create going forward. We looked at Joe and noted that he was not writing anything. He was simply staring at a blank sheet of paper. Our first assumption was that he had checked out of the workshop. However, we noticed that this judgment was our reactivity to him, so we walked up to him and asked, "We notice that you are not writing. Is there anything we can help you with?"

He looked up, aggressively jerked his thumb in the direction of the door and said, "Let's take this outside." We were not sure if he wanted to talk or punch us out.

When we stepped outside the room, he said rather aggressively: "Let me tell you what I got from this workshop. If you want me to write down on that sheet of paper a list of results, that is a no-brainer. I do that every day. But, if you want me to write down what I really want, I don't know. That is what I got from this workshop, and I got it from the 360° feedback and from the stories you told about your own lives."

What he next said is a vintage example of the Socialized, outside-in, Reactive Level Mind in the form of Controlling-Protecting, being seen perhaps for the first time. You can also read, in what he says, the Creative Mind starting to boot up. Joe's next words to us are an example of the vulnerable and courageous inner work that goes on in this transition.

He continued: "When I was a boy, my dad told me to go to college. So I did. When I was in college, they told me that the highest job availability was in engineering, so I became an engineer. No one asked me if I wanted to be an engineer, but I did so. When I started working as an engineer, they told me that I should be a manager, so I became a manager. When I became a manager, they said I was better off if I moved up the ladder, and so I began to climb. Now I sit at the top of a very large organization and I can chase results with the best of them. So, if you want me to write on that sheet of paper a list of results, that is no problem. I do that every day. But, if you want me to write *what I really want*, I don't have a clue. What do I do with this?"

Joe was now looking at us, wide-eyed, like a deer in the headlights, and his eyes were misty as he said, "What do I do with this?" Needless to say, we worked with him to create a supportive plan going forward.

In this story, you can hear Joe describe his Socialized Mind and how it was formed. You can hear him describe the core of his identity, "I can chase results with the best of them," which is code for, "That is who I am. If I am not that, who am I?" Given this self-definition, you can understand the source of his aggressive and autocratic way of leading. It makes perfect sense. You can also see him start to take a perspective on the limitations of his externally defined and driven Reactive Structure of Mind. "I can chase results, but I do not know what I really want." You can hear in the core organizing questions of the Creative Mind. "Who am I if I am not my ability got get results? What do I really want? What would I do if I could?" You can also hear the courage and vulnerability of a leader facing these questions.

This is the Hero/Heroine's Journey. In this story, you can hear the old self disintegrating and the new self that has not yet emerged. This is what makes the transition so scary, a crisis. Joe is messing with the core of the operating system that has brought him the success he has achieved. He is not sure that if he dismantles this way of being it will work out well for him. He does not yet have any experience with the new Creative Mind. He will not know the benefits of Creative Mind for some time. All he has is the question that naturally arises from the Creative Mind to initiate the transformation, "What do I really want?" While Joe does not know where this question will lead, he intuitively knows that this is the right question. Joe does not yet know that this transition is *not* asking him to give up his hard-won capability to get results. He does not yet realize that he is hanging that gift on a Reactive Structure, and that in doing so is limiting the gift and introducing liabilities (evident in his 360° results). Joe has not yet experienced that, in the transition to Creative Mind, you keep your gift and jettison the liabilities. As a result, you get your gift in a higher form. The Creative capacity to achieve far outperforms what can be achieved from his Reactive *Controlling-Protecting* mindset. Joe does not know any of this yet. All he can say is, "What do I do with this?" So he is faced with the courageous choice to go forward on a journey with no guarantees, or to retreat back into his Reactive Mind. That choice will define the future of Joe's leadership.

TALKING ABOUT IT WITHOUT KNOWING IT

The leadership literature has described Creative Leadership for decades, but without the framework of Adult Development. This has limited our ability to understand what it is, what makes the Reactive and Creative Mind so different, and how to support the evolution.

Robert Fritz masterfully described the difference between the Creative and Reactive orientations. However, he did not place each orientation within a vertical development framework. Larry Wilson did the same thing. He described these same two orientations as play-not-to-lose and play-to-win, but did not see these as progressively developing structures of mind. This is true of most of the good leadership theory and research.

In the work that led up to his book, *The Empowered Manager*, Peter Block started out trying to get the bathroom conversation into the meeting room (Block, 1987). In the bathroom, people say how they are really experiencing the meeting. When the meeting reconvenes, everyone agrees that things are going fine. This is usually not the conversation that happened in the bathroom at break. To address this, and to get the truth to appear in the meeting room, Peter began to work on teaching the necessary authentic "political" skills.

As Peter engaged leaders in the skill-practice of telling the truth in meetings, he ran into caution. Peter constantly heard leaders say, "If I stand up, I will get shot." In order to address this cautious, play-not-to-lose game, Peter realized that he needed to help leaders discover a vision or purpose that was bigger than their fear—worth the risk. This led him to challenge leaders with the question of vision: what would you do if you could? These questions (How am I playing not-to-lose? How am I getting in my own way? What do I really want? What would I do if I could? How would I lead if I knew I could not fail or would not be fired?) are key developmental questions for the evolving Creative Mind. If asked frequently and with searing honesty, they reliably boot up the Creative Mind.

Peter was on to something. He and others were describing Creative Mind and how to develop it without seeing or describing the vertical process of development. The Leadership Development field is a random collection of great stuff—models, frameworks and research. Each is useful, but partial. Most of it describes the leadership that emerges at the Creative Mind, without attributing it to a natural, sequential process of development.

In his book, *In Over Our Heads*, Bob Kegan made a game-changing statement. He said that most of the leadership literature describes the kind of leadership that naturally emerges on Creative Mind (Kegan, 1998). The leadership literature and competency research is quite clear in describing effectiveness. Effective leaders are purpose driven and translate their deep sense of purpose into a clear and compelling vision and strategy, which become the focus of execution and decisions. Leaders are systems-aware, redesigning systems to produce higher-order results. They are authentic and courageous in their conversations, lead with integrity, and are self-aware, emotionally intelligent, interpersonally skillful, and relationally competent—fostering high teamwork and trust, as well as mentoring and developing others. Kegan says that such leadership is vintage Creative, Self-Authoring Mind (Kegan and Lahey, 2009). He concluded that these leadership competencies arise naturally on Creative Mind, but do not reliably boot up on Reactive Mind. Our research corroborates Kegan's conclusion.

The leadership literature has described Creative Mind without knowing it. This has led us to approach Leadership Development primarily as an outer game of skill development and ignore the maturity of the inner game. Meanwhile, a well-researched understanding of the process of development, and the vertically sequential structures of mind, was being incubated in the field of Developmental Psychology, outside the mainstream of the Leadership Development field. Stage Development theory needs to move to the center of the Leadership Development conversation. It is at the center of the Leadership Circle Profile and the Universal Model of Leadership.

CREATIVE STRUCTURE

The Reactive Mind creates an oscillating pattern of performance over time, the natural tendency of which is to seek equilibrium and return to normal (Figure 10.3).

The natural tendency of the Reactive Mind is to establish hierarchical, patriarchal structures, dynamics, and cultures. Such organizations do not perform as needed today.

The Creative Mind creates a different pattern of results. In the story of the insurance salesman, we mentioned that he talked about the problem, his disgust with himself, and his swinging into gear, but he never talked about his vision or why he cared about selling. He expressed no overarching passion, which is the heart of the Creative Mind. Creative Mind orients on Purpose. The core of the Creative IOS is a constant focus on a desired future vision, and amid the current reality (with all its mixed messages and hurdles) taking authentic, collaborative action to bring that vision into being over time. Creative Leadership is about creating an organization that we believe in, creating outcomes that

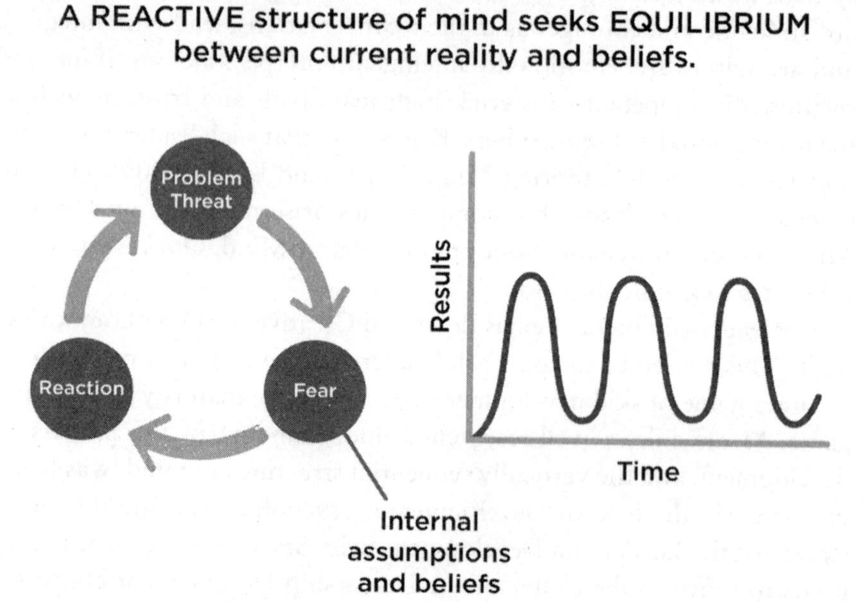

FIGURE 10.3 Reactive Structure of Mind

matter most, and enhancing our collective capacity to create a desired future. It is designed for change, to bring into being what is envisioned (Figure 10.4).

The Creative Mind starts from purpose and vision, not with a problem. There are plenty of problems to deal with as we create the futures we want, but the driving focus is on creating a vision that we care about, a vision worthy of our deepest commitment. Not any vision will do. If it does not matter, it generates no energy. The energy that fuels the Creative Mind is passion. Love is not too strong a word.

While fear is naturally present when creating what we want (the spark behind fear), fear is not running the show. The focus on purpose and vision generates a passion, love, and commitment that is bigger than the fear. Love is superordinate to fear. It is more powerful, and, thus, Creative Structure supersedes the Reactive play-not-to-lose game.

The focus on vision, fueled by passion, results in action, not reaction. In Creative Structure, we do not take action to eliminate what we do not want. Nor is action a reaction to fear—trying to attenuate it. In the Creative Mind we do not react, but we act to bring into being what we

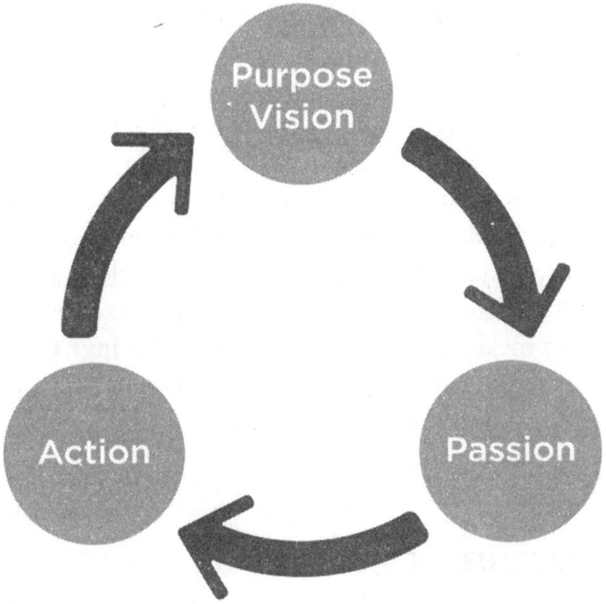

FIGURE 10.4 Creative Structure of Mind

most care about. This mind structure is fundamentally different from Reactive Mind and gets a different pattern of performance over time.

The Creative Structure is not a balancing loop. It does not seek equilibrium or have a natural tendency to oscillate. In System Dynamics language, the Creative Structure is a growth loop—each time you cycle through the loop, it grows (Figure 10.5).

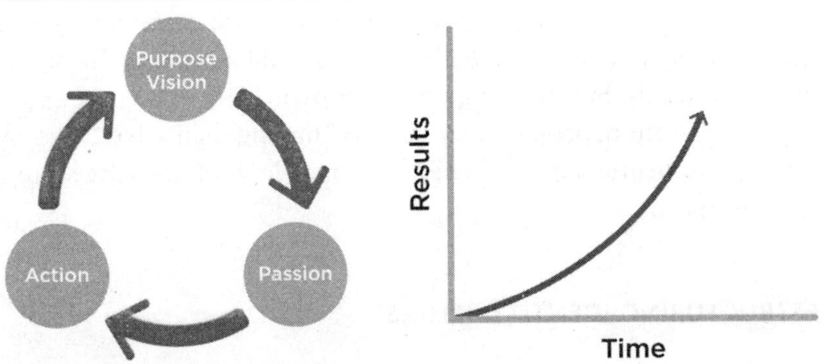

FIGURE 10.5 The Creative growth loop

As we get clearer about our purpose and translate that into a clear picture of the future we want, passion naturally grows. As passion grows, the tendency to take the action necessary to creating our desired future also grows. As we take action to create what we want, we either get closer to our vision or clearer about it. Then our passion grows again (or stays high). As passion grows, the tendency to take additional action also grows, which takes us farther in the direction of our vision. This is a virtuous growth cycle. Each time through the cycle, it grows and funds future growth (unlike the Reactive Mind, where each time through the loop, it reverses the direction of results, thus oscillating). Creative Mind is designed to seek vision, not equilibrium. It is designed for the complexity of leading change and creating new futures. It is the minimum system requirement for mastering leadership.

CREATIVE STRUCTURE OF IDENTITY

The Creative Structure is inside-out. It marches to the beat of a different drummer. It is not driven by what we are socialized to think is in our best interest. We live and lead from our own internally discerned sense of purpose, values, and vision. This is why Kegan calls it *Self-Authoring* (Kegan and Lahey, 2009), Covey calls it *Independent* (Covey, 1989), and Susanne Cook-Greuter calls it *Individualist* (Cook-Greuter, 2004). We call it *Creative* because it is designed to create what matters most.

In the transition to the Creative Self, we experience a shift from an externally based identity that is dependent on outside validation to an internally based identity. In this identity, we do not base our self-esteem, worth, and security on how others see us. Our self-esteem, worth, and security are in our own hands. We establish them, not by living up to others' standards, but by living up to our own.

In this transition, people often refer to "finding themselves," discovering their "authentic self," and enjoying a new level of inner freedom and creative capacity.

RESTRUCTURING IDENTITY BELIEFS

The new level of creative capacity that comes with this transition results from a rewriting of the IOS code. Reactive beliefs are structured and depend on outside validation: "I am okay if you like me, accept me, see me as smart, or as the one who is in control and gets results. If I am not that, who am I?" These beliefs can be structured to Comply, Protect, or Control, depending on how we have organized our character/ego structure, with what core strengths/gifts we are identified—heart, head, or will.

At the Creative Stage, these assumptions are not running on autopilot. We are not subject to them. We can intervene and challenge them when the fear that they produce hits our bodies. Instead of reacting to the fear as if it is real, we think: "I know this is when I always go into fear and say to myself, 'If I stand up, I will be shot,' but, now I know that voice of fear in me like an old familiar friend. I now know that this fear comes from the illusion that my future is in your hands and, thus, I constantly need you to like me and think highly of me, or else. I now know that this is not the truth."

This ability to, in the moment, gain perspective on the old Reactive assumptions and to challenge their illusions is one hallmark of the Creative Mind. It is now running the show. It is managing the limitations that come with hanging our gifts on a Reactive Structure.

As this perspective-taking and challenging process unfolds, we develop new assumptions that are structured from the inside-out, not dependent on outside validation. The belief that "my future is in your hands" is replaced with "I am responsible for, and capable of, creating my own future." The belief that "I am okay only if you always like or admire me" is replaced with "I am okay whether or not you like and admire me." The belief that "to be is to be successful and, thus, failure is not an option" is replaced with "I create results; I am not my results. Failure and mistakes are part of the process of creating success." As we see, challenge, and rewrite earlier Reactive assumptions, we upgrade the Reactive IOS into a Creative Level IOS. Consciousness is the operating system of performance. Since structure determines performance, and since consciousness is the deep structure of performance, this restructuring process transforms how we lead and live.

Rob's story (from Chapter 3) has all the elements of this restructuring process, as well as the corresponding shifts in performance that come with it. Rob was the manager that we called two years after debriefing his LCP with him. What Rob said to us illustrates this shift of mind, the ability to take a perspective on the old Reactive IOS, the ability to intervene and challenge the old assumptions when they reassert themselves, and the presence of new assumptions that do not depend on outside validation.

As you recall, Rob's 360° feedback clearly indicated that he was a strong Controlling-Protecting type. He described himself as "The Ogre." He told us that *if he had not changed, he would have failed.* Listen to what the transformation from Reactive to Creative sounds like.

> When I returned to the office, I did a lot of soul searching and observing of myself. I saw more clearly all the stuff that we had talked about. I realized that I am hard-wired for results. I care about people, but when problems erupt, I explode and take over. I am constantly worried about what others will think if we fall short of expectations. Fear of failure runs me. I measure myself by always succeeding. So, when problems hit the fan, I become the Ogre!
>
> About six months ago, I received a promotion. I am now in charge of all supply-side management for the start-up of our new plant in another country. I could not have been successful here had I not changed. This is a different culture. It is very relational. People hug each other when they come into work. They look each other in the eye when they say hello. Had I led the way I used to lead, it would have been game over.
>
> What is even more amazing is that it would be okay with me if I am not the guy. If I fail here, I will be okay. It would not be the end of the world. Consequently, when problems come up, I can deal with them. Instead of blowing up, blaming people, and taking over, I work with and through the team. I am direct and firm, but in a way that builds accountability, trust, relationship, and teamwork.
>
> Sure, I still feel the urge to blow up. I feel that fireball erupt in my chest, but now I manage it—it does not manage me. I am not as defined by my results now, and that enables me to be more effective at achieving them.

Rob then told us that before he worked for his current company he worked for another company in Detroit. He told us how painful it was to live though the downturn in the industry, the closing of plants, and the impact of all of that on people and their families. Rob began to cry as he said: "Now I can have a positive impact in another community. I am becoming the leader I have always dreamed I could be. I am a much happier person."

In this story, you can hear Rob's ability to take a perspective on his earlier IOS. He finds humor in how he was subject to it. It took him over and he became the Ogre. You can hear his insight into the structure of his socialized mind. He describes himself as having been hardwired for results, convinced that failure was not an option, in constant worry about what others would think if results were off, etc. He is no longer subject to these assumptions. He has them. They do not have him. He can intervene when they reassert themselves. He has learned to manage the fear and the "fireball" of anger that comes up in him when these assumptions are triggered.

In this story, you can also hear the presence of the newly written Creative code. The new Creative level assumptions are evidenced when he says: "And what is even more amazing is that it would actually be okay with me if I am not the guy. If I fail here, I will be okay. It would not be the end of the world." Here he is describing that he is no longer as dependent on outside validation. He is responsible for this and is managing it.

Finally, in this story you can hear that he has shifted from a fear driven, problem focus to a vision focus. "Now I have the opportunity to have the opposite, positive impact in another community. I am finally becoming the leader I always knew I could be." This focus on vision and his ability to manage his fear and anger puts Rob more consistently in the Creative growth loop. This is the structure that is now determining his performance.

Rob is experiencing a restructuring of mind and identity and re-optimizing the tension between purpose and safety. Thus, he is less subject to the oscillations of the Reactive Mind. Purpose and vision are now leading, and he is managing his Reactive Tendencies. He has not lost his gift of getting results. He keeps his gift and jettisons the liabilities that come with identifying with those gifts (hanging them on a Reactive Structure). He is getting his gifts and strengths in a higher, more effective form. He is now capable of meeting the adaptive challenge presented by the plant start-up in a foreign culture, in a way that works. He will never go back to his earlier Reactive mindset.

DESIGNED FOR LEADING CHANGE

The Leadership literature has been describing the leadership capabilities that naturally arise on the Creative Structure of Mind and the kind of effectiveness and business performance that go with it. Where the Leadership field has missed the point is not noticing the structure of the IOS that enables such high performance.

Figure 10.6 describes Rob's shift. It shows the relationship between Levels of Mind, Structures of Mind, and the patterns of performance associated with those structures. From this diagram, we clearly see why Creative Mind is more adapted to lead.

Once people experience the new capability and freedom of the Creative Self, very few regress to an earlier stage because the Creative Self is far more adapted for the challenges of adult life. It is far more capable of leading amid escalating complexity. It can create desired results much more effectively and with lower energetic cost.

The developmental challenge, as we move from adolescence into the Reactive Mind, is to merge with the current culture, to take on its mental models about how things work, and to define our self in a way that will succeed within the current culture and system. The developmental

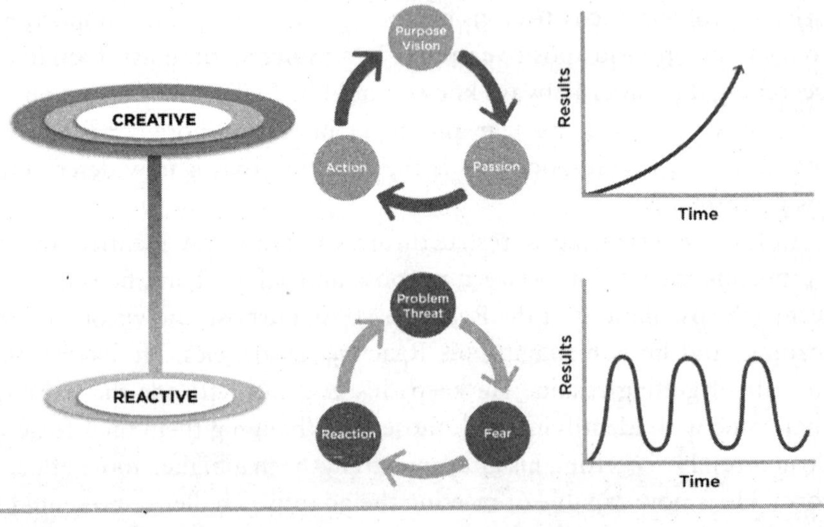

FIGURE 10.6 Two Structures of Mind and Leadership

challenge is to develop an outside-in operating system. As such, it is designed to perpetuate current reality, not change it.

Because the Creative Mind is not governed by the dictates of the surrounding environment, it is free to change it. The developmental challenge in the transition to Creative Mind is to individuate from the Socialized Mind—to become our authentic self (inside-out) amid current realities and, thus, become the envisioned change. Creative IOS is inside-out precisely because we discern, out of all the environmental messages, what we stand for. This internally constructed self is not dependent on outside validation. It is, by design, focused on a vision of a desired future that matters. As such, it is free to lead in ways that create a new, more agile, innovative, creative, empowered, and high-performing culture while bringing the best of the old culture forward. In changing from the old to the new, when old Reactive Tendencies reassert themselves, individually and collectively, and create a force for going back to normal, Creative leaders now have the inner resources to manage these Reactive Tendencies and stay the course. This is why the Creative Structure of Mind is designed to lead and sustain change.

CREATIVE MIND AND PERFORMANCE

Not only is Creative Mind designed to lead change, but it is highly effective. The circular diagram below shows the correlation of every dimension on the LCP and in the Universal Model of Leadership to Leadership Effectiveness. Much can be learned from this diagram about the Universal Model and about what helps or hinders effective leadership. All the key Creative Competencies that naturally arise on the Creative IOS and do not boot up well on Reactive IOS are strongly and positively correlated to Leadership Effectiveness. Reactive dimensions are mostly inverse. Draw your own conclusions (Figure 10.7).

Note that the two most highly correlated dimensions to Leadership Effectiveness in the outer circle are the dimensions of *Purposeful Visionary* (.91) and *Teamwork* (.89). These are the two strongest correlations in the 29 dimensions that make up the outer circle of the LCP. When these two variables are plugged into a multivariate regression equation, their combined correlation to Leadership Effectiveness is .94. No other combination of variables in the outer circle explains so much of what it

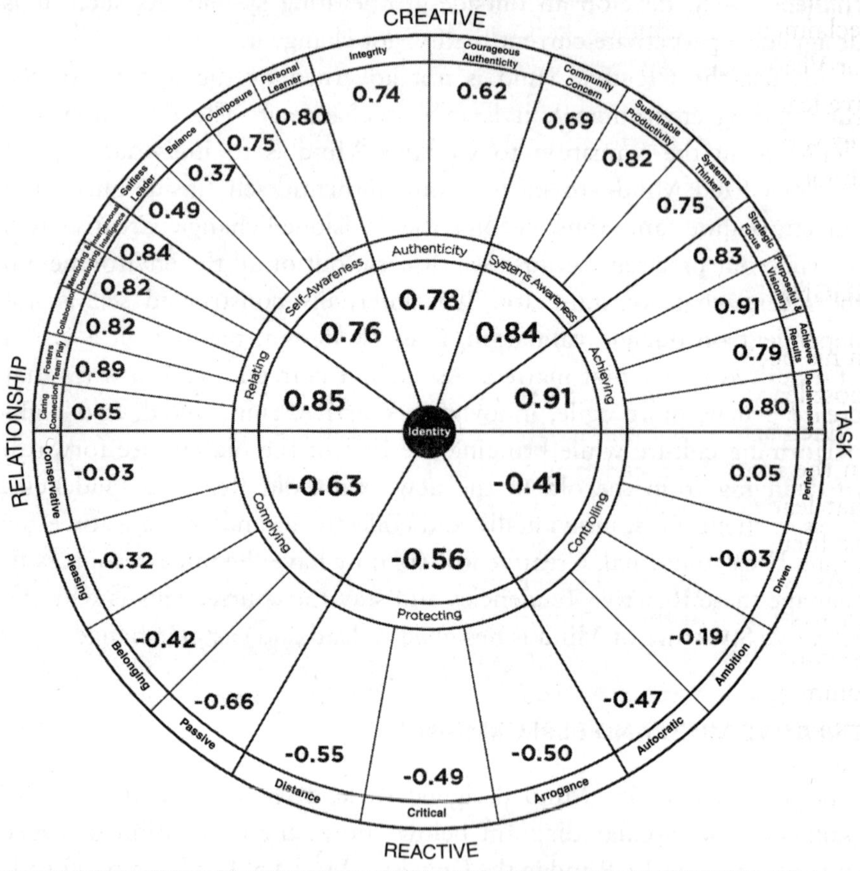

FIGURE 10.7 Correlations to Leadership Effectiveness

takes to be an effective leader. If you lead from a deep sense of purpose, translate that into clear vision, and build alignment among key stakeholders (teamwork) in the realization of that vision, you are highly likely (.94 correlation) to be an effective leader.

Also, these two dimensions are on opposite sides of the circle. As found in the Ohio State Leadership Studies in the 1950s, the development and balancing of Task and Relationship capability are fundamental to effectiveness. *Purposeful Visionary* is task focused. Vision is the driver of task accomplishment in the *Creative Achieving* Structure of Mind. Achieving is *power with* not *power over*. Achieving builds alignment in order to accomplish vision. Likewise, when *Complying* evolves into *Relating*, it naturally develops teamwork and high alignment. The power that is reclaimed as Complying shifts to Relating is put in service of advocacy for Vision. Consequently, if you do nothing else to become a more effective leader, work toward building high alignment and teamwork among key stakeholders by focusing them on a vision that they collectively care about.

ALIGNMENT

In his book, *The Fifth Discipline*, Peter Senge describes the condition of most leadership teams with the image in Figure 10.8 (Senge, 1990).

Each arrow (within the larger arrow) symbolizes an individual leader on the Extended Leadership Team. The length of the arrow represents that leader's personal power and the direction of the arrow represents the focus of that leader's activity and impact.

As we can see, the organization will make forward progress as all arrows point to the right. However, the sum of the vectors is not very potent. There is much wasted energy going into misalignment. This common condition of leadership teams led Senge to make his infamous statement that "the collective intelligence of most teams is beneath the average intelligence of its members." The level of collective effectiveness in this group is simply not high enough to result in the collective intelligence being higher than the average intelligence. This leadership team is likely to be caught in a host of Reactive dynamics that undermine its effectiveness. Patrick Lencioni says much about this in his book, *The Five Dysfunctions of a Team* (Lencioni, 2002). These Reactive

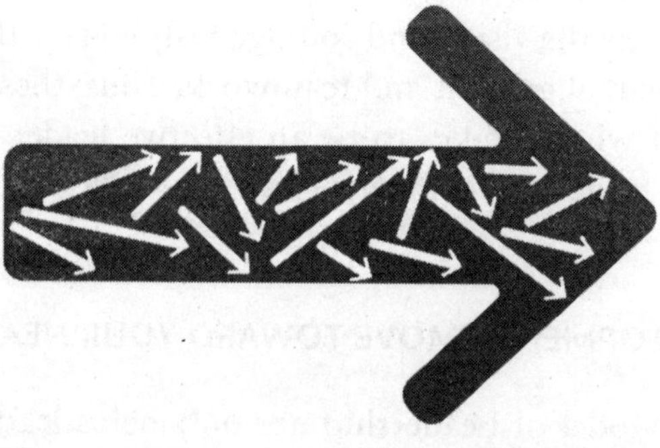

FIGURE 10.8 The condition of most leadership teams

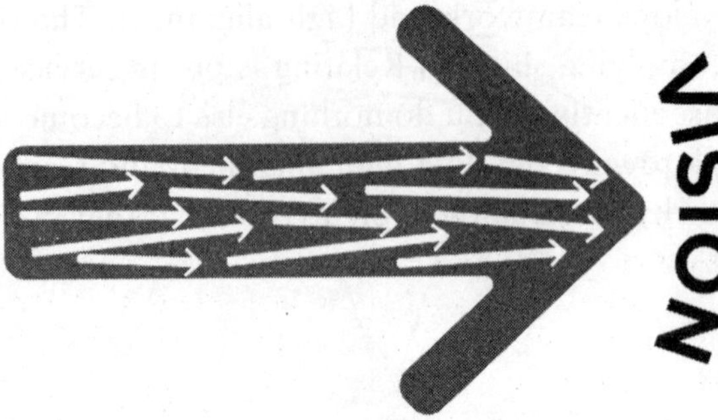

FIGURE 10.9 Alignment

Tendencies lower the Leadership Quotient to less than one—a competitive disadvantage.

Senge was also clear, from his experience consulting to Senior Leadership Teams, that the fastest way to move a group into alignment is to get them focused on a vision that they collectively care about. When members of the team can see that they can pursue their personal purposes by achieving the organization's vision, they fall into alignment. This condition is represented in Figure 10.9.

Any leader receiving LCP feedback should ask two simple questions: How is the combination of my Creative Competencies and Reactive Tendencies contributing to my standing clearly for a vision of greatness for the organization? How is my combination of Creative Competencies and Reactive Tendencies serving to support, or undermine, building alignment among key stakeholders toward that vision?

Addressing these two questions could clarify how a leader might become more effective and boot up Creative Mind, since the heart of the Creative Structure is purpose and vision as well as the authenticity required to embody the vision and courageously engage the conversation that results in high alignment and teamwork. Thus, these two variables explain more of what it takes to be an effective leader than any other combination of leadership competencies.

PATH OF DEVELOPMENT—MOVE TOWARD YOUR NEAR ENEMY

The Universal Model of Leadership not only helps leaders gain breakthrough insight, it also points out the direction of development. In this

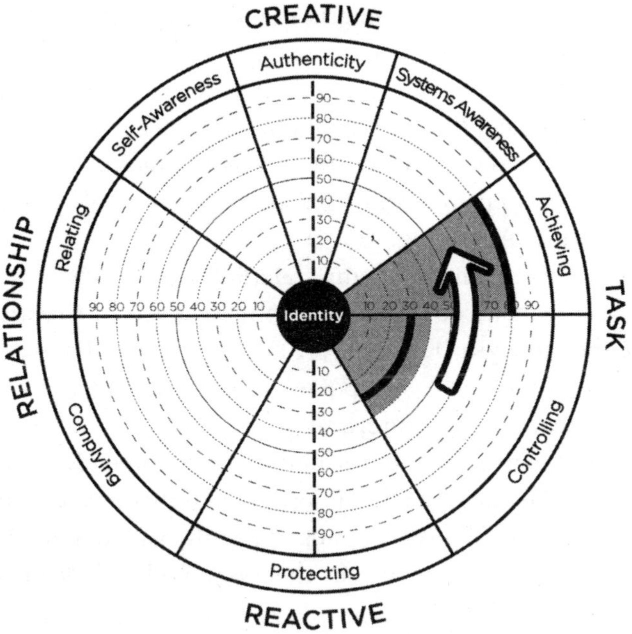

FIGURE 10.10 Controlling's path of development

model, the Path of Development into Creative Mind is to mature your core gift—to leverage the strengths that are hung on a Reactive Structure. This focus of development is counterintuitive and runs opposite to how we usually attempt to improve our leadership.

In the East there is a teaching story that goes: "It is not the enemy out there that you most need to fear. That enemy you are prepared for, you have counted their numbers, you have built your defenses, and you have studied their tactics. The enemy you most need to fear is the *Near Enemy*, the one in your own camp, the one that you think is working for you, but is not in the way that you think. That is the enemy you most need to fear."

In the Universal Model, *near enemies* are next to each other. For example, the near enemy of *Achieving* is *Controlling* (Figure 10.10). If you ask high *Controlling* managers why they need to be so controlling, they say that they do it to get results. Yet Controlling is inverse to results as measured by Achieving (–.24). While this is not a strong correlation (because Controlling and Achieving share the gift of driving for results), it is inverse.

This suggests that Controlling is not working for you the way you think it is. Controlling works against results and undermines its own gift. Controlling is the near enemy of Achieving. Achieving out-performs Controlling as evident from Controlling's inverse correlations to Leadership Effectiveness (–.41) and Business Performance (–.21) and Achieving's high correlations to both (.91 and .61, respectively). Controlling is the near enemy of Achieving.

Counterintuitively, near enemy relationships provide the optimal direction of a leader's development from Reactive to Creative because they share the same gift (Figure 10.10). The gift of both Controlling and Achieving is the will, or use of power, to get results. Controlling hangs this gift on a Reactive Structure, and this creates liabilities. Since the Will type is all about getting results, the natural direction of development is to keep the gift and jettison the liabilities. In the transformation from Reactive to Creative, the Will type is most naturally suited and open to shift from Controlling to Achieving. In this way, Will type leaders leverage their core strengths.

The same is true of the relationship between Relating and Complying (Figure 10.11). If you ask a Complying type why they comply, they will talk about creating harmony and teamwork. They do it, in part, to preserve relationship. However, Complying is solidly inverse to relationship, as measured by Relating (–.44). Complying actually undermines its core gift. It works against relationship. Complying is the near enemy of Relating. Relating outperforms Complying, as can be seen from Complying's inverse correlations to Leadership Effectiveness (–.63) and Business Performance (–.40) and Relating's high correlations to both (.85 and .50, respectively). Complying is the near enemy of Relating.

Finally, the same "near enemy" analysis can be made of the relationship of Protecting to the Awareness dimensions above it in the circle (Figure 10.12). Protecting is rationally gifted. It seeks to know. In its Reactive form, it uses its knowing brilliance to prop up its self-esteem, put others down, and place itself above others. In so doing, it undermines its own gift. The off-putting style of the Protector limits the transfer of knowledge and wisdom that is the Protecting type's core gift. These gifts come into full form as Self-Awareness, Authenticity, and Systems-Awareness. The correlations bear this out. Protecting is inverse to Self-Awareness (–.74), Authenticity (–.38), and Systems-Awareness (–.51) while each of these is highly correlated to Leadership Effectiveness (.76, .78, .84, respectively)

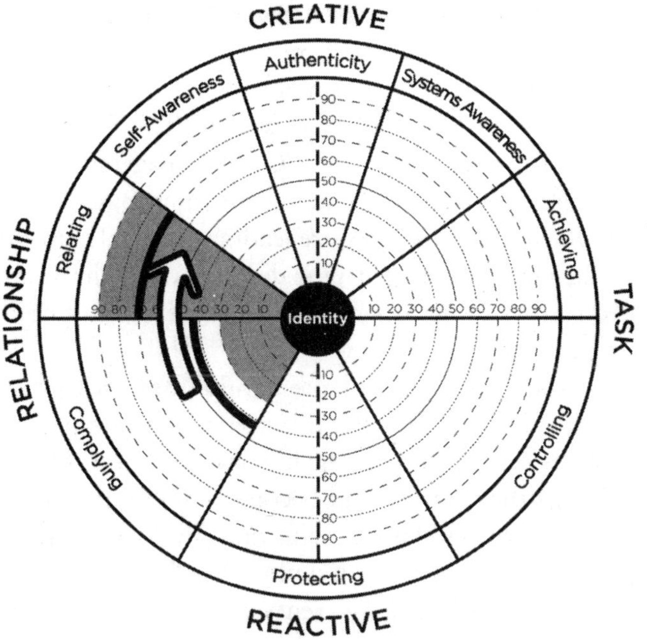

FIGURE 10.11 Complying's path of development

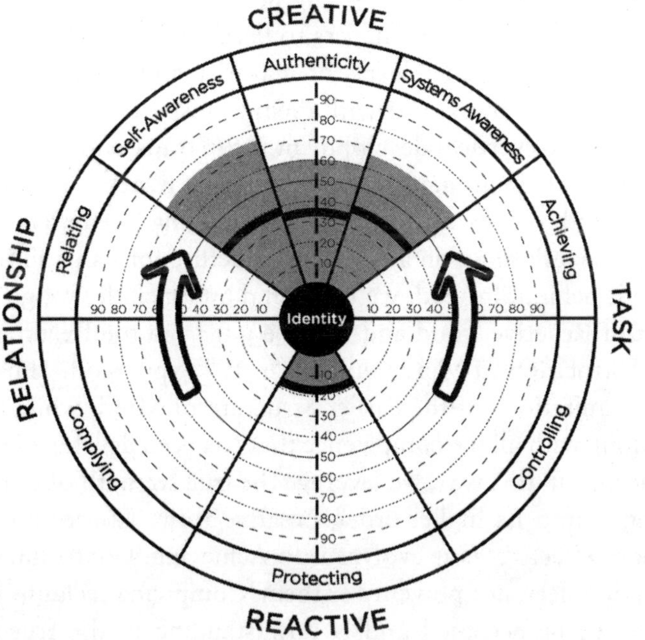

FIGURE 10.12 Protecting's path of development

and Business Performance (.48, .50, .57, respectively). The near enemy of Awareness and Authenticity is Protecting.

In the Universal Model, the optimal path of development is to move toward the near enemy and leverage its gift. The first move is to get insight into the Reactive near enemy. Once managers gain deep insight into how they are leading, what they want to change, and the identity beliefs that influence the way they are leading, the circle also suggests the direction of their development. This is depicted through the layout of the circle. The direction of development is to move directly up, more than up and across, the circle.

This is important because it is more natural for a Heart type Complying person to focus on developing the strength of Complying. Complying then matures into Relating, which is more natural than asking that person to change their nature and become a Will type Achiever. When Complying evolves into Relating, Achieving develops nicely. When Controlling evolves into Achieving, Relating develops as well. When Protecting evolves into Authentic Awareness, Achieving and Relating come along with it.

This converts The Leadership Circle into a powerful development system. It works with a manager's strength, even when it is being reactively over-used. It does not ask managers to become different, but to develop their strengths into higher levels of maturity and mastery. It does not ignore weaknesses, but works with them to foster deeper insight.

The promise of vertical development is to "transcend and include." In development, we do not ignore the liabilities of Reactive styles as is popular today with our over-emphasis on leveraging strengths. Nor do we reject the strength hung on a Reactive Structure for its liabilities. We do not leave it behind. Instead, we transcend and include; we go right into the heart of Reactive Mind and free the gift from the Reactive assumptions and Structures of Mind that limit its full expression. Thus, we transcend the limitations of the earlier Structure of Mind, while harvesting the gift along with all the competence that has been developed in learning to use the gift. In this way, we leverage the true strength of our core type and bring it into its higher-order Creative form. Controlling becomes much more effective as it evolves into Achieving. Controlling becomes power with others, not power over them. Complying reclaims the power it gave up to be accepted and is now standing in the true power of Relating. As such, it is much more effective than Complying. Protecting harvests its rational strengths and becomes highly Self-Aware, Authentic, and Systems-Aware. Each type, as it transforms from Reactive to Creative, gets its core strength in a higher-order form. The correlations in the Inner Circle Table substantiate this, as do the correlations to Leadership Effectiveness and Business Performance.

TYPE THROUGH STAGE

The Universal Model of Leadership can be summarized as a Type through Stage Model: three core types (Heart, Head, Will) evolving through sequential Stages of Development (Reactive, Creative, Integral, Unitive). This model does not ask leaders to change their type—their core nature—it encourages leaders to evolve that essential nature into higher-order Structures of Mind. With each evolution in the Structure of Mind, leaders leverage their core strengths and gifts while jettisoning the liabilities of the earlier Structure of Mind. In so doing, they become more effective even as life gets more complex.

The Universal Model describes the differences between the core types at each level of development, how these types relate to each other, and, thereby, establish relational, team, and cultural dynamics that can hinder (at Reactive) or support (at Creative and higher) teams and organizations in effectively creating the future to which they aspire. The model is designed to provide developmental insight and to point out the direction of optimal development. Since it does this individually and collectively, it is very useful in developing the individual and collective effectiveness and intelligence required for high performance.

CREATIVE ORGANIZATIONS

The design of systems, structures, and cultures have their origins in the structures of consciousness that create them. The cultures and structures that most organizations are moving toward are Creative Structures. They are thus designed, led, and sustained by leaders functioning out of a Creative Mind. The natural tendency of Reactive Mind is to create and recreate patriarchal and overly hierarchical organizations. Creative Mind tends to establish systems, structures, and cultures that are creatively unique and different. These change efforts have many different labels—lean, agile, adaptable, fast, innovative, flexible, empowered, involving, inclusive, participative, engaging, self-managed, intrapreneurial, creative, fluid, flat, purpose-driven, visionary, and so on. We are moving to these types of organizations because the worldwide leadership experience strongly suggests that they can better compete in today's environment of constant change and escalating complexity.

Creative Mind is more adapted to lead this kind of change. Reactive Mind too readily defaults to old patterns of leadership. Reactive Mind is not mature enough to lead change into a Creative organization design. This requires Creative Level Mind or higher.

INTEGRATION

Figure 10.13 summarizes the transition from Reactive to Creative. It shows how identity shifts from outside-in to inside-out as the tension between purpose and safety is re-optimized by a choice to live and lead from purpose and accept the inherent risk that leading entails. The game changes from playing-not-to-lose to playing-on-purpose.

The diagram also shows how this identity shift changes the Structure of Mind from one designed to oscillate and return to normal (instituting and re-instituting current reality both individually and collectively) to one designed to create new vision.

Because Creative Leadership is designed for change, it is the first level of leadership adapted for leading toward a more Creative culture. It does this more effectively, efficiently, and with far less energetic cost individually and organizationally. Because Creative Leadership is designed to create an equilibrium between current reality and vision, it can create and sustain shifts in culture and business performance (not returning to the normal of the old culture and starting over with a new flavor of the month).

Such Creative Leadership is what the literature has been describing in various ways with lots of good models and research. What the leadership literature has largely missed is that this kind of leadership requires a shift of mind. The literature, until very recently, has not understood leadership from a developmental perspective. Developmental Psychology has much to add to our understanding of what makes for effective leadership and how it develops. Understanding the development of leadership effectiveness as a heroic journey of transformation through an invariant sequence of Stages and Structures of Mind has the potential to greatly

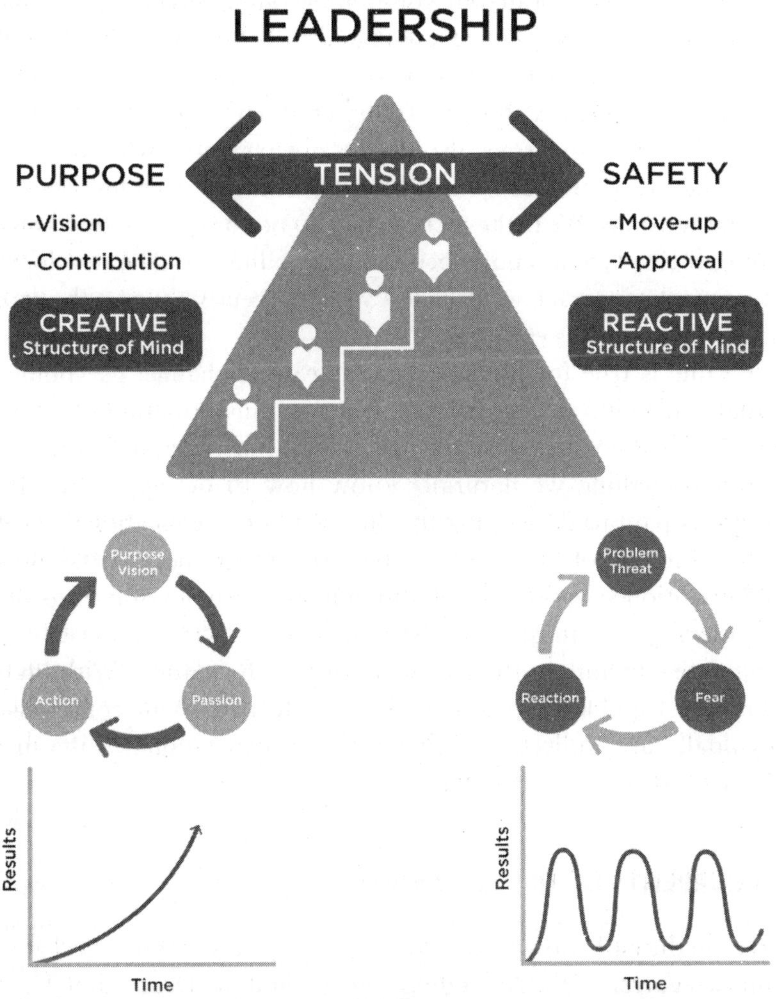

FIGURE 10.13 The transition from Reactive to Creative

accelerate the pace at which we can develop leaders for a future so greatly in need of both wise and effective leadership.

LITERACY IN THE PATHWAYS OF TRANSFORMATION

Most leaders lack literacy when it comes to effecting inner—personal and cultural—transformation. Lack of literacy does not mean lack of intelligence or competence; it means we don't know what we don't know.

As parents, we celebrate our children becoming literate in our native language. First, they recognize letters and then learn the sounds of each letter. Letters become words and words become sentences, which in turn become paragraphs and books. Young children do not know they are illiterate, but they are. They also do not always know why they should become literate. From our view as parents, we know what literacy means and what it brings. We make it clear they do not have an option and that claiming their place in adult society requires literacy. The development of literacy takes years if not decades. So we fervently support the process because we know it is essential.

The same is true for literacy regarding inner change: psychological, spiritual, and cultural. This is literacy in the transformation of the Inner Game. It is literacy in soul-work. We are not born literate in soul-work. It is not something we naturally know how to develop. Little to no attention is paid to developing this literacy in our educational systems. The development of inner literacy requires intentional efforts and sustained attention supported by skillful guidance. To develop transformative leadership, we must be transformed. As leaders, we must become soul-literate—literate in the pathways of transformation. With literacy, we become capable of pursuing the transformation in consciousness (individually and collectively) that makes organizational shifts in performance possible and sustainable.

TWO CURRENTS OF TRANSFORMATION

Literacy in the pathways of transformation requires that we excel at navigating two currents: the Ascending Current and the Descending Current (see Figure 10.14). Learning to navigate the Ascending Current means orienting our life and leadership on our highest aspirations. It means giving ourselves over to the purpose that wants to have its way in our lives. The soul is a jealous lover. It refuses to invest itself in a compromise. We either move toward the spark of our longing, turning it into vision after vision, or the body fills with dense smoke. This discipline of stalking our longing—our purpose and our highest aspirations—is literacy in navigating the Ascending Current.

Navigating the Ascending Current is only possible if we can also navigate the Descending Current. The pursuit of purpose brings us face-to-face with the ways we are playing-not-to-lose. Literacy in navigating

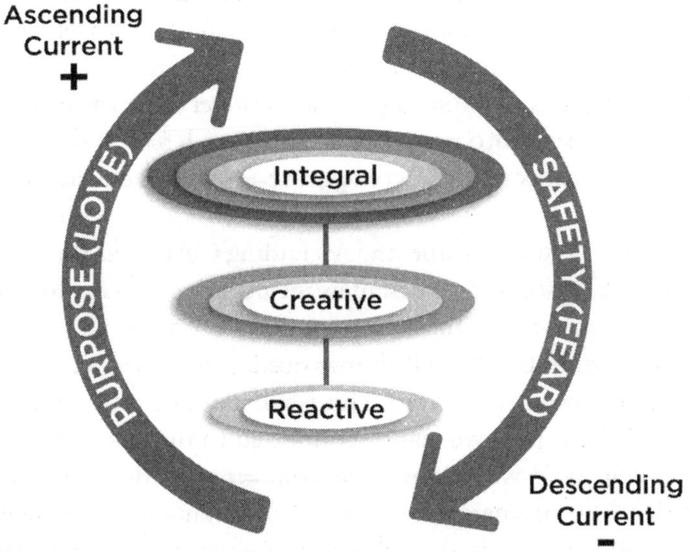

FIGURE 10.14 Two currents of transformation

the Descending Current means facing our fears head-on, becoming a student of our fears by descending into them. Ken Wilber calls this current "descent in service of transcendence." Transformation requires that we see the illusory beliefs at the core of our fears. As we descend into our doubts and fears, we see that they are not what we thought they were. We see that the old self is too small for the purpose and vision that want to come through. We also discover that there is a much larger self that is fully capable of creating the future to which we aspire.

The Two Currents of Transformation are built into the Universal Model. The Ascending Current leads from the Reactive bottom half of the circle to the Creative top half of the circle. The Creative half of the circle is oriented on Purpose and Vision, the heart of the Growth Loop Structure of Creative Mind. This purposeful orientation is the ascending pull of our highest aspirations. As we navigate this current, we come into the fullness of our authenticity, the centerpiece of Self-Authoring development. We also become more self-aware, emotionally intelligent, relationally competent, and systemically wise. We become that to which we aspire. As Rob indicated, we finally become the kind of leader we always knew we could be. This is the Ascending Current that is built into the Model.

The Descending Current leads from the Creative top half of the circle into the Reactive bottom half of the circle. As we step up to new possibilities for our leadership and orient on a vision of greater contribution, we face parts of ourselves that are not yet up to the challenge. We then have to descend into the parts of ourselves left in Reactivity. As we transform these aspects, we become more powerful, effective, and wise leaders.

In Figure 10.14, we also label the Ascending Current as the positive (+) current and the Descending Current as the negative (−) current. Electrical circuits are composed of these two currents (and the neutral ground). In order for energy to flow, all that is needed is to connect the positive current with the negative current. This is what happens when you turn on a light switch—the positive lead is connected to the negative lead. Work happens when the positive energy is connected to the negative energy. To stop the flow of energy, to turn off the lights, or stop work from happening, all you have to do is disconnect either the positive lead or the negative lead.

Metaphorically, if we disconnect from the Ascending Current of our highest aspirations, the passionate, generative energy stops flowing. If we disconnect from the negative current, of descent in service of transcendence, we block the flow of our lives and live in an illusion that is too small for the purpose that is trying to come through us. Disconnect from either the spark or the fear and the body fills with dense smoke. Navigating transformation requires mastery with both currents.

This is the transformative process. We are pulled into transformation by the call to become more, to create a vision of the future that is consistent with our highest values and aspirations. That call is always in a relationship with greater organizational or societal need for change. We are called to a vision of service. As we move toward that purpose and vision, we inevitably face the limitations within us. If not faced and transformed, these limitations cause us to hold back, play small, and remain stuck in Reactive strategies that are incapable of authoring the future we want. To become the person/leader who can act on the vision in every encounter, we must face the parts of our self that are too small, too scared, too controlling, too protected, too compliant, and too caught up in playing not-to-lose. If we do not face this person, we will return to normal and compromise our vision.

The old self must be dismembered and disintegrated so that a higher level of integration and structure can emerge. The practice of seeing the illusion in our fears and facing the truth about the false nature of our Reactive identity is an acquired taste. It is not for the faint of heart. Developing literacy in these two currents of transformation is truly a hero/heroine's Journey. This heroic transformative journey happens when we give ourselves over to the pull of purpose and ride the Descending Current down to where we see the illusion of our Reactive Self. The process of descent enables us to rewrite our Reactive code and empower ourselves for the realization of our purposeful vision.

The Biblical Hero's Journey story of *Jonah* describes this process precisely. Jonah is walking along the beach one day, minding his own business, when God says to him: "Jonah, I want you to be a leader. I want you to be my prophet to Nineveh."

Jonah tries to deflect the request: "My calendar is a little busy. Sorry, can't make it."

God repeats the request more insistently.

Jonah responds with: "Are you kidding me? If I go to Nineveh and speak for you, they will hand me my head." This is the corporate equivalent of, "If I stand up, I will get shot."

God scratches His head, and then decides that Jonah's leadership is less evolved than He thought. God concludes that Jonah is in need of some serious leadership development. And so, a whale rises from the ocean and swallows him.

Jonah is now riding the Descending Current. He has to go into the deep and the dark to find his light. Jonah probably does not know this. All he knows is that he is stewing in a lot of digestive juice. And this is the perfect metaphor. The old self—the self that is too small, scared and Reactive to lead—must be digested. That self must come apart, and its nutrients made available for forming the new, higher-order self. Jonah is now like the butterfly in the cocoon, becoming the goo out of which the butterfly emerges.

We are not sure what happens for Jonah in the belly of the whale, but we suggest that he is riding both currents of transformation. Goethe wrote a poem called *The Holy Longing* (Bly, 1980) about this very transformative process. As you read Goethe's poem, notice his facility with the two currents of transformation.

The Holy Longing

Tell a wise person, or else keep silent,
because the mass man will mock it right away.
I praise what is truly alive,
what longs to be burned to death.
In the calm water of the love-nights,
where you were begotten, where you have begotten,
a strange feeling comes over you,
as you watch the silent candle burning.
Now you are no longer caught in the obsession with darkness,
and a desire for higher love-making sweeps you upward.
Distance does not make you falter.
Now, arriving in magic, flying,
and finally, insane for the light,
you are the butterfly and you are gone.
And so long as you haven't experienced this: to die and so to grow,
you are only a troubled guest on the dark earth.

Conscious evolution is a disintegration–reintegration process—a death to the self you currently are to enable a higher self to emerge. The wisdom traditions are clear about this, and much is at stake if we resist the journey. Describing the spark behind fear, David Whyte says, "If the spark remains unlit, the body fills with dense smoke." Goethe puts it even more starkly: "And so long as you have not experienced this: to die and so to grow,/you are only a troubled guest on the dark earth."

Great leadership is more than mere effectiveness. It is mastery; it is a higher level of lucidity, maturity, and consciousness. It is wise, ethical, visionary, compassionate, and courageous. The evolutionary journey of conscious leadership is how we become leaders that can make a positive difference to the future. The world is desperate for great leadership, and great leadership is only possible by taking the journey into higher-order consciousness. As we develop mastery in navigating the two currents of transformation, we orient on the purpose for which we were born and leave that as the legacy of our life and leadership. We also meet our own limits and transform them into elements of the new, higher-order self that is ever more capable of fulfilling the Promise of Leadership.

TAKING STOCK

- Doesn't everything die at last and too soon? Tell me, what is it you plan to do with your one wild and precious life (Mary Oliver, 1990)?
- What's worthy of your life's blood?
- What must you be about with your life, else you are living someone else's life?
- What would be lost in the world if you were to deny your purpose?
- What would you do if you could? If you knew you could not fail and would not be fired?

Chapter 11

Six Leadership Practices

Spiritual Boot Camp for Leaders

Leadership is a set of practices. The notion of practice is simple: To master anything, you need to practice; to become more effective in our leadership, we must continually practice and improve both our outer game and our inner game.

Here we describe six essential leadership practices that, if approached as ongoing disciplines, reliably mature the inner game and develop outer-game capabilities. These practices, taken together, are a *spiritual boot camp* for leaders. They are spiritual because they the call forth the highest and best in us. They are a *boot camp* because they change and restructure us, making us more fit to lead. They reliably transform Reactive Mind into Creative Mind and beyond.

PRACTICE 1: DISCERNING PURPOSE

Life is purposeful. Leadership is purposeful. A primary task of a life creatively led is to discern the purpose of our life. Creative Mind orients itself on the purpose that seeks to come through us. Great leaders stand for what matters and create it. In his book, *On Becoming a Leader*, Warren Bennis writes: "Leaders are made, not born, and made more by themselves than by any external means. No leader sets out to be a leader per se, but rather to express him/herself freely and fully. Becoming a leader is synonymous with becoming yourself. It is precisely that simple, and also that difficult. First and foremost, find out what it is you're about, and be that" (Bennis, 1989).

I Am Not Becoming Who I Am

Bob: I started my career making hog food and dog food. I managed production in the most technologically advanced livestock feed and pet food processing plant in the United States at the time. We were in start-up (code for *nothing worked*). Late one night, we were trying to get the plant back on-line. I was frantically working in the receiving bay emptying a railroad car filled with feed ingredients needed to get the plant back in production. When the car was empty, I climbed inside to sweep it out. As I finished, I propped my feet up in the hopper bottom to catch my breath. Out of my mouth, in a loud authoritative voice, completely unrehearsed, came the words, "I am not becoming who I am." I knew immediately that I had spoken a truth about myself that I could not take back. That moment began my practice of *Discerning Purpose.*

A few weeks later, I received a book by Rainer Maria Rilke titled *Letters to a Young Poet* (Rilke, 1993). This book is a series of letters that Rilke, the great German poet, wrote to an aspiring young poet. The young poet had sent Rilke samples of his work for critique. Rather than critique the poems, Rilke responds with some advice about why one would write poetry in the first place, and in so doing, gave a powerful description of the practice of *Discerning Purpose*.

> You ask whether your verses are good. You ask me, and others before me. You send them to magazines. You compare them with other poems, and you are disturbed when certain editors reject your efforts. Now, since you have allowed me to advise you, I beg you to give up all that. You are looking outward. Nobody can counsel and help you, nobody. There is only one single way. Go into yourself. Search for the reason that bids you write; find out whether it is spreading out its roots in the deepest places of your heart, acknowledge to yourself whether you would have to die if it were denied you to write. This above all—ask yourself in the stillest hour of your night: *Must* I write? Delve into yourself for a deep answer. And if this should be affirmative, if you may meet this earnest question with a strong and simple "*I must*," then build your life according to this

> necessity; your life even into its most indifferent and slightest hour must be a sign of this urge and a testimony to it.

When I read this, I knew that I had to discern my "Musts." I started by creating a list of *Musts*—the deepest and highest aspirations for my life. Each night after work, I would write about these *Musts*. As I did, I knew that if I admitted what I really wanted my life to be about, I was crossing a threshold from which I could not go back. I realized that I had to be about this life, the one emerging on the pages of my journal. Otherwise, I would be living someone else's life, not my own. When I finished writing, I set about creating the life that I felt born to live.

Fifteen years later, I found this journal in the attic. As I reread it, I began to weep because everything I had written was happening in my life in ways I never could have imagined at the time. I then realized the full power of the Creative Mind set on purpose.

This practice has the power to boot up with Creative Mind. When we get clear about who we are and what we must do, magic happens. Joseph Campbell (Campbell, 2008) says that when we step into the adventure of living on purpose "the universe will open doors where there were only walls."

W.H. Murray could not be clearer on this subject (Murray, 1951):

> Until one is committed, there is hesitancy, the chance to draw back, always ineffectiveness. Concerning all acts of initiative (and creation) there is one elementary truth, the ignorance of which kills countless ideas and splendid plans: that the moment one definitely commits oneself, then Providence moves too. All sorts of things occur to help one that would never otherwise have occurred. A whole stream of events issues from the decision, raising in one's favor all manner of unforeseen incidents and meetings and material assistance, which no man could have dreamed would have come his way. I have learned a deep respect for one of Goethe's couplets: "Whatever you can do, or dream you can, begin it, / Boldness has genius, power, and magic in it."

Creative Mind harnesses this genius, power, and magic in a way that Reactive Mind cannot. Creative Mind moves the levers that cause creation while Reactive Mind looks in the rear view mirror trying to navigate forward by fixing what it does not want in order to stay safe.

Stalking Your Longing

Creative Leadership springs from the pursuit of purpose, from discerning and defining a personal purpose worthy of our deepest commitment. Purpose is longing—love for what the soul wants to pursue most in this life. The Greeks called it *Eros*, the capacity to follow what is most intensely missing or unfinished in our lives. Purpose wells up from within. It is not something we invent. It finds us, if we pay attention. The primary task of life is to let it live us.

Discerning purpose is a practice of attention, much like tracking a deer through woods. The deer leaves signs if we know how to read, track, and stalk them. Discerning purpose requires attention to the trail, to the minute, subtle, and detailed clues our life is leaving as we live it (or as it lives us). Life has been speaking to us for a long time about what matters most. It has been leaving a trail. It remains for us to have the courage and the discipline to pay attention.

This practice is about learning to trust those moments of clarity when purpose is speaking. We exist as multidimensional beings. Since the deepest, truest parts of ourselves know what we are up to here, we need to be in conversation with them. Life speaks in times when we are most alive, when we are doing something that lights us up. Joseph Campbell's admonition is to "follow your bliss." He states: "If it brings you joy do more of it" (Campbell, 2008). The purpose of our life is leaving clues in periods of joy, excitement, enthusiasm, meaning, and fulfillment. These are the times when we feel most alive, moments when the soul is speaking about who we are and what we care most about, pointing us in the direction of our highest aspirations. It speaks of our *Musts*. Learning to stalk these moments is the practice of discerning purpose.

Life is also speaking in the moments when we are least alive, when life is not working, when it is as bad as it gets, when we are miserable, bored, restless, and flat. Life is letting us know, in these periods, what is most intensely missing. This too informs us about what we must be about. As David Whyte once said in a lecture, "The first step toward the fire is noticing how cold you are."

When we sift the times we are most and least alive, we can extract the themes, patterns, and clues that forge our purpose. Paying attention to these clues, letting them point the way to our deeper longings, and defining which of these longings are *musts* is the work of this discipline. When we do this, we stalk our longing—navigating the pull of the Ascending Current.

Purpose is not discovered in a vacuum. Our purpose is not merely about our personal fulfillment. It is about contribution and service. Albert Schweitzer said: "I don't know what your destiny will be, but this I know: the only ones among you who will be really happy are those who have sought and found how to serve" (Schweitzer, 1935). Our purpose is about what brings us meaning and joy, but it is also about what the world most needs. We are born and live into a set of circumstances: families, societies, cultures, and organizations. The circumstances of our lives are no accident. Our purpose is connected to the needs of those around us, of the organizations, society, and world in which we live and work. In each of us, there is an intersection between our unique passion, curiosity, and talent and a world in need, a contribution only we can make, and when we find that intersection, we are on to the purpose of our lives.

Viktor Frankl discovered his purpose in a Nazi concentration camp. He learned that those who had a purpose for living had a much higher survival rate. He also discovered the meaning of his own life. Frankl survived, founded a school of psychotherapy he called Logotherapy, and wrote his classic book, *Man's Search for Meaning*. In it, he says, "Everyone has his own specific vocation or mission in life; everyone must carry out a concrete assignment that demands fulfillment. Therein he cannot be replaced, nor can his life be repeated, thus, everyone's task is unique as his specific opportunity to implement it" (Frankl, 1959). Each of us must find our inevitable work—the work we came into this life to do.

Connecting the Dots

In his commencement speech at Stanford, Steve Jobs said: "You can't connect the dots looking forward; you can only connect them looking backwards. This practice requires that we trust that the dots will somehow connect in your future. You have to trust in something—your gut, destiny, life, karma, whatever. This approach has never let me down, and it has made all the difference in my life."

In the feed plant, I started stalking my longing. When I left that job, I did not know how things would unfold or even what shape my life and career would take. I did not even know about the Leadership and Organizational Development profession. Now, 35 years later, as I look back over my life, and see all that has unfolded from what I wrote in my *Musts* journal, I can see how all the dots connect. I used to think that I was stalking my longing. I realize now that *the longing was stalking me the whole time.*

So, practice paying attention to what your life is trying to tell you about who you are and what you are here to do. Stalk the longing that is stalking you. Then, exercise the courage to submit to the purpose that wants to have its way with your life.

Purpose is something bestowed—and received. It arises in our lives and in us. We must notice it and inquire what it wants from us. It is not something we rationalize and choose, though we must choose to follow it. It is something we receive and to which we surrender. This practice is an inside-out dialogue with life as it spontaneously arises in our interaction in the world.

This practice is not something we do once; it is a life-long discipline to remain in dialogue with our purpose. The soul has a way of moving on as soon as we complete one phase of the journey having realized the vision that emerges from our purpose. About the time we feel we have lived into our purpose, it requires us to discern our purpose again. The soul is a jealous lover; it refuses to invest itself in a compromise. We either step toward "the spark behind fear recognized as life" or "the body fills with dense smoke." Discerning purpose is a core practice for living and leading from our Creative Edge. There is no safe way to do that.

Creative Leadership

The ongoing discovery and exploration of our sense of purpose is the central discipline of the Creative, Self-Authoring Mind and the starting place for true leadership. The power to create what matters in the face of difficult circumstances comes from within, from passion and conviction. Passion is the energizing force of the Creative Mind and of the creative tension it takes to lead. Passion has its source in knowing our purpose: what we are here to learn, become, and do with our lives. If we are unfamiliar with this abiding sense of purpose, we have not integrated a discipline of spiritual attention into our lives. As long as deep conviction and passion are uncommon, so will genuine, creative, and authentic leadership remain uncommon.

The soul knows where it wants to go, and it does not compromise. Leadership requires the spiritual discipline to be led by our higher purpose. This discipline provides the staying power required to transform ourselves and our organizations in spite of the vulnerability of change, the political risks, the self-doubt, the fear, and the possibility of failure. We will only see it through if it matters enough—if it is worth the risk. Our purpose is worth the risk.

To lead, we must optimize the tension between purpose and safety by orienting on purpose and letting the chips fall where they may. There is no safe or risk-free way to do this, no sure formula for success. However, great power lies at the source of Creative Leadership. As leaders, our first task is to cultivate purpose, translate that into vision, and sustain that creative tension in ourselves. Our second task is to cultivate and sustain this creative tension for the organization. This is the path of transformation. We transform ourselves into an embodiment of our purpose and vision, and then we stand for it in the midst of the current realities and shifting political currents. We act it out in every encounter, and, thus, transform not only ourselves into our highest self, but also the organization into its higher purpose. This is the Promise of Leadership.

PRACTICE 2: DISTILLING VISION

The second practice that reliably develops Creative Leadership is the ongoing discipline of translating purpose into a vision of our desired future, both individually and collectively. Every credible authority on leadership (Bennis, Collins, Covey, Wilson, Senge, Fritz, Block, Peters, Drucker, Kouzes/Posner, and Cashman, to name a few) describes *vision* as the centerpiece of effective leadership. In the LCP, the dimension of *Purposeful Visionary* most correlates to Leadership Effectiveness. The Creative Mind is focused on creating vision; thus, the discipline that most evolves Creative Mind is the challenge of self-authoring a vision of greatness for ourselves and for the organization. Being a person of vision and leading the organization into its desired future is the first Promise of Leadership.

Five Elements of Vision

Vision is personal, specific, lofty, strategic, and collective.

Vision is personal. Vision, in the Reactive Mind, is given or authored by others, and then it is adopted, however enthusiastically. Vision at the Creative level is self-authored. Creative Leadership is the act of articulating and acting in pursuit of a vision that flows from our personal commitment to higher purpose. Vision is the picture of how that purpose wants to actualize in meaningful and tangible ways. Vision describes the specific direction our soul longs to go.

Vision is specific. It is specific enough that we would recognize it when we realize it. Recently, as we consulted with a healthcare organization, we encouraged the leadership team to take a three-day off-site to get clear and aligned on their vision. As we introduced the meeting agenda, the CFO said, "I am concerned that this will be a huge waste of our time. What do you mean by *vision* and what might we say about it that could possibly take three days?"

We responded, "You will create a specific and detailed picture of the healthcare organization that will exist in this community five years from now." The CFO said, "If we could do that, it would be amazing. We have never had that conversation."

For vision to be useful it needs to be specific enough to set direction, focus strategy, drive action, and guide decision-making. We need to specify the result you have in mind, in enough detail that everyone knows when the vision is attained.

Vision is strategic (but it is not strategy). Strategy charts the course of how to get from wherever we are to the vision. Vision is the capstone of strategy, a description of the business, as we most want it to exist at some point in the future. Vision is a response to the current reality of the marketplace, but it is not limited by the constraints of that reality. It is strategic because it sets a direction that enables the organization to excel in its current environment and well into the future. Vision defines the organization's unique contribution to real needs, real markets, and real social and cultural imperatives. It sets the organization on course to thrive and contribute.

Vision is lofty. It captures our highest aspirations for our lives and work. It is unashamedly spiritual and fundamentally imaginative. A lofty vision grabs us at a deeper level than does the promise of profit or market share. While a vision will often include these, by *lofty* we mean that it appeals to our deepest values, higher aspirations, and personal purposes. As such, a lofty vision also makes the pursuit of it meaningful and worthwhile. Lofty vision is worthy of our deep commitment. It is worthy of our life's blood. Lofty vision magnifies the creative capacity of the organization by drawing people into alignment.

Vision is collective. Vision catalyzes alignment. If purpose is the source from which great leadership springs, vision is the leader's primary contribution. By expressing his or her vision, the leader causes others to reflect on what they stand for. It is difficult to remain neutral in the presence of strong, visionary leadership. When we encounter it, we are challenged to examine and evaluate our own interests, values, stance, and direction. Alignment happens when members of the organization can see that they are able to fulfill their own personal purposes by achieving the organization's vision.

Leaders enroll others in their vision, but *enrollment* has little to do with getting others to buy in to our vision. This notion is a vestige of our Reactive, patriarchal roots. Enrollment, as a Creative process, happens in dialogue. When, as leaders, we articulate and embody our vision, we stimulate reflection in others. If we then engage in dialogue about our individual aspirations, we find common ground. We enable the true purpose and vision of the organization to rise to the surface. Alignment develops naturally as the dialogue continues. Thus, the practice of Distilling Vision requires that leaders initiate and sustain this dialogue—that they are willing to influence and be influenced. Such a dialogue ups the probability of a collective vision emerging that expresses the highest aspirations of the organization: one that excites, humbles, and fulfills its members, as well as one that contributes to the success of the business.

The *Purposeful Visionary* dimension on the LCP is the dimension most highly correlated with *Leadership Effectiveness* at .91. Since a lofty and strategic vision catalyzes alignment, it is highly correlated to *Teamwork* at .89. The combination of *Purposeful Visionary* and *Teamwork* is the combination of dimensions that is most highly correlated (.94) to *Leadership Effectiveness*. Distilling Vision is the primary Promise of Leadership.

This discipline requires that we create a purpose-connected vision of results, embody that vision, and encourage others to do the same. It also requires that we distill and refine a collective sense of purpose and vision through honest dialogue. The resulting vision taps the spiritual power of purpose and brings a generative force to bear on the creation of meaningful personal and organizational results. Since vision is the focus of the Creative Mind, this discipline awakens the Creative, Self-Authoring Mind. As leaders embody this practice, they fulfill on the Leadership Agenda and imperative, developing a Creative Leadership System.

PRACTICE 3: KNOWING YOUR DOUBTS AND FEARS

Bob: Early in my career, I did not know that I was a flaming perfectionist who was subject to his Reactive Mind. I was functioning at a mid-Reactive level as an *expert perfectionist,* meaning, "there's a right way to do everything, and I know what it is."

About this time, I became interested in assessments. I became fascinated by one assessment in particular, and my enthusiasm was an early clue to my life's purpose and vision. In fact, I was so interested in this assessment that I called the company and told them that I wanted to learn from them. In order to expedite my learning, I invited them to come and work with one of the leadership teams in the organization. They sent the founder's wife! She was quite talented, but she had a different model of how to lead the work than the one in my head. Of course, since I am an *expert perfectionist*, she was wrong and I was right. She could not find a way to work with me, and so, eventually, we parted company. Effectively, I ran her out of the organization.

Ten years later, I created a workshop to help senior leaders become aware of their Reactive patterns and see how they tend to recreate patriarchal systems even as they try to transform them. In this workshop, we used the aforementioned assessment. I wanted my colleagues, who would be leading this workshop, to be well-grounded in it. So, I asked the founder of the assessment company (let's call him Doug) to teach us the elements of the assessment. Doug was a brilliant man, a walking encyclopedia on leadership, how to measure it, and how to see it in action. After one extraordinary day with him, we decided to schedule a second day.

A month later, we met again. I said something to start the meeting, and Doug quickly interrupted me, saying in his gruff voice, "Bob, can I give you some feedback?"

I said, "Yeah, sure."

He said, "Well, after our last session, I went home and talked to my wife! We searched our database to see if there were any other Bob Andersons from Toledo, Ohio, that we worked with 10 years ago. We could not find any, and so we concluded that you are the same Bob Anderson. Is that accurate?"

I said, "Yes."

He said, "Do you still want the feedback?"

I said, "Yes."

He said, "You are not the same asshole you used to be."

A bit stunned by this statement, I looked around the room and everybody in the group was nodding in agreement as if to say, "Yeah, he is right about that."

Since Doug was an astute observer of human behavior, he precisely described the shift he saw in me over 10 years. Again the group nodded in agreement. After giving me this feedback, he said, "I do not know what you are doing, but keep doing it because it is working."

When he said this, I went "click, click, click" in my head—this practice, this practice, and this practice. I knew exactly what I was doing. I knew the practices that had caused this change in the way I was now leading. I had a regular practice of distilling vision, of focusing on what I most wanted to create and to become. I also had a practice of exploring my underlying Reactive beliefs and assumptions whenever I noticed that I was getting in my own way.

In the practice of *Knowing Our Doubts and Fears*, we face what Ralph Stayer, the CEO of Johnsonville Sausage, called "terrible truth number one"—I am the problem" (Belasco, 1993).

We learn to notice (perhaps with the help of feedback from others) when we are not acting on our vision or acting in ways that do not support its realization. Then we take the path of descent in service of transcendence. We enter into the fear, anxiety, or inner conflict that is reactively running behavior that is inconsistent with our vision. In this practice, we move toward our doubts and fears. We become a student of them. We get beneath them and listen to the silent inner conversation we have with ourselves. We track that conversation to its source: the identity beliefs and assumptions that run our Reactive IOS. We face these beliefs and assumptions fiercely and compassionately until we see the illusion in them, and we see how this illusion is causing us to behave, act, and lead in ways that are inconsistent with the person we want to be, the results we are pursuing, and the vision we are creating. We are then liberated to act in ways that embody more of what we want.

This practice means learning to navigate the *Descending Current*. To be transformed, we must descend into the parts of ourselves that are not yet ready to embody our vision—that are too small, too scared, too reactive, too controlling, too cautious, etc. This is descent in service of transcendence.

We often hear people say, "The key to transformation is to get rid of the Reactive, or fix your Reactive, or get out of your Reactive." No! This approach is, in itself, Reactive (fixing or getting away from what we do not want). The Path of Descent is Creative if it is in service of creating what matters. We are the agent of creation, and so, when we discover that we are the obstacle to our own vision, we must do the work of freeing ourselves up to, as Gandhi said, "be the change we want to see in the world."

Our vision depends on this practice. We stalk our longing until it distills into vision. The vision then challenges us to transform ourselves into an effective and powerful vessel for realizing the vision. The new vision will challenge the status quo of who we are, how we live and lead, and how our organization is performing. Vision challenges and evolves the current state of things. If we cannot see our contribution to the current state of things and change our mind (rewrite the IOS code that runs us on autopilot), then we will likely continue to act in ways that undermine the very thing to which we are committed. The inner game runs the outer game.

We are never "done" with purpose or vision. If we are tracking it and stalking it, it keeps pulling us toward becoming the ever-larger person/leader that wants to emerge. It stretches us. When we are stretched by vision, when we choose to "step up," we meet our doubts and fears at the door. The spark behind fear smolders inside—always this energy, always this tension.

Every time we go to a new edge, we are terrified. However, we have learned to not take that story so seriously. Reactive Mind is governed by fear. We react to those unconscious assumptions because they have us, and we believe their story is true. When this happens, we are into our favorite habitual Reactive strategy before we know it. We have chosen comfort over challenge, but it is not really comfortable. What appears to be a choice for comfort and safety is actually a managed level of anxiety. When we choose safety over purpose, we override the fragile sense of purpose. The vision is compromised without notice, and we are left wondering why it is so hard to make progress.

The alternative is to continue to give ourselves over to the pull of purpose, distill it into vision, and then deal with the fear and the doubt that inevitably arise. These three practices work together. Purpose gets discerned and then distilled into vision. Vision challenges us to think and act differently, perhaps in ways that are not supported by our current set of beliefs and assumptions. When vision outstrips our current mental models and contradicts our well-worn identity structures, we feel fear, doubt, and other forms of inner conflict.

This natural feeling simply means that we are being adaptively challenged to re-think ourselves, to be restructured. Restructuring happens when we reframe our limited Reactive ways of understanding ourselves. As we reframe our self-limiting assumptions we boot up a new, creatively structured operating system designed to manifest the vision we are holding. Creative structure seeks vision. Since we are designing our Creative IOS in relationship to our Self-Authored vision, we are tailoring its design to optimally support the unique purpose and vision coming through our lives and leadership.

The best description for how to work with the Reactive parts of ourselves comes from a book called *Feeling Good* by David Burns (Burns, 1980). In his *Vertical Thinking* process, he gives precise instructions on how to listen beneath Reactive feelings to the silent thinking that is running our habitual patterns of behavior. He shows how to track that thinking back to its source—the core identity beliefs that are running the show. Finally, he shows how to rewrite, over time, our IOS code at the Creative Structure of Mind. We have found no better source for learning how to navigate the Descending Current as we transition from Reactive to Creative Mind.

Each of us is a unique spiritual entity. With that comes our own unique longings, gifts, and a passion for expressing that uniqueness in the world. We also have a host of experiences and waves of conditioning that make our uniqueness difficult to identify and take seriously. We are acculturated and taught to define our self-worth and safety upon getting ahead, winning, gaining approval, and meeting others' expectations. When pursuing our purpose, as vision conflicts with these maps of identity, it is easy to lose sight of our deeper longings. Our soul is then held captive by our well-conditioned Reactive Mind, making it impossible to stalk our purpose, let alone stand for it, when we are in the habit of reacting to stay safe.

Again, we cannot pursue both safety and purpose simultaneously. We must make a choice. The soul is not interested in safety. The soul knows what it longs for, it is up for the adventure, and it is unwilling to compromise. This is the key choice we make in life. It will determine the nature and quality of our leadership. Without a practice of descent, to know our doubts and fears, it is likely that we will live a compromise.

PRACTICE 4: ENGAGE IN AUTHENTIC, COURAGEOUS DIALOGUE

There is no safe way to be great. And there is no great way to be safe. Transformation requires courage. There is no way around it. Reactive Mind orients on safety in whatever form that takes (Complying, Protecting, or Controlling). The practice of Authentic Courage directly confronts all our play-not-to-lose strategies and, if practiced, reliably catalyzes the evolution of Creative Mind.

The courage required in organizations is not the courage required on the battlefield. We do not risk life and death, although it may feel that way at times. Mostly, the courage required is the courage to tell the truth. Honest conversation happens in organizations, but mostly in the bathroom, not in the meeting room. In the meeting room, we all agree that we are making great progress. In the bathroom, we often hear a different story. When caution prevails, the truth is obscured. Collective effectiveness and intelligence rapidly erode. Performance suffers. We fall short of the vision we espouse. Change efforts come off the rails.

Since authentic, courageous conversation is the lifeblood of high performance, this dimension is top-dead-center on the LCP. Authenticity in the LCP combines *Courage*, the willingness to bring up difficult issues and engage them in a great way, and *Integrity*, embodying our values by walking the talk. *Authenticity* is highly correlated to *Leadership Effectiveness* (.80), to *Purposeful Visionary* (.82) to *Teamwork* (.68) and to *Business Performance* (.50). It is one of the central defining capabilities of Creative Mind.

This Practice requires the previous three practices. Courage requires that we are committed to something bigger than our fears, something worth the risk (Discerned Purpose and Distilled Vision). It also requires that we know our fears and that we can separate real risk from the fear we make up when subject to our Reactive illusions.

Bob: Five years after I discovered that I needed everyone to like me as a leader, I was consulting to a large manufacturing organization. One day we met with the top 80 managers. I was not leading the discussion because they wanted to explore a topic that was outside my area of expertise, so I called in another consultant to work with me. I made a few comments before the morning break. At the break, my client, the CEO, a rather rough and tumble type, took me aside and said, "Bob, I was just talking to my Vice Presidents at break, and frankly, they did not appreciate your comments. I think it best if you just keep your mouth shut the rest of the day."

I was shocked. I wondered, "What could I have said that was so controversial?" I went back to my seat licking my wounds and said nothing for the next few hours.

Mid-afternoon an amazing "coincidence" happened. A woman stood up and said, "I feel like it is not safe to say what you really think in this room. After meetings like this, the senior managers caucus and discuss who said what. They make conclusions about us that impact our credibility and our future here." No one knew quite what to say. Then the conversation continued, and within 30 seconds the group swept the issue under the rug by concluding that it was safe to say what you really think, that there was no issue with speaking up in this group.

In the meantime, my heart is beating loudly. What this woman had just described happened to me today. I found myself in a moment of choice: courage or safety. Mind you, I am sitting right across the table from the CEO. How am I going to play it?

While the group was disposing of this issue, I was riding the Ascending and Descending Currents of the first three practices. "How do I want to show up in this moment? What is my vision of great consulting in a moment like this? How do I best serve my client? What do I care about that is worth the risk?" These questions reminded me of well-practiced clarity that had come from the practices of Discerning Purpose and Distilling Vision. I was also riding the Descending Current. So this is the point where I always make up that if I stand up I will get shot. I know this familiar voice of caution all too well. I know that I constantly tell myself that my future depends on always being liked, admired, and valued. I do not have to listen to that voice in this moment. I chose to speak up. I stood and said, "What you said (pointing to the woman who had raised the issue) happened to me today. A meeting happened at the break and someone in senior leadership, and I will not mention names, took me aside and said that it was probably best if I kept my mouth shut the rest of the day." The group gasped. "No way! It could not happen here." I said, "Yes. It did happen here. It happened to me today."

The group then had a two-hour discussion about the level of honesty, caution, truth telling, authenticity, and inauthenticity that was in the room. It was a breakthrough conversation for them. As they left the meeting, they agreed that the last two hours had been the best conversation they had ever had as an Extended Leadership team.

As the group was leaving, quite exuberant over their breakthrough conversation, I was trying to pack up and make it out of the room without making eye contact with the CEO. I caught myself in the act. This is the practice. I noticed that I was afraid to face him. Ascending Current: What is my vision of service to my client in this moment? Descending Current: What am I telling myself is at risk? Oh, that same familiar voice of caution again.

Choice: I looked the CEO in the eye and said, "What did you think about what I said?"

He responded, "What do you mean?"

I said, "Well you told me it would be best if I kept my mouth shut."

He said, "You were talking about me?!!"

When he asked this, I envisioned myself laughing and saying, "No. Never mind." Instead, I said, still looking him in the eye, "Yes, I was talking about you."

He responded, "Well I was just looking out for your welfare. I need what you are bringing to this organization, and I want you to live to fight another day!"

I pondered this comment and then said, "I get that you were looking out for my welfare. I appreciate your intent. Here is what I would like you to get: In that moment, you were a conduit to me for all the caution and fear that was just expressed in your leadership team."

He glared at me for what seemed like a long time and for a moment I honestly thought this might well be my last day consulting with this organization. He then said, "Huh! I did do that, didn't I? Wow. That was helpful! I need more of that from you. When is our next meeting?"

Courage is the willingness to be authentic, to speak and act in ways that express and embody our vision of greatness. The whole culture is going on in every meeting: the level of honesty or withholding, caution or courage, vision or compromise, integrity or manipulation, clarity or lack of clarity. It is all happening in every meeting. To change the culture is to change the moment. The vision lives or dies in moments of courage. We either opt for purpose and take the risk of saying what we really think and feel, or we opt for safety. In this choice we either advance the vision or hold it back. The power to create the culture we want lies in authenticity.

The *Promise of Leadership* cannot be fulfilled if leaders cannot tell the truth to one another. Most of our work with senior teams is long term. After a year of working with them, we often hear this feedback: "The difference that has made all the difference is that we can now tell the truth to one another. A year ago, too many issues were un-discussable and caught in the politics of caution and ambition. Now we can readily cut through complex issues, and it is fun."

Authentic, courageous conversation is necessary for high performance. Collective effectiveness lives or dies with the ability to speak honestly and with high integrity to each other. Collective intelligence depends on it. This practice is a hallmark of Creative Mind and leadership and practicing it as a discipline evolves Creative Mind and leads to Integral Mind.

PRACTICE 5: DEVELOP INTUITION, OPEN TO INSPIRATION

Finding leverage points within systems that are so complex they defy rationality—or as Peter Senge says are *un-figure-out-able*—requires that leaders trust a way of knowing that is beyond rationality and deductive logic. Leaders must learn to use data and rational analysis as far as it can go and then listen to their gut, their intuitive knowing about the best or right thing to do. This requires a level of maturity in the IOS that can balance reason with intuition for guiding the development of the organization's vision, strategy, decision-making, and creative innovation.

We do not Discern Purpose or Distill Vision solely with the rational mind. We do not balance our checkbook with intuition. Mastery in most disciplines, including leadership, requires strong rational capability balanced by strong access to intuitive knowing. Purpose, vision, insight, innovation, creativity, authenticity, and wisdom characterize great leaders. None of these capabilities are merely rational. They depend on intuition as the source of inspiration.

Daniel Webster defines *Intuition* as, "The power or faculty of attaining direct knowledge or cognition without reference to data, evident rational deduction, or inference." In other words, we just know, and we do not know why or how we know. Most of us have experience with this kind of knowing and we also have experience with what happened when we did and did not follow it. Intuition is a capability we all have and it can be developed. Like any talent, intuition is normally distributed; some are more gifted than others, but all of us have the capability.

Intuitive capability atrophies in most of us. Usually our cultural bias tells us to ignore our intuition (unless we are from a rare culture that is deeply intuitively informed). Intuition is largely discounted in the workplace. As such, we limit our leadership effectiveness, individual and collective. Most cultures are primarily Reactive, and Reactive Mind is conditioned to dismiss intuitive insight as irrelevant and untrustworthy. Reactive Mind, in pursuit of safety and predictability, wants proof. It is designed to think "within the box," not to make innovative leaps "out of the box." Intuition, in most of us, lies fallow until consciousness develops beyond Reactive Mind.

Since it is an innate capability, intuition can develop at any stage, but it typically begins to emerge as a powerful leadership capability as Creative Mind evolves. In his book, *Value Shifts*, Brian Hall suggests that intuition does not develop until the Self-Initiating phases of development (another label for what we call Creative Mind) (Hall, 2006). Creative Mind develops intuition as a powerful tool. This intuitive capability tends to reach its full potential at the Integral level.

Bob: Intuition can be a powerful tool in many situations. It can be helpful, for example, in a courageous conversation when we do not know what to say next to move the conversation forward. I was once coaching a senior executive in a program at the University of Notre Dame. We administered the LCP and then conducted a one-on-one debrief session with each manager. It was my last coaching session of the day. I had started at 6:30 a.m., and it was now 6:00 p.m. When I walked into the coaching room, the man was looking down at the table. He did not look up at me. As I sat across from him, he pushed the LCP binder across the table at me and said, "I do not understand this arrogance crap—explain to me what these results mean."

I tried to talk to him about what *Arrogance* meant and how it may show up in leadership. Nothing I said landed. I was getting nowhere. He was arguing with me at every turn. I was at a loss for what to say to him that would be helpful, and then, an idea popped in. When it did, I immediately had the gut sense that this idea held the key to our conversation. I then knew what I needed to say/do, but the idea scared me because it required that I trust my gut and take a risk with him. After double-checking my intuitive insight, I said, "Let me show you what arrogance looks like. When I walked into the room, here is how you looked (I put my head down and stared at the table). Most people would make eye contact, perhaps smile, or shake my hand. Knowing that I have been in these coaching sessions for 11 hours, they might even say, 'Man, it has been a long day for you, how are you doing?' Instead, you pushed this binder at me with your head down and said, 'Tell me about this arrogance crap.' That is what arrogance looks like."

He rocked back in his chair, glared at me for a minute, and said, "You know if people see me outside of work, they do not recognize me."

I asked, "What do you mean?

He said, "When I am not at work, I have my ball cap on, a beer in one hand, and a smile on my face. I am actually a fun guy, but when I walk into work, I put my game face on. At work no one really knows me. I make sure of that."

We then went on to have an extraordinary conversation. In fact, the conversation was so transformative that when he stood up, and started to walk out of the room, he stumbled slightly and said, "Oh, I need to be careful. I feel a little woozy."

I said, "Yeah, that was a big shift."

In order to lead effectively, we need access to every kind of information available to us. We need access to forms of perception beyond the bounds of our usual organizational rationality. We need to see relationships and interconnections that are invisible to linear, logical methods. This discipline of leadership asks us to take intuition seriously, to recognize that intuition is real, that we all have it, that it can be developed through practice, and that, in the words of the philosopher Schopenhauer, "there is in us something wiser than our head" (Schopenhauer, 1974).

In the book, *The Intuitive Manager*, Roy Rowan indicates that most successful leaders rely heavily on intuition (Rowan, 1986). They learn to trust their gut with key decisions, decisions that define their careers and set the course for their success. They have done so even when the data does not seem to support the intuitive direction. However, they seldom talk about it, because it feels illegitimate in our data-driven world. That said, many leaders have spoken about how they have learned to trust their intuition. For example:

- I began to realize that an intuitive understanding and consciousness was more significant than abstract thinking and intellectual logical analysis ... **Intuition is a very powerful thing, more powerful than intellect, in my opinion**. That's had a big impact on my work. —Steve Jobs
- Steve Jobs, "... was, indeed, an example of what the mathematician Mark Kac called a magician genius, someone whose insights come out of the blue and require intuition more than mere mental processing power."—Walter Isaacson, author of the book *Steve Jobs* (Isaacson, 2007)
- The intuitive mind is a sacred gift and the rational mind is a faithful servant. We have created a society that honors the servant and has forgotten the gift.—Einstein
- The intellect has little to do on the road to discovery. There comes a leap in consciousness, call it intuition or what you will, the solution comes to you and you do not know how or why.—Einstein
- Dull minds are never either intuitive or mathematical.—Pascal
- The insight never comes hit or miss, but is born from unconscious levels exactly in the areas in which we are most intently consciously committed . . . where information is not consciously available. Although the realization may arrive at a seemingly magical moment, it comes usually after a long hard pondering of a problem ... It is through science that we prove, but through intuition that we discover.— Jules Henri Poincaré. (Singh, 2006)
- Have the courage to follow your heart and intuition. They somehow already know what you truly want to become. Everything else is secondary. —Steve Jobs
- We lie in the lap of immense intelligence, which makes us receivers of its truth and organs of its activity.—Ralph Waldo Emerson (Emerson, 1936)

Intuition is the practice of opening to a deeper knowing, a higher sensory perception, a calling, an inner voice that says, "Stay with this," or, "Do this now," or, "This is who you are, what you stand for, what you need to move toward in your leadership." Intuition is the gateway to the higher more spiritual dimensions of our selves. We are multidimensional beings. We are more than a physical body and brain. We are beings that exist simultaneously on unseen dimensions (traditionally called psyche, soul, and spirit). Intuition is the gateway to these higher dimensions. It gives us access to knowing at these levels of ourselves. When we tap into these dimensions we know things we did not know we knew. Insights come in wholes. The solutions to problems are immediately and completely comprehended. Intuition is the source of breakthrough insight, wisdom, and transformative vision. It is the source of most great innovative advances.

Intuition, balanced with rational analysis, is a key capacity of the Creative Mind. Developing it opens us to uncommon insight, wisdom, and creative capacity for innovation. Creative Leadership is courageous, authentic, purpose-driven, visionary, strategic, emotionally intelligent, and inspirational. All of this is informed by intuition.

PRACTICE 6: THINK SYSTEMICALLY

In the presence of a new and compelling vision, structures and systems must evolve. When structural change is ignored, visions fail. Great leaders have the capacity to think systemically and to design systems for high performance. Developing Systems Thinking stimulates the evolution of Creative and Integral Mind.

Culture eats strategy for lunch every day. Structural forces are more powerful than individual commitment. Only when leaders courageously meet the challenge of structural change head-on can they make their vision a reality. Systems have a powerful immune system that seeks homeostasis or equilibrium, and they push back hard when change is introduced. This tendency to resist change helps to ensure the survival of the system; it also makes systems difficult to change. As Warren Bennis writes: "The reason why so many experiments in change fail is that the leaders have failed to take into account the strong undertow of cultural (structural) forces. Leaders who fail to take their social architecture into account and yet try to change their organizations resemble nothing so much as Canute, the legendary Danish monarch who stood on the beach and commanded the waves to stand still as proof of his power" (Bennis, 2009).

Again, *structure determines performance*. Individually and organizationally, you are designed perfectly for the performance you are getting. Significant changes in individual and collective performance must first take place at the level of structural design. Since organizational and societal systems are created at the level of collective consciousness that created them, personal transformation in the level of Mind of individuals must precede transformation in organizational and societal structures. When organizational structures are designed at a higher order of complexity and performance than an individual's consciousness, they encourage individual consciousness to develop to that same order of complexity. Thus, systemic and personal transformations are interdependent.

In the Reactive Mind, we react to fix problems. This strategy is wholly inadequate for redesigning systems. Structures are not changed by attempting to "fix" the problems that are arising from inadequate design. To use another metaphor, the disease is not cured by attempting to resolve its symptoms. Only changes to underlying structure can, in the long run, lead to significantly different outcomes.

What changes systems is *leveraged action*: strategically focused action aimed at particular points of leverage that may be far removed in time and space from the symptoms that infuriate us at the moment. These points of leverage are where we get a multiplied return in improved performance on our efforts at change. Finding *leverage points* requires us to see and explore the dynamic "system-ness" of our current reality. When we create new vision, we establish a creative tension between our current level of performance and our envisioned results. In holding this tension over time, we are more likely to see the systemic structure of current reality, not just symptoms and problems. We need to resist reacting to the hot or loud symptoms closest at hand, to focus attention on redesigning the system that can more naturally manifest the vision, and to live with the anxiety of not responding to all the problems as we search for leverage. This capacity arises naturally on Creative Mind and is beyond the design capacity of Reactive Mind.

The ability to not react to problems and symptoms, hold creative tension over time, use intuition to find leverage in the midst of unfathomable complexity, and have the courage it takes to authentically advocate for fundamental change in structures is why Reactive Mind is incapable of

Systemic Thinking and Design. Creative Mind is required. Integral Mind is preferred. Brian Hall suggests that the Visionary Strategic capability matures as Creative Mind evolves and opens into Systems Awareness (Hall, 2006). Systems Awareness, thinking, and design begin to emerge in the late Creative Stage of Development and reach maturity at the Integral Stage. Learning about and practicing Systems Thinking evolves Creative Mind into Integral Mind.

The *Systems Awareness* dimension is highly correlated (.65) to the Stage of Development out of which the leader is operating. The more mature the leader's Structure of Mind, the more likely it is that they are systemically aware. *Systems Awareness* is the dimension on the LCP most highly correlated to *Leadership Effectiveness* as seen by bosses (.81). When CEOs evaluate the leaders who work for them, they most want to see a leader who is thinking systemically, has the big picture, understands the relationship between the business environment and business, and redesigns systems to solve multiple problems at once to achieve higher performance. It is little wonder that Systems Awareness is also strongly correlated to Business Performance (.57) and to Achieving (.88). Systems Awareness is a Creative Leadership capability required to lead change.

One of leadership's primary roles in executing the vision is as an architect of structure. Architects do not do the construction; they guide the process. Senior leaders ensure that processes are in place so that the organization learns to think systemically and to redesign itself over time. It does not mean that senior leaders do the redesign and then require others to adapt to new roles and processes. The real challenge is to develop a change strategy that gets broad-based involvement in the ongoing renewal of the system. In addition, the deeper work of leadership development needs to go on side-by-side with system redesign. When the Leadership Development Agenda is integrated into a well-conceived strategy for redesigning whole systems, visions become reality. People grow and translate that growth directly into organizational improvement.

This systems architect role of leadership requires courage. People may ignore or disagree with your vision, but when you address the system, you must be prepared for conflict. The underpinning of any tangible structure is an invisible structure of thought, belief, philosophy, or theology. Tangible structures simply mirror the thinking, assumptions, and beliefs that gave birth to them. Changing tangible structures, therefore, almost always confronts the thought and identity structures to which people currently adhere. This is why structural change is often so tenaciously resisted. It upsets the apple cart.

Rollo May states: "Whenever there is a breakthrough of a significant idea . . . [it] will destroy what a lot of people believe is essential to the survival of their intellectual and spiritual world… As Picasso remarked, 'Every act of creation is first of all an act of destruction.' The breakthrough carries with it also an element of anxiety. For it not only broke down my previous hypothesis, it shook my self-world relationship. At such a time I find myself having to seek a new foundation, the existence of which I as yet do not know" (May, 1975).

Structure change is both conflictual and ambiguous. No one has answers because systems are so complex. Moving forward in ambiguity, while challenging the cherished thinking that built the old order creates conflict. Such conflict, compassionately engaged in, is a sign of life. It is the process by which visions get tested and improved (or changed) and through which the old structures evolve and become new. The leader is at the forefront of the controversy and must be willing to be a controversial figure.

The ambiguous and controversial nature of the change agent role brings the leader up against all the previous practices. Systems evolution happens in the presence of purposeful vision. Design innovations and leverage are discovered as much by intuition as by rational analysis. It takes the courage to engage in the authentic dialogue needed to forward the vision, find leverage, and implement fundamental structural change. There is no safe, risk-free way to do this and so, as Creative leaders, we must be able to see through our fears in order to refrain from reacting to symptoms, returning to old Reactive behavior patterns that are likely to stymie progress, and stay the course in the midst of pressures to compromise.

PATH OF MASTERING LEADERSHIP

There is no safe way to be great and no short cut to greatness. Boot camp is often required. These six practices, if practiced as ongoing disciplines, reliably evolve the mind from Reactive to Creative and beyond: These practices are interdependent. They each build on the others and depend on the others. Taken together, they transform consciousness. Transformed leaders then transform the organizations that they lead. If practiced regularly, these six practices do two things: 1) they transform consciousness from Reactive to Creative and from Creative to Integral; and, 2) they create high performance individually, collectively, organizationally.

The first purpose of life is to be a person of vision—the essential act of all great leaders. As we do this, we come face-to-face with our need for wholeness and confront that which limits us from offering our contribution. Thus, the second purpose of life is to overcome the obstacles that block us, many of which are within our own structure of beliefs. Our task in life is to keep a polar tension between a vision of the unique meaning that is striving for expression in our lives and to remain honest about the un-integrated side of ourselves that are incapable of living out the vision. To combine these two purposes, to serve and to heal, is to be a leader. Engaging in these six practices with discipline, honesty, and authenticity as a committed student of oneself and one's circumstances moves us toward leadership and true empowerment, toward greatness, and toward organizations, nations, and a global community that reflect and fulfill our highest aspirations. This is mastering leadership.

TAKING STOCK

- Follow your bliss. If it brings you joy, do more of it. What brings you joy, brings you alive? How could you do more of it? (Campbell, 1949)
- What is your vision of the compelling future that serves generations to come?
- What if you started your next important meeting with the question, "What are we not going to tell the truth about today?" What's your answer?
- If courage is the willingness to move forward in the face of disapproval, who are you going to disappoint?
- What is the deeper intuitive knowing, hunch, or gut sense that you must now usher in through your leadership?
- What is it that most wants and needs to happen in the system in which you find yourself?

Chapter 12

Integral Leadership

Built for Complexity, Designed for Transformation

If you want to be whole,
let yourself become partial.
—Lao Tzu, Tao Te Ching[1]

Bob: Several years ago, my Uncle Tom was dying. His brother, my Uncle Dick, went to visit him daily. On one visit on a particularly bad day, Tom said, "Dick, dying is not for sissies."

Transformation is not for sissies, either. It is a big deal. It is a death–resurrection process if we see it through—if we go full circle.

The Hero/Heroine's journey does not stop with Creative Mind. The transformation from Creative Mind to Integral Mind is yet another metamorphosis, ushering in a higher-order consciousness that can go well beyond the limits of the Creative Mind. Transformation is the process by which we are remade, over and over, into Integral and Unitive leaders.

The Integral Mind is built for complexity, designed for leading change within complex systems amid volatile, ambiguous, and rapidly changing environments. By the time leaders evolve to the Integral Stage, their leadership is likely to be extraordinarily effective, if not masterful

[1]Excerpts from #22 [2 I.]., #67 [6 I] from Tao Te Ching by Lao Tzu, A New English Version, with Foreword and Notes, by Stephen Mitchell. Translation copyright © 1988 by Stephen Mitchell. Reprinted by permission of HarperCollins Publishers.

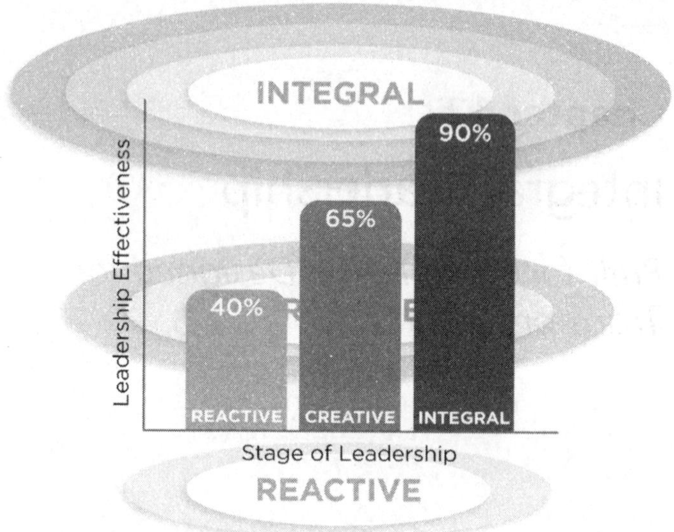

FIGURE 12.1 Stages and effectiveness

(see Figure 12.1). One leader who was measured at the Integral Mind in the Stage of Development study told us about an incident that happened when he was president of a large healthcare system. He mentioned that every time he took on a new position or department, outcomes improved dramatically: operating room efficiencies increased dramatically, costs fell, patient outcomes improved, and medical staff, employee, and customer satisfaction scores increased. His track record was so impressive that the CEO asked him to share the secrets of his effectiveness. My friend looked him in the eye and said, "Do you really want to know what I know?" The CEO, intuitively sensing that he was being asked if he was willing to transform his way of leading, declined the invitation.

Only 5% of leaders function from Integral Mind. It is rare, but when we see it, it is often extraordinary. Integral Mind far exceeds the structural limits of Reactive Mind. It can navigate complex "whitewater" in a way that Reactive Mind cannot. In the study conducted with the University of Notre Dame, the Leadership Quotient (LQ) of Reactive Mind is less than 1.0. Creative Mind more than doubles this, averaging a LQ of around 2.0. Integral Mind far exceeds the capacity and capability of Creative Mind, as Integral level leaders' average LQ score is 9.0. Integral

Mind is a huge competitive advantage. It is built for complexity because it is a far more powerful operating system.

BRIEF SUMMARY OF STAGES

The Reactive Mind is designed to establish competence in a chosen profession, to merge with the current organizational and cultural realities, and to succeed within them. From this stage, we build a life and learn to make our way in the world on its terms. If this does not happen, development derails and the leader is severely career limited. At this stage, we learn many of the capabilities that we will need in life. If we are developing into a leader, we are learning the management craft of executing and getting results. These skills must be developed, honed, and included as we jettison the Reactive for a Creative Mind.

In the transition, the competent manager becomes the visionary leader. The focus on fixing problems evolves into a focus on creating vision. Solutions become more comprehensive and longer term as the Creative Leader translates vision into strategy. The Creative leader has harvested the competence developed at the Reactive Stage (transcend and include) and is, therefore, capable of translating strategy into execution for results. The internal operating system has gone through a structural metamorphosis from outside-in to inside-out. It has moved on from a preoccupation with safety to an abiding commitment to purpose. It has shifted from a fear-driven, play-not-to-lose inner game to the passion of a purpose-driven inner game (see Figure 12.2).

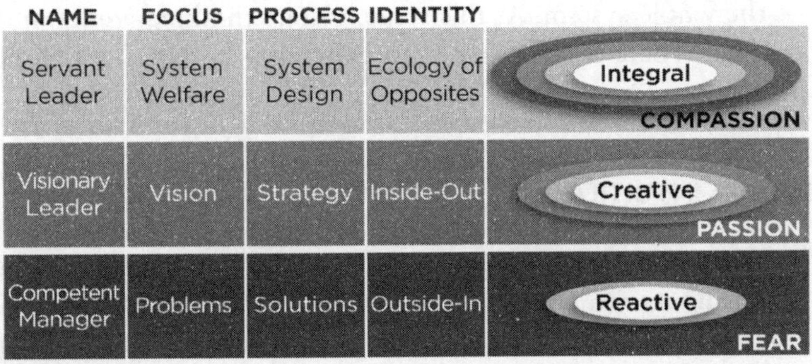

FIGURE 12.2 Stage summary

SERVANT OF THE SYSTEM

In the shift from the Creative to Integral Mind, the person/leader is competently self-authoring his/her life and leadership and again is riding the Ascending and Descending Currents of transformation. This is now a well-established practice, as the self is now authoring its own, ongoing transformation. This is why Bob Kegan calls the Integral Stage, *Self-Transforming* (Kegan and Lahey, 2009). This self-transforming capacity is precisely what enables the leader to be system-transforming.

In the transition to Integral Mind, the Ascending Current opens up into a larger, systemic vision. It focuses on wholes rather than parts, pulling the leader into a larger commitment and passion for the welfare of the whole. The visionary leader becomes the Servant Leader. The focus is both on the success of the organization that we are leading (the hallmark of Creative Leadership) and on the interdependent welfare of that organization and its larger system. The visionary leader becomes the servant of the whole system and all of the interdependencies that, together, co-construct the welfare of all stakeholders.

With this transition, both time horizons and organizational perspective expand. The strategist becomes the system architect. This is also a transcend-and-include process. The well-honed visionary and strategic capability developed at the Creative Stage, and the professional-managerial competence (to solve problems, execute strategy, and get results), which developed at the Reactive Stage, are now put in service of a larger, systemic vision. Strategic capability evolves into Systemic Awareness. The strategist becomes the System Architect. The leader is now focused on optimizing the design of the whole system for the welfare of the whole system. At this stage, system thinking comes into full bloom, and Whole Systems redesign capability becomes a well-honed competency.

MATURING INTUITION

At the Creative Stage, access to intuition, the willingness to trust it, and balancing it with reason are developing. At the Integral Stage, intuitive capability matures into a powerful skill. Complexity often defies rationality. Intuitive insight is often required to find leverage points in the system. Integral Leadership takes rationality as far as it can go and then trusts the intuitive insight that emerges in the creative unresolved tension.

Integral leaders often create results that seem impossible for others. It looks like magic. Integral *magic* derives from the creative power of systemic intuitive insight—systems awareness and vision supported by highly developed intuition.

SEEING THE ENTIRE DEVELOPMENT SPECTRUM

Integral leaders now understand the entire trajectory of development. They have lived through several transformative transitions and can now look back over their life and remember the time when Reactive Mind moved to Creative Mind. They remember going through the Integral transformation process, or they have enough self-awareness to know that they are in the midst of another metamorphosis. They now understand the progressive development process and its stages. Each Stage of Development before the Integral Stage rejects the earlier stage as immature and dismisses the later stages (that have not yet been experienced) as irrelevant—not in the "real world." In part, this is what limits the effectiveness of leaders at earlier stages—they are too dismissive of others' level of perspective-taking to optimize collective effectiveness and intelligence. The Integral leader is more capable of, as Covey says, "seeking first to understand," (Covey, 1989) and as Peter Block says, "treating the other person's perspective as valid—for them" (Block, 1987). This makes the Integral leader capable of working effectively with people of all Types (Heart, Head, and Will) and with people at all levels.

Understanding the trajectory of development enables these leaders to lead and mentor change more effectively. They are capable mentors because they know the developmental territory and can guide others through it. They can mentor leaders who are limited by Reactive assumptions, beliefs, and perspectives. They can support Creative Leaders as they transform to Integral mind. *Mentoring and Developing* is one of the most highly correlated dimensions on the LCP to Stage of Development. Integral leaders are good mentors.

Integral leaders can also resolve the inevitable conflict between people at different levels of development. Since earlier stages reject or dismiss other stages, conflict inevitably results when leaders at different development levels work together on complex issues. Leaders at different levels are in different "real worlds," often unable to take a perspective on each other's "real worlds," and, thus, dismiss the others' perspectives as irrelevant. Integral leaders work invisibly in the spaces between people at different levels to form bridges of understanding. They form and hold the field of interaction at a very high level of effectiveness and intelligence.

Integral leaders also know the relationship between consciousness and the structure and culture of the organization. Therefore, when leading systemic change, they implement new system designs at the level of system that can be operationalized by the level of consciousness of the leaders in the system. They do not get too far out ahead of what the Leadership System can digest. They time and progressively implement systemic change at a pace that stimulates other leaders to evolve, but not so fast as to set the organization up for failure. Because they understand that leaders create the culture, they readily engage the Leadership Agenda with a systemic approach to the development of the leadership system as an integral part of transforming business structures for improved performance.

HOLDING UNRESOLVEDNESS, CONFLICT, AND TENSION

Leading systemic change requires leaders to hold a high level of conflict, tension, ambiguity, and unresolvedness. Integral Mind can hold huge opposites in tension over a sustained period of time, thus allowing the dialogue of key stakeholders to arrive at breakthrough, high-leverage solutions to complex problems. These solutions usually take the form of elegant systemic interventions or design changes in the structure of the system. These structural breakthroughs enable the system to naturally perform such that all parts of the system thrive.

Recall that redundant polarities are sets of conflicting opposites that are interdependent and must be resolved simultaneously in order for the whole system to cohere and perform at a high level. Integral Mind is the first Structure of Mind complex enough to consistently resolve such complexity into high-leverage change, in part because of its capability to hold opposites in tension. Integral Mind can hold conflicting visions and points of view without championing one and making the others invalid. It holds both competing ends of the conflict as a healthy and creative tension. It is capable of synthesizing out of this tension (between thesis and antithesis) a higher-order solution where all sides win and where the best intentions of all are realized.

AS WITHIN, SO WITHOUT

The ability to hold large conflicts, opposite visions, and redundant polarities in tension without reacting to them, trying to problem-solve them, or turning them into win-lose battles reaches its zenith at the Integral Stage. These leaders can do this with effectiveness, mastery, and wisdom because the self has gone through yet another metamorphosis, another profound internal transformation in identity. Its inner game has gone from inside-out to an *ecology of opposites*.

The transformation in the inner game happens because the inner game must evolve to enable the leader to lead amid complexity and unresolvedness. Both the inner and outer games must mature at the pace of escalating complexity if the leader is to remain relevant and effective. In the outer game, as the Ascending Current pulls the leader into being the servant of the larger system, a corresponding and commensurate shift is required in the inner game. For leaders to hold tremendous conflict and tension in the outer world, they must do so in the inner world.

For every action, there is an equal and opposite reaction. So, the inner world must match the upward pull of the Ascending Current in the outer world. Consequently, the Descending Current must go deeper. As the CEO of a large leadership consulting firm said to us in a meeting, "The CEO must be the most self-aware person in the organization. If you want to go higher, you must go deeper." Thus, the Descending Current drops into the *Shadow*, the opposite of everything we think we are. Our identity is challenged to expand and hold the inner conflict, oppositeness, and unresolvedness within ourselves. As goes the inner world, so goes the outer world. As we hold and integrate our inner, unresolved oppositeness, we become leaders who can do the same in the larger system of organizational life and in the world.

The descent into shadow is fierce work. This is the second phase of the Hero/Heroine's Journey. It, too, is a death–resurrection process, and the self that dies is the Creative Self—the authentic, purposeful, and visionary self comes apart. It is not that we lose these capabilities and attributes, although it may seem so; rather, we transcend and include them. What we lose is our identity as *only* an authentic visionary. The hard-won and well-practiced authentic, visionary self begins to fray at the edges as the Creative Self begins to notice that it is not only that self, it is also a self that is just the opposite. The Creative Self fragments into an ecology of many selves.

A MEETING OF TWIN OPPOSITES

Bob Kegan (1998) uses the image of a cylinder to describe this transformation. At the Creative Stage, we are identified with the vertical, singular cylindrical mass of the cylinder. Like martial artists who develop their art by moving from center (around the body's vertical centerline or "Hara Line"), at the Creative Stage, we are identified with the hard-won authentic self. At the Integral Stage, we notice that the space of the cylinder is defined by two holes at the opposite ends of the cylinder. Identity shifts from "I am this one, singular, authentic self" to "I am many selves, an ecology of opposites in tension." We realize that we are both ends of the cylinder. We are that authentic self, and its opposite. This is the stage where Jekyll meets Hyde, where the male meets his inner female (and vice versa), where saint meets sinner, and where the hard-earned authentic, visionary Creative self meets its shadow self.

HAVE YOU EVER ONCE ASKED ME WHAT I WANT?

Bob: I remember the moment that I mark as the beginning of my transition to Integral Mind. Years ago, I was a seasoned consultant who had built his career by helping organizations build high engagement, empowering leadership cultures. Then, I met my inner controller. I was in my office one day developing a new and expanded vision for the business. As a sole proprietor, I was doing this by myself (something I coach my clients not to do). I was excited by the emerging possibilities of where we could take the business. I called a close colleague named Barbara to run the vision by her and share my excitement. After 10 minutes of monologue, I noticed that she had not said a word; there was nothing but silence on the other end of the line. I stopped and said, "Barbara, you do not sound very excited."

Barbara was skilled at courageous authenticity. She said, "I am not."

I asked, "Why not?"

She said, "It is your vision."

I said, "I know it is my vision, but why are you not excited?"

She said, "Bob, think about it. It is your vision. It has always been your vision. In the five years that I have worked closely with you, have you, even once, asked me what I want through my association with you?"

I was stunned, and I quickly ended the call. I knew that she had flagged something very important about my leadership, and I was angry. At this point, I was practiced at navigating the Descending Current, so I sat down, pulled out a note pad and began to write everything I heard myself saying inside my angry reaction: "There is no way I would ever turn over this business to the *likes of them*! They have no idea what it takes to build a business. They would run it into the ground. My financial future is all tied up with this business. If I let go, even just a little, it is game over. The business will fail, and I will fail with it. That is not an option."

As I reflected on what I wrote, I realized that I am as controlling as any of the high-control managers that I had ever "tried to fix." I had spent my career with a log in my own eye. I made leaders wrong for their high-controlling ways, not noticing that I was just like them—projecting my shadow self on to them—making them wrong for acting out a part of myself that I was unwilling to acknowledge as part of me. I had met the enemy, and it was me.

It took me years to integrate this learning. As I did so, I became far more effective in many ways, particularly at consulting to high-control managers. Instead of approaching them as a problem to fix, I simply smiled, and said, "Oh, you too? Welcome to the club." As I came to accept that shadow part of myself, I became more accepting of that quality in others. With acceptance, that controlling quality no longer needed to live in shadow and could be integrated into me. I became a more effective leader. Later, as the transformation progressed, I was also able to harvest the gift of power (the Controller's gift) that was hidden in shadow.

The *shadow* is sometimes described as any part of ourselves that we do not see. Because we do not see it (are subject to it and do not yet have it as an object of our reflection and self-management) it is said to be in shadow. We do not define shadow this way. With this definition, the core organizing identity beliefs, unseen by Reactive Mind, would be classified as shadow. This misrepresents what Jung meant by shadow. These core organizing identity beliefs form the core of the Reactive Level identity or ego. The shadow self is the opposite self. Jung defined the shadow as the opposite choice of the choices we make (Jung, 1976). In the math of the psyche, shadow works like this: If we identify with A as good, then the opposite of A (Z) is bad. If A makes us worthwhile, then Z makes us worthless. If A makes us safe, Z makes us unsafe. Given this inner mathematics, if we are identified with A, we reject Z. Z-like qualities have no place in us and get disowned and rejected. They are pushed into shadow and assumed not to exist in us. This is how Jung defined the shadow—all the parts of myself seen as opposite to the core of my ego identity.

Jung also says that *most of what is in shadow is solid gold*, meaning that much of what is rejected is a strength we possess, but we neither know we have it, nor do we accept it. Harvesting the shadow means reclaiming these disowned gifts and strengths. In transforming from Reactive to Creative Mind, we dis-identify with our ego's core organizing and self-limiting assumptions. We replace them with more empowering assumptions that enable Creative, Self-Authoring leadership to emerge. In the transition from Creative to Integral, we descend into the shadow to do the same work with what has been rejected and disowned as unacceptable and even contemptible. This is hugely empowering because we are freeing and developing additional gifts and strengths, ones that complement those that came into full bloom at the Creative Stage.

SHADOW SIDE OF THE UNIVERSAL MODEL

The Universal Model of Leadership was designed to help leaders gain insight into what is in shadow, if they are ready for that (in transition from Creative to Integral Mind). A leader operating out of an Integral Mind could have a profile like the one in Figure 12.3.

This profile is the one produced by the Extraordinary Leaders in our Stage of Development Study reported earlier. It is a profile with an LQ of 9.0. It is also high on the dimensions designed into the profile to assess Integral Leadership Competencies such as *System Awareness*, *Personal Learner*, *Selfless Leader*, and *Community Concern*. Integral leadership is highly effective in complex situations precisely because it is high on these more systemic, subtle, complex, and powerful competencies.

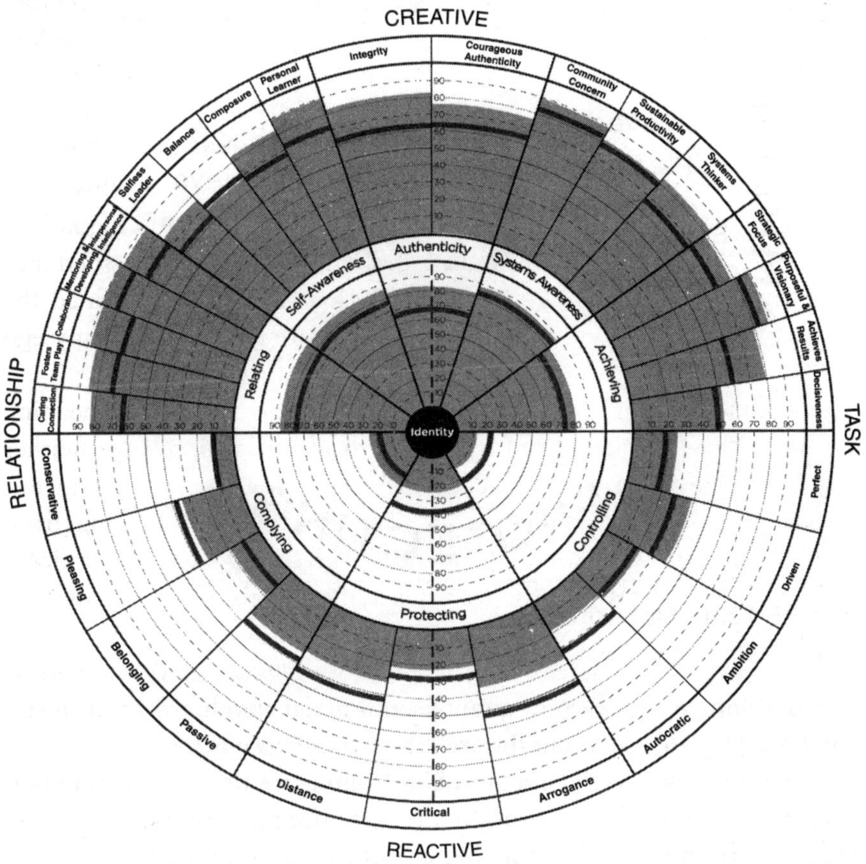

FIGURE 12.3 Extraordinary Leaders' Profile

The bottom half of the profile was designed to provide insight into shadow. The Extraordinary Leader Profile is extraordinary, in part, because of the absence of shadow. Integral level leaders have harvested a lot of shadow and, thus, it may not show up in their Profiles. Such is not the case with many Profiles.

The three types (Heart, Head, and Will) are built into the structure of the LCP and in the bottom Reactive half of the profile. Each type chooses strengths out of which to build its core identity. Reactive beliefs equate these strengths with being good, right, safe, successful, and worthwhile. The linkage of that gift to safety and identity leads to compulsive

FIGURE 12.4 Opposite types

over-development of certain qualities and under-development of others. The under-developed strengths are left in the shadows.

In Figure 12.4, *Complying* and *Controlling* are drawn opposite each other because they are structurally the same but mirror image opposites. They are structurally the same because the core organizing belief equations have the same structure, Identity = X. They are mirror-image opposites because these two types fill in opposite Xs.

Complying types define relationships as what makes them good, safe, and worthwhile. They give up power for safety, sensing power is dangerous. The exercise of will and power is not okay—it is dangerous, untrustworthy, troublesome, selfish, and, therefore, bad. The strengths of power will go underdeveloped in the shadow.

Controlling types take on power to get ahead, to win, and to succeed. They believe: *Power makes me safe and getting results makes me good and worthwhile.* This is how they establish themselves as right, good, safe, and worthwhile. They, therefore, eschew anything that might compromise their power, especially relationships: *Relationships are soft and vulnerable and, therefore, dangerous. They cost me power, which funds my capacity to get results. Loss of power is weakness and not okay. It is wimpy, and, therefore, bad.* Since the opposite strengths of relationships are considered unsafe and illegitimate, they are underdeveloped and disowned.

Shadow Boxing

When working with senior teams, we ask, "What do Controlling types call Complying types?" We get a long list of derogatory descriptors: *wimp, woosie, push-over, weak, unreliable*, etc. Then we reverse the question, "What do these Complying types call Controlling types?" Again, we get a long list of derogatory descriptors: *Animal, control freak, jerk, boss*, etc. We all have a good laugh with this, but we know something is true about what is coming to light.

Such name-calling (*shadow boxing*) goes on all the time. We saw this shadow boxing play out dramatically with Ken and Jack when we discussed Type Dynamics earlier. Jack had nothing good to say about Ken and called him a *useless wimp*. Ken called Jack an *animal*, a big hairy ape who sat in meetings all day beating his chest. Their relationship was dysfunctional—a classic example of the deep mistrust between opposite types who have a lot in shadow.

Since *Protecting* does not have an opposite, it is pictured in the center of the diagram. Protecting types pursue safety in rationality while remaining neutral. They fear vulnerability from either the softness of relationship or the risk of taking on power. The disowned opposite strengths of the Protector can be either strengths of relationship or willpower, or both. Because Protecting is neutral, it tends to gravitate its energy either toward *Complying* or *Controlling*. If it leans toward *Complying*, the strengths it leaves undeveloped in the shadow are those of power. If it leans toward *Controlling*, it leaves relationship strengths undeveloped in its shadow. Protecting-Complying types typically disengage from the risk associated with driving results. The Protecting-Controlling types tend to eschew the vulnerability of relationship. If both relationship and power are disowned, the Protector is largely disengaged and lives in a rational ivory tower, not trusting either the Complying types or Controlling types.

The structure of how each type forms its ego identity, and what it leaves undeveloped in the shadow (and thus mistrusts in others), creates a lot of organizational fireworks. Shadow boxing happens when we see our inner opposite being played out by someone else. We tend to see, in the opposite type, all that we have labeled as illegitimate. The opposite nature of the other is seen, to some degree, as unacceptable. Mistrust easily develops. Each type's Reactive tendency is triggered by the opposite type, such that when we come together, we easily fall into ineffective patterns. Complying types see the Controller as acting out the part of themselves that they have disowned—that is illegitimate, dangerous, and bad. Controlling types look back at the Complier and do the same thing. The Complier is operating from the very stance that Controllers assume will get them killed. Each type sees the opposite way of being as dangerous, irresponsible, and illegitimate. Each type can deeply mistrust the other and disparages them.

Shadow boxing may go on dramatically, as was the case with Ken and Jack, or it may form an undercurrent of mistrust. Either way, it is costly. Collective effectiveness erodes and collective intelligence falls to the lowest common denominator, below what it takes to consistently find leverage in complex systems. At the Integral Stage, we work these un-integrated aspects of ourselves and become more effective at working with those who are different. This enables us to effectively lead complex systems with embedded conflict and opposites in tension.

Shadow Flags

When these types of shadow dynamics are strongly in play within the person and are driving a leader's style of leading, they often show up clearly in Profiles. The Profile "flags (points out) the shadow." Mary's Profile (Figure 12.5) is a good example.

As you can see, Mary's profile is very Reactive. Mary is a strong Controlling-Protecting type, and her leadership style reflects it. Mary is completely identified with getting results and is highly and rationally protected in the way she engages. Relationship is in the shadow. This is seen in her profile in two ways—by the very low scores on Relating and Complying. In the LCP Model, when a Reactive score is very low in relationship to a strongly opposite pattern in the rest of the profile (as in Mary's profile), that low score can be flagging a shadow element—disowned opposite strength. Mary has compulsively over-developed her task-driven result-orientation, and she is actively pushing the softer side of life away. This is the ego-shadow dynamic within Mary.

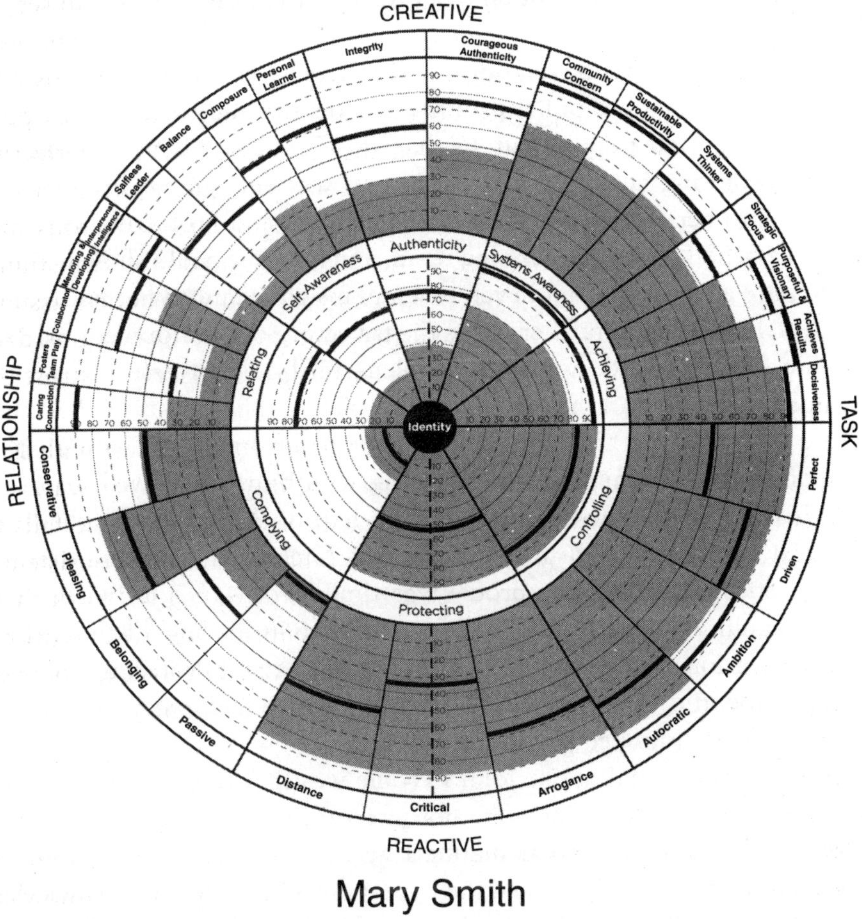

FIGURE 12.5 Mary Smith's profile

Mary came to us a year after having been fired. In her last position, she had led a successful turnaround in a sizable business. The company honored Mary for her success with a celebration banquet, then fired her the next day with no explanation. Mary had spent the last year of her life trying to figure out what had happened to her. Before contacting us, she had taken four other 360° assessments, administered as a part of Executive Development programs at leading universities. Since most leadership development is skill-based, Mary had learned little. After taking the LCP, she said, "Finally I know what happened to me. They were right to fire me." Mary went on to gain more insight into herself and her leadership.

Because Mary was navigating the Reactive to Creative transition by discovering the nature of her primary ego identity and Reactive Mind, it was inappropriate to point out the shadow flag at Complying and engage her in exploring her disowned shadow. It was enough for her to gain insight into her Reactive Mind, her Controlling and Protecting Tendencies, the beliefs that were running them, and how she could show up and lead more effectively. That developmental insight changed her life. Some leaders, however, are further along the trajectory of development, where dealing with the shadow in their profile is a helpful conversation.

Bob: I recently had the privilege of debriefing John on his LCP. At the time, John was a senior partner in a large consulting firm with global responsibility. The night before meeting with him, I reviewed his profile. It was very Creative—the entire top half of the circle was filled in. He had strong task and people skills. His raters had evaluated him as a very effective leader. His profile was similar to Mary's in that it had some significant extensions in the Reactive, bottom half of the circle. The dimensions most extended were Controlling and Protecting (Ambition, Autocratic, Arrogant, and Critical). He also had a shadow flag at Complying that looked just like Mary's.

What was unusual about John's Profile was that the higher scores at Controlling and Protecting were not interrupting Relating, or anything else in the top half, for that matter. I was a bit puzzled about how to explain this to him and formed the hypothesis that he had outgrown the need for these Reactive Tendencies, as he had developed such Creative Competency, but still resorted to them too often. He could let go of these old patterns of leadership behavior and trust that the Creative Competencies would not only carry him, but would outperform the Reactive Tendencies. He could improve his effectiveness by letting them go; he did not need them anymore.

This was my initial read of John's Profile. Since I was unsettled with this read, I decided to sleep on it and re-look at his profile the next morning. When I looked again at his profile, I had an immediate intuitive hit: *This conversation is not about the Reactive to Creative transition. This is an Integral transformation conversation.* I then placed more emphasis on the interpretation of his profile on the extremely low *Complying* score. I did not know if I would bring this up to him, but I was ready to talk about this potential shadow element in his Profile.

Our conversation was an extraordinary one. As is often the case with extraordinary leaders, he was engaged, curious, and open to feedback. We talked about my initial hypothesis that he could let go of his Controlling and Protecting strategies and trust his well-developed Creative capability. He realized that if he did this, he would be more effective and we discussed some example situations where he might experiment with a more effective approach. He found the conversation insightful and helpful.

He then asked, "Bob, is there anything else in this Profile that I should be aware of?"

I did an intuitive gut check and, sensing that I should talk about his shadow flag at Complying, I said, "Your very low score at Complying is a shadow flag."

"What does that mean?" he asked.

When I explained what is meant by shadow and what this low score might mean in his case, he did not find my explanation helpful. I tried a couple of times to suggest what this score might be indicating and I could tell by his response that little of what I was saying was helpful. As this was going on, I was getting an intuitive sense of what I needed to say, but it felt risky to say it. Finally, as my explanations were not helping much, I said to him, "I am going to take a risk here. I have no idea what this will mean to you, but here is what I am getting intuitively: Inside you there is a beautiful, tender, big-hearted little boy who got hurt, and you want nothing to do with him."

He was quiet for a moment and then said, "I know exactly what you are talking about. Thank you. That is most helpful. I also know what I need to do about it."

Harvesting the Shadow

Two years later, I had dinner with John in Sydney, Australia. I asked him about our debrief conversation. He told me that the conversation had profoundly changed his life. Shortly after, he sought out one of the top Shadow Work consultants in the world and did considerable work with this person. He said he is now freer, happier, and more effective as a result. He told me that he was able to harvest all the soft, feeling, vulnerable, emotionally intelligent parts of himself that he had previously rejected and labeled as weak, irrelevant, and ineffective. He thanked me profusely for the profound impact this conversation had made on his life and his leadership.

When I met John in Sydney, he was well along in *harvesting the shadow*. Diving into the shadow means dropping into all that is unfinished within us. This is akin to opening Pandora's Box. It is also a bottomless lake. In the epic Hero's Journey story, *Beowulf*, the shadow is described fiercely as the lake where Grendels live (Heaney, 2000).

> They live in secret places, windy cliffs and wolf dens where water pours from rocks and then runs underground. And the groves of trees hanging out over their lake are all covered with frozen spray that wind down snakelike roots that reach as far as the water and help keep it dark. At night that lake burns like a torch. No one knows its bottom. No wisdom reaches such depth. A deer, driven through the forest by packs of hounds, a stag with great horns, prefers to die on that shore, refuses to save its life in those waters. It is not far from here, nor is it a pleasant spot.[2]

Engaging and harvesting the shadow is the second leg of the Hero's/Heroine's journey. Ken Wilber called the Integral Stage the *Centaur Stage* (Wilber, 2000). The centaur is the Greek mythological figure that is half human and half animal. At the Integral Stage, we take on our opposite nature. We reengage what has been repressed. Much of what has been repressed is the opposite side of our typology, but there is much more in the shadow, all of which has been deemed unacceptable. Much of this has to do with our animal nature and all of its desires that seem to exist, like the centaur, in the lower half of our bodies.

The insurance salesman had a money shadow: "I have been taught all my life that it is bad to have money." Money, sex, power, vulnerability, and intimacy are often in shadow. When we dive into the lake where Grendels live, we do not pick and choose what we find there. We take it all on. This is what John was encountering when he told me that he had been doing shadow work. He was discovering that he had many selves within him. Some want to love, and some want to kill. Some care about

---

[2]From *Beowulf*, tranlslated by Seamus Heaney. Copyright © 2000 by Seamus Heaney. Used by permission of W. W. Norton & Company Inc.

others, and some don't give a crap. Some are masculine, and some are feminine. Some want peace, and some want war. Some seek forgiveness, and some want revenge. These opposites are always in tension within us. Realizing that there are many fiercely competing selves within each of us, and reconciling these opposites, is the work of the Integral Stage.

The Integral Self is an *ecology of opposites* in the same way that a forest is an ecology. A forest's diversity enables it to thrive. That diversity is full of opposites in tension. Some species within the forest are growing while other species are either symbiotically or parasitically feeding on that growth. Other species are feasting on and digesting dead life. Their excrement creates the nutrients for new life. This is an ecology. Death and life co-exist interdependently and quite fiercely in an ecology. The interdependence of opposites in tension is precisely what makes the forest so resilient, healthy, and thriving. The Integral Mind is also an ecology of opposites—light and shadow, male and female, friend and foe. This is precisely what makes it so effective and powerful. This inner diversity needs to be embraced for the full power of the Integral Self to emerge. The shadow can, and must, be harvested.

When the Creative Self first meets the shadow self, it is quite a shock. Eventually, however, this meeting of the inner opposite is not a meeting of opposition or rejection. It may be in the early stages of the Integral transformation because this shadow self is a most unwelcome guest. However, as the transformation proceeds and that guest refuses to leave, the possibility opens of accepting and integrating the disowned opposite self into a higher-order construction of the self—an Integral ecology of opposites. For that to happen, this meeting of opposites needs to be held by a larger self-acceptance and compassion.

The last stanza of one of Rilke's poems profoundly expresses the fierceness, power, and beauty of the Integral Self (Bly, 1980):

> I am the rest between two notes,
> which are somehow always in discord
> because death's note wants to climb over—
> but, in the dark interval, reconciled,
> they stand there trembling.
> And the song goes on, beautiful.

In this poem, you can hear Rilke's facility with the Ascending and Descending Currents of transformation. You can feel the self-compassion in his confession that these two notes are "somehow *always* in discord." Rilke also expresses that his Integral Self is not about trying to fix itself. Nor is he trying to eliminate what seems to be opposite to himself. He discovers the surprise of Integral development: that the work of *harvesting the shadow* is much more elegant than all that fixing and self-improving. It is reconciliation, forgiveness, and compassion for all that is forever unfinished. Rilke discovers that, like the forest, this partialness is wholeness, and the song goes on, beautiful.

The song goes on beautiful for a couple of reasons. First, as Jung said, most shadow is solid gold—gifts to be harvested. Second, the ecologically constructed Integral Self is far more capable of serving, healing, and making whole the larger system. Let's explore both.

Path of Development—Gifts in Shadow

Recall that the path of development into Creative Mind is up, not across the circle (see Figure 12.6).

We do not ask leaders to develop their opposite side right away. That is the path of most resistance, as it goes right through the shadow.

What is the typical prescription for a highly controlling leader like Mary? Typically, we send her to charm school and try to help her become a kinder, gentler version of herself. We work on her weakness instead of leveraging her strength. This is asking Mary to go directly into her shadow—the side of herself she mistrusts the most. She is armed to the teeth against doing that. Mary is hard-wired for results, so let's have a results conversation with her. Let's help Mary understand the difference between Controlling and Achieving. If we can help Mary unhook her natural strengths and gifts from Reactive Structure and evolve a more mature relationship with those gifts, she becomes a highly Creative-Achieving Leader. In so doing, she moves from *power over* people to *power with* people. She develops a clearer stand for an organizational purpose and vision for which she cares. She is then challenged to help people get on the same page with her and to build alignment among key stakeholders. Mary is now building relationships that serve her passion for results. This is the developmental path of least resistance for Mary to boot up her Creative Mind. Once this movement is mature, the Integral phase of her journey becomes available. At this phase, Mary will engage more directly with her disowned opposite strengths. She will enter more

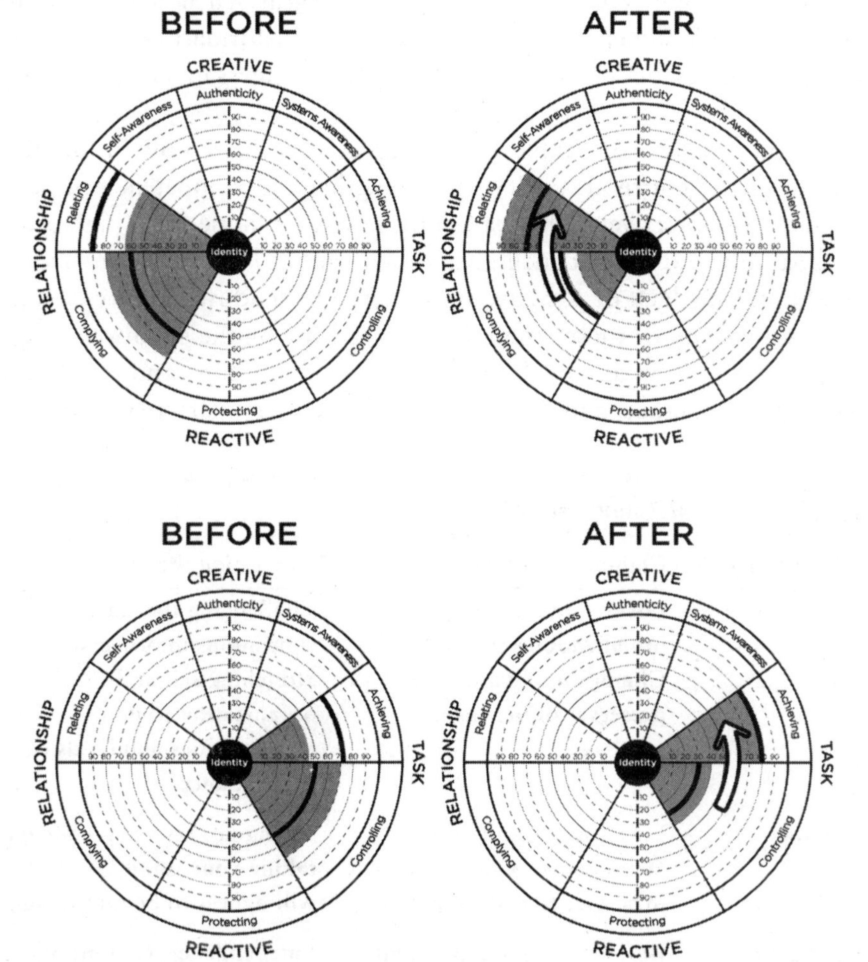

FIGURE 12.6 The Path of Development

deeply into the soft and vulnerable parts of herself, bring those gifts to maturity, and become an even more extraordinary and effective leader.

This same path of least resistance is available for each type. Complying moves toward Relating first, and then, as the journey progresses, takes on its disowned aggression and power. Protecting types move toward Courage—learning how to tell their considerable truth with respect. In so doing, they harvest their Creative strengths of Awareness (self and system) and Authenticity. As the Integral journey unfolds, they develop their disowned strengths (either taking on the risk of using their power, or the vulnerability of relationship). The Integral Self not only gets its primary gift in higher-order form (from the transformation from Reactive to Creative), but now it gets its opposite giftedness in its higher-order form.

As you can see from Table 12.1, Integral leaders are now in full possession of the entire array of gifts, strengths, and competencies that it takes to lead effectively. Their strengths have been honed to a high order of capability and are not encumbered by Reactive limitations or shadow liabilities. This lack of Reactive limitation and shadow liability enables them to use any of these strengths as called for by the situation. These leaders can pull on any of these capabilities at any time and as needed, with elegance, grace, and mastery, making them very effective leaders.

TABLE 12.1 Harvesting the shadow

COMPLYING	Claiming Your True Gift	Harvesting the Shadow
Conservative	Loyalty and fidelity to the organization's purpose. Champion of values and preserver of heritage.	Challenging the status quo; continuous improvement. Stretching self and organization to new opportunities and levels of performance.
Pleasing	Love for self and others. Willingness to give of oneself in service to others' needs.	Saying no, asserting yourself, taking your stand, willingness to be unpopular.
Belonging	Builder of community and organization, committed purpose.	Independence. Championing directions that are counter to the status quo.
Passive	Service. Non-attachment, acquiescing to the needs of others, egoless.	Achievement for the enjoyment of it. Asserting yourself. Leading, being a creative force in your own and the organization's future.
PROTECTING	**Claiming Your True Gift**	**Harvesting the Shadow**
Distance	Wisdom through detachment, care, and reflection.	Engagement. Self-confidence and assertion. An active group member.

Critical	Discernment through being inquisitive and challenging limited thinking.	Supporting and encouraging others. Valuing what is best about the other's position.
Arrogance	Strength of character without the need for credit. Mentoring others into their own "bigness."	Egolessness. Willingness to be unseen and unnoticed so that others can grow into their greatness.
CONTROLLING	Claiming Your True Gift	Harvesting the Shadow
Perfect	Constant pursuit of continuous improvement balanced with acceptance for things/people as they are. Desire to create outstanding results.	Gentle treatment of self and others. Acceptance of self and others. Detachment from the outcome. Stepping back that others may learn and grow.
Driven	Willingness to work and risk for what you love. Doing whatever it takes to realize your deepest longings.	Receptiveness. Slowing down to reflect and renew. Bringing wisdom into action.
Ambition	Desire to create outstanding results. Personal energy to pursue worthy results.	Loyal fellowship, collaboration, mutuality in relationships. Stepping back that others may learn and grow.
Autocratic	Service through personal strength, persistence, and influence. The integrity to do what is needed even if it is controversial.	Sensitivity to self and others. Respect and care, willingness to experience and share vulnerability—intimacy. Loyal fellowship and collaboration.

FIERCE COMPASSION, THE DANCE OF ENEMIES

The Integral Self is both fierce and compassionate. Fierce compassion heals. David Whyte says: "The blade is so sharp it cuts things together, not apart" (Whyte, 1992). The inner work of the Integral transformation is shadow work—work that integrates shadow elements into a larger, more inclusive construction of the self. This "cutting things together, not apart" can only happen with searing honesty, self-compassion, and forgiveness. It is just this honest compassion for the inner conflict and unresolvedness within oneself that enables the leader to hold the conflicted visions and redundant polarities in the outer world with equanimity, tolerance, and compassionate forgiveness. This fiercely embodied compassionate leadership is now mature enough to call forth conflicting stakeholders and hold them in a dialogue with the level of tolerance, urgency, acceptance, resolve, forgiveness, humility, and courage that allows for higher-order systemic resolution to emerge. When leaders reach this stage, they are capable of orchestrating a high level of collective effectiveness and intelligence. As a result, new, sustainable future visions, as well as the systemic design innovations required to realize them, naturally emerge.

As shadow is reintegrated, the leader no longer makes others who are different, or who hold very different visions, into enemies. This ability to meet significant diversity, conflict, and divisiveness within the system of the self becomes a capability the leader has to meet and heal systemically—in the larger system beyond the self.

Integral leaders become capable of holding and healing large systemic division, incongruity, and conflict for two reasons. First, the system and the self are not separate. Leaders all too often sponsor change, but they are not changed by the change they sponsor because at earlier levels they see themselves as separate from the system—as the antidote to the system's problems. Integral leaders see the unresolvedness, conflict, and dysfunction "out there" as a mirror of what is "in here." "*I am a microcosm of the system I am trying to change. Thus, I need to do most of the changing.*" The ability to see the system's need for transformation interdependently with one's own need for transformation is what makes Integrally-led change efforts succeed and actually achieve the intended results and sustain those performance shifts over time.

A second reason why Integral leaders can successfully lead systemic change is that they are no longer projecting their shadow. Shadow projection (seeing in others a projection of our shadow self and making them into enemies, and not seeing all the damage that our shadow, individually and collectively, is causing) goes on all the time in relationships, team dynamics, organizational dynamics, and world politics. It is inherently divisive, erodes trust, and lowers collective effectiveness and intelligence to such a degree that damage is done. This is what we often see in and between governments—vilifying the opposing side when both sides have an unseen and unacknowledged contribution to the dysfunction. All of this is shadow projection and it is doing terrible damage worldwide.

Unless leaders in positions of power evolve to Integral leadership, we are not likely to resolve the complex knot of perilous global issues that we now face. Reactive Mind has a lot in shadow; therefore, it does not see its contribution to those problems, sees others as the main cause of the problems, and has a lot of enemies. Since its orientation is to fix what is wrong, the basic dynamic at the Reactive level is the need to convert you, fix you, or destroy you. Problems need to be eliminated.

Creative Mind has also not yet seen into its shadow. However, it is not so oriented toward fixing and eliminating problems. Instead, it is oriented toward championing its vision. For the Creative leader, the conflict between opposites takes the form of trying to convince each other of the rightness of its perspective, not noticing that the other's perspective has validity, and that validity may well be in my shadow. So, neither Reactive nor Creative leadership is mature enough to hold the tension of conflicting opposites to enable breakthroughs to emerge. This comes with integrating the shadow, meaning that I no longer turn you into an enemy. I take the log out of my own eye and see you clearly. "You are not my enemy. You are the part of me that I make into an enemy. We are not so different, you and I. I am a microcosm of the health and dysfunction in the whole system. So are you. As such, I am more like you than I care to admit. I have met the enemy, and they are us. We are both a part of the problem and part of its resolution. For transformational change to happen, I must be transformed. I must do most of the changing. I must be the change I want to see in the world." When adversaries come together with this Integral level of awareness, peace breaks out.

We once met a man who was deeply involved with Ronald Reagan and Mikhail Gorbachev, behind the scenes, in preparing for the meeting at Reykjavik. Reagan and Gorbachev were in different discernment processes at the time. While Reagan was name-calling (Evil Empire), Gorbachev was starting to see the whole system. He was seeing what we call "the Dance of Enemies" and his and the Soviet Union's part in it. His analysis went like this: "You build bombs. So, we build bigger bombs. Then, you build even bigger bombs, and we build even bigger bombs. You call us names, so we call you different names that mean much the same. We are not so different, you and I." Gorbachev was taking an Integral perspective on the arms race.

At the same time, Peter Senge and the folks in the MIT Systems Dynamics Lab were modeling the Arms Race. They had come to a disconcerting conclusion. They were stumped. They could find no way, from within the assumptions and structure of the arms race, to stop it from escalating. Nor could they find a way to make it spiral down; it perpetually spun up.

Gorbachev found the hidden point of leverage in the system of the arms race where a simple and small change in structure makes a large and lasting change in performance over time. He showed up at Reykjavik and said to Reagan, "I am here to deprive you of an enemy." In effect, he was saying: "I see the whole game (system) we are in together. I have my contribution. You have yours. I am the enemy you accuse me of being. So are you. We are not so different. I will change the game. I will deprive you of an enemy. I disarm—unilaterally. Deal with that."

Reagan and Gorbachev left that meeting as friends, and the arms race began to spin down.

One statement, "I am here to deprive you of an enemy," was so full of Integral insight and wisdom that it changed the world. Gorbachev saw that the dysfunction and conflict "out there" in the larger system was also mirrored "in here." He saw the log in his own eye. He had met the enemy in himself and in his country. He could reconcile these discordant opposites with forgiveness and compassion. He gave Reagan nothing to fight against. "I am the enemy you accuse me of being. You are my shadow and I am yours. I own my shadow and make no requirement that you do the same. I disarm. I am stopping my part in the game. Your move."

We suggest that Gorbachev's insight, and the clear statement of his stance/strategy, "I am here to deprive you of an enemy," could only be found from an Integral Structure of Mind. Only Integral Leadership is complex enough (seeing the whole system, the interdependence of the inner and outer system, and how the whole system lives in me and in you) to come up with this. This statement could not have been sourced from within Reactive Mind. It is too oppositional, too binary, too focused on fixing the external problem ("out there"), and too good and bad, right and wrong oriented to ever come up with "I have met the enemy and they are us."

Reactive Mind is responsible for the politics of blame that has Washington, D.C. in gridlock. Reactive Mind is capable of statements like those made by George W. Bush after 9/11: "If you're not for us, you're against us. Let's get them on their soil before they get us on ours." Much of the war on terrorism is being fought between a pre-Reactive mindset and a Reactive one. Neither is mature enough to change the game fundamentally.

Gorbachev's statement is also not likely to have been sourced from Creative Mind. It is too focused on the rightness of its vision and values. It does not yet see its shadow (the log in its own eye). Therefore, it is less likely of coming to the inner reconciliation between the "two notes which are somehow always in discord." It still projects its shadow on the other and makes it into an enemy. It may not be an enemy we have to kill, but it must be converted to our vision. Creative Mind is often too focused on championing a vision of greatness to be able to "seek first to understand" as St. Francis required. Creative Leadership is not yet complex enough to do what Gorbachev did. This kind of systemic wisdom—seeing the whole system, seeing my/our contribution to the conflict, reconciling inner opposites so that the outer opposites in conflict may be reconciled, summoning genuine compassion for the shadow of conflicting parties, seeing clearly that the dysfunction and unresolvedness out there is a manifestation of the dysfunction and unresolvedness in me/us, finding in all this the one hidden place of leverage that can change everything—only reaches its full possibility with the transformation to Integral Mind.

Integral Mind is capable of changing the world. It is Gorbachev at Reykjavik. It is Nelson Mandela ending Apartheid and healing the Nation of South Africa. It is Gandhi fasting to end the riots between Muslims and Hindus in Calcutta. It is Aung San Suu Kyi, leading a successful, non-violent, democratic revolution from a prison cell in Burma. Only Integral Mind or higher is complex enough to lead truly large-scale, sustainable, systemic change.

WHY IS CHANGE SO DIFFICULT?

We have been asking—and answering—this question throughout this book. The leadership of complex systemic change requires leadership of a matching complexity of mind.

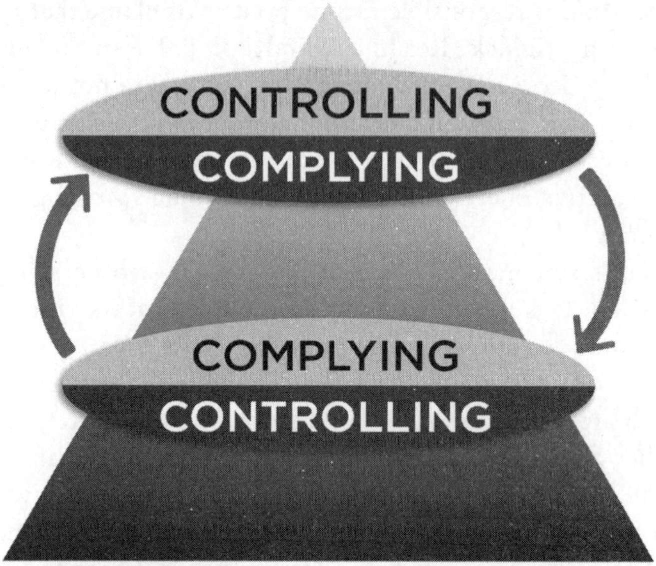

FIGURE 12.7 Patriarchy's shadow—the challenge of transformation

Most organizations are challenged to move from Patriarchy to Partnership (Figure 12.7). In this transition those at the top, mostly Controlling types, are required to share power and let go of control (the scariest thing they can do). To whom do they let go of control? Complying Types. Their shadow—the part of themselves they mistrust the most. Complying types are challenged to take on power and to take more risk (the scariest thing they could do). With whom must they step into power? Controlling types. Their shadow—the part of themselves they mistrust the most. We wonder why it is hard? In movement from Patriarchy to Partnership everyone is required to upgrade their operating system. That is the Development Agenda. If it does not happen, we all collude in going back to normal.

INTEGRAL LEADERSHIP IMPERATIVE

In this book, we have explored the link between leadership effectiveness and business performance, between mastery and maturity, between mastery in the outer game and maturity of the inner game. We have explained why the complexity of mind, individual and collective, must evolve at the pace of change and escalating complexity to remain relevant and effective today. We have shown how each progressive level of leadership is designed to get a predictable pattern of results. We put forth six practices that transform leadership from one stage to the next, and we have described a systemic approach to developing the leadership system, all as an extended argument for the Leadership Imperative facing every organization.

Later Stages of Mind are required to navigate the complexity we are now facing in the business environment and in the world. Most leaders are running a Reactive level IOS. It is not complex enough. Creative Mind may not even be complex enough. It is a necessary and required evolution, but may not yet be complex enough to lead and sustain radical systemic change. Integral Mind is optimized for this task. It is capable of navigating through the complex and interdependent issues we face in our global business environment as well as geopolitically. The Leadership Imperative we face in our businesses and in our world today is that only 5% of leaders are operating from Integral Mind.

Integral level leadership is highly effective for navigating the complex change and thorny interdependent global issues we face today because it has:

- Developed the requisite problem solving, management, and execution skills of the Reactive Stage.
- All the Self-authoring, Visionary, Authentic, Emotionally Intelligent, Self-awareness and Systems Awareness competency of the Creative Mind.
- The mastery to ride the Ascending and Descending Currents of transformation such that now the leader is self-transforming and system transforming.
- Opened up into a larger vision of Systemic interdependence and welfare.
- Become the Servant Leader—servant of the system's welfare and its architect.
- Cultivated the intuition required to find leverage in the midst of complexity.
- The seeming magic to see, intuitively around corners in making decisions in a way that sometimes defies logic.

- Seen the whole trajectory of development and is capable of working at any level within that trajectory to foster transformation, individual and collective.
- Matured the ability to hold huge conflict in tension, the ability to see the unresolvedness "out there" as its own unresolvedness.
- Stopped projecting its shadow and making enemies out of others who hold different perspectives.
- The ability to meet the enemy and see that "they are us," to take the log out of its own eye, to meet the enemy as myself and to meet it with compassion.

This is why Integral Mind is built for complexity and capable of leading systemic change. The Integral Mind has included and transcended all the competencies developed as it came through the Reactive and Creative Structures of Mind. It has harvested the gifts and strengths of the shadow. It can now use all of these strengths with the mastery and maturity required of the moment with an unparalleled acceptance of difference and a unique compassion for the bitterness of conflict that has ensued from earlier levels of consciousness.

The Unified Model of Leadership and its metrics point to the conclusion that accelerating the development of leadership is an imperative in today's world, that this must be systemically approached from a developmental perspective, and that we must hasten the day when we have more Integral level leaders than Reactive level leaders. This is a tall agenda. Our world depends on it.

TAKING STOCK

- What's your contribution to the problems that so frustrate you?
- How are you the enemy? The enemy you see in others?
- What are you laying your life down for?
- How much compassion do you practice on a daily basis for yourself and others? How willing are you to forgive yourself and others?
- How are you destroying the world? How are you saving the world?

Chapter 13

Unity

Journey's End, Development Turned Upside Down

We have explicated a Universal Model of Leadership Development, a consciousness-based model grounded in experience, theory, research, and psychometrics. However, any complete description of human development would be inadequate if not inclusive of, and grounded in, the Wisdom Traditions that describe the highest reaches of human consciousness.

Unity Consciousness is the highest *level* of consciousness in human experience. We do not consider it a *Stage of Development*, since from the Unitive perspective there are no stages. This paradox turns the development world upside down. The mind is unable to wrap itself around the *unknowable*—that which is prior to mind altogether.

This chapter will be brief for four good reasons: 1) it could be an entire book; 2) it seems wrong to write a lot of words about *oneness*; 3) we know very little about it; and 4) the vast majority of us are not living in Unity—we operate at other consciousness levels.

Hence, we can claim no authority about what we write here. We can only report from those who live from a Unity Consciousness and from our glimpses into that Unity—what can be seen, known, and experienced in these short tastes of the *One Taste*.

Moreover, we will make little attempt to relate Unity Consciousness to leadership, effectiveness, or mastery. We will provide no statistics or research. Honestly, we have no way of knowing how Unity Consciousness relates to leadership in practical terms. However, what we do know is that those people who have most moved the world—Jesus, Buddha, Krishna, etc.—spoke from and as Unity Itself. The great saints and spiritual masters have given us a glimpse of what leadership looks like when the self is no more.

Although logic cannot apprehend Unity Consciousness, thinking about it logically may help. *Unity* means *one*—not two, not many, not diversity—only one. If there is Unity, then, there is only one. Therefore, when there is Unity Consciousness, there is awareness of only one. In this state of awareness, you and I are not two, but only one.

WAVES ON THE OCEAN

The best metaphor we can think of for describing our relationship to Unity is that we are like waves on the ocean, not separate from the ocean. We are the *ocean-ness* itself. If we are identified with being separate waves, then we experience ourselves on a journey across the ocean. We are surfing on the ocean, and it is an adventurous ride. *Ocean* is seen to be separate from our *wave-ness*. As separate waves, we experience the ups and downs of wave life. We love the ups and strive for them. We fear the downs and work to avoid them.

From the perspective of our wave-ness, it appears that we are separate from other waves; after all, they are *over there* and look different. Looking out at other waves creates comparison. We want to be *more than*, *bigger than*, *faster than* other waves, and we think we are better off if we are. This creates desire for gains and fear of loss. Some waves appear friendly; other waves may appear to threaten our ability to get what we want, and so we fear them. We may even make them into an enemy. In addition, some waves are different enough that we think they are less of a wave. Therefore, we think they are not worthy of wave life. We enslave or ethnically cleanse these waves. We may treat them with bigotry and prejudice. Some waves are treated as second-class citizens and denied certain privileges or access to opportunity simply because they appear different. While some waves are privileged, other waves are allowed to live in poverty because they are *over there*, different, and not part of us. Competition, conflict, and even wars break out between waves. Such is ocean life when we lose touch with our ocean-ness.

As we travel, we wonder what happens when we reach the shore. We know this waveform has an end, and we fear our demise. Do we exist after our death? All of this causes us to wonder if there is an Ocean. We search for the Ocean and strive to be in relationship with the Ocean in order that we might join the Ocean after we die. As we search for the Ocean, we suffer the loss of our ocean-ness. We may even forget altogether our inherent unity with the Ocean and with all waveforms arising on and as the ocean. Thus, we long for something, and we know not what. We long for forgotten Union. We try to fill in this longing with more of almost everything, but it does not fulfill. So we suffer.

When we suffer, we are like *thirsty water*. Striving for Unity Consciousness is like water trying to quench its thirst. As a separate wave, we are thirsty because we are caught in the illusion that we are separate from our source condition. We search for water to quench our thirst, not realizing that *we are the water,* and there is, in reality, no thirst. The search to become our *selves* is driven by this thirst. All longing, all desire, is for the *one* that we already are; therefore, all of our striving and searching for fulfillment to quench our thirst is in vain. It can never fulfill.

Ultimate fulfillment happens when we awake from the dream of our separate wave-ness. When we awake, the search ends. We realize that we never needed to search. All of the problems and dilemmas that seemed so important and unsolvable in the dream simply evaporate. We realize that we were always one with the Ocean, that we were never separate, and that all waves are one; we are all each other. There is only Ocean. We also realize that we are the eternal ocean itself, and, as this Unity, we know that there is no death. What we call *death* is only a change of form. The struggle and fear of separate ego life ends. There is only abiding love, bliss, joy, and freedom.

Simply put, there is only Unity, only the One. Nothing is other than this simplicity, not even you. You are not who you think you are. In fact, you have no idea who you are. As long as there is a you, you do not know who you are. Once you know who you really are, there is no you left to know.

NO SELF, ALL GOD

In the Western spiritual traditions, the highest levels of experience are described as *union with God*. God is commonly referred to as a duality—a self in relationship to a Divine other. Yet if we are in union, then there is only one. To be completely in union is to be completely one with that with which we are in union. In Unity, then, duality dissolves.

Meister Eckhart, the great 13th century Christian mystic, once said in a sermon that his most fervent prayer is, "God rid me of God" (Fox, 2014). He went on to describe his experience of Unity and the pain of slipping out of that state of union back into his separate ego self-sense. In praying, "God rid me of God," he was praying to be permanently realized in God. In the state of Unity, it is as accurate to say that *there is no God* (as traditionally experienced as a self-other relationship) as it is to say that *there is only God*, and as accurate to say that *there is no you* as it is to say that *there is only you*. There is only *one*, and nothing is other than that *One*. In Divine union, only the Unity is astonishingly experienced as prior to the *God–you* duality, prior to *I–Thou*, prior to relatedness and all difference. This is why some Eastern spiritual traditions do not speak of God, only of the experience beyond mind, beyond self, beyond knowing, and beyond all difference. This is Satori, Nirvana, and the Kingdom of Heaven.

Taoist writer-philosopher Wei Wu Wei is credited with this provocative statement (Wei, 2002):

> Why are you unhappy?
> Because 99.9 percent of everything you think,
> And of everything you do,
> Is for yourself—
> And there isn't one.

In Unity, the self is surrendered. The *self* moves from subject to object and, as an object, it is seen as mirage. From that perspective, the story of separate self, all of its gains and losses, desires and fears, problems and dilemmas are simply noticed as dreams from which we have awakened. The mirage of the ego, then, simply evaporates, and we are no longer subject to an ego at all. There is no objective, separate self, and there never was. There is only subject, only the ground of being, only the pure, undifferentiated Unity out of which all diversity arises. In this awareness, all diversity is recognized as a Unity. This is astonishingly obvious. This is the most joyous, free, love-blissful experience imaginable. It is *rapture*. It so obvious that it is no big deal. It is simply the utter nature of reality. There is only one. All diversity, including ourselves, arises from and as Unity. In that Unity, there is only joy, only love, only freedom, only bliss, only light, only silent stillness, and an emptiness that is radiant. This is the "pearl of great price."

DEVELOPMENT TURNED UPSIDE DOWN

The individual self is not the truth. This book has been about the journey of ego development as it relates to leadership effectiveness. Each progressive Structure of Mind is a more mature ego-identity structure. The movement into Unity is different. The ego is not *matured* into Unity—it is *surrendered*. You must forget yourself. Unity Consciousness is not a higher-order Structure of Mind, of ego, or identity. Unity Consciousness is identity-less.

In Unity, the individuated self—however mature, developed, and accomplished—is seen as not ultimate, not the truth. This is what turns developmental theory upside down. If there is no *self*, then *self-development* cannot lead to the highest Consciousness.

No amount of self-development work can help. You cannot get there from here. You cannot surrender the self by working hard to improve the self. In fact, all efforts at self-improvement actually prevent the transformation into Unity Consciousness. Seeking and striving do not help either. Only the separate self can seek and strive, and the seeking itself maintains the ego self that is searching. Seeking to improve, to change, to create, to move on, to become is all a defense against the ultimate surrender of the self. In this transformation, you are at journey's end, and there is nothing you can do except to surrender your very self.

With the end of ego, we are now living in and as the Unity that is always already inherently present. In this awareness, we realize that the Stages of Development were all part of the dream. There never was a separate ego self, and it was only from the perspective of the separate ego self that it appeared that we went on a development journey. The Structures of Mind through which we seemed to evolve were just structures of ego mind. Now we are living from and as our inherent Unity, which is beyond mind, prior to mind. We still have a body and a brain. We still think and act. However, we are not identified with any of that. We now view our wave-ness from the abiding perspective as the Ocean. We, our individuated forms, are just forms arising from and as Unity itself. That Self never went on a journey and never needed development.

Does this invalidate the first 12 chapters of this book (and all of the psychological, personal, and leadership development theory, research, and practice)? Perhaps. We cannot really know unless we are living from and as Unity.

TWO ARGUMENTS FOR DEVELOPMENT

Here is how we hold the dilemma of developing the self that is no-self. We will make two arguments for the necessity of development.

First, no amount of Unity Consciousness will equip you to design an aircraft if you have not deeply studied calculus, physics, and the principles of aeronautical engineering. By the same token, if you want to develop mastery in the art of leadership, a mature Structure of Mind is required. Most of us will not realize Unity Consciousness in this lifetime. So, we need something to do that helps. Why not develop? Why not become more effective? Furthermore, living as Unity will not necessarily make you a more effective leader. You still have to live, work, and lead in the complexities of the current business environment. You still need a complex Structure of Mind through which to translate insight into action and results. In other words, development is necessary to being effective and is insufficient for realizing Unity.

Second, only the mature ego can be surrendered. Egos too deeply caught in Reactivity can never surrender. Even if we glimpse, for a moment, a state experience of Unity, we quickly snap back to the center of gravity of our current Structure of Mind. In other words, we fall back asleep into the same dream we were having before we momentarily awakened. Integral Mind is the most evolved Structure of Mind that has been researched. We think that Integral Mind is mature enough and inclusive enough to surrender the illusion of diversity. Once we see that "we have met the enemy and they are us," the illusion of the separate self is now transparent enough to be seen through. As Rilke says in a poem, "And then God, from his place of ambush, leaps out" (Rilke, 1982). The highest and most hard-earned levels of human maturity may just be the optimal "place of ambush" where ego dies and we, astonished, see into our inherent Unity. In short, we think development into mature Structures of Mind and Identity is preliminary to the breakthrough to Unity. Development helps, but it is only preliminary practice for the arduous work of surrendering identity altogether.

NOT ME, NOT ME

In Eastern tradition, the phrase used for this transformation is *Neti-Neti* (*not me, not me*). As we progress through the Stages of Development, each transformation is a *Neti-Neti* realization. In the transition from adolescence to Reactive Mind, we realize we are not merely this independent capability to meet our egocentric needs. In the transition from Reactive to Creative Mind, we realize that we are not merely this externalized identity that depends on outside validation for worth and security. In the transition from Creative to Integral Mind, we realize that we are not just this hard-earned, self-authoring, authentic version of ourselves. We are many selves, perhaps even all selves.

Each Stage of Development is the death of a small version of our self for a larger version of our self. In the surrender into Unity, we face the big *Neti-Neti*. The separate self that we have worked so hard to improve is not me. This time, we do not surrender into a large version of our self, but we surrender the self altogether and live as Unity Itself. All prior surrenders of a smaller self for a larger self are simply practice rounds for the surrender of self-hood altogether.

UNITY LEADERSHIP

When the consciousness that animates us and our leadership is that of Unity, *justice* is our natural state: non-violence toward, acceptance of, and tolerance of difference is effortless. The other waves are not different. We are one Ocean. We are each other.

This is the state of being from which Jesus said, "Love your neighbor as yourself," since your neighbor is your *Self*. When we live from the consciousness that we are all each other, war, poverty, bigotry, prejudice, and hatred simply cannot arise. We know that the suffering of another, *over there*, is our suffering. Another father/mother's children are our children. We become intolerant of systems that are not inclusive and keep *our children* worldwide trapped in poverty, injustice, and lack of opportunity. We become servants of humanity. We see that all creatures are one in that Unity, and we become stewards of the planet.

We will not reach a tipping point soon where a critical mass of leaders live and lead as Unity. This will not happen in time to prevent the global calamity for which we are heading. We believe that what is needed is for mature leadership to emerge that can make the critical difference in the outcome on this planet. We are convinced that this requires, at a minimum, Integral Mind leading from the presumption of our inherent Unity. Integral Mind is mature enough and complex enough to match wits with the complexities of global challenges. If that mature leadership capability can lead and function from the presumption of our inherent and prior Unity, then we can find the global systemic solutions that usher in a thriving future for all inhabitants on the planet and for the planet itself. This is the Leadership Imperative.

The Mission Statement for The Leadership Circle and for the Full Circle Group is:

> We exist
> to evolve the conscious practice of leadership
> to steward the planet
> and to awaken us all to our inherent unity.

We invite you to take on the Leadership Agenda for your organization and evolve the effective and conscious leadership, in yourself and others, that is so needed in the world.

TAKING STOCK

- What ego strategies have you exhausted and which ones continue to exhaust you? How would you live if you knew that ego fulfillment is an illusion?
- To what are you attached, that if you let go of, would set you free?
- Have you opened your love to the great love? Are you are helping people you have never known and may never see? (Barks, 2004)
- Have you ever been introduced to the "you" that pre-dates you, that wants for nothing, that has nothing to lose, and that does not need development and never did?

Appendix 1

Leadership Circle Profile Dimensions

Relating summary dimension measures the leader's capability to relate to others in a way that brings out the best in people, groups, and organizations. It is composed of:

- **Caring Connection**, which measures the leader's interest in and ability to form warm, caring relationships.
- **Fosters Team Play**, which measures the leader's ability to foster high-performance teamwork among team members who report to him/her, across the organization and within teams in which s/he participates.
- **Collaborator**, which measures the extent to which the leader engages others in a manner that allows the parties involved to discover common ground.
- **Mentoring & Developing**, which measures the leader's ability to develop others through mentoring and maintaining growth-enhancing relationships.
- **Interpersonal Intelligence**, which measures the interpersonal effectiveness with which the leader listens, engages in conflict and controversy, deals with the feelings of others, and manages his/her own feelings.

Self-Awareness summary dimension measures the leader's orientation to ongoing professional and personal development, as well as the degree to which inner self-awareness is expressed through high integrity leadership. It is composed of:

- **Selfless Leader**, which measures the extent to which the leader pursues service over self-interest, where the need for credit and personal ambition is far less important than creating results that serve a common good.
- **Balance**, which measures the leader's ability to keep a healthy balance between business and family, activity and reflection, work and leisure—the tendency to be self-renewing and handle the stress of life without losing the self.
- **Composure**, which measures the leader's ability, in the midst of conflict and high-tension situations, to remain composed and centered and to maintain a calm, focused perspective.
- **Personal Learner**, which measures the degree to which the leader demonstrates a strong and active interest in learning and personal and professional growth. It measures the extent to which s/he actively and reflectively pursues growing in self-awareness, wisdom, knowledge, and insight.

Authenticity summary dimension measures the leader's capability to relate to others in an authentic, courageous, and high integrity manner. It is composed of:

- **Integrity**, which measures how well the leader adheres to the set of values and principles that s/he espouses; that is, how well s/he can be trusted to "walk the talk."
- **Courageous Authenticity**, which measures the leader's willingness to take tough stands, bring up the "undiscussables" (risky issues the group avoids discussing), and openly deal with difficult relationship problems.

Systems Awareness summary dimension measures the degree to which the leader's awareness is focused on whole system improvement, productivity, and community welfare. It is composed of:

- **Community Concern**, which measures the service orientation from which the leader leads. It measures the extent to which s/he links his/her legacy to service of community and global welfare.

- **Sustainable Productivity,** which measures the leader's ability to achieve results in a way that maintains or enhances the overall long-term effectiveness of the organization. It measures how well s/he balances human/technical resources to sustain long-term high performance.
- **Systems Thinker,** which measures the degree to which the leader thinks and acts from a whole system perspective as well as the extent to which s/he makes decisions in light of the long-term health of the whole system.

Achieving summary dimension measures the extent to which the leader offers visionary, authentic, and high achievement leadership. It is composed of:

- **Strategic Focus,** which measures the extent to which the leader thinks and plans rigorously and strategically to ensure that the organization will thrive in the near and long term.
- **Purposeful & Visionary,** which measures the extent to which the leader clearly communicates and models commitment to personal purpose and vision.
- **Achieves Results,** which measures the degree to which the leader is goal-directed and has a track record of goal achievement and high performance.
- **Decisiveness,** which measures the leader's ability to make decisions on time and the extent to which s/he is comfortable moving forward in uncertainty.

Complying summary dimension measures the extent to which a leader gets a sense of self-worth and security by complying with the expectations of others rather than acting on what s/he intends and wants. It is composed of:

- **Conservative,** which measures the extent to which the leader thinks and acts conservatively, follows procedure, and lives within the prescribed rules of the organization with which s/he is associated.
- **Pleasing,** which measures the leader's need to seek others' support and approval in order to feel secure and worthwhile as a person. People

with strong needs for approval tend to base their degree of self-worth on their ability to gain others' favor and confirmation.

- **Belonging**, which measures the leader's need to conform, follow the rules, and meet the expectations of those in authority. It measures the extent to which s/he goes along to get along, thereby compressing the full extent of his/her creative power into culturally acceptable boxes.
- **Passive**, which measures the degree to which the leader gives away his/her power to others and to circumstances outside his/her control. It is a measure of the extent to which s/he believes that s/he is not the creator of his/her life experience, that his/her efforts do not make much difference, and that s/he lacks the power to create the future s/he wants.

Protecting summary dimension measures the belief that the leader can protect himself/herself and establish a sense of worth through withdrawal and remaining distant, hidden, aloof, cynical, superior, and/or rational. It is composed of:

- **Arrogance**, which measures the leader's tendency to project a large ego—behavior that is experienced as superior, egotistical, and self-centered.
- **Critical**, which measures the leader's tendency to take a critical, questioning, and somewhat cynical attitude.
- **Distance**, which measures the leader's tendency to establish a sense of personal worth and security through withdrawal, being superior and remaining aloof, emotionally distant, and above it all.

Controlling summary dimension measures the extent to which the leader establishes a sense of personal worth through task accomplishment and personal achievement. It is composed of:

- **Perfect**, which measures the leader's need to attain flawless results and perform to extremely high standards in order to feel secure and worthwhile as a person. Worth and security are equated with being perfect, performing constantly at heroic levels, and succeeding beyond all expectations.
- **Driven**, which measures the extent to which the leader is in overdrive. It is a measure of his/her belief that worth and security are tied to

accomplishing a great deal through hard work. It measures his/her need to perform at a very high level in order to feel worthwhile as a person. A good work ethic is a strength of this style, provided that the leader keeps things in balance and is able to balance helping others achieve with his/her own achievement.

- **Ambition**, which measures the extent to which the leader needs to get ahead, move up in the organization, and be better than others. Ambition is a powerful motivator. This scale assesses if that motivation is positive, furthering progress—or negative, becoming overly self-centered and competitive.
- **Autocratic**, which measures the leader's tendency to be forceful, aggressive, and controlling. It measures the extent to which s/he equates self-worth and security to being powerful, in control, strong, dominant, invulnerable, or on top. Worth is measured through comparison; that is, having more income, achieving a higher position, being seen as a most/more valuable contributor, gaining credit, or being promoted.

Appendix 2

Theorists Integrated into The Leadership Circle Universal Model of Leadership

Foundational Thought Leaders That Form the Core of the Universal Model of Leadership

Thought Leader	Theory/Research	TLC Universal Model of Leadership
William and Cindy Adams	Whole System Approach	Systems Awareness Dimension; Creative and Integral Level Leadership
Peter Block	Authenticity; Caution; Control; Political Scripts	Authenticity Dimension; Reactive Dimensions
David Burns	Cognitive and Rational Emotive Psychology	All Reactive Dimension; Underlying, Self-limiting Belief and Assumptions and associated behavior
Robert Fritz	Creative and Reactive Orientations	Two Stages of Development; top half and bottom half of the LCP circle
Karen Horney	Character Structure; Three Core Types	Heart, Head, Will Types; Complying Protecting, Controlling; Relating, Awareness, Achieving

Foundational Thought Leaders That Form the Core of the Universal Model of Leadership		
Thought Leader	Theory/Research	TLC Universal Model of Leadership
Robert Kegan and Lisa Lahey	Developmental Psychology; Stages of Adult Development; Immunity to Change	Kegan's Development Model is the vertical axis of the LCP; Immunity to Change describes Reactive Structure's pattern of performance
Peter Senge	Systems Thinking and Systems Dynamics; Personal Mastery	Systems Awareness Dimension; Reactive Structure and Creative Structure
Ken Wilber	Integral Model	The Universal Model of Leadership is an Integral Model. Ken's seminal work has greatly influenced its development

Stage of Adult Development Thought Leaders		
Thought Leader	Theory/Research	TLC Universal Model of Leadership
Don Beck	Spiral Dynamics	Stages of Adult Development
Susanne Cook-Greuter	Maturity Assessment Profile and Stage Model	Integrated with Kegan's Stage Model, Used to Research the Relationship of the LCP to Stage of Development
James Fowler	Stages of Faith	Stages of Spiritual Development
Carol Gilligan	In a Different Voice	Stages of Development; Different Types/Voices moving through Structures of Mind
Brian Hall	Value Shift	Stages of Adult Development; Stages of Organizational Development, at which stage vision, strategy, intuition, and systems thinking typically develop

Stage of Adult Development Thought Leaders

Thought Leader	Theory/Research	TLC Universal Model of Leadership
Bill Joiner & Steven Josephs	Leadership Agility	Stages of Adult Development
Robert Kegan & Lisa Lahey	Developmental Psychology; Stages of Adult Development; Immunity to Change	Kegan's Development Model is the vertical axis of the LCP; Immunity to Change describes Reactive Structure's Pattern of Performance
Bill Torbert	Action Logics	Stages of Adult Development

Other Integrated Thought Leaders, Framework, and Spiritual Traditions

Thought Leader	Theory/Research	TLC Universal Model of Leadership
Wes Agor	Intuitive Management	Intuition Practice
Warren Bennis	On Becoming a Leader	Leadership Practices; Creative Level Leadership, Purposeful Visionary Dimension
Kevin Cashman	Inside-out Leadership	Inner Game, Leadership Practices
CCL, PDI, DDI	360 Competency Research	Key Creative Leadership Competencies
Jim Collins	Level 5 Leadership	The Polarity of Fierce Resolve with Ambition; Hedgehog Concept
Stephen Covey	Seven Habits of Successful People	Leadership Practices, Stages of Ego Development—Dependent, Independent, Interdependent
Mihaly Csikszentmihalyi	Flow	Creative Level Leadership, Mastery, Intuition
Max Dupree	Inclusive Organization	Systems Awareness Dimension, Creative Level Leadership

Other Integrated Thought Leaders, Framework, and Spiritual Traditions

Thought Leader	Theory/Research	TLC Universal Model of Leadership
Albert Ellis	Rational Emotive Therapy	Reactive Dimensions, core identity beliefs and assumptions, Leadership Practices
Viktor Frankl	Man's Search for Meaning; Logo Therapy	Purposeful Visionary Dimension; Creative Structure of Mind
Tim Gallwey	Inner Game Theory	Inner Game, Operating Systems, Reactive and Creative Structures of Mind
Daniel Goleman	Emotional Intelligence	Self-Awareness Dimension
Robert Greenleaf	Servant Leadership	Creative to Integral Level Leadership
Michael Hammer	Organization Redesign	Systems Awareness Dimension
Kathleen Hurley & Theodore Dobson	Enneagram	The Enneagram framework is foundational to the Universal Model; Reactive Structure of Mind, and Pathway of Development
William James	As a Man Thinketh	Creative and Integral Structures of Mind
Joe Jaworski	Synchronicity	Intuition, Creative Consciousness
Barry Johnson	Polarity Theory	Polarities across the LCP Circle; Ability to manage polarities increases with Stage of Development
Carl Jung	Ego Shadow Dynamics	Type Shadow Dynamics

Other Integrated Thought Leaders, Framework, and Spiritual Traditions

Thought Leader	Theory/Research	TLC Universal Model of Leadership
Robert Kaplan	Beyond Ambition	Controlling Dimension, Sustainable Productivity Dimension
Kouses and Posner	Integrity	Integrity Dimension
Clay Lafferty	Life Styles Instrument	Reactive Dimension and the brilliance of displaying data in a circle
Patrick Lencioni	The Five Dysfunctions of a Team	Reactive Structure of Mind played out collectively
James MacGregor-Burns	Transactional vs. Transformational Leadership	Reactive and Creative Leadership
Abraham Maslow	Hierarchy of Need, Self Actualization	Hierarchy Model is a Stage Model; Self-Awareness Dimension
David McClellend	Achievement Motivation	Achieving Dimension
Douglas McGregor	Theory X, Theory Y	Internal Assumptions impact on leadership style and effectiveness; polarity between Relating and Controlling
Otto Scharmer	Presence, Theory U	Integral Level Mind, Systems Awareness Dimension, Self Awareness Dimension Intuition
Will Schutz	The Truth Option, FIRO-B	Authenticity Dimension, Complying and Controlling Dimensions

Other Integrated Thought Leaders, Framework, and Spiritual Traditions

Thought Leader	Theory/Research	TLC Universal Model of Leadership
Lao Tzu	Tao Te Ching	Self-Awareness Dimension
Marvin Weisbord	Whole System Redesign	Systems Awareness Dimension
Meg Wheatly	Leadership and the New Science	Systems Awareness Dimension, The kind of Systems Thinking that emerges at the Integral Structure of Mind
Larry Wilson	Play To Win; Play-Not-To-Lose	Creative and Reactive Structures of Mind
Wisdom Traditions	Spiritual Development	Unity Consciousness, Stages of Consciousness Development
Zenger-Folkman	Extraordinary Leadership	Leadership Competencies, research on extraordinary leaders

References

Abrams, Jeremiah, and Connie Zweig. *Meeting the Shadow: The Hidden Power of the Dark Side of Human Nature*. New York: Penguin Putnam, 1991.

Adams, Cindy, and W. A. Adams. *Collaborating for Change: The Whole Systems Approach*. San Francisco: Berrett-Koehler Publishers, 2000.

Adams, W. A., and Michael Bowker. *The Whole Systems Approach Involving Everyone in the Company to Transform and Run Your Business*. Provo, UT: Executive Excellence Pub., 1999.

Agor, Weston H. *Intuitive Management: Integrating Left and Right Brain Management Skills*. Englewood Cliffs, N.J.: Prentice-Hall, 1984.

Allen, James. *As a Man Thinketh*. Chicago: Science Press, 1905.

Anderson, Robert. *Leadership the Uncommon Sense*. Position Paper, theleadershipcircle.com, 1990.

Anderson, Robert. *Pathways to Partnership*. Position Paper, theleadershipcircle.com, 1995.

Anderson, Robert. *Mastering Leadership*. Position Paper, theleadershipcircle.com, 1991.

Autry, James A. *Love and Profit: The Art of Caring Leadership*. New York: Morrow, 1991.

Barks, Coleman. *The Essential Rumi: New Expanded Edition*. New York: Harper Collins Publishers, 2004.

Beck, Don, and Christopher C. Cowan. *Spiral Dynamics: Mastering Values, Leadership, and Change: Exploring the New Science of Memetics*. Cambridge, Mass., USA: Blackwell Business, 1996.

Beesing, Maria, and Robert J. Nogosek. *The Enneagram: A Journey of Self-discovery*. Denville, N.J.: Dimension Books, 1984.

Belasco, James A., and Ralph C. Stayer. *Flight of the Buffalo: Soaring to Excellence, Learning to Let Employees Lead*. New York, NY: Warner Books, 1993.

Bennis, Warren, and Burt Nanus. *Leaders: The Strategies for Taking Charge*. New York City: Harper & Row, 1985.

Bennis, Warren. *On Becoming a Leader*. New York City: Addison Wesley, 1989. Latest edition: Bennis, Warren. *On Becoming a Leader*. 4th edn. New York City: Basic Books, 2009.

Beowulf: A New Verse Translation. Trans. Seamus Heaney. New York City: Norton, 2000.

Berger, Jennifer Garvey. *Changing on the Job Developing Leaders for a Complex World*. Stanford, Calif.: Stanford Business Books, an Imprint of Stanford University Press, 2012.

Berger, Jennifer Garvey, and Keith Johnston. *Simple Habits for Complex Times: Powerful Practices for Leaders*. Stanford, CA: Stanford University Press, 2015.

Block, Peter. *The Empowered Manager: Positive Political Skills at Work*. San Francisco: Jossey-Bass Publishers, 1987.

Block, Peter. *Stewardship: Choosing Service Over Self-interest*. San Francisco: Berrett-Koehler, 1993.

Bly, Robert. *Iron John: A Book about Men*. Reading, Mass.: Addison-Wesley, 1990.

Bly, Robert. *News of the Universe: Poems of Twofold Consciousness*. San Francisco: Sierra Club Books, 1980.

Bonhoeffer, Dietrich, and Manfred Weber. *Meditations on the Cross*. Louisville, Ky.: Westminster John Knox Press, 1998.

Burns, D. *Feeling Good: The New Mood Therapy*. New York City: Signet, 1980.

Campbell, Joseph, and Bill Moyers. *The Power of Myth*. New York City: Anchor, 1991.

Campbell, Joseph. *The Hero with a Thousand Faces*. New York City: Pantheon Books, 1949.

Campbell, Joseph. *The Hero with a Thousand Faces: The Collected Works of Joseph Campbell*. 3rd edn. Novato: New World Library, 2008.

Capitalizing on Complexity: Insights from the Global Chief Executive Officer Study. http://www-01.ibm.com/common/ssi/cgi-bin/ssialias?infotype=PM&subtype=XB&htmlfid=GBE03297USEN. Retrieved June 15, 2015.

Cashman, Kevin. *Leadership from the Inside Out: Seven Pathways to Mastery*. Provo, UT: Executive Excellence, 1998.

Collins, Jim. "Good to Great." *Fast Company*, September 30, 2001.

Collins, Jim. *Good to Great: Why Some Companies Make the Leap … And Others Don't*. New York City: Harper Business, 2001.

Cook-Greuter, Susanne R. "Making the Case for a Developmental Perspective." *Industrial and Commercial Training* 36, no. 7 (2004).

Covey, Stephen. *The 7 Habits of Highly Effective People*. New York City: Simon & Schuster, 1989.

Csikszentmihalyi, Mihaly. *Flow: The Psychology of Optimal Experience*. New York: Harper & Row, 1990.

Csikszentmihalyi, Mihaly. *The Evolving Self: A Psychology for the Third Millennium*. New York, NY: HarperCollins Publishers, 1993.

Depree, Max. *Leadership Is an Art*. New York: Doubleday, 1989.

Ellis, Albert. *How to Stubbornly Refuse to Make Yourself Miserable about Anything–yes, Anything*. New York: Carol Publishing, 1988.

Ellis, Albert, and Melvin Powers. *A New Guide to Rational Living*. Chatsworth: Wilshire Book Company, 1961. Latest edition: Ellis, Albert, and Melvin Powers. *A New Guide to Rational Living*. Chatsworth: Wilshire Book Company, 1975.

Emerson, Ralph Waldo. *Nature*. Boston: James Munroe and Company, 1936.

Fowler, James W. *Stages of Faith: The Psychology of Human Development and the Quest for Meaning*. San Francisco: HarperSanFrancisco, 1995.

Fox, Matthew. *Meister Eckhart: A Mystic-Warrior for Our Times*. Novato: New World Library, 2014.

Frankl, Viktor. *Man's Search for Meaning*. New York City: Washington Squares Press, 1959.

Fritz, Robert. *The Path of Least Resistance*. New York City: Fawcett-Columbine Books, 1989.

Gallway, W. Timothy. *The Inner Game of Work: Focus, Learning, Pleasure, and Mobility in the Workplace*. New York City: Random House, 2000.

Gilligan, Carol. *In a Different Voice: Psychological Theory and Women's Development*. Cambridge: Harvard University Press, 1982.

Goethe, Johann Wolfgang von. "The Holy Longing". In *News of the Universe*. Trans. Robert Bly. Oakland: University of California Press, 1980.

Goleman, Daniel. *Emotional Intelligence: Why It Can Matter More Than IQ*. New York City: Bantam, 1995. Latest edition: Goleman, Daniel. *Emotional Intelligence: Why It Can Matter More Than IQ*. 10th Anniversary ed. New York City: Bantam, 2005.

Greene, Robert. *Mastery*. New York: Viking, 2012.

Greenleaf, Robert K. *Servant Leadership: A Journey into the Nature of Legitimate Power and Greatness*. New York: Paulist Press, 1977.

Hall, Brian P. *Values Shift: A Guide to Personal and Organizational Transformation*. Eugene: Wipf & Stock Publishers, 2006.

Heifetz, Ronald. *Leadership Without Easy Answers*. Boston: Harvard University Press, 1998.

Hersey, Paul, and Blanchard, Ken. "Life cycle theory of leadership." *Training and Development Journal*, 23 (1969): 26–34.

Hill, Napoleon. *Think and Grow Rich*. Meriden: The Ralston Society, 1937.

Horney, Karen. *Our Inner Conflicts*. New York City: W.W. Norton & Company, 1945.

Hudson, Frederic M. *The Adult Years: Mastering the Art of Self-renewal*. San Francisco: Jossey-Bass, 1991.

Hurley, Kathleen V., and Theodore Elliott Dobson. *What's My Type?: Use the Enneagram System of Nine Personality Types to Discover Your Best Self*. San Francisco: HarperSanFrancisco, 1991.

Isaacson, Walter. *Steve Jobs*. New York City: Simon & Schuster, 2011.

Jaworski, Joseph. *Synchronicity: The Inner Path of Leadership*. San Francisco, CA: Berrewt-Koehler Publisher, 1996.

Jobs, Steven. *"You've got to find what you love," Jobs says*. Stanford: Stanford Report, 2005.

Johansen, Bob. *Leaders Make the Future: Ten New Leadership Skills for an Uncertain World*. San Francisco: Berrett-Koehler Publishers, 2009. Latest edition: Johansen, Bob. *Leaders Make the Future: Ten New Leadership Skills for an Uncertain World*. 2nd edn. San Francisco: Berrett-Koehler Publishers, 2012.

Johanson, Gregory J., and Ron Kurtz. *Grace Unfolding: Psychotherapy in the Spirit of the Tao-te Ching*. New York: Bell Tower, 1991.

Johnson, Barry. *Polarity Management: Identifying and Managing Unsolvable Problems*. Amherst: HRD Press, 2014.

Jung, Carl. *Psychological Types: The Collected Works of C. G. Jung. Vol. 6*. Princeton: Princeton University Press, 1976.

Kaplan, Robert. *Beyond Ambition: How Driven Managers Can Lead Better and Live Better*. San Francisco: Jossey-Bass, 1991.

Kauffman, Draper. *Systems 1: An Introduction to Systems Thinking*. Future Systems, 1980.

Kegan, Robert. *The Evolving Self*. Boston: Harvard University Press, 1982.

Kegan, Robert. *In Over Our Heads: The Mental Demands of Modern Life*. 4th printing edn. Boston: Harvard University Press, 1998.

Kegan, Robert, and Lisa Laskow Lahey. *Immunity to Change: How to Overcome it and Unlock Potential in Yourself and Your Organization*. Boston: Harvard University Press, 2009.

Kelly, Walt. *Pogo: We have met the Enemy and He is Us*. New York City: Simon and Schuster, 1972.

Klein, Eric, and John B. Izzo. *Awakening Corporate Soul: Four Paths to Unleash the Power of People at Work*. Lion's Bay, B.C.: Fairwinds Press, 1998.

Kohlberg, Lawrence. *The Philosophy of Moral Development: Moral Stages and the Idea of Justice*. San Francisco: Harper & Row, 1981.

Kouzes, Jim, and Barry Posner. *The Leadership Challenge: How to Keep Getting Extraordinary Things Done in Organizations*. San Francisco: Jossey-Bass, 1995.

Kouzes, Jim, and Barry Posner. *Leadership Challenge*. 3rd edn. San Francisco: Jossey-Bass, 2002.

Kurtz, Ron. *Body-centered Psychotherapy: The Hakomi Method: The Integrated Use of Mindfulness, Nonviolence, and the Body*. Mendocino, CA: LifeRhythm, 1990.

Lafferty, J. Clayton, and Robert Cooke. *The Life Styles Inventory and the Guttman Scale: Using the Items to Help the Focal Individual Identify Strategies for Developing Constructive Thinking and Behaviour.* Australia: Human Synergistics International, 2009.

Laloux, Frederic. *Reinventing Organizations: A Guide to Creating Organizations Inspired by the Next Stage of Human Consciousness*. Millis: Nelson Parker, 2014.

Lao-tzu. *Tao Te Ching*. Trans. S. Mitchell. Radford: Wilder Publications, 2008.

Lencioni, Patrick. *The Five Dysfunctions of a Team: A Leadership Fable*. San Francisco: Jossey-Bass Publishers, 2002.

MacGregor Burns, James. *Leadership*. New York City: Harper Collins, 1978.

Marion, Jim. *Putting on the Mind of Christ: The Inner Work of Christian Spirituality*. Charlottesville, VA: Hampton Roads Pub., 2000.

Maslow, Abraham. *Motivation and Personality*. New York City: Harper and Row, 1954.

May, Rollo. *The Courage to Create*. New York: Norton, 1975.

McClelland, David. *The Achievement Motive*. New York City: Appleton-Century-Crofts, 1953.

McClelland, David. *Human Motivation*. Cambridge: Cambridge University Press, 1988.

McGregor, Douglas. *The Human Side of Enterprise*. New York City: McGraw-Hill, 1960.

Mitchell, Stephen. *Bhagavad Gita: A New Translation*. New York: Harmony Books, 2000.

Mitchell, Stephen. *Tao Te Ching: A New English Version*. New York: Harper & Row, 1988.

Moore, Thomas. *Care of the Soul: A Guide for Cultivating Depth and Sacredness in Everyday Life*. New York, NY: HarperCollins, 1992.

Murray, W. H. *The Scottish Himalayan Expedition*. Denver: J. M. Dent & Company, 1951.

Oliver, Mary. "The Summer Day." In *House of Light*. Boston: Beacon Press, 1990.

Palmer, Helen. *The Enneagram: Understanding Yourself and the Others in Your Life*. San Francisco: Harper & Row, 1988.

Peters, Thomas J. *Thriving on Chaos: Handbook for a Management Revolution*. New York: Knopf, 1987.

Rilke, Rainer Maria, and Stephen Mitchell (Trans). *The Selected Poetry of Rainer Maria Rilke*. New York: Random House, 1982.

Rilke, Rainer Maria. *Letters to a Young Poet*. Trans. M.D. Herter Norton. New York City: W. W. Norton & Company, 1993.

Rogers, Carl. *On Becoming a Person: A Therapist's View of Psychotherapy*. Boston: Houghton Mifflin Company, 1962.

Rooke, David, and William R. Torbert. "Organizational Transformation as a Function of CEOs' Developmental Stage." *Organizational Development Journal* 16, no. 1 (1998): 11–28.

Rowan, Roy. *The Intuitive Manager*. New York City: Little, Brown and Company, 1986.

Schaef, Anne Wilson, and Diane Fassel. *The Addictive Organization*. San Francisco: Harper & Row, 1988.

Schopenhauer, Arthur. *Parerga and Paralipomena Short Philosophical Essays, Vol. 1*. 1st edn. Oxford: Clarendon Press, 1974.

Schutz, Will. *The Truth Option*. Will Schutz Associates, 1984.

Schutz, Will. *Profound Simplicity*. Will Schutz Associates, 1982.

Schweitzer, Albert, in a speech to the students of Silcoates School, Wakefield (along with "a number of boys and girls from Ackworth School"), on "The Meaning of Ideals in Life," at approximately 3:40 p.m. on December 3, 1935. "Visit of Dr. Albert Schweitzer" (as translated from the French of the address by Dr Schweitzer's interpreter), *The Silcoatian,* New Series No. 25 (December, 1935): 784–785 (781–786 with 771–772 ("Things in General")).

Senge, Peter. *Systems Principles for Leadership*. Cambridge, Mass.: Massachusetts Institute of Technology, 1985.

Senge, Peter. *The Fifth Discipline: The Art and Practice of The Learning Organization*. New York City: Doubleday, 1990. Latest Edition: Senge, Peter. *The Fifth Discipline: The Art and Practice of The Learning Organization*. Revised edn. New York City: Doubleday, 2006.

Senge, Peter M. *Presence: Exploring Profound Change in People, Organizations, and Society*. New York: Doubleday, 2005.

Singh, M. P. *Quote, Unquote: A Handbook of Famous Quotations*. New Delhi: Lotus Press, 2006. 172

"Success Is the Enemy" and Other Truths The CEO of Johnsonville Foods Inc. Preaches His Management Mistakes and Methods to Those Looking to Improve. Madison: The Wisconsin State Journal, 1997.

The New Jerusalem Bible. Ed. Susan Jones. New York: Doubleday, 1985.

Torbert, William R. *Action Inquiry: The Secret of Timely and Transforming Leadership*. San Francisco, CA: Berrett-Koehler, 2004.

Torbert, W. *The Power of Balance: Transforming Self, Society, and Scientific Inquiry*. Newbury Park: Sage, 1991.

Van Dusen, Lani. "Leadership: The Next Productivity Frontier." Lecture, Leadership and Human Capital Management, 53rd Annual Convention from Equipment Leasing and Finance Association, San Diego, October 21, 2014.

Van Dusen, Lani. "The Importance of Investing in Leadership." *Journal of Equipment Lease Financing*, Spring 2015.

Vries, Manfred F. R., and Danny Miller. *The Neurotic Organization*. San Francisco: Jossey-Bass, 1984.

Wade, Jenny. *Changes of Mind: A Holonomic Theory of the Evolution of Consciousness*. Albany: State University of New York Press, 1996.

Wei, Wu Wei. *Ask the Awakened*. Boulder: Sentient Publications, 2002.

Weisbord, Marvin. *Productive Workplaces Revisited: Dignity, Meaning, and Community in the 21st Century*. San Francisco: Jossey-Bass, 2004.

Wenger, Michael. *Wind Bell: Teachings from the San Francisco Zen Center 1968–2001*. Berkeley, Calif.: North Atlantic Books, 2002.

Wheatley, Margaret. *Leadership and the New Science: Discovering Order in a Chaotic World*. San Francisco: Berrett-Koehler, 2006.

Whyte, David. *Songs for Coming Home: Poems*. Revised edn. Langley, Wash.: Many Rivers Press, 1989.

Whyte, David. *Where Many Rivers Meet: Poems*. Langley, Wash.: Many Rivers Press, 1990.

Whyte, David. *Fire in the Earth: Poems*. Langley, Wash.: Many Rivers Press, 1992.

Whyte, David. *The Heart Aroused: Poetry and the Preservation of the Soul in Corporate America*. New York: Currency Doubleday, 1994.

Whyte, David. *Crossing the Unknown Sea: Work as a Pilgrimage of Identity*. New York City: Riverhead Books, 2001.

Whyte, David. *River Flow: New and Selected Poems*. Langley, Wash.: Many Rivers Press, 2012.

Wilber, Ken. *One Taste: Daily Reflections on Integral Spirituality*. Shambhala, Boston, USA, 1999.

Wilber, Ken. *Integral Psychology: Consciousness, Spirit, Psychology, Therapy*. Boston: Shambhala, 2000.

Wilber, Ken. *A Theory of Everything: An Integral Vision for Business, Politics, Science, and Spirituality*. Boston: Shambhala, 2001.

Wilson, Larry, and Hersch Wilson. *Play to Win!: Choosing Growth Over Fear in Work and Life*. Austin: Bard Press, 1998. Latest edition: Wilson, Larry, and Hersch Wilson. *Play to Win!: Choosing Growth Over Fear in Work and Life*. Revised edn. Austin: Bard Press, 2004.

Zenger, Jack, and Joseph Folkman. *The Extraordinary Leader: Turning Good Managers into Great Leaders*. 2nd edn. New York City: McGraw-Hill Professional Publishing, 2009.

About the Authors

ROBERT J. ANDERSON

Robert J. Anderson is the Founder, Chairman and Chief Development Officer of The Leadership Circle. He is also the Co-founder and Chairman of Full Circle Group. Over the past 35 years, Bob has dedicated his career to exploring the intersections between leadership and mastery, competence and consciousness, spirituality and business.

Bob is the creator of The Leadership Circle Profile^{TM}, an integrated and innovative leadership assessment tool. A culmination of years of research, The Leadership Circle Profile and its associated assessment tools are used by thousands of organizations around the world. The Leadership Circle and Full Circle Group earned first place in the Large Leadership Partner and Provider category of the HR.com 2015 Leadership 500 Excellence Awards. Bob is a true pioneer in the field of leadership development and research.

Bob works with CEOs and leadership teams to help them improve their leadership effectiveness. He has also partnered with independent consultants and coaches around the world to help them master the skills of coaching and developing executives to achieve greater personal and organizational effectiveness. Bob's practical wisdom, humility, creativity, humor, and expertise provide a rare and transformative experience for the leaders, coaches, and consultants with whom he works.

Bob serves as adjunct faculty for the Executive Education Center at the University of Notre Dame Mendoza College of Business. There he assists diverse groups of leaders in navigating their own leadership transformations. In 2005, Bob received the Partner in Innovation faculty award.

Bob holds a Bachelor's Degree in Economics from John Carroll University and a Master's Degree in Organizational Development from Bowling Green State University. Bob and Kim, his wife of 32 years, make their home near Toledo, Ohio. The two enjoy traveling the globe for both work and play with their three adult children.

WILLIAM A. ADAMS

Bill Adams is the Co-founder and CEO of Full Circle Group, North America, and CEO of The Leadership Circle. Bill has an uncanny way of bringing clarity and wisdom that distills moments of truth, creates solid direction, and builds confidence as he creates lifelong relationships and friendships with his clients. He is extensively sought out as a trusted advisor to CEO's, top executives and teams around the world. Being passionate about relationships, leadership, and business, Bill has devoted the past 35 years to supporting leaders through complex business challenges. He is known for successfully partnering with leaders to unlock breakthrough performance, develop deep leadership capability and produce systemic, transformational business results. His clients range from Fortune 500 corporations to start-ups across multiple industries.

Bill sits on numerous boards in the for-profit, education, and nonprofit worlds. A serial entrepreneur, he has started, sold, and merged multiple businesses. In 1991 his consulting firm, Maxcomm, Inc., received the Small Business of the Year Award and in 2015, The Leadership Circle and Full Circle Group earned first place in the Large Leadership Partner and Provider category of the HR.com 2015 Leadership 500 Awards.

With a passion for creating a world of work where people thrive, Bill teaches and applies time-proven principles that translate into bottom line results, effective organizations, and personal fulfillment. His keen focus on external business drivers, combined with a whole systems approach for evolving internal business systems, creates cultures where people are committed to investing their discretionary energy, while assuming personal responsibility for the results they produce. Bill authored *The Whole*

Systems Approach: Involving Everyone in the Company to Transform and Run Your Business (with his wife and co-author, Cynthia Adams) and *The Quest for Quality: Prescriptions for Achieving Service Excellence* (with co-authors Phil Wexler and Emil Bohn). He and Cindy contributed to two editions of *The Change Handbook: Group Methods for Shaping the Future* (Peggy Holman and Tom Devane), and he contributed to *Managing Quality in America's Most Admired Companies* (Jay Spechler). Bill has also led the joint venture conferences – Self-Organizing Systems: The New Science of Participation™ – with Meg Wheatley.

Bill holds a Master's Degree in Interpersonal and Organizational Communication from the University of Montana. Bill and Cindy make their home in the mountains of northern Utah. The two are most at home in the outdoors, working with youth leadership and spending time with their four children and a growing crew of grandchildren.

Index